Content-Based Curriculum for High-Ability Learners

Content-Based Curriculum for High-Ability Learners

edited by
Joyce
VanTassel-Baska
and
Catherine A.
Little

A Service Publication of
The National Association for Gifted Children
1707 L Street NW, Suite 550
Washington, DC 20036
(202) 785-4268   http://www.nagc.org

PRUFROCK PRESS, INC.

ISBN 1-882664-78-7

Prufrock Press, Inc.
P.O. Box 8813
Waco, Texas 76714-8813
(800) 998-2208
Fax (800) 240-0333
http://www.prufrock.com

To models
for curriculum thought—
Dr. Mortimer Adler
Dr. Hilda Taba
Dr. Ralph Tyler

To mentors
on curriculum
for gifted learners—
Dr. James J. Gallagher and
Dr. A. Harry Passow

Table of Contents

List of Tables   xii
List of Figures   xiiii
List of Sample Lessons   xv

Acknowledgments   xvii

Chapter 1
Content-Based Curriculum   **1**
for High-Ability Learners: An Introduction
by Joyce VanTassel–Baska

What is a Differentiated Curriculum? 2
Philosophies of Curriculum 4
Rationale for an Integrated Curriculum Model
   for Talent Development 6
Curricular Reform Design Elements 11
Implementation Considerations 15
Conclusion 20

▬▬▬ **Section I**   **25**

Chapter 2
Accelerating Learning Experiences   **27**
in Core Content Areas
by Joyce VanTassel-Baska and Beverly Sher

Classroom-Based Acceleration 29
Issues in Implementing a Diagnostic-Prescriptive Approach 32
Accelerated Learning Across Grade Levels 33
Applications of Accelerated Patterns: Case Studies 36
Who Can Work With Accelerated Learners? 42
Making Acceleration a Useful Option 44
Conclusion 44

Chapter 3
Incorporating Higher Order Process Skills Into Content 47
by Jeanne M. Struck

Why Teach Higher Order Process Skills? 49
Thinking Critically and Creatively 50
Complexity of Outcomes: Bloom's Taxonomy 51
A Model of Socratic Teaching 54
A Model of Problem Solving 56
A Model for Reasoning 58
A Model for Research 69
Metacognition 73
Conclusion 76

Chapter 4
Developing Creative Student Products 79
by Janine M. Lehane

Judging the Quality of an Artwork 81
Fostering Students' Ability to Develop Quality Products 82
Discipline-Based Product Development 84
Judging Quality Via Assessment 86
The Role of the Teacher in Creative Production 87
Application to Literature 88
Sensitivity to Gifted Students' Perfectionism 90
Shaping Quality Products 90
Judgments About Student Products 93
Conclusion 96

Chapter 5
Concept Development and Learning 101
by Linda D. Avery and Catherine A. Little

The Importance of Concept Learning 102
What is a Concept? 104
Supporting Student Concept Development 106
Moving From a Lesson to a Curriculum 113
Assessing Concept Learning 118
Using Concepts to Design Interdisciplinary Curricula 119
Conclusion 121

Section II 125

Chapter 6
Adapting Language Arts Curricula for High-Ability Learners 127
by Catherine A. Little

Learner Outcomes of Significance 129
Habits of Mind 130
Authentic Assessment 132
Conceptually Oriented Curricula 134
Higher Order Reasoning 135
Substantive Content 141
Constructing Meaning 142
Multicultural/Global Emphasis 144
Intradisciplinary and Interdisciplinary
  Connections 146
Materials and Resources 148
Technology Relevant 149
Inquiry-Based Learning and Other Models 151
Metacognition 152
Conclusion 155

Chapter 7
Adapting Mathematics Curricula
for High-Ability Learners
by Dana T. Johnson

161

Learner Outcomes of Significance 164
Placement and Assessment 164
Habits of Mind 168
Substantive Content 169
Conceptually Oriented Curricula 173
Higher Order Reasoning 174
Inquiry-Based Learning 183
Materials and Resources 184
Intradisciplinary and Interdisciplinary
  Connections 184
Constructing Meaning and Metacognition 185
Technology Relevant 186
Conclusion 187

Chapter 8
Adapting Science Curricula
for High-Ability Learners
by Beverly T. Sher

191

Learner Outcomes of Significance 192
Substantive Content 196
Problem-Based Learning: Integrating Content,
  Process, and Concepts 198
Scientific Habits of Mind and Inquiry-Based Learning 205
Constructing Meaning and Metacognition 206
Materials and Resources 207
Conclusion 216

Chapter 9
Adapting Social Studies Curricula   **219**
for High-Ability Learners
by Molly M. Sandling

Learner Outcomes of Significance
  and Habits of Mind 220
Higher Order Reasoning 223
Conceptually Oriented Curricula 233
Substantive Content 235
Multicultural/Global Emphasis 238
Intradisciplinary and Interdisciplinary
  Connections 243
Technology Relevant 244
Inquiry-Based Learning 245
Constructing Meaning 247
Materials and Resources 248
Authentic Assessment and Products 250
Metacognition 252
Conclusion 252

▬▬▬▬▬ **Section III**   **255**

Chapter 10
Selecting Resources and Materials   **259**
for High-Ability Learners
by Linda D. Avery and Li Zuo

Curricular Selection Process 261
Curricular Resources for High-Ability Learners 270
Conclusion 274

Chapter 11
Making Appropriate Instructional Choices   **279**
by Jeanne M. Struck and Catherine A. Little

The Influence of Content 281
The Influences of Students 286
The Influences of the Teacher 290
The Influence of Context 293
Conclusion 300

Chapter 12
Assessing Student Learning   **305**
by Li Zuo and Joyce VanTassel-Baska

Technical Considerations in Assessment 306
Authentic Assessment 309

Issues in Assessing Gifted Students' Learning 312
Models for Assessment 312
Conclusion 323

Chapter 13
Aligning Curricula for the Gifted With Content Standards and Exemplary Secondary Programs
327
by Catherine A. Little and Wendy T. Ellis

Using Content Standards as a Basis
  for Curriculum Development 329
Aligning Existing Curricula With Existing Standards 333
The International Baccalaureate Diploma Programme 340
The College Board Advanced Placement Program 349
Conclusion 352

Chapter 14
Implementing Innovative Curricular and Instructional Practices in Classrooms and Schools
355
by Joyce VanTassel-Baska

Curriculum Effectiveness Research 356
Staff Development 365
The Importance of Innovation in Schools 370
Creating a System of Learning 371
Conclusion 372

Appendix: Standards for the English
  Language Arts Aligned
  With Curricular Emphases
377

About the Authors
381

Index of Names
385

Index of Subjects
389

List
of Tables

Table 1.1 Curricular Philosophies   **5**
Table 1.2 Application of Integrated   **12**
           Curriculum Model to William
           and Mary Science, Language Arts,
           and Social Studies Curricular Units
Table 2.1 Archetypal Features of Candidates   **35**
           for Acceleration Matched
           With Intervention
Table 2.2 Acceleration Pattern   **41**
Table 5.1 Sample Concepts Useful   **105**
           in Curriculum Development
Table 6.1 Goals and Outcomes of Significance   **131**
Table 7.1 Outcomes of Significance   **165**
Table 8.1 Alignment of Learner Outcomes   **194**
Table 8.2 Curricular Indications of Mrs. Hollis'   **200**
           Differentiated Response
Table 9.1 Key Goal and Related   **222**
           Learner Outcomes
Table 12.1 Table of Specifications   **308**
Table 12.2 Assessment Tools for Writing   **311**
Table 13.1 Social Studies Unit Aligned   **335**
           with State Standards
Table 13.2 Language Arts Curriculum   **336**
           Aligned With State Process Standards
Table 13.3 Social Studies Unit Aligned   **338**
           With Local School District Standards
Table 14.1 Persuasive Writing Scoring Rubric   **362**
Table 14.2 Classroom Observation Form: **369**
           Critical Thinking Strategies

List of Figures

Figure 1.1   Integrated Curriculum Model   **8**
for Gifted Learners

Figure 1.2   A Model for Curricular Reform   **15**

Figure 2.1   Mathematics and Reading Packaged   **31**
Curricula for High-Ability Learners

Figure 3.1   Paul's Wheel of Reasoning: **59**
The Eight Elements

Figure 3.2   Social Studies: Battles of the   **65**
Revolutionary War

Figure 3.3   Science: The Issue of Human   **66**
Cloning

Figure 3.4   Language Arts: Literature Study   **67**

Figure 3.5   Teacher Assessment   **68**
of Student Thinking

Figure 3.6   William and Mary Center   **70**
for Gifted Education Research Model

Figure 3.7   Developing an Issue   **71**

Figure 3.8   Research Project Rubric   **75**

Figure 4.1   Sample Student Writing Preassessment   **86**

Figure 4.2   Sample Rubric   **92**
for Assessing Artistic Products

Figure 4.3   Sample Assessment Activity   **96**

Figure 5.1   The Change Model   **111**

Figure 5.2   Student Example 1   **112**

Figure 5.3   Student Example 2   **113**

Figure 5.4   Concept Development Model   **114**

Figure 5.5   Change Matrix   **116**

Figure 5.6   Initial Steps of Concept Map   **117**
on Isolation in *The Secret Garden*

Figure 5.7   Disciplinary Applications   **120**
of Concepts

Figure 6.1   Hamburger Model   **139**
             for Persuasive Writing
Figure 6.2   Dagwood Essay Model   **140**
Figure 6.3   Literature Web   **143**
Figure 6.4   Vocabulary Web   **153**
Figure 7.1   Hyacinths in the Pond   **167**
Figure 7.2   Mathematical Mosaic   **173**
Figure 8.1   Need to Know Board   **203**
Figure 9.1   Reasoning About a Situation or Event   **224**
Figure 9.2   Concepts in the Social Sciences   **235**
Figure 9.3   Analyzing Primary Sources   **237**
Figure 10.1 Model of the Curricular   **262**
             Review Process
Figure 13.1 Differentiation Features Checklist   **333**
Figure 13.2 IB Diploma Programme   **341**
             Curricular Model
Figure 13.3 IB–MYP Curricular Model   **344**
Figure 13.4 IB–PYP Curricular Model   **345**
Figure 13.5 K–12 Program Framework   **347**
             Reflecting IB and the ICM
Figure 14.1 Assessment Tools   **364**
             for Language Arts Units
Figure 14.2 Assessment Tools for Science Units   **365**
Figure 14.3 The Center for Gifted Education's   **367**
             Staff Development Model
Figure 14.4 Systemic Model for Implementation   **372**

List of Sample Lessons

Elements of Reasoning   **63**
  as Applied to a Problem Situation
Learning From Experience   **94**
The Concept of Change   **108**
Reflections on Change in Poetry   **136**
Patterning   **171**
Exponential Growth   **175**
Properties and Operations   **178**
Patterns of Rational Numbers   **179**
Tensions in the Former Yugoslavia   **225**
Sacco and Vanzetti   **229**
Chinese Thought and Education   **239**

Acknowledgments

The editors would like to thank past and present staff and consultants of the Center for Gifted Education at the College of William and Mary for their insightful contributions to this text in the form of suggestions, commentary, and individual chapter material.

We are also indebted to the Javits Program of the United States Department of Education, Office of Educational Research and Improvement, for providing funding for much of this work over the past 12 years.

We are also deeply grateful to Dawn Benson for her work with typing and retyping several versions of the manuscripts.

Chapter 1

Content-Based Curriculum for High-Ability Learners: An Introduction

by
Joyce VanTassel-Baska

The intention of this book is to provide a clear and cogent way to approach the development of curricula for gifted and high-ability[1] learners that is substantive, rigorous, and keeps with the structure of the disciplines as they have been defined by the standards in each subject domain taught in schools. For reasons too numerous to mention, the field of gifted education has strayed rather far away from a strong content emphasis in its curricular models, especially at the elementary level. Many of the extant

---

1. The term *gifted* used throughout the text refers to students identified for district gifted programs on multiple criteria, including ability, achievement, and aptitude. According to *National Excellence*, a report developed by the United States Department of Education (1993), this group of learners constitutes 12% of the local district populations offering such programs. The term *high ability* used throughout the text refers to students comprising the top 20% academically of the student population in schools, including gifted learners.

models in the field represent an emphasis on higher level processes and creative production without a concomitant linkage to a high-level curricular base. While such an approach was possible in the early days of the field, such artificial separation of curricular emphases can no longer be tolerated in the age of standards and accountability for learning. Thus, we hope this text breaks new ground in demonstrating that it is possible to develop high-powered, rich, and complex curricula that treat content, process, and product considerations as equal partners in the task of educating gifted learners. Moreover, the model on which the text is based represents a further meta-level of development in that an overarching concept or theme binds the curricular study together within and across areas of learning so students can appreciate the world of ideas as a superordinate bridge to understanding their world.

This introductory chapter will explore several facets of conceptualizing curricula, instruction, and assessment for gifted learners. It will begin by defining a differentiated curriculum for this population. A discussion of various curricular paradigms will be discussed as a prelude to arguing for an integrated approach to the development of curricula. Next, the chapter presents the Integrated Curriculum Model (ICM) with the types of applications made in curricular units developed by the Center for Gifted Education at the College of William and Mary. Key curricular reform elements are presented to illustrate how they have been incorporated into the structure of these units. Finally, a discussion of implementation considerations explores the respective role of the nature of the learner and the context variables of flexibility, grouping, climate, and teacher quality.

What is a Differentiated Curriculum?[2]

Typically, a curriculum is organized according to grade levels, with each subsequent grade-level expectation being more demanding than the preceding. In this way, we can calibrate level of difficulty to ensure that students are working in their zone of proximal

---

2. Throughout this text, the terms *adaptation* and *differentiation* are both used to refer to the modifications made to curricula to serve the needs of gifted learners. Although *adaptation* is a more general term, while *differentiation* reflects a closer analysis of individual students and groups of students and their instructional needs, both imply application of the reform principles and curricular characteristics discussed in this chapter.

development (Vygotsky, 1978). When we differentiate curricula for the gifted, we must move to a higher level of expectation in respect to content, process, and concept demands. Thus, one way of accommodating higher expectations effectively is to make *more advanced curricula* available at younger ages, ensuring that all levels of the standards are traversed in the process. In language arts, for example, this should mean reading more challenging books that are above the functional reading level of gifted learners. Differentiating curricula then requires attention to level of functional learning matched to advanced expectations. Adaptation of advanced learning expectations needs to occur, as well. It may be insufficient to merely move students through the next stage of the curriculum without a concomitant appreciation for depth and complexity of the underlying experiences to be provided. Thus, the curricular level for gifted learners must be adapted to their needs for advancement, depth, and complexity.

Another aspect of differentiation that needs clarification is in the *choice of instructional strategies*. In many respects, there are no strategies that are differentiated only for the gifted. Rather, strategy use is inextricably tied to the nature and level of the curriculum being addressed. Thus, the reason that the diagnostic-prescriptive approach to instruction is so powerful with the gifted is that it allows for a process by which curricular level can be efficaciously discerned and addressed in an adaptive fashion. Yet, we know that some strategies are highly effective with the gifted in combination with an advanced curriculum. For example, questioning can be a powerful tool for evincing high-level discussions in gifted clusters if the stimulus reading or viewing is also challenging. Use of open-ended activities can also prove effective if they are of requisite difficulty. Problem-based learning (PBL), because of the sheer demands of working on ill-structured problems, poses a particularly appropriate instructional approach for gifted program use. Thus, strategy differentiation involves a set of techniques that need to be matched to advanced curricula in order to be effective for advancing the learning of gifted students.

An additional element of differentiation for the gifted relates to challenge, which can best be provided through careful *selection of materials* for use in classrooms. We have a strong evidential base that suggests that materials constitute the curriculum in most classrooms (Apple, 1991) and that most basal materials are inappropriately geared to challenging gifted students (Johnson, Boyce, & VanTassel-Baska, 1995). Taken together, these findings suggest the need for careful selection of materials that meet basic specifications for exemplary curricula in the subject area in question, as well as appropriate curricula for the gifted based on differentiation features. While the selection of nationally available materials meeting these specifications for the gifted may be small, such materials do exist (see Chapter 10) and should be used to guide the differentiation process for curricula.

Finally, it may be important to acknowledge that *project work* needs to be carefully differentiated for the gifted, as well, in order to meet the criterion of creativity. As more emphasis is placed on collaborative project work at all levels of schooling, it is critical that educators of the gifted use a set of standards to judge whether or not such work is sufficiently challenging for this group of learners and whether or not the contextual settings in which the work is carried out will promote sufficient growth for them. Differentiation of project work may be judged based on the medium in which the project is done and the variables and skills addressed by the demands of the work. Provision of alternatives for student products also enhances the creativity dimension of the curriculum. For example, students might write a poetry book using their choice of poetry forms.

Philosophies of Curriculum

Several philosophies abound about the purpose of curricula in programs for gifted learners. In a sense, each of these philosophies contributes a competing paradigm. Table 1.1 attempts to describe the elements of each of these paradigms and their links to influential writers and conceptualizers.

While these paradigms may be viewed as competitive, they also may be seen as complementary when translated into the context of classroom practice. In fact, many gifted programs try to be eclectic in their curricular orientation, never ascribing totally to one view over another. Yet, clearly our extant curriculum for the gifted tends to employ a singular orientation more often than not. For example, a partial list of curricular models suggests these relationships to distinct paradigms of curricular thought:

Table 1.1
Curricular Philosophies

Curricular Paradigm	Ontology	Epistemology	Axiology	Methodology	Influences/Precursors
Traditionalist (academic rationalism)	Reality is manifested in representational modes.	The world is knowable through studying the products of the past.	Quality matters.	Reading and discussion of ideas, issues, and themes.	Adler (1982)
Social reconstructionist	Reality is socially constructed.	The world is knowable through social actions that promote equality or inequality.	Equity matters.	Challenging existing social order.	Banks (1975)
Cognitive constructivism	Reality is individually constructed.	The world is knowable by experiencing and applying key skills and concepts.	Direct experiences, mediated by social interactions, matter.	Cooperative/collaborative learning that is engaging.	Vygotsky (1978)
Behavioristic positivism	Reality is observation and perception of behaviors with mastery as a goal.	The world is knowable by verification of observations and incrementalism.	Skepticism matters.	Scientific method; emphasis on assessment of learning to reflect mastery.	Skinner (1967)
Postpositivism	Reality is limited to consensual communities.	The world is knowable "through a glass darkly."	Person–context interaction matters.	Depth of understanding; use of schemas and scaffolds to enhance connections and sense making.	Gardner (1983)

Model	Paradigm
• Renzulli's Enrichment Triad Model	• Cognitive constructivist
• Stanley's D–P model of acceleration	• Behavioristic positivism
• Ford's multicultural curriculum model	• Social reconstructionist
• VanTassel-Baska's Integrated Curriculum Model (ICM)	• Traditionalism
• Gardner's teaching for understanding	• Postpositivist

Rationale for an Integrated Curriculum Model for Talent Development

A new approach to talent development has been explored through the development of curricula for grades K–12 that demonstrate alignment with the curricular reform paradigm and is responsive to students talented in traditional academic areas (VanTassel-Baska, 1994b; VanTassel-Baska, Gallagher, Bailey, & Sher, 1993). This approach has relied on the key factors of curricular reform to guide the development process. It also has employed an integrated curriculum model that emphasizes talent development.

While many approaches have been used by schools in their programs for the gifted, the use of systematic challenging curricular intervention has been lacking. Moreover, planned curricular experiences have not been sustained over time. What the field has lacked is a comprehensive and cohesive curricular framework that uses good curricular design, considers the features of the disciplines under study, and sufficiently differentiates for talented students. Thus, it is time to consider an integrated model of curricula for gifted learners, one that is sensitive to all aspects of their learning needs. Salient characteristics of the gifted learner may be handled simultaneously in such a scheme, attending to precocity, intensity, and complexity as integrated characteristics representing cognitive and affective dimensions. Integrating curricular approaches allows for this more broad-based response to student needs.

A second reason for an integrated curriculum relates to current delivery models. As pull-out programs have decreased in number, more gifted students are being served in heterogeneous or self-contained settings, contexts in which integrated curricular approaches can work well if applied diligently and systematically. Since an integrated curriculum represents a total curricular package in an area of learning, rather than an add-on curriculum, it provides the needed differentiation within traditional areas of learning for which schools are accountable.

A third reason for an integrated approach rests with the recent research on learning. Studies have documented that better transfer of learning occurs when higher order thinking skills are embedded in subject matter (Perkins & Salomon, 1989) and teaching concepts in a discipline is a better way to produce long-term learning than teaching facts and rules (Marzano, 1992). Our understanding of creativity also has shifted toward the need for strong subject matter knowledge as a prerequisite (Amabile, 1996).

A fourth reason for using an integrated model is related to a clear shift of emphasis in the field from the focus on the individual gifted learner to the process of collective talent development for all learners. As this shift has occurred, curricular principles important for the gifted have been seen as the province of all learners developing talents in both traditional and nontraditional domains, accomplished through employing interdisciplinary, concept-based curricula and higher order thinking. This development calls for a close alignment of meaningful subject matter with its higher order manipulation of skills and ideas.

For all of these reasons, an integrated curriculum model offers a cogent exemplar for curricular design and development for gifted learners at the dawn of a new century.

The Integrated Curriculum Model

The Integrated Curriculum Model (ICM), first proposed in 1986 and further explicated in subsequent publications (VanTassel-Baska, 1992; 1994a; 1998; in press), is comprised of three interrelated dimensions that are responsive to very different aspects of the gifted learner (see Figure 1.1). These dimensions may be thought of as:

Emphasizing advanced content knowledge that frames disciplines of study. Honoring the talent search concept, this facet of the model would ensure that careful, diagnostic-prescriptive approaches were employed to ensure new learning as opposed to remedial instruction. Curricula based on the model would represent appropriate advanced learning in

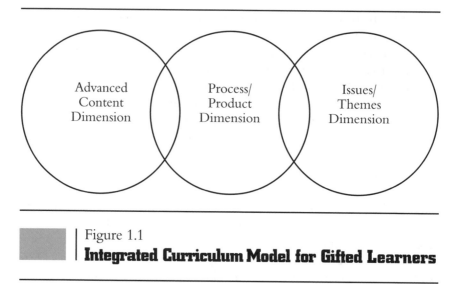

| Figure 1.1
| **Integrated Curriculum Model for Gifted Learners**

that area. For example, teachers would routinely determine what students already know about their yearly instructional plan by testing them on end-of-year or end-of-chapter material before it is taught and then adjusting classroom instruction to their level of learning.

Providing higher order thinking and processing. This facet of the model would promote student opportunities for manipulating information at complex levels by employing generic thinking models like Paul's Elements of Reasoning (1992) and more discipline-specific ones like Sher's Nature of the Scientific Process (1993). This facet of the ICM also implies the utilization of information in some generative way, whether it be a project or a fruitful discussion. For example, students may use the reasoning element "point of view" to discuss and write about a short story by William Faulkner. Students may conduct a science experiment reflecting on whether or not their findings supported their research question, and if not, why?

Focusing learning experiences around major issues, themes, and ideas that define both real-world applications and theoretical modeling within and across areas of study. This facet of the ICM honors the idea of scaffolding curricula for talented learners around the important aspects of a discipline and emphasizing these aspects in a systematic way (Ward, 1981). Thus, themes and ideas are selected based on careful research of the primary area of study to determine the most worthy and important issues and ideas for curriculum development; a theme consistent with new curricular specifications (American Association for the Advancement of Science, 1990; Perkins, 1992). These ideas become an important framework for curriculum development. The goal of such an approach is to ensure deep understanding of ideas, rather than superficial responding.

This model synthesizes the three best approaches to curriculum development and implementation documented in the literature for talented learners (Benbow & Stanley, 1983; Maker, 1982; Ward, 1981). Recent reviews of curricular models for the gifted have found the greatest effectiveness prevailing in the accelerative approach, guided by content modification (Johnsen, 2000; VanTassel-Baska & Brown, 2000). The fusion of these approaches is central to the development of a coherent curriculum that is responsive to diverse needs of talented students while also providing rich challenges to all for optimal learning.

Translation Into Curricula
The ICM has been translated into a curricular framework and set of teaching units in the areas of science, language arts, and social studies, the last of which has just completed an initial 3-year development cycle. To date, these three curricular areas represent the best examples of a deliberate effort to translate the model into written materials. The translation of the ICM was accomplished by developing a curricular framework addressing each of its dimensions in an integrated way. In order to satisfy the need for advanced content, the language arts curriculum (Center for Gifted Education, 1999), developed for grades K–12, used advanced literature selections that were 2 years beyond grade reading level, used advanced language, and contained multiple levels of meaning. The writing emphasis was placed on persuasive essays that developed an argument, which is a more advanced form of writing than is typically taught at elementary levels. Use of advanced vocabulary and the mastery of English syntax at the elementary level was also stressed.

The process/product dimension of the curriculum was addressed by embedding the Elements of Reasoning developed by Paul (1992) and by using a research model developed to aid students in generating original work (Boyce, 1997). Products were encouraged through both written and oral work.

The issue/theme dimension of the curriculum was explicated by focusing on the theme of change as it applied to works of literature selected for the unit, the writing process, language study, and learners reflecting on their own learning throughout the unit. Additionally, studying an issue of significance was emphasized as a part of the research strand for each unit. To date, six units have been developed, validated, piloted, and revised using this framework (Center for Gifted Education, 1999; VanTassel-Baska, Zuo, Avery, & Little, 2002).

The translation of the ICM to the National Science Curriculum Project for High-Ability Learners was driven by the overarching theme of systems, which became the conceptual organizing influence in each of the seven units of study (Center for Gifted Education, 1997). Students learned the elements, boundaries, inputs, and outputs, as well as the interactions of selected systems. Through a problem-based learning approach, they also learned about how science systems interact with real-world social, political, and economic systems. The process/product dimension of the curricular model was addressed through engaging students in a scientific research process that led them to create their own experiments and design their own solutions to each unit's central problem. The advanced content dimension was addressed by selecting advanced science content for inclusion in each unit and encouraging in-depth study of selected content relevant to understanding the central problem of the unit. These units are being used in classrooms across the country to incorporate the new science emphasis and have been found successful in heterogeneous settings, as well as with more restricted groups (VanTassel-Baska, Bass, Reis, Poland, & Avery, 1998).

The translation of the ICM to social studies was also driven by the theme or concept of *systems* for several units, with the concepts of *change* and *cause and effect* explored in additional units. The concept of *systems* was applied to understanding structures in society, such as economic and political systems; other units emphasized connected chains of causes and effects to help students understand multiple causation in history and to recognize that historical events were not inevitable. As in the language arts, the process/product dimension of the model was addressed through embedded use of Paul's (1992) Elements of Reasoning, as well as through a heavy emphasis on historical analysis. Products included written and oral presentations of research efforts and other activities. The advanced content dimension was addressed through the selection of advanced reading materials, including many primary source documents, as well as secondary sources and historical fiction, and through early introduction of advanced skills and ideas.

An example of the translation of the ICM to the specific disciplines may be found in Table 1.2, which portrays the ICM as it has been applied to the exemplary curricular units developed at the Center for Gifted Education at the College of William and Mary. These curricular units will be discussed further as examples of content-based curricula for high-ability learners throughout this text, with explorations of the same emphases in the fourth major content area, mathematics, as well.

Curricular Reform Design Elements

These national curricular projects for high-ability learners were developed with an understanding of appropriate curricular dimensions for gifted students, but they also demonstrate the use of key design features of curricular reform strongly advocated by the national standards projects (O'Day & Smith, 1993) and the middle school movement (Erb, 1994). Thus, the curricular projects employ the following emphases:

- *Meaning-based,* in that the curriculum emphasizes depth over breadth, concepts over facts, and is grounded in real-world issues and problems that students care about or need to know. In science, students study the implications of acid spills on interstate highway systems. In language arts, they relate to how the impact of the treatment of minorities in this country has changed over a 60-year period. In social studies, students examine documents within context and explore the influence of various individuals and groups to understand the complexity of historical events and decisions. Moreover, the pedagogy of the curriculum is constructivist in orientation, helping students to construct their own meaning from the events, artifacts, and problems studied.
- *Higher order thinking and reasoning* is integral to all content areas. The units provide students opportunities to demonstrate their understanding of advanced content and interdisciplinary ideas through strategies such as concept mapping, persuasive writing, and designing experiments.

Table 1.2

Application of Integrated Curriculum Model to William and Mary Science, Language Arts, and Social Studies Curricular Units

Dimension	Science Units	Language Arts Units	Social Studies Units
Advanced Content	• Student-determined mastery of science content through problem-based approach. • Formative and summative assessment of science content learning.	• Advanced reading selections. • Corresponding advanced vocabulary work. • D-P approach used to teach grammar. • Expository/personal essay writing.	• Advanced in-depth study of key periods in U.S. and world history that were influential, with an emphasis on the use of primary sources.
Process/Product	• Use of scientific process embedded in problem-based learning. • Preparation of problem resolution and presentation to class.	• Use of writing process model coupled with self, peer, and teacher assessment approaches. • Use of Paul's Elements of Reasoning (1992) to explore meaning in literature and to conduct real-world research. • Production of research project/oral presentation of findings.	• Emphasis on Paul's Elements of Reasoning (1992) as a basis for oral and written argument in the analysis of complex social and historical issues. • Emphasis on historical analysis skills applied to primary and secondary sources.
Issues/Themes	• Organized around the concept of *systems*. • Teaching to underlying generalizations about systems.	• Organized around the concept of *change*. • Teaching to underlying generalizations about change.	• Organized around the concept of social, geographical, political, and economic systems that define the history of ancient and modern civilizations. • Subconcepts of structure, function, pattern, and cause and effect are also explored. • Emphasis on complexity of causality in human interactions throughout history.

- Emphasizes *intradisciplinary and interdisciplinary connections* through using overarching concepts, issues, and themes as major organizers. Thus, students study systems of cities, government, economies, and language, as well as chemistry and biology. The concept of *change* in language arts is relevant to literature, writing, and language, as well as to mathematics, art, and music.
- Provides opportunities for *metacognition*—student reflection on learning processes. Students are involved in consciously planning, monitoring, and assessing their own learning for efficient and effective use of time and resources. In social studies, for example, students pursue alternative paths to a real-world problem resolution in their particular area of study through a deliberative group process that engages them in metacognitive skills.
- Develops *habits of mind* through cultivating modes of thinking that resemble those of professionals in various fields with respect to skills, predispositions, and attitudes. In science, curiosity, objectivity, and skepticism are openly nurtured. In language arts, the mode of reflection and revision is consistently encouraged. In social studies, experiences develop awareness of the complexity of causality, the importance of exploring bias, and the need to avoid present-mindedness and ethnocentrism.
- Promotes *inquiry-based learning and problem solving* by having students take charge of their own learning. In the problem-based science units, students find out what they know, what they need to know, and how to pursue important knowledge in working on a real-world problem in small investigatory teams. In language arts, students team to discover how language functions and is structured. In social studies, students work together to explore different aspects of a culture or historical period and then share their findings.
- Uses various new *technologies as tools* for the learning process, from doing library research via the Internet, to composing at the word processor, to communicating with students around the world by e-mail. The units of study in each area incorporate activities that require these applications.
- Framed on *learner outcomes of significance*, those that advance higher level skills and conceptual understandings. Expectations for learning are identified at targeted grade levels that reflect the priorities of the new curriculum for being broad-based, conceptual, and relevant to real-world application. In each set of units,

learner outcomes reflect content, process/product, and concept emphases.

- Employs *authentic assessment* by tapping into what students know as a result of meaningful instruction. Using approaches like portfolios and performance-based activities, the units engage learners in assessment as an active part of the learning process.
- Sensitive to *multicultural and global concerns*. In the case of language arts and social studies, it ensures a strong representational pattern of multicultural readings and materials, as well a focus on the important skill of viewing issues from multiple perspectives. History is deliberately taught from the viewpoint of both minority and majority groups.
- Focuses on an overarching *concept* as a frame for development and implementation. Language arts units employ the concept of *change*, while science and social studies work with the concept of *systems* with the overlap of change over time and cause and effect in the study of history.
- Employs *multiple resources and materials* that allow flexibility, variety, and sophistication in delivery patterns. Students may read different texts, for example, yet respond to a common set of questions about them.
- Focuses on *substantive content*: key ideas, principles, and structures that students need to master in the discipline in order to become proficient. The content is organized to provide an understanding of the structure of language arts, science, and social sciences.

All of these reform elements formed the basis for initial curriculum development work. A model of the elements taken together may be seen in Figure 1.2. The puzzle represents a holistic way to represent the interlocking nature of these elements, yet it reveals the clear boundaries of each that may be used in teacher training.

Systematic tailoring of the curriculum for gifted learners occurred through ensuring the following kinds of additional emphasis:

- provisions for acceleration and compression of content;
- use of interrelated higher order thinking skills (e.g., analysis, synthesis, and evaluation);
- integration of content by key ideas, issues, and themes;
- advanced reading level of materials employed;
- opportunities for students to develop advanced products;

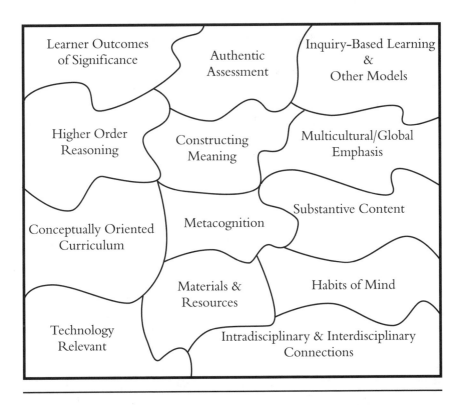

 Figure 1.2
A Model for Curricular Reform

- opportunities for independent learning based on student capacity and interest; and
- consistently focused use of inquiry-based instructional techniques.

Thus, the systematic fusion of integrated curricular considerations with reform principles was effected.

Implementation Considerations

The implementation of any curricular model is based on several considerations in the school setting. Most important among them is the nature of the learner. For talented students, regardless of the richness of the core curricular base, there will be a need to address certain powerful characteristics through flexible implementation of a model.

The Learner: Characteristics, Aptitudes, and Predispositions

There are many characteristics of gifted learners on which one might focus for a discussion of creating an optimal match between learner and curriculum. Several lists have been discussed as a basis for curricular work (e.g., Maker, 1982; VanTassel-Baska, 1994a). However, in studies of curricula, it has become apparent that three such characteristics remain pivotal for purposes of curricular planning and development: precocity, intensity, and complexity.

Precocity. The precocity of the learner is a key characteristic to consider in curriculum development. Gifted learners, almost by definition, evidence advanced development in some school-related curricular area. The most commonly tested areas for such development are in the verbal and mathematical subject domains. Most students identified for gifted programs are at least 2 years advanced in one or both areas. Such evidence of advanced development provides a basis for curricular planning at a more advanced level and the expectation that such students can master new materials in one-third to one-half the time of typical learners. For acutely gifted learners, there is a powerful motivation to learn fast and move ahead.

Intensity. In addition to precocity, another key characteristic that deserves attention for curriculum development is the intensity of gifted learners. This intensity may be manifested affectively in the realm of emotional responsiveness when students react strongly to the death of a pet or the classroom injustice committed by a teacher. But, this characteristic also has saliency in the cognitive realm. Students exhibit intensity through the capacity to focus and concentrate for long periods of time on a subject that fascinates them or an idea they find intriguing. Such a characteristic can just as quickly become dissipated in uninteresting busywork or lack of depth in the exploration even of a subject of interest. This characteristic, like precocity, needs curricular attention.

Complexity. The third learner characteristic of curricular interest is complexity, the capacity of gifted learners to engage in higher level and abstract thinking even at young ages. It also refers to their preference for hard and challenging work, often at levels beyond current functioning. They also enjoy working on multiple levels simultaneously, such as when solving complex real-world problems that have many parts and perspectives to study. Just as with precocity and intensity, the characteristic of complexity in the gifted demands curricular responsiveness because it is openly desired by the learner and often indicated by his or her behavior in the classroom.

These three characteristics each dictate an approach to the curriculum that honors the various facets of the gifted mind and personality. While other curricular models have addressed a particular facet of the gifted learner, the Integrated Curriculum Model represents a fusion of several approaches such that the most powerful characteristics of the gifted are directly reflected in the curricular intervention.

While this model has salience for all learners, based on a talent development paradigm, the variable of time becomes crucial in implementation. Not all learners will be ready at the same stage of development in each area for the advanced, intensive, and complex study required by the curriculum. For example, reading selections in the language arts curriculum may be appropriate for high-ability fifth graders, but too difficult based on reading level for average fifth graders. Teachers, then, would need to decide whether to substitute more accessible literature and still employ the unit with all students or to differentiate instruction in the classroom, using the unit only with a cluster group of high-ability learners. The judicious application of this curricular model for all learners is thus advised.

The Context Variables

While the need for a match between the learner and the intervention has already been described, it is also important to highlight important contextual considerations that could impact the successful use of this curricular model in school settings. There are at least four variables that must be considered: flexibility in student placement and progress, grouping, teacher training, and climate of excellence.

Flexibility in Student Placement and Progress. Even an enriched and accelerated curriculum developed for high-ability learners that addresses all of the educational reform principles cannot be used without careful consideration of entry skills, rate of learning, and special interests and needs. Thus, ungraded multiage contexts in which high-ability learners access appropriate work groups and curricular stations represent a critical component of the implementation context. Pretesting of students on relevant skills is a central part of the Center for Gifted Education's curricular projects, and diagnosing unusual readiness or developmental spurts that may occur in a curricular sequence is also important. Schools may notice and use such data as a basis for more in-depth work in an area of a particular teaching unit.

Grouping. As a curriculum for high-ability learners is implemented, attention must be paid to the beneficial impact of grouping for instruction. As Kulik's (1993) latest reanalysis of the grouping data demonstrated, when curricula are modified for gifted students, the positive effects of grouping become more prominent. Moreover, recent classroom studies have verified that little differentiation is occurring in heterogeneous classrooms for gifted students (Archambault et al., 1993) and the majority of teachers in our schools are not trained to teach gifted learners (Westberg, Archambault, Dobyns, & Salvin, 1993). Thus, forming instructional groups of gifted students for implementation of a differentiated curriculum is clearly the most effective and efficient way to deliver it. Whether such grouping occurs in separately designated classes or in regular classrooms is a local consideration.

Teacher Training. Based on recent data confirming the significant role of teacher training in providing differentiated instruction for the gifted (Hansen & Feldhusen, 1994; Tomlinson et al., 1994) and the availability of coursework in the education of the gifted (Parker & Karnes, 1991), there is good reason to place gifted students with teachers who have received at least 12 hours of professional training. The benefits to gifted learners become greater when a differentiated curriculum is handled by those sensitive to the nature and needs of such students. Some training in the direct implementation of curricular materials to be used is also desirable. For example, in our experience with the Center for Gifted Education materials, about 3 days of training in the various approaches employed in the materials have generally supported initial implementation, depending on the experience of the teachers involved.

What teacher characteristics are essential for implementing content-based curricula with gifted learners? Obviously, knowing the content area being taught is a primary consideration, coupled with a deep understanding of how gifted students learn differently from other students and even each other. Such a combination requires important human characteristics in a teacher of the gifted, such as openness to experience, a personal passion for learning, and a curiosity about how the minds of these students work. Such characteristics must also be matched, however, by a strong grasp of the structure of the discipline in which one is teaching and the security to employ different methods as they are required. Facilitating learning for these students must involve careful questioning and probing, coupled with the regular presentation of challenging stimuli.

Can we educate teachers to possess these characteristics? In part, we may be able to. Yet, my questionnaire to high school gifted seniors about choosing education as a career has convinced me that finding teachers with these qualities is a difficult challenge. One student wrote in response to the question of what would be an incentive to go into teaching, "Having teachers who do not follow formulaic teaching styles . . . "

Access to high-quality, well-trained teachers in specific subject areas who can provide challenge and nurturance for our best learners is clearly a critical issue in appropriate education of the gifted. Without thoughtful teachers, the best curricula will lie dormant in classrooms, unable to be energized and vivified by expert instruction. Teachers with only strong management skills also will fail to excite the gifted if lack of knowledge is apparent.

Climate of Excellence. In order for gifted learners to perform at optimal levels, the educational context must offer challenging opportunities that tap deeply into students' psychological states (Csikszentmihalyi, Rathunde, & Whalen, 1993), provide generative situations (VanTassel-Baska, 1998), and also demand high standards of excellence that correspond to expectations for high-level productivity in any field (Ochse, 1990). More than ever, the climate of a school for excellence matters if curricular standards are to be raised successfully for any student. For gifted students in particular, such a climate must be in place to ensure optimal development, positive attitudes toward learning, and engagement. Such a climate is also essential for disadvantaged gifted youth who are put more at risk by lowered expectations for performance (House & Lapan, 1994).

Conclusion

This opening chapter has established the landscape of what constitutes appropriate curricula for the gifted and why such a multidimensional approach is required. Succeeding chapters will provide concrete applications of the ICM at work with gifted students across subject areas, levels of instruction, and dimensions of learning. Only through careful curriculum development practices can we help promote optimal learning opportunities for minds of promise.

Key Points Summary

❑ Differentiated curricula for the gifted involve the features of advanced level, choice of instructional strategies that promote thinking, selection and purchasing of appropriate materials, and generative project work.

❑ Curricular paradigms used in gifted education include the following: traditional, social reconstructivist, cognitive constructionist, behaviorist, and postpositivist. Such views carry their own inherent assumptions about reality, knowledge, methods, and values of a school-based curriculum.

❑ Curricula for the gifted should employ the features of the Integrated Curriculum Model (ICM) since it is consistent with multiple paradigms and existing research on learning and gifted learners.

❑ Curricula for the gifted should align with existing state and national standards to be effective and exemplary of key reform features.

❑ Implementation of a curriculum must honor the specific characteristics of the learners being taught and provide a flexible and supportive environment for learning.

References

Amabile, T. (1996). *Creativity in context*. Boulder, CO: Westview Press.

American Association for the Advancement of Science. (1990). *Science for all Americans*. New York: Oxford University Press.

Apple, M. W. (1991). The culture and commerce of the textbook. In M. W. Apple & L. K. Christian-Smith (Eds.), *The politics of the textbook* (pp. 22–40). New York: Routledge.

Archambault, F. X., Jr., Westberg, K. L., Brown, S., Hallmark, B. W., Zhang, W., & Emmons, C. (1993). Regular classroom practices with gifted students: Findings from the Classroom Practices Survey. *Journal for the Education of the Gifted, 16*, 103–119.

Banks, J. A. (1975). *Teaching strategies for ethnic studies*. Boston: Allyn and Bacon.

Benbow, C. P., & Stanley, J. C. (Eds.). (1983). *Academic precocity: Aspects of its development*. Baltimore: Johns Hopkins University Press.

Boyce, L. N. (1997). *A guide to teaching research skills and strategies for grades 4–12*. Williamsburg, VA: Center for Gifted Education, College of William and Mary.

Center for Gifted Education. (1997). *Guide to teaching a problem-based science curriculum*. Dubuque, IA: Kendall/Hunt.

Center for Gifted Education. (1999). *Guide to teaching a language arts curriculum for high-ability learners*. Dubuque, IA: Kendall/Hunt.

Csikszentmihalyi, M., Rathunde, K., & Whalen, S. (1993). *Talented teenagers: The roots of success and failure*. New York: Cambridge University Press.

Erb, T. (1994). The middle school: Mimicking the success routes of the information age. *Journal for the Education of the Gifted, 17*, 385–406.

Gardner, H. (1983). *Frames of mind: The theory of multiple intelligences*. New York: BasicBooks.

Hansen, J., & Feldhusen, J. (1994). Comparison of trained and untrained teachers of the gifted. *Gifted Child Quarterly, 38*, 115–123.

House, E., & Lapan, S. (1994). Evaluation of programs for disadvantaged gifted students. *Journal for the Education of the Gifted, 17*, 441–466.

Johnsen, S. K. (2000, Summer). What the research says about curriculum. *Tempo*, 25–30.

Johnson, D. T., Boyce, L. N., & VanTassel-Baska, J. (1995). Science curriculum review: Evaluating materials for high-ability learners. *Gifted Child Quarterly, 39*, 36–43.

Kulik, J. (1993). *An analysis of the research on ability grouping: Historical and contemporary perspectives*. Storrs: The National Research Center on the Gifted and Talented, University of Connecticut.

Maker, C. J. (1982). *Curriculum development for the gifted*. Rockville, MD: Aspen Systems.

Marzano, R. (1992). *Cultivating thinking in English*. Urbana, IL: National Council for Teachers of English.

Ochse, R. (1990). *Before the gates of excellence: Determinants of creative genius*. Cambridge, England: Cambridge University Press.

O'Day, J. A., & Smith, M. S. (1993). Systemic reform and educational opportunity. In S. H. Fuhrman (Ed.), *Designing coherent educational policy* (pp. 250–311). San Francisco: Jossey-Bass.

Parker, J., & Karnes, F. (1991). Graduate degree programs and resource centers in gifted education: An update and analysis. *Gifted Child Quarterly, 35*, 43–48.

Paul, R. (1992). *Critical thinking: What every person needs to survive in a rapidly changing world.* Rohnert Park, CA: Foundation for Critical Thinking.

Perkins, D. (1992). Selecting fertile themes for integrated learning. In H. Hayes Jacobs (Ed.), *Interdisciplinary curriculum: Design and implementation* (pp. 67–75). Alexandria, VA: Association for Supervision and Curriculum Development.

Perkins, D., & Salomon, G. (1989). Are cognitive skills context bound? *Educational Research, 18*, 16–25.

Sher, B. T. (1993). *Guide to key science concepts.* Williamsburg, VA: Center for Gifted Education, College of William and Mary.

Skinner, B. F. (1967). *Science and human behavior.* New York: Free Press.

Tomlinson, C., Tomchin, E., Callahan, C., Adams, C., Pizzat-Timi, P., Cunningham, C., Moore, B., Lutz, L., Robertson, C., Eiss, N., Landrum, M., Hunsaker, S., & Imbeau, M. (1994). Practices of preservice teachers related to gifted and other academically diverse learners. *Gifted Child Quarterly, 38*, 106–114.

United States Department of Education Office of Educational Research and Improvement. (1993). *National excellence: A case for developing America's talent.* Washington, DC: U.S. Government Printing Office.

VanTassel-Baska, J. (1986). Effective curriculum and instructional models for the gifted. *Gifted Child Quarterly, 30*, 164–169.

VanTassel-Baska, J. (1992). *Effective curriculum planning for gifted learners.* Denver: Love.

VanTassel-Baska, J. (1994a). *Comprehensive curriculum for gifted learners* (2nd ed.). Boston: Allyn and Bacon.

VanTassel-Baska, J. (1994b). Development and assessment of integrated curriculum: A worthy challenge. *Quest, 5*, 1–5.

VanTassel-Baska, J. (Ed.). (1998). *Excellence in educating gifted and talented learners* (3rd ed.). Denver: Love.

VanTassel-Baska, J. (in press). *Curriculum planning and instructional design for gifted learners* (2nd ed.). Denver: Love.

VanTassel-Baska, J., Bass, G., Ries, R., Poland, D., & Avery, L. D. (1998). A national study of science curriculum effectiveness with high-ability students. *Gifted Child Quarterly, 42*, 200–211.

VanTassel-Baska, J., & Brown, E. (2000). An analysis of gifted curriculum models. In F. A. Karnes & S. M. Bean (Eds.), *Methods and materials for teaching the gifted* (pp. 91–131). Waco, TX: Prufrock Press.

VanTassel-Baska, J., Gallagher, S. A., Bailey, J. M., & Sher, B. T. (1993, September/October). Scientific experimentation: The importance of strong science education for all students is a concern to schools. *Gifted Child Today, 16*(5), 42–46.

VanTassel-Baska, J., Zuo, L., Avery, L. D., & Little, C. A. (2002). A curriculum study of gifted student learning in the language arts. *Gifted Child Quarterly, 46*, 30–44.

Vygotsky, L. S. (1978). *Mind in society: The development of higher psychological processes*. Cambridge, MA: Harvard University Press.

Ward, V. (1981). *Differential education for the gifted*. Ventura County, CA: Office of the Superintendent of Schools.

Westberg, K. L., Archambault, F. X., Jr., Dobyns, S. M., & Salvin, T. J. (1993). An observational study of classroom practices used with third- and fourth-grade students. *Journal for the Education of the Gifted, 16*, 120–146.

Section I

Introduction

This section of the book explicates the Integrated Curriculum Model (ICM) in all of its elements. It begins with a discussion of the need for an emphasis on an accelerated curriculum for precocious learners that uses appropriate diagnostic and prescriptive approaches to ascertain areas and levels of readiness. VanTassel-Baska and Sher also explore the implications of acceleration in all of its forms as students progress through school. Their chapter focuses on two diverse case studies in which accelerated study was essential for each student's development. In the second chapter in this section, Struck tackles the issue of infusing higher order process skills into content and demonstrates through the presentation of various models the efficacy of doing so. In the treatment of specific models of learning, such skills are used to demonstrate the importance of the continued use of one model to build student automaticity and the internalization of the model for use in any problem situation. The Lehane chapter on student products exemplifies the issues associated with facilitating the development of original student work and assessing it in such a way that students can see the growth potential for themselves in continuing to refine a product. This chapter uses the humanities as a content base to explore appropriate differentiated product demands along with a helpful discussion on the concept of quality as it relates to the development of aesthetic products. The Avery and Little chapter explores the world of concepts and themes as a fundamental aspect of curricular structure for the gifted. They thoughtfully probe the essence of what concepts are, how to teach them, and their importance in understanding how the world works.

Each of the chapters is linked to specific research-based curricular and teaching models that have been used with gifted learners and found to be effective. Taken together, these chapters demonstrate the power of the ICM in responding to the primary needs of gifted learners for advanced work, higher level work that is in-depth and creative, and conceptual work that challenges them at complex levels of thought.

Accelerating Learning Experiences in Core Content Areas

by
Joyce VanTassel-Baska
and
Beverly Sher

You are a primary teacher of the gifted and have just begun your third year of teaching. Because you are now off probation, you feel you can begin to experiment a bit with the curriculum, especially as you have noticed that some of your students seem bored and distracted by what constitutes grade-level curriculum. In fact, the mother of one of your students has already scheduled an appointment with you to discuss how you plan to differentiate for her child in the regular classroom. Yet, you have 22 other students whose needs must also be considered. How do you satisfy the needs of advanced learners and their families while also attending to the full range of student needs?

Acceleration of gifted students is the first consideration in planning an appropriate curriculum for them. Each of these learners is typically identified based on advanced development in one or more areas of the curriculum to begin with. This higher level of functioning demands that the level of curricular challenge be raised to ensure a good match to the child's readiness pattern for learning. Thus, acceleration has to precede enrichment within core areas of learning.

There are several myths associated with the advancement of children beyond grade-level expectations. The following list is typical in that it explores various misconceptions about acceleration that both educators and parents hold.

Myth #1: Gifted children will become social and emotional misfits if they are accelerated. No studies suggest that acceleration causes such problems in the gifted (Gross, 1994; Kulik & Kulik, 1984). Ironically, just the opposite may be true. When forced to be socialized with age mates in a lower level curriculum, gifted children may become socially with-drawn and alienated over time.

Myth #2: Gifted children benefit more when their learning is controlled, even when advancement is a part of the plan. For example, students may go ahead a half year in math, but no more. This myth is dangerous in that it implies a one-size-fits-all mentality when working with the gifted. Individual differences prevail in ways that make artificial boundaries for learning a subject inhibitory. Each student should be encouraged to learn as much as possible in subject areas for which he or she must demonstrate proficiency (Schiever & Maker, 1997).

Myth #3: Gifted children benefit from enrichment more than acceleration. Studies over the past century have continued to demonstrate that acceleration is twice as powerful as enrichment when dealing with gifted students (e.g., Kulik & Kulik, 1992). Moreover, gifted students enjoy moving at a fast pace through subject material, gobbling up new facts as they go. For many gifted students, their major interest area is also the area of learning in which they are most precocious, thus adding to their desire for advanced work in that area.

Myth #4: Gifted children will run out of curriculum or have to repeat in later years because of early exposure to advanced level work. The new stan-dards have clearly demonstrated the scope of material that needs to be mastered in each subject area, an amount requiring more instructional time than is currently available in schools (Marzano, 1999). Consequently, there will always be more to learn even for the gifted at every stage of development. Schools need to be sensitive, however, to K–12 curricular planning for the gifted that would allow for effective use of school time in a subject area augmented with outside opportunities.

Myth #5: Gifted children will be more normalized by staying with age mates. The reality of giftedness is its unique trajectory for learning that does not conform to age-grade expectations. Consequently, staying with age mates and being discouraged from learning at one's own comfortable rate invites underachievement patterns of behavior, including acting up and out, refusing to do assigned work, and loss of motivation for learning (Gallagher & Gallagher, 1994).

These are but a few of the common ideas we hold about the dangers of acceleration of gifted learners. In truth, our gifted programs are far less effective than they might be if strong acceleration policies were enacted.

Classroom-Based Acceleration

For the clear majority of gifted and high-ability learners in school, the use of classroom-based acceleration practices are an essential part of making learning meaningful for them. A system for diagnosing and prescribing the appropriate level of instruction for these learners was developed in the 1970s by Julian Stanley and has been used worldwide in programs for the gifted ever since (Benbow & Stanley, 1983; VanTassel-Baska, 1996). For a teacher with gifted and high-ability children in the class, what approaches are essential to employ? The core of the approach may be summarized in three steps: diagnostic assessment, cluster grouping, and follow-up curricular intervention.

Step 1: Diagnostic Assessment

Perhaps the central strategy that is called for is effective diagnostic assessment of those learners who a teacher suspects of having advanced abilities in the core areas of learning: reading and math. This diagnostic assessment should be buttressed by the previous year's achievement data and other records. Utilizing multiple sources of data for making decisions is important. Possible sources of diagnostic data include the following:

- *End-of-year assessments to be employed at your grade level.* In September, give your students the end-of-year reading comprehension test, the spelling test, and the English usage test in language arts; in math, give them the end-of-year computation, measurement, and number theory assessment. In each of these areas, your high-ability learners are likely to score 75% or higher, necessitating the need for compressed instruction and advanced work on other aspects of the language arts and math curricula.
- *Formal diagnostic instruments.* Give your students the Gates-Mcginitie diagnostic reading test and the Orleans-Hanna math test to assess functional level in these skill areas. Teachers may also administer an individual achievement test in these key areas of learning.
- *Chapter tests that cluster items across topics in math.* Because of the incremental nature of math study, you may want to assess students on more discrete aspects of the curriculum as the year progresses. While this approach inhibits accelerative practices, it does allow students to avoid being remediated.

Such diagnostic assessment is a crucial first step in finding students who need advanced instruction in basic areas of the curriculum.

Step 2: Cluster Grouping

Follow-up instructional intervention must then be based on the diagnostic results. These results should be analyzed for patterns within and across student profiles. Students who are reasonably close in scores (i.e., within 10 percentage points) should be cluster-grouped for advanced instruction. These groups may range from two to five students in number. If a teacher has only one student who is very advanced, that student should be cluster-grouped with other students at a comparable level either at the same grade level or at the next grade level for instruction in reading, math, or both. It is not appropriate to have gifted students working independently throughout the year in a core area of the curriculum when they could be working with intellectual peers and learning more.

Step 3: Intervention With Curricular Materials

Beyond the instructional grouping decision lies the issue of a differentiated instructional plan for these students in reading and

Mathematics

Target group:
Advanced students whose results suggest 1–2 years beyond grade-level expectations.

Curricular interventions:
- Fast-paced use of math text in gap areas, working out of the current and next 2 years text materials in the district
- Compression of the math standards for the group, consistent with diagnostic results
- Use of leveled materials as supplementary resources (e.g., Techniques of Problem Solving [TOPS] materials)
- Use of math manipulatives
- Use of games and puzzles in a structured math center

Reading

Target group:
Advanced students who score 1–3 years beyond grade level expectations in reading skills and comprehension.

Curricular interventions:
- The Center for Gifted Education Language Arts units
- Junior Great Books as supplementary reading material
- Compression of the state language arts standards that relate to reading skills, including analysis and evaluation of text
- Independent reading program, based on tailored bibliographies

Figure 2.1

Mathematics and Reading Packaged Curricula for High-Ability Learners

mathematics. Figure 2.1 suggests packaged curricular materials that could be employed with these cluster groups to address a differentiated plan for learning. Such interventions should make the delivery of the differentiated instructional plan feasible, as materials that are already differentiated can be put in student hands, relieving the teacher of the necessity of creating activities and projects from scratch.

The combinatory power of diagnostic testing, cluster grouping based on results, and follow-up intervention with proven materials would be a major improvement in all classrooms and ease the concerns of parents of the gifted whose children feel trapped by grade-level work. By the same token, the use of prepared materials eases the teacher's burden of creating differentiated lessons on the fly. Moreover, it provides enough curriculum for a year's worth of work.

Issues in Implementing a Diagnostic-Prescriptive Approach

Many teachers find that they can only accommodate limited numbers of classroom groups successfully. If a teacher can maintain three such groups, it is sufficient to the tasks outlined above. Teachers should provide direct instruction to such groups on a rotating model so that instructional time is shared equally across the classroom. Gifted and high-ability students need direct instruction, too, just at their level of learning.

Teachers often complain that they have no support for these techniques from other teachers or the principal. These approaches require the support of whole schools in order to make them work. Individual teachers cannot effectively implement these strategies in the absence of cross-grade collaboration and principal approval and support. Consequently, careful up-front planning is necessary across staff to make the model work effectively.

Across multiple years, schools must articulate their work with high-ability learners to the next level of learning in the school district, typically middle and high schools. Curriculum coordinators in each of the disciplines must be made cognizant of the implications for accelerated learning and become supportive of such efforts.

Sometimes, the cluster-grouping model used initially in each area is insufficient in terms of containing students ready to do the advanced work. Adding and removing students from the cluster should be ongoing as new students surface who can handle the challenge and current students fail to perform.

Teachers frequently feel they lack the skill to work with an advanced group in their classroom. This problem may be alleviated by differentiating the staffing within a school such that the most skilled teacher in a particular area like math can be assigned to work with the math high-ability clusters at least one day a week or obtain the use of expert volunteers in a similar capacity. Resource teachers of the gifted may also be employed in this fashion.

Accelerated Learning Across Grade Levels

A basic principle of instruction for gifted students is that many of them need content acceleration continuously and at a number of specific stages in their development (VanTassel-Baska, 1986, 1998). Although a district's programs may include classroom-based adaptations of basic materials and activities that enrich, expand, and enhance learning opportunities such as have just been described, it must be recognized that a student's need for accelerated learning will extend beyond what a given teacher can provide. It may be difficult to obtain a program that is consistently fast-paced, enriching, and well organized. Yet, such goals must be targeted if the students' needs are to be met. As an example, in a comprehensive language arts program for elementary students reading at advanced levels, the following program attributes would be appropriate:

- use of advanced reading materials such as those suggested;
- participation in an inquiry-based study of appropriate children's literature (e.g., Junior Great Books);
- inclusion of a writing program that encourages elaboration and incorporation of ideas from literature into stories;
- use of supplementary materials for the development of vocabulary skills;
- reading of selected biographies and books in the content areas (including subjects dealing with multicultural issues);
- inclusion of experiences in foreign language;
- emphasis on the development and use of logic and critical thinking;
- spelling work derived from both basal and literary reading selections;
- telling stories and reading personal works; and
- encouragement and provision of time to pursue free reading based on children's interests.

Although the overall emphasis of the program is an integrated language experience with a strong emphasis on enrichment of the basic curriculum, the underlying issue of appropriate level of instruction is stressed through careful assessment of reading-skill levels at various stages each year, access to advanced reading materials, and a vocabulary and spelling program that corresponds with the level of reading instruction. This list of interventions for gifted learners at the elementary level shows the scope of activities that acceleration should provide in setting the curricular pattern in a given content area.

Subject matter acceleration in other content areas also has importance for students in the elementary grades. In mathematics, for example, there is also the need to consider the following instructional emphases across years:

- a focus on developing spatial skills and concepts through geometry and other forms of spatial problem solving;
- a focus on problem-solving skills with appropriately challenging problems;
- an emphasis on the use of calculators and computers as tools in the problem–solving process;
- more emphasis on mathematical concepts and less on computational skills;
- focus on logic problems that require deductive thinking skills and inference;
- emphasis on applications of mathematics in the real world through creation of projects that provide experience;
- emphasis on algebraic manipulations; and
- work with statistics and probability.

For many gifted students, accelerative options are necessary outside the regular classroom and over the developmental course of their K–12 years. Table 2.1 contains options that educators and parents need to consider as a core part of curricular planning for high-ability and gifted learners. Again, the accelerated curriculum is balanced with a strong enrichment element; but, at the same time, it allows for skills, concepts, and requisite materials to be at a challenging level for the child, rather than being geared to grade-level considerations.

Table 2.1
Archetypal Features of Candidates for Acceleration Matched With Intervention

Early Admission	Content Acceleration	Grade Advancement	Early Exit From High School
Developmentally advanced in all academic areas by at least 2 years; identified by parents and confirmed by a psychologist.	Precocity in verbal areas; above average in other academic endeavors; identified by teachers during the primary years of schooling.	Developmentally advanced in all academic areas with above-average (not outstanding) grades; is bored by the school's regular and gifted program; identified by parents/self through talent search participation at junior high level.	Highly motivated student who is excelling in all areas at the high school level; identified by teachers and awards.
Suggested Intervention: Early entrance to kindergarten with an appropriately advanced curriculum, careful monitoring of progress throughout early elementary years. Additional acceleration will probably be warranted by junior high school. Early graduation from high school may also be considered (Proctor, Black, & Feldhusen, 1986).	*Suggested Intervention:* Content acceleration to appropriately challenging levels in reading; early application of verbal abilities to writing, dramatics, and debate; formation of literary discussion group that provides a peer-group context (Davis & Rimm, 1988).	*Suggested Intervention:* Grade acceleration to high school; course selection and program guided by academic strengths and interests; careful monitoring of performance in advanced classes to ensure both challenge and success (Stanley, 1979).	*Suggested Intervention:* Early graduation from high school with emphasis on career counseling and college selection of liberal arts study (Stanley, 1979).

Applications of Accelerated Patterns: Case Studies

The following two case studies have been drawn from the authors' direct experience with gifted children and their developmental trajectories of learning. Each case reflects very different student profiles and predispositions for schoolwork. Each profile also accentuates the need for different accelerative opportunities based on aptitude areas and levels. Finally, the case studies illustrate the uniqueness of gifted students' development and, to some extent, the lack of predictability in it.

Acceleration Case Study #1

Lewis was an intellectually precocious infant. He was fascinated by books by the age of 6 months, and he would listen to his parents read for hours at a time by 12 months. He knew all of the upper-case and lower-case letters and their sounds by 18 months, and he was reading before age 2. He also showed signs of mathematical talent, as he was doing double-digit addition and subtraction in his head at 26 months. He could count past 1,000 at age 2½.

He entered Montessori preschool 4 months before his fourth birthday. Montessori was an excellent fit for him: He loved working at his own pace on reading, math, and geography. By kindergarten, Woodcock-Johnson testing revealed that he was working at the late elementary level in all subject areas, and his Montessori teacher had created an individualized, advanced curriculum for him.

At 6, he entered a Montessori elementary program as a first-year student. His teachers brought advanced math work down from the upper-elementary classroom for him; he loved extracting square roots using the Montessori materials. He also enjoyed working with the school's periodic table materials, usually used by upper-elementary students to "build" atoms of different elements by adding the proper number of protons and neutrons to the nucleus and the proper number of electrons to the electron shells surrounding the nucleus.

By second grade, he had exhausted the Montessori elementary math materials, which included algebra and geometry work. Fortunately, the Education Program for Gifted Youth (EPGY) became available as a distance-learning program from Stanford that year. He started the EPGY K–8 math sequence at the second-grade level in October and had finished the eighth-grade level by Christmas. He took the EPGY Logic of Algebra and Spatial Visualization courses to finish off his second-grade year.

In third grade, he was promoted to the upper-elementary class-room, normally reserved for fourth through sixth graders. He took the EPGY Algebra I and Algebra II courses, earning As. In fourth grade, he did essentially no math. He spent the year finishing the Montessori grammar boxes and polishing his essay skills; he became a competent chess player, an adept Civilization II strategist, and a Civil War buff. He enjoyed Bruce Catton's Civil War books and Winston Churchill's multivolume history of World War II. The Montessori school agreed to skip him a grade so he could participate in The Johns Hopkins' Center for Talented Youth's (CTY) Drama course for young students in the summer, where he read Ibsen, Chekhov, and Shakespeare.

In sixth grade, Lewis took EPGY's precalculus course, earning an A, and worked through Harold Jacobs' geometry textbook on his own in his Montessori classroom. He qualified for Johns Hopkins' Study of Exceptionally Talented (SET) program with a 790 on the SAT-M just after his 11th birthday; he earned a 600 on the SAT-V. He took CTY's Bay Ecology course over the summer.

His parents felt that his intellectual and social needs could not have been met in a traditional elementary school program. In Montessori school, he was able to work at his own rapid pace in all subject areas, but was also able to socialize with other elementary students in a multiage classroom. The noncompetitive Montessori environment kept his intellectual accomplishments from making other students (and their parents) feel threatened; this smoothed his social path through elementary school.

After graduating from his Montessori elementary program, Lewis moved on to public middle school at age 11. Because he was working so far ahead of grade level, the middle school agreed to skip him a second grade, and he entered middle school as an eighth grader. The middle school allowed him to take an exceptionally flexible schedule, hoping to meet both his social and his intellectual needs. He split his school day between the local university, eighth-grade classes, and sixth-grade classes.

At the university, he took the first two semesters of college calculus, earning As. At the middle school, he took the eighth-grade Spanish I course and the eighth-grade world history course. He used Bay Ecology to place out of middle school science and used CTY's Level III distance writing tutorial in place of middle school English. He took physical education, beginning band (he started French horn that fall), and other "specials" with his sixth-grade age peers. He moved to the eighth-grade band at the end of the first semester and was first chair French horn in the top middle school band by the end of the school year. He participated in MathCounts, a middle school mathematics team competition offered in selected school districts nationally (MathCounts Foundation, 2000). His team won the regional competition and placed fourth in the state; he was second in the regional individual competition and seventh in the state individual competition.

Middle school was a less happy experience for Lewis than Montessori elementary school had been. He found his middle school classes slow and boring, and he was bullied by some of the other students. Fortunately, he had allies in the building: The gifted resource teacher was always available to help him, and he found social acceptance in the band and on the MathCounts team. Now, he sees his year in middle school as being the equivalent of military boot camp: It was tough, but it taught him the public school social skills needed for survival in high school. At the end of eighth grade, though, he was convinced that he wanted to skip high school and go straight to college. His parents convinced him to give high school a try for a year, and they promised that he could go on to the local university at the end of ninth grade if he wanted to; the admissions office at the university supported this plan.

In ninth grade, Lewis took the multivariable calculus and differential equations courses at the university, earning As. He took CTY's Level IV writing tutorial in place of ninth-grade English. He used CTY's Fast-Paced High School Biology course, taken the previous summer, to place out of high school biology. Other classes included Art Foundations (a mistake, for social reasons), chemistry, Advanced Placement economics, Spanish II and III, and band. He was the second chair French horn in the All-District Symphonic Band and placed 40th out of 57 in All-State Band/Orchestra auditions. He also played in the local youth orchestra. He participated in Math League competitions and took CTY's Number Theory course in the summer.

Compared with middle school, high school seemed like "paradise" to Lewis. He had a social niche in band and had a supportive gifted resource teacher. He found his schedule adequately challenging, thanks to his college math courses and his AP course. He decided that he wanted to stay in high school for the full 4 years and graduate with his class.

In 10th grade, Lewis took the university's introductory computer science course for majors and Foundations of Mathematics, the last course required for math majors, earning As. He finished EPGY's linear algebra course, which he had started the previous spring, earning an A. His high school courses included English 10, AP biology, Spanish IV, Advanced Spanish Conversation, and band. He started the high school world geography course, which was required for graduation, but found it much too easy, so he compacted out. He took two high school world history courses through the University of Missouri's distance-learning program to meet high school graduation requirements. He continued to participate in Math League competitions and others. He was first chair French horn in the top band at school, as well as in All-District Symphonic Band and All-State Symphonic Band, also continuing to play French horn in the local youth orchestra. He placed third in All-State Band/Orchestra auditions.

Lewis plans to continue splitting his time between the university and the high school for another 2 years. He plans to take almost every AP class offered by the high school and to continue taking the math and computer science courses required for an applied math major at the university. Currently, he is ranked first in his high school class, with straight As and a large number of weighted courses on his transcript. He looks forward to another 2 years in the high school music program, and he is thinking of adding the university's orchestra to his list of outside activities. High school has been a happy experience for him, both socially and intellectually, and he sees no reason now to leave before graduation.

Acceleration Case Study #2

A second, less radical acceleration case study involves Samantha, a young girl who evinced early signs of verbal giftedness by learning the alphabet at age 2, memorizing whole books for recitation as early as age 3, and reading by age 5. Early testing (age 5) on the Peabody Individual Achievement Test revealed high verbal and general information scores (99%) with lower levels in math problem solving and concepts (85%). The Ravens Matrices showed her to be at 99% for her age group on both the Colored and Standard forms. An individual Stanford-Binet administered at age 10 revealed a 155+ score, with clear superiority in verbal areas. While standardized achievement and aptitude measures revealed potential and capacity for high performance, she struggled in school, typically receiving Bs instead of As at most stages of development. Habits of procrastination, not completing assignments, and experiencing difficulty with math were also chronic problems. SAT results in seventh grade revealed strong aptitude in both math and verbal areas, qualifying her to participate in summer programs sponsored by Northwestern University. High school assessment results continued to show high-level performance, with PSAT scores at 1370 and SAT scores of 1360, each favoring high verbal performance (720 on the PSAT and 750 on the SAT).

Attendance at a Montessori school from ages 2–5 characterized early development. Participation in Saturday and summer programs at two local universities also characterized extra school enrichment opportunities from age 5 on. Courses taken in the two university programs were broad-based, including two courses in mathematics, one in science, an art course, a geography course, journalism, and literature and writing options.

The public school accommodations for gifted children in elementary and early middle school years were minimal, with participation in a 45-minute once-a-week pull-out experience of limited educational value. The Saturday and summer experiences were necessary augmentations to keep interest in learning high. Family travel also spurred interest at these ages. Private school placement at middle school levels was also important in receiving a more personalized education, albeit not a stronger one academically. Acceleration in foreign language coursework and participation in a nongraded drama group that included students from grades 7–12 promoted both interest and accelerated skill development during these years. The need for a math tutorial became apparent when Samantha began taking Algebra I as an eighth grader.

She attended a small, private parochial school from eighth grade through her sophomore year in high school. Advantages of this particular setting for her included the opportunity to work with a superb Latin teacher and a strong math teacher, the drama opportunities mentioned earlier, the establishment of social interaction with other gifted young people, and the smaller, more structured environment. Disadvantages for Samantha at this school included a lack of school flexibility regarding course taking beyond the institution, a narrow view of education, and a disdain for students with atypical problems and learning needs. The last year and a half of high school were spent in a large, public institution that offered greater flexibility, but lacked necessary structure and attention to individual needs.

Block scheduling proved overwhelming in respect to keeping up with homework expectations as Samantha was diagnosed as having

Table 2.2
Acceleration Pattern

Grade	Accelerated Options
7	Homeschooling/tutorial (Latin I)
	Northwestern University—Literary Analysis (summer)
8	Latin II
	Northwestern University—Creative Writing (summer)
9	Latin III
	Northwestern University—AP English (summer)
10	AP Latin IV (Vergil)
	College French I & II (summer)
11	AP Latin V Catullus & Horace (independent study)
	French III & IV (block schedule at high school)
	AP American History
12	AP Government
	Dual enrollment (French)
	Early graduation (January)

both a learning disability and Attention Deficit Disorder (ADD) in her junior year. Advanced Placement courses, while a joy during her summer experience at Northwestern University and during her sophomore year at the private school, became drudgery on the block model. Because of summer course credits and dual enrollment, she was able to graduate in January of her senior year and begin college work, much to her relief. Despite her problems, awards and honors typified Samantha's experiences in school. She usually was on the honor roll, had won fourth place in the regional spelling bee in fourth grade, and had received both music and drama awards. She also was a Commended Scholar in the National Merit Program and an AP scholar by junior year. She received Latin awards for the National Latin Exam for 5 consecutive years, recording a perfect score her freshman year on the Latin III exam. She was one of 43 students selected statewide to participate in the Governor's School Latin Academy at the end of her junior year.

Table 2.2 characterizes the path of acceleration employed in Samantha's case, starting in seventh grade. For Samantha, the benefits of accelerated study included early college entrance, earning 17 college credits, earning 15 high school credits during 3 weeks in the summer, and courses waived at the university, including a freshman writing seminar.

Samantha hopes to obtain her doctorate some day. In the meantime, she plans to become an English major and classics minor at a selective public university where she currently resides. Her goals, however, have been hampered by the persistence of learning problems, coupled with more recent ancillary health difficulties.

Both Lewis and Samantha represent atypical gifted learners in respect to aptitudes, interests, and developed skills. Lewis is clearly functioning at a highly gifted level, such that schooling must be arranged around him. Samantha, while also highly gifted verbally, has a somewhat uneven profile of abilities and learning problems that lower her level of functioning. Yet, over the years, both were buoyed by accelerated experiences that impacted them positively in growth and development in all spheres of learning—the cognitive, affective, social, and aesthetic.

Who Can Work With Accelerated Learners?

Good teachers can accommodate the placement of a precocious child in their classes. If, however, an instructional option is seriously intended to provide an opportunity to accelerate a capable child's learning, it will take a teacher who is trained in gifted education and sensitive to some central issues. For many educators of the gifted, even acceleration is not a program option of choice (Southern & Jones, 1991). Therefore, there are several important qualities that should be sought in teachers of accelerated students:

- *Eager backing of acceleration options for able learners.* The attitude of the teacher toward acceleration will have a critical influence on the adaptation and progress of accelerated students. Whereas accelerants are likely to have difficulties in classes in which teachers attribute most problems to their young age, it should also not be expected that they will fare well in classrooms where their advanced placements are merely tolerated. A teacher should be able to rise to the challenge of accelerating the learning of capable students. Such a teacher will furnish educational activities, plan and follow strategies, and set expectations that will promote and maintain accelerated achievement. Teachers need to carry out frequent assessments of the accelerant's achievement and adjustment. If difficulties appear, they should be analyzed and dealt with promptly and rationally.

- *Capability to adapt and modify a curriculum to provide accelerative experiences.* Teachers chosen to work with these students need to understand how to compress material, select key concepts for emphasis, and share knowledge systems with their students. They should not double the homework amount or "cover" more material in class (VanTassel-Baska & Olszewski-Kubilius, 1988).

- *Adequate training and competence for teaching in the content area of the program.* Capable learners should have teachers who are eminently prepared to teach subject matter. This is especially true of accelerated learners. Their exceptional aptitudes will allow them to acquire new skills and knowledge rapidly and also to explore issues that students in the regular class programs will not have time to address. Teachers need to prepare for incorporating appropriate content expertise (Gallagher & Gallagher, 1994), arranging mentorships, and arranging alternate learning placements, such as laboratories, clinics, and internships (VanTassel-Baska & Olszewski-Kubilius, 1988).

- *Preparation in organizing and managing classroom activities.* A teacher of an accelerated program of study must be particularly conscious of the differences within an accelerated group of learners. Some will be capable of moving quite rapidly; others may wish to explore an area of interest in depth. Classroom environments should be flexible enough to accommodate for such individual differences. Skill in the use of cluster grouping and regrouping within an accelerated program is highly desirable for such teachers. Teachers of accelerated students can use student contracts, academic centers in the room, independent reading time, and library-based study to assure integration of the range of student needs.

Making Acceleration a Useful Option

School districts will need to plan and prepare carefully to assure that accelerative experiences will have beneficial effects for students. Networks of content area experts, artists, and educators from all levels and sectors of the community should be developed to discuss acceleration issues, produce cooperative plans, and identify mentors and resource persons. Preschool educators and university experts in early childhood should be involved from the beginning because early referral is an important aspect of any acceleration plan. Such a task force should, for example, address the need to devise appropriate curricula and to examine logistical issues regarding early-entrance and early-exit options.

In order to maximize curricular and program flexibility, it may be appropriate to develop written policy statements regarding acceleration. Indefensible restrictions should be removed to assure that capable students have maximum opportunities in the educational system, rather than being merely confined in it. Provisions need to be considered for at least the following opportunities:

1. continuous progress based on ability and performance, not age or grade, in individual curricular areas;
2. early entrance to school;
3. appropriate credit, placement, or both for advanced coursework taken off campus, given validation of proficiency; and
4. early involvement in college work through the College Board Advanced Placement program, International Baccalaureate program, or dual-enrollment options with institutions of higher education.

Conclusion

Although educators have every reason to show concern about the practice of acceleration, there is little basis in either research or effective practice not to utilize it with selected individuals or groups of gifted and high-ability learners in the area of proven competency. Candidates for acceleration vary among themselves, and the nature of the acceleration practice should be responsive to those individual variations. Schools, however, need to ensure that support structures for accelerative practice are in place and that competent teachers are available to carry out such programs. Only then will the high-ability learner be well served in our schools.

Key Points Summary

❑ Accelerating gifted and high-ability learners requires teachers to set aside harmful myths about the process and employ research-based practices.
❑ Accelerating students in the classroom involves a three-step process of diagnostic assessment, cluster grouping based on results, and follow-up curricular intervention.
❑ Acceleration beyond the classroom involves programmatic emphasis in each curricular area that would be available to gifted learners over the K–12 years of schooling.
❑ Use of accelerative practices such as early admission, content acceleration, grade advancement, and early exit from high school depend on the individual and group profile of learners.
❑ Students with different profiles can benefit from varied forms of acceleration at key stages of development.
❑ Teachers who work with accelerative practices must understand the nature of the learner, as well as the content area(s) involved.

References

Benbow, C. P., & Stanley, J. C. (Eds.). (1983). *Academic precocity: Aspects of its development.* Baltimore: Johns Hopkins University Press.

Davis, G. A., & Rimm, S. B. (1988). *Education of the gifted and talented* (3rd ed.). Englewood Cliffs, NJ: Prentice-Hall.

Gallagher, J. J., & Gallagher, S. A. (1994). *Teaching the gifted child* (4th ed.). Boston: Allyn and Bacon.

Gross, M. U. M. (1994). Radical acceleration: Responding to academic and social needs of extremely gifted adolescents. *Journal of Secondary Gifted Education, 5,* 27–34.

Kulik, J. A., & Kulik, C. C. (1984). Synthesis of research on effects of accelerated instruction. *Educational Leadership, 42*(2), 84–89.

Kulik, J. A., & Kulik, C. C. (1992). Meta-analytic findings on grouping programs. *Gifted Child Quarterly, 36,* 73–77.

Marzano, R. (1999). *An analysis of national standards in relationship to instructional time.* Aurora, CO: McRel.

MathCounts Foundation. (2000). *MathCounts in a nutshell.* Retrieved October 8, 2001, from http://www.mathcounts.org/Program/nutshell.html

Proctor, T. B., Black, K. N., & Feldhusen, J. F. (1986). Early admission of selected children to elementary school: A review of the literature. *Journal of Educational Research, 80,* 70–76.

Schiever, S. W., & Maker, C. J. (1997). Enrichment and acceleration: An overview and new directions. In N. Colangelo & G. A. Davis (Eds.), *Handbook of gifted education* (2nd ed., pp. 113–125). Boston: Allyn and Bacon.

Southern, W. T., & Jones, E. D. (Eds.). (1991). *Academic acceleration of gifted children.* New York: Teachers College Press.

Stanley, J. C. (1979). The study and facilitation of talent for mathematics. In A. H. Passow (Ed.), *The gifted and talented: Their education and development. 78th yearbook of the National Society for the Study of Education* (pp. 169–185). Chicago: University of Chicago Press.

VanTassel-Baska, J. (1986). Acceleration. In C. J. Maker (Ed.), *Critical issues in gifted education* (pp. 179–196). Rockville, MD: Aspen.

VanTassel-Baska, J. (1996). Contributions of the talent-search concept to gifted education. In C. P. Benbow & D. Lubinski (Eds.), *Intellectual talent* (pp. 236–245). Baltimore: Johns Hopkins University Press.

VanTassel-Baska, J. (Ed.). (1998). *Excellence in educating gifted and talented learners* (3rd ed.). Denver: Love.

VanTassel-Baska, J., & Olszewski-Kubilius, P. (Eds.). (1988). *Patterns of influence on gifted learners.* New York: Teachers College Press.

Incorporating Higher Order Process Skills Into Content

by
Jeanne M. Struck

You are a teacher at an urban school that was placed on notice by the state department. If your standardized test scores do not increase, your school will lose state accreditation. It was determined that test scores were low due to a weakness in student higher order process skills. You know that thinking critically is important for all students; however, you are interested in teaching strategies that will "tap" the potential giftedness you encounter in some of your students each day. You also want to investigate ways to incorporate such strategies fully into your core content curriculum for efficiency and strengthening of skills.

Throughout the United States, the accountability movement and national standards have caused many teachers to experience angst about whether or not the content they teach is learned and retained. Many districts are seeking more viable strategies to impart knowledge. The present philosophy of education in many schools emulates Dewey's (1938) notion that education be experience-based. Eisner (1988) observed that humans construct meaning, rather than discover it. Meanings are represented through an array of forms, with each form representing meaning in unique ways. Literacy within these forms can only be achieved with educational programs designed to promote meaningful experiences. This being the case, curricula in today's classrooms should include instructional strategies that employ higher order process skills.

This chapter contains explanations of how to provide high-ability learners with meaningful experiences through integrating higher order process skills such as critical thinking, problem solving, and research into any given content area under study. This chapter includes higher order process models and strategies that can be applied within and across subject areas when teaching selected state learning standards. Bloom's (1956) taxonomy will be discussed as a starting point for creating meaningful outcome objectives that are measurable. Since Socratic teaching is a powerful strategy that fosters critical thinking, this chapter also includes a discussion on how to become an effective Socratic questioner and conduct Socratic seminars.

Throughout life, individuals are confronted with issues and questions; therefore, students need to be taught how to formulate judgments and propose creative solutions to problems. Paul's (1992) Elements of Reasoning are discussed as an instructional model that effectively engages students in reasoning about any content under study. Since creative problem solving (CPS) involves both convergent and divergent thinking processes that produce innovative solutions (Daupert, 1996), the CPS model is also highlighted.

Since inquiry (or the asking of questions) and making judgments are critical elements of research, the above instructional strategies are precursors for students conducting research. Information strategies, reasoning, metacognition, and research are interrelated, reiterative processes; they are not separate and linear as they may sometimes appear in lesson plans. Therefore, an illustration of the complete research process will be described using the Center for Gifted Education's research model (Boyce, 1997).

Why Teach Higher Order Process Skills?

What distinguishes humans from other animals is our capacity for higher order mental activity. Reasoning is part of every individual's daily activities. The abilities to reason, make decisions, problem solve, analyze, interpret, and think creatively are necessary to survive in today's world of work and to deal with complex family, community, and societal issues. This being the case, supporting students in thinking critically benefits both individual and societal needs. Seiger-Ehrenberg (1985), who developed several thinking skills programs, stated:

> By the time students graduate from high school, they should be able to consistently and effectively take intelligent ethical action to accomplish the tasks society legitimately expects of all its members and to establish and pursue worthwhile goals of their own choosing. (p. 7)

By "intelligent ethical action," Seiger-Ehrenberg meant an individual's ability to arrive at a decision using rational thought processes, while taking into account the well-being of others who will be affected. She proposed that these outcomes could only be accomplished through incorporating the teaching of higher order process skills within curricula.

A Nation at Risk (National Commission on Excellence in Education, 1983) cited higher order process skills as a major weakness in U.S. education: "American students lack rigorous thought and perhaps even thinking is not valued in our schools" (p. 2). The main message in most U.S. schools is to provide "the right answer." Data from the National Excellence report (U.S. Department of Education, 1993) confirmed the prevailing viewpoint that schools offer unchallenging curricula and have low academic expectations for students. Top U.S. students had unimpressive results on assessments requiring higher level thinking. The report noted that "Students going on to a university education in other countries are expected to know more than American students and to be able to think and write analytically about that knowledge on challenging exams" (p. 12). In response to these reports, educational reformers have advocated repeatedly for intellectually challenging instruction in U.S. schools that is deeply rooted in the academic disciplines (Cohen & Spillane, 1993).

Educators should integrate higher order process skills into the content they teach each day. Many times, strategies and models that invoke critical thinking are taught in isolation, even though research suggests that such skills should be embedded in content (Feldhusen, 1994b). However, higher order reasoning is an integral piece of all content-based curricula. The teaching of higher order reasoning provides a link between learner outcomes of significance and a curricular base so that students have a viable approach for constructing meaning of substantive content.

Yet, higher order thinking strategies should be integrated into the curriculum with care. The nature of the content and the intended understandings should drive what higher order thinking strategy to use. A vertical alignment of higher order thinking models should exist across the grade levels. With continued practice and feedback, children will routinely analyze, synthesize, and evaluate problems using the models with which they are most familiar.

Thinking Critically and Creatively

Critical and creative thinking skills are part of everyone's daily repertoire. Broadly speaking, critical thinking is reasonable, reflective, and focuses on deciding what to believe or do (Ennis, 1985), whereas creative thinking is "the ability to form new combinations of ideas to fulfill a need" (Halpern, 1984, p. 234). When individuals are thinking critically, they may also be thinking creatively. According to Paul and Elder (2001), critical thinking is comprised of three phases: the ability to analyze thinking, the ability to assess thinking, and the ability to improve thinking. Therefore, when an individual thinks critically, he or she is analyzing, evaluating, and being creative. For example, when planning a vacation, most people gather material pertaining to the places they would like to visit. When in the process of deciding where to stay, what route to travel, and what places to tour (analysis thinking), the people traveling make decisions based on how much money they have to spend, their personal preferences, and how much time they will have for vacation (evaluative thinking). Many travelers become very creative in their thinking when they are deciding what route to follow; they map out routes that will "beat the traffic" and get them to their destination sooner, or they find new ways to combine sites during a single day's travel (creative thinking).

When individuals are thinking critically or creatively, they are utilizing similar cognitive operations, such as observing, comparing, and inferring (Marzano et al., 1988). Higher order processes are more complex, multifaceted, and involve both critical and creative thinking skills, such as analysis, evaluation, and synthesis. Some other higher order processes include concept formation; problem solving, including creative problem solving; decision making; research; reasoning; and metacognition.

Complexity of Outcomes: Bloom's Taxonomy

Most educators are familiar with Bloom's (1956) taxonomy of cognitive objectives. Teachers may utilize this framework when formulating meaningful educational activities, developing outcome objectives that instill awareness and knowledge in specific domains, and linking student assessment. Even though the taxonomy was originally designed to classify instructional objectives and test items in a hierarchical fashion, many educators have adopted it as a model for "conceptualizing higher level thinking skills in gifted learners" (Feldhusen, 1994b, p. 303). Remember that the taxonomy is a tool for the teacher to categorize activities, not a model that develops higher order processes per se.

Level one of Bloom's taxonomy is the *knowledge* level. At this level, individuals use simple cognitive skills that include remembering information and processes. This encompasses many types of information, such as facts, terminology, criteria, details, generalizations, conventions, methodology, trends and sequences, classifications and categories, principles, generalizations, and theories (Feldhusen, 1994b; Gronlund, 1998). At this first level of the taxonomy, teachers may ask students to

- list the branches of the government and the duties of those people elected or assigned to each branch;
- describe the phases of the water cycle; or
- outline the steps of the scientific method.

At level two, known as the *comprehension* level, learners are engaged in higher cognitive activities, such as translation, interpretation, and extrapolation. The following are examples of these types of activities:

- explaining the events that led to the Revolutionary War;
- converting a mathematical problem using manipulatives into a numerical or algebraic equation; and
- distinguishing between historical fiction and a nonfiction book pertaining to an historical event.

Level three, known as the *application* level, involves activities in which the students apply principles, concepts, theories, and generalizations in new situations. At this level, students transfer their knowledge and use it to solve new problems as in the following examples:

- demonstrating how to solve an algebraic equation using manipulatives;
- using the principles of bridge design to construct a stable span; and
- using a word-processing program to rewrite a handwritten report and editing the paper using computer tools.

Level four is referred to as the *analysis* level. At this level, learners are expected to dissect problems, sort their aspects into categories, gather facts and opinions, compare the present situation to other situations, and research an issue and develop questions about it (Maker, 1982). The following are examples of activities students might perform at this level:

- diagramming and explaining the mechanisms of a compound machine;
- reading about the battles of the French and Indian War and inferring why each battle was won or lost; and
- estimating how many linked tabs from soda cans would stretch around the walls of the school building.

Level five is called the *synthesis* level. Here, students are engaged in thinking skills in which they "combine or integrate ideas, concepts, principles, or information into unified wholes that represent a new pattern or structure" (Feldhusen, 1994b, p. 304). Due to the creation of new ideas or products, creative thinking is a component of the thinking process. For example, students might

- paint a picture integrating the techniques of Monet and Renoir;
- design a brochure to inform the public about an infectious disease or chronic ailment; or
- write a story about schools in the United States today from the perspective of a teacher or student from the colonial era.

The *evaluation* level is the final level of the taxonomy. At this level, students are required to judge, criticize, compare, justify, conclude, discriminate, or support ideas, situations, problems, events, or issues using standards or criteria. The following are examples of activities at this level:

- comparing the writing styles of Gary Paulsen and Judy Blume and explaining which they prefer and why;
- picking a way of solving a mathematical equation and justifying why that method was chosen; and
- criticizing and debating the President's tax plan.

Gifted learners acquire more knowledge without much practice and are proficient at using information at higher levels (Maker, 1982). With this in mind, activities for gifted learners should reflect higher level, more complex thinking skills. The following is an example of a lesson that uses Bloom's taxonomy as a framework and is appropriate for gifted learners at the fifth- or sixth-grade level.

While reading *The Phantom Tollbooth* by Norton Juster (1961), direct the students in learning different types of figurative language that include simile, metaphor, hyperbole, personification, alliteration, and onomatopoeia (knowledge level). As the students are reading, ask them to identify various uses of figurative language and explain each use and meaning in the sentence (comprehension level). After reading the novel, read aloud some stories that include figurative language and allow the students to identify the type (application level). At this point, you may ask each to pick a particular type of figurative language to research. Tell the students to compare and contrast different authors' uses of the same figurative language to express an idea (analysis). Next, tell the students they are to write a story or poem incorporating several types of figurative language (synthesis). As a culminating activity, allow the students to share their products with the class and evaluate themselves and each other using a set of standards and criteria set by the class before the research began (evaluation).

To reiterate, teachers must be cognizant that Bloom's taxonomy is only a framework for constructing meaningful lessons; it is not an organized curriculum that teaches higher order process skills. It does not systematically examine concepts common to different disciplines of study, nor does it assist in analyzing the relationships among the disciplines with regard to the concepts. Therefore, teachers need to incorporate other models that will infuse higher order process skills into all the curricular areas they teach.

A Model of Socratic Teaching

Many teachers of the gifted use action verbs associated with the taxonomy levels when formulating questions, but powerful inquiry goes beyond that technique. Socratic teaching is one of the oldest and most effective teaching strategies for cultivating higher order process skills. By using Socratic discussion and questioning techniques, instructors can continually probe students' thoughts on a subject. A response elicits a question and another response, followed by a question and a response, "which forces the students to think more deeply about the heart of an issue and explore its many sides" (VanTassel-Baska, 1992, p. 113).

According to Adler (1982, 1983), Socratic questioning brings students' ideas to birth, while the awakening of creative and inquisitive powers stimulates imagination and intellect. Socratic discussion enhances clarity of thought, as well as critical and reflective thinking. While engaging in discourse, learners continually analyze their own and others' values and ideas.

Before engaging in discourse on a topic, students should have read various types of literature on the topic. These might include historical, scientific, and philosophical books, poems, short stories, essays, plays, and authentic documents. The literature should be "products of human artistry" (Adler, 1982, p. 29) and not textbooks. According to Adler, in-depth reading of a topic will assist the students in coming to the discussion with a common vocabulary of ideas.

A way of engaging in Socratic teaching is to have Socratic seminars (Horn, 2001). A Socratic seminar is an opportunity for thoughtful and collaborative dialogue to take place within an open-ended discussion. It is a time when multiple viewpoints are respected and a shared understanding is established.

Based on successful implementation of Socratic seminars, the Fairfax County Public School District in Virginia has outlined some viable suggestions on how to conduct this type of seminar (Horn, 2001). Before engaging in a Socratic seminar, guidelines should be established. Let the students know it is okay to refer to the text when needed; to "pass" if asked to contribute; and, if confused, to ask for clarification. Every person involved in the seminar should have read the short story, poem, historical document, or play, or studied the art print under discussion at least once in class and, preferably, a second time at home. The piece of writing or art should address complex issues and ideas, connect to the curriculum, and be ambiguous, challenging, and lead to enduring understandings.

Effective Socratic questioners: (1) allow students to have "wait time" to consider the question and frame an answer before requesting a response, (2) maintain an intellectual discussion, (3) ask probing questions that stimulate in-depth thinking, (4) occasionally summarize what has and has not been discussed, and (5) encourage as many students as possible to participate in the discussion.

Three types of questions may be asked during a Socratic seminar. The lowest level of questioning asks the students to gather or recall information. This type of questioning is useful in gaining clarity, sequencing, and asking for details. For example, a teacher might use Paul Revere's etching of the Boston Massacre (see Archiving Early America, 1996) and related primary source accounts and secondary source retellings in a social studies lesson. In such a lesson, the first level of questioning might include the following: *What is the definition of a massacre?* and *What facts from the written accounts of the incident are not portrayed in the etching?*

The next type of questioning asks the students to make sense of the information they gathered, assists them in processing it, and is helpful for analyzing. Continuing the specific example lesson from above, sample questions at this level might include: *How did Paul Revere use color to make the portrayal more powerful?* and *Is the etching an example of propaganda? Why or why not?*

The first question posed at the Socratic seminar should be at the highest level. It should be open-ended and result in students' applying and evaluating information. This type of question should lead the students to cite rich and significant details and to have insight on the issue at hand. Examples of this type of questioning for the sample social studies lesson are as follows: *How do you think the patriots or the loyalists would interpret Paul Revere's etching? and Why do you think that the etching was such an effective piece of propaganda?*

Each of these levels of questioning represents an important component of an effective Socratic seminar, but not all questions for such a seminar can be prepared in advance. A key element of Socratic questioning is the teacher's skill at probing student responses to the questions with further questions, moving among the questioning levels to elicit deeper, more carefully reasoned and complex thoughts from students.

The Socratic seminar is a powerful teaching and learning strategy for all children, but it can be particularly effective when used with gifted children. Teachers guide, as well as challenge, their students to use critical and creative thinking skills to understand important ideas and concepts.

A Model of Problem Solving

Creative problem solving (CPS), developed by Parnes (1967), is a complex problem-solving model that promotes creative thinking. When solving problems using CPS, an individual or group of individuals rely on both convergent and divergent thinking to arrive at new, viable solutions. The CPS model is comprised of six steps or processes:

1. mess finding;
2. data finding;
3. problem finding;
4. idea finding;
5. solution finding; and
6. acceptance finding.

Mess finding is the process of sorting through a problem situation—a situation in which there is an uncertainty about just what exactly the problem is or an undefined situation. For example, a teacher might tell a class of students that they are in charge of the program for a Parents' Night at school. During mess finding, the students may decide what the major areas to address in planning should be and divide into groups of three or four, each of which will address a major planning issue.

In *data finding,* the learners brainstorm what they know about the problem situation, what more they need to know, and where they can find the information. At this stage, the participants decide what relevant pieces of information each is responsible for gathering and sharing with the group. In the example situation, it might range from gathering information about a specific topic to share with parents, to talking with cafeteria and custodial personnel about possibilities for serving food and cleaning up from the event. According to Daupert (1996), during data finding a "mess statement" can help to clarify the steps or direction taken in solving the problem.

In *problem finding,* the students formulate a specific problem statement. Daupert (1996) suggested that participants brainstorm a list of possible problem statements beginning with "In what ways might we . . ." For the various problems involved with the sample situation, problem statements might include the following:

- In what ways might we advertise the event to encourage more parents to attend?
- In what ways might we involve all the members of the class in the presentation of the program?
- In what ways might we organize the information to present everything within a reasonable time frame?

When *idea finding,* the students search for many solutions to a problem or parts of a problem. In the above example, the learners "sift" through their many ideas of what to present and how to present it with everyone involved in a brief period of time. During this stage, students write down creative ways of addressing their problems. Some things to consider might be the talents of the individuals in the group and the availability of facilities and resources.

The processes of evaluating and judging the ideas are part of the *solution finding* stage. Students look at each idea and decide what they would need in order to carry it out successfully. What materials would be needed? Are they affordable? Do we have enough time to work on the idea? What might we need that we have not already considered? Which idea is the most interesting to work on? According to the group, which idea would be the most effective?

In *acceptance finding*, a plan is developed for implementing the solution. Students imagine how their completed event will look and begin taking steps to achieve it, beginning by listing what must be done. Students may brainstorm the list first and then prioritize it, placing the steps on a chart, numbering them, and checking them off as they are completed.

Future Problem Solving is an adaptation of the CPS model (Feldhusen, 1994b). Students are engaged in solving issues that may impact the future of the nation or the world. For example, teachers may tell students they are members of the city council and they are faced with the following situation: The girls' soccer team needs a field, and, in 2 weeks, they will meet with the mayor to decide the best location for the field. Their goal is to develop a presentation that will convince the mayor and other city council members that a given location is the best.

Thinking creatively is an important part of higher order processes. When implementing the CPS model to solve a problem, individuals are analyzing the problem when engaged in mess finding, data finding, problem finding, idea finding, solution finding, and acceptance finding. Throughout the process, evaluation and decision making are taking place, as well as the creative fashioning of a feasible solution for implementation. Such a model provides students with an important thinking tool for many life applications beyond the classroom.

A Model for Reasoning

The content taught in schools is based on various disciplines, which are grounded in specific habits of mind; therefore, content should be taught as a skilled way of thinking (Foundation for Critical Thinking, 1996). Paul's (1992) Elements of Reasoning, known as the Wheel of Reasoning in a visual format (see Figure 3.1), comprise a model of key aspects of thought that are the building blocks of productive thinking. Working together, these building blocks provide a general logic to reasoning. In document interpretation and listening, they assist in making sense of an author or speaker's reasoning. Through attention to the Elements of Reasoning, authors and speakers are able to strengthen their arguments.

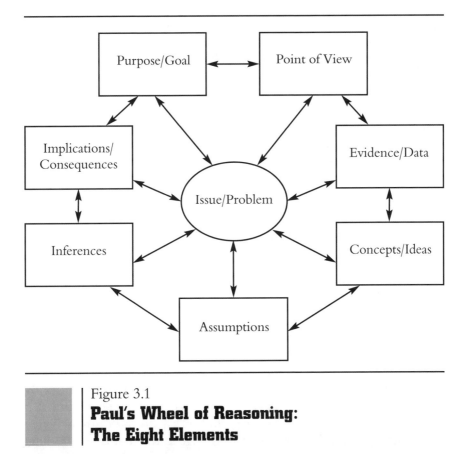

Figure 3.1
Paul's Wheel of Reasoning:
The Eight Elements

Note. From *The Miniature Guide to Critical Thinking Concepts and Tools* (p. 2), by R. Paul & L. Elder, 1999, Dillon Beach, CA: Foundation for Critical Thinking. Copyright © 1999 by Foundation for Critical Thinking, http://www.criticalthinking.org., e-mail cct@criticalthinking.org. Adapted with permission.

The Elements of Reasoning

The following Elements of Reasoning are implicit when we gather, conceptualize, apply, analyze, synthesize, or evaluate information (Foundation for Critical Thinking, 1996; Paul, 1992):

Purpose, Goal, or End in View. Individuals reason to achieve some objective, satisfy a desire, or fulfill some need. For example, if my computer is not working when I arrive at work, the purpose of my reasoning is how to get it fixed and how to complete the day's work. Reasoning is often poor due to a defect at the level of goal, purpose, or end. If the goal is unrealistic, contradictory to an individual's other goals, or muddled in some way, then the reasoning used to achieve it is problematic. If we are clear on the purpose of a writing or speech, it will help to focus the message in a coherent direction.

Question at Issue (or Problem to Be Solved). When individuals attempt to reason something out, there is at least one question at issue or problem to be solved (if not, there is no reasoning required). If a person is not clear about what the question or problem is, it is unlikely that he or she will find a reasonable answer or one that will serve his or her purpose. As part of the reasoning process, a person should be able to formulate the question to be answered or the issue to be addressed. For example, why won't my computer work? Or, should libraries censor materials that contain objectionable language?

Points of View or Frame of Reference. As individuals take on an issue, they are influenced by their own point of view. For example, parents of young children may have a different point of view pertaining to censorship of books than librarians do. The price of a car may seem low to one person and high to another due to different frames of reference. Any defect in a person's point of view or frame of reference is a possible source of problems in his or her reasoning. An individual's point of view may be too narrow, not precise enough, unfairly biased, and so forth. By considering multiple points of view, individuals may sharpen or broaden their thinking. Arguments for or against an issue can be strengthened when others' points of view are acknowledged. In listening and reading, individuals need to identify the perspective of the speaker or author and understand how it affects the message being delivered. In writing and speaking, an individual's careful exploration of his or her own point of view and acknowledgement of the points of view of other stakeholders are important in presenting a reasoned argument.

An individual's point of view can be influenced by many factors. Among them is the generation of the person: Is he or she young or old? Prior knowledge or lack of prior knowledge based on one's culture can also influence a person's point of view. In addition, how much actual experience the person has had with an issue, problem, or event can skew his or her thinking. Lastly, an individual's emotional involvement based on his or her values can influence perspectives.

Experience, Data, Evidence. When people reason, they must be able to support their point of view with reasons or evidence.

Evidence is important in distinguishing opinions from reasons and creating a reasoned judgment. Individuals can evaluate the strength of an argument or the validity of a statement by examining the supporting data or evidence. Experiences can also contribute to the data of a person's reasoning (e.g., data from surveys or published studies or previous experiences with starting a computer may contribute to the reasoning process that is necessary to resolve the problem).

Concepts and Ideas. Reasoning requires the understanding and use of concepts and ideas (including definitional terms, principles, rules, or theories). When individuals are learning content, they should ask themselves, "What are the key ideas presented?" Thoughts should be examined and organized around the substance of concepts and ideas. Some examples of concepts are freedom, systems, and survival.

Assumptions. People need to take some things for granted when they reason, but they need to be aware of the assumptions they have made and the assumptions of others. If individuals make faulty assumptions or presuppositions, this can lead to defects in their reasoning. Reasoning involves self-assessment of an audience or the message that is being conveyed. For example, a person might assume that others share his or her point of view or assume that the audience is familiar with the First Amendment when reference is made to First Amendment rights. As a reader or listener, an individual should be able to identify the assumptions of the writer or speaker.

Individuals formulate assumptions based on beliefs and presuppositions. When reasoning, it is important to clarify in your mind the points of view and assumptions of different stakeholders affected by the issue. The distinction between assumptions and inferences may cause problems when reasoning. Remember that assumptions are based on beliefs, such as assuming that others share our same point of view and that the audience or listeners know and understand what we know and understand. To reason effectively, identify and examine your assumptions carefully. Inferences provide small steps in our reasoning, or tentative conclusions based on the data or evidence we have collected, along with prior experiences. During the reasoning process, try to distinguish between the actual experiences and the interpretations of those experiences.

Inferences. Reasoning involves inferences by which conclusions are drawn and meaning is given to data. An inference is a small step of the mind in which a person makes a conclusion based on available evidence. For example, if we know that a train departs for our destination at 7:00, that it takes 30 minutes to get from our current location to the train station, and that it is now 6:45, we can infer that we will miss the train. The conclusions are interpretations of raw data; thus, they depend on the skill of the individual making sense of his or her situation and also on the reliability of the data available. Many inferences are justified and reasonable, but some are not. People need to distinguish between the raw data of their experiences and their interpretations of those experiences. They must also come to understand that a person's point of view and assumptions heavily influence inferences.

Implications and Consequences. The ability to reason well is measured in part by an ability to understand and articulate the implications and consequences of the reasoning. When individuals argue and support their perspectives on issues and questions, solid reasoning requires that they consider the implications of following that path and what the consequences are of taking the course they support. When individuals read or listen to an argument, they need to ask themselves what follows from that way of thinking. They should also consider consequences of actions that characters in stories take. For example, if a student does not do the assigned homework, then he or she will have to stay after school; if I put gas in the car when it has a quarter of a tank left, then my car will take longer to run out of gas. Explain to the class that, when they have an issue or problem, they need to look carefully at the information surrounding it, form a point of view, and be able to express reasons for their inferences about the issue based on facts.

Using the Model for Reasoning

With students, the Elements of Reasoning may be introduced through application to a particular problem situation relevant to the students' own lives. For example, the sample lesson on pages 63–64 demonstrates questions about each element as it relates to the scenario given.

Paul's Wheel of Reasoning can be utilized as a framework for developing lessons in various subject areas based on each discipline's habits of mind. For example, in history class, students should think like an historian; in biology class, like a biologist; and, in English class, like a writer. Figures 3.2, 3.3, and 3.4 are examples of applications of the model in social studies, science, and language

Sample Lesson
Elements of Reasoning
as Applied to a Problem Situation

Instructional Purpose:

- To introduce the elements of reasoning.
- To reason about a problem situation.

Scenario:

It's the end of August, and you need to buy a new pair of athletic shoes for school. Your dad wants you to buy good shoes that he can afford, but you want the most expensive brand that you know "everyone" at your school will be wearing.

Questions and Sample Responses:

What is the problem or issue?
- You and your dad are not agreeing on the brand of athletic shoe to buy.

Why are we reasoning about it?
- A decision needs to be made that is agreeable to both you and your dad as to what brand of shoes to buy.

What are the different points of view?
- Point of View #1: Dad has a budget and he knows the impact advertising has on young people.
- Point of View #2: You have an image to keep and you don't want your self-esteem to decrease. You believe the top shoes will help you to jump high like Michael Jordan or run fast like Marion Jones. You want to be a professional sports star.

What evidence supports each point of view?
- You want some data to present to your dad to support your point of view. When you are at the pool, park, and church, you poll other children and ask them what brand name of shoes they will buy for the start of school.
- Your dad collects information about the different athletic shoes from consumer magazines and Internet sites and shows you reports on the quality of the athletic shoe.

- You and your dad read a book about Michael Jordan or Marion Jones so you both can learn how talent was developed and how the athlete became a star.

What inferences can be made from the evidence?
- Inference #1: You may infer from the survey that everybody at school will be buying the brand of shoes you want.
- Inference #2: Your dad infers from his past experience that you will grow out of these shoes in 6 months or less or, because of wear, you will need a new pair of shoes before the school year is over.
- Inference #3: You wrongly infer from the commercials that the athlete gained his or her talent from the shoes.
- Inference #4: You may infer from reading a story about the athlete of choice that talent is developed through many hours of hard work, practice, and training.

What assumptions are being made?
- Assumption #1: You are assuming that almost everyone in your class has (or wants) the desired brand of athletic shoes and that a certain amount of status comes with wearing these shoes.
- Assumption #2: You think that wearing a certain brand of shoes will give you more athletic talent and will help you become a sports star.
- Assumption #3: Your dad is assuming the advertising companies have done a good job brainwashing youth into thinking they cannot live without certain brand names.
- Assumption #4: Your dad thinks that the less-expensive shoes are just as good as the more-expensive brand-name shoes.

What are the implications and consequences of your thinking?
- Implications: You may decide from your research on the subject that it is okay to buy a less-expensive shoe. You may also reason that, if the shoes you buy are not so expensive, there may be money left over to buy another item that is needed for school.
- Consequences: If you insist on buying the more-expensive brand name, you may have to get a job or do chores around the house to earn the money to pay for them. You may have to wear the shoes longer, even if they are worn out or out of style.

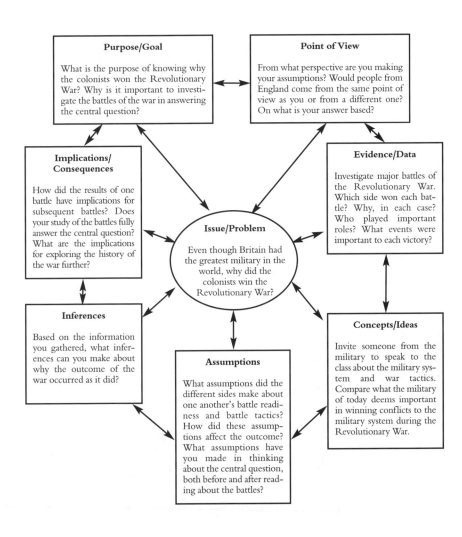

Purpose/Goal

What is the purpose of knowing why the colonists won the Revolutionary War? Why is it important to investigate the battles of the war in answering the central question?

Point of View

From what perspective are you making your assumptions? Would people from England come from the same point of view as you or from a different one? On what is your answer based?

Implications/ Consequences

How did the results of one battle have implications for subsequent battles? Does your study of the battles fully answer the central question? What are the implications for exploring the history of the war further?

Evidence/Data

Investigate major battles of the Revolutionary War. Which side won each battle? Why, in each case? Who played important roles? What events were important to each victory?

Issue/Problem

Even though Britain had the greatest military in the world, why did the colonists win the Revolutionary War?

Inferences

Based on the information you gathered, what inferences can you make about why the outcome of the war occurred as it did?

Concepts/Ideas

Invite someone from the military to speak to the class about the military system and war tactics. Compare what the military of today deems important in winning conflicts to the military system during the Revolutionary War.

Assumptions

What assumptions did the different sides make about one another's battle readiness and battle tactics? How did these assumptions affect the outcome? What assumptions have you made in thinking about the central question, both before and after reading about the battles?

Figure 3.2
Social Studies:
Battles of the Revolutionary War

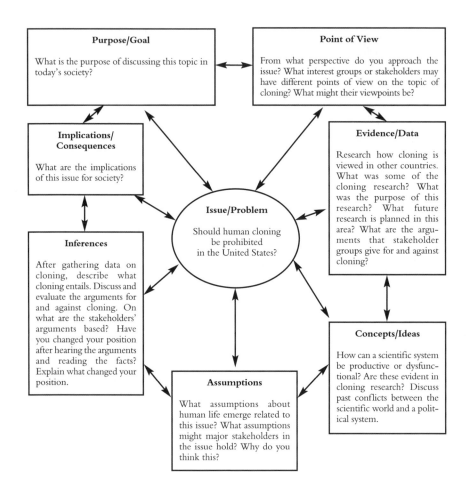

Purpose/Goal

What is the purpose of discussing this topic in today's society?

Point of View

From what perspective do you approach the issue? What interest groups or stakeholders may have different points of view on the topic of cloning? What might their viewpoints be?

Implications/Consequences

What are the implications of this issue for society?

Evidence/Data

Research how cloning is viewed in other countries. What was some of the cloning research? What was the purpose of this research? What future research is planned in this area? What are the arguments that stakeholder groups give for and against cloning?

Issue/Problem

Should human cloning be prohibited in the United States?

Inferences

After gathering data on cloning, describe what cloning entails. Discuss and evaluate the arguments for and against cloning. On what are the stakeholders' arguments based? Have you changed your position after hearing the arguments and reading the facts? Explain what changed your position.

Concepts/Ideas

How can a scientific system be productive or dysfunctional? Are these evident in cloning research? Discuss past conflicts between the scientific world and a political system.

Assumptions

What assumptions about human life emerge related to this issue? What assumptions might major stakeholders in the issue hold? Why do you think this?

Figure 3.3
Science:
The Issue of Human Cloning

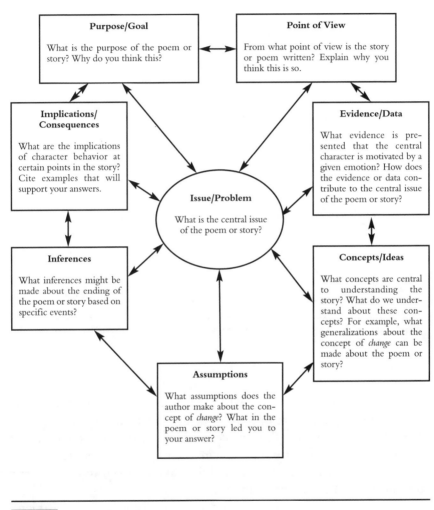

Purpose/Goal

What is the purpose of the poem or story? Why do you think this?

Point of View

From what point of view is the story or poem written? Explain why you think this is so.

Implications/ Consequences

What are the implications of character behavior at certain points in the story? Cite examples that will support your answers.

Evidence/Data

What evidence is presented that the central character is motivated by a given emotion? How does the evidence or data contribute to the central issue of the poem or story?

Issue/Problem

What is the central issue of the poem or story?

Inferences

What inferences might be made about the ending of the poem or story based on specific events?

Concepts/Ideas

What concepts are central to understanding the story? What do we understand about these concepts? For example, what generalizations about the concept of *change* can be made about the poem or story?

Assumptions

What assumptions does the author make about the concept of *change*? What in the poem or story led you to your answer?

Figure 3.4
Language Arts:
Literature Study

Directions: Rate each standard according to the following:

3 = Strong   2 = Adequate   1 = Needs Improvement

1. Are there *enough reasons* to make a convincing argument? One or two reasons might not be enough to show your point of view so as to be understood fully.

2. Is the evidence *correct or right*?

3. Are the reasons *clear*? Is the meaning understandable by anyone who reads or hears the argument? Are they explained well, or is more information needed?

4. Are *specific* reasons or examples included, rather than vague generalizations?

5. Are the arguments and reasons *strong and important*? Or do they seem to be included just to have something to say?

6. Is the thinking *logical*? Does the paragraph follow an understandable path, or is it just a disconnected group of statements? Do the sentences seem to go together and to be in the right order?

 Figure 3.5
Teacher Assessment of Student Thinking

Note. From *Literary Reflections* (p. 111), by the Center for Gifted Education, 1998, Dubuque, IA: Kendall/Hunt. Copyright © 1998 by the Center for Gifted Education. Reprinted with permission.

arts that are designed to engage students in modes of thinking specific to professionals in the aforementioned fields of study. The elements of thought do not have to be analyzed in order; however, one should identify the assumptions that guided thinking after inferences have been made. This process will assist the thinker in gaining command over thinking. When coming to a conclusion, the thinker should identify the underlying assumption and ask, "Are the inferences I made justifiable?"

Assessment of student thinking is essential for monitoring student progress in a subject area; it assists teachers' future curricular planning by identifying students' strengths and weaknesses. Figure 3.5 is an authentic assessment tool, adapted from Paul's (1992) Standards of Reasoning, that can be implemented when students write persuasive essays about a given issue.

A Model for Research

Many gifted learners have intense interests in certain disciplines. They sometimes collect numerous fascinating facts about a topic, but cannot articulate the relevance of those facts to societal issues. Students should be provided with strategies that assist them in understanding and contributing research findings to arguments that surround important, real-world issues (Boyce, 1997).

Learners should be engaged in researching significant issues and should incorporate the Elements of Reasoning as guideposts. When identifying an issue for class, it is important to remember the core aspects of a good issue for research. Issues have various characteristics:

- *An issue is a component of the real world.* It is a controversy or problem people are discussing or should be discussing. It is ambiguous, with no clear-cut or easy solutions. As a person gathers new information, the problem changes.
- *An issue has multiple points of view.* Different people or groups have different perspectives or points of view about an issue. Depending on how the issue is resolved, various groups and individuals—stakeholders—stand to win or lose tangible things, such as income and property, or intangible things, such as solitude and freedom of speech.
- *An issue is researchable with substantial information available.* To develop a convincing argument, students will need multiple sources of information and data. Important issues and real-world problems are informed by historical and contemporary information sources and by the collection and analysis of a variety of data.
- *An issue is on a worthy topic and has personal involvement.* Research offers the opportunity to ask questions about things that matter. While asking questions and seeking solutions, students have the chance to consider the arguments of others and contribute their personal perspective and original thinking. When a person cares about an issue, he or she is willing to spend time digging for evidence, taking a stand, developing an argument, and proposing a resolution to the problem.

The Center for Gifted Education's research model (Boyce, 1997), outlined in Figure 3.6, provides students with a framework to follow in investigating a real-world research issue. An example of a real-world

Directions: Refer to the list below to guide your research of a problem or an issue.

Identify the issue or problem.
- What is the issue or problem?
- Who are the stakeholders and what are their positions?
- What is my position on this issue?

Read about the issue and identify points of view or arguments through information sources.
- What are my print sources? What are my media sources? What are my people sources?
- What primary and secondary source documents might I use?
- What are my preliminary findings based on a review of existing sources?

Form a set of questions that can be answered by a specific set of data. For example:
- What would be the results of _____ ?
- Who would benefit and by how much?
- Who would be harmed and by how much?
- My research questions:

Gather evidence through research techniques such as surveys, interviews, or analysis of primary and secondary source documents.
- What survey questions should I ask? What interview questions should I ask?
- What generalizations do secondary sources give?
- What data and evidence can I find in primary sources to support different sides of the issue?

Manipulate and transform data so that the information can be interpreted.
- How can I summarize what I found out?
- Should I develop charts, diagrams, or graphs to represent my data?

Draw conclusions and make inferences.
- What do the data mean? How can I interpret what I found out?
- How do the data support my original point of view?
- How do they support other points of view?
- What conclusions can I make about the issue?

Determine implications and consequences.
- What are the consequences of following the point of view that I support?
- Do I know enough or are there now new questions to be answered?

Communicate findings. (Prepare an oral presentation for classmates using note cards and a written report.)
- What are my purpose, issue, and point of view, and how will I explain them?
- What data will I use to support my point of view?
- How will I conclude my presentation?

Figure 3.6
William and Mary Center for Gifted Education Research Model

Note. From *A Guide to Teaching Research Skills and Strategies in Grades 4–12* (pp. 10–11), by L. N. Boyce, 1997, Williamsburg, VA: Center for Gifted Education, College of William and Mary. Copyright © 1997 by the Center for Gifted Education. Reprinted with permission.

State the issue:	
Identify the stakeholder groups:	Describe each group's position:
State your initial position:	

Figure 3.7

Developing an Issue

Note. From *A Guide to Teaching Research Skills and Strategies in Grades 4–12* (p. 24), by L. N. Boyce, 1997, Williamsburg, VA: Center for Gifted Education, College of William and Mary. Copyright © 1997 by the Center for Gifted Education. Reprinted with permission.

issue for student investigation is the question of whether or not a school should adopt a uniform policy; the model is discussed below with reference to this sample issue.

The exploration commences with identification of the issue itself and of key stakeholders—including students, parents, teachers, administrators, school board officials, local stores, and others in the example—with discussion of what those stakeholders' positions are likely to be. Students should also consider and state their own initial position on the issue, to bring to consciousness assumptions and biases already present in their approach to the issue. This step of the process may be organized graphically as illustrated in Figure 3.7.

At the next stage, students gather preliminary information on the issue from a variety of sources. Resources should include print material, the media, and individuals with some expertise on the issue. At this stage and throughout the research process, a central responsibility of the teacher is to facilitate students' data collection and to guide them in evaluating the sources they select. Teachers and media specialists should incorporate mini-lessons on source finding and on judging information accessed, especially through online sources. Encouraging students to be critical consumers of research is an important and challenging part of the overall process of developing young researchers.

During stage three of the research process, students should formulate a set of questions that can be answered by a specific set of data. For example:

- What would the results be if our school enforced the wearing of school uniforms?
- Who would benefit from this rule and by how much?
- Who would be harmed by the enforcement of this rule and by how much?

In addition, the students may add any other questions of interest that can be answered by a specific set of data.

At stage four of the model, the class should gather evidence through research techniques, such as surveys, interviews, or experiments. With the issue at hand, the students should create a questionnaire that probes the points of view of the various stakeholders: the boys and girls who are students in the building, members of the staff, parents, and community members. Also, they could interview selected stakeholders using prewritten interview questions, such as "In your opinion, how do uniforms impact education?" or "What are potential benefits and problems in requiring students to wear school uniforms?"

From information that was gathered, at stage five the students manipulate and transform data so that they can be interpreted. They should summarize their findings and develop charts, diagrams, or graphs that depict the data collected. A graph of differential responses to each question by stakeholder would illustrate interesting findings (e.g., younger students may be in favor of the uniform code, while students in the upper grades may be against it).

From this information, students enter into stage six of the research process, drawing conclusions and inferences. At this stage, they determine what the data mean and interpret the results. Results might suggest, for example, that parents support uniforms more than students do for many specific reasons that students can explain.

At stage seven, students determine what the implications and consequences of the results are in light of the problem at hand. From their implications and consequences, they decide whether their initial questions have been answered or if they need to seek data to answer new questions that were formulated. For example, students should be able to present data and support the answer to the question of school uniforms.

The final stage of the research model involves communicating results to an audience. For example, students may write a persuasive essay stating their point of view or conduct a debate. Have them state whether their initial position on the issue has changed. From the data they collected, do they think that uniforms should become a rule at their school?

The Center for Gifted Education's research model assists students in higher order and creative thinking, relating to Paul's eight Elements of Thought (Paul & Elder, 2001). Students identify an issue or problem that generates questions. By investigating multiple positions on an issue, points of view are explored. Students analyze and evaluate information during the data-collection phase, draw conclusions and inferences from data-collection results, and determine implications and consequences. When they communicate the results of their investigation in an effective manner, students are employing both critical and creative thinking.

Metacognition

A crucial aspect of research and one that is often overlooked is the application of metacognitive thinking for independent and interdependent learning. Both cognition and metacognition are mental processes of knowing. Cognition includes learning knowledge, comprehending, perception, reasoning, and judging, whereas metacognition is the "process of developing awareness of one's own thinking and techniques for controlling and improving thinking activities" (Feldhusen, 1994b, p. 320). Metacognition requires cognitive processes; however, cognition does not necessarily mean someone is thinking metacognitively.

For example, you may be reasoning about what athletic shoes to buy for the beginning of the school year. A poll of children between the ages of 10 and 17 is taken, and the results show that 85% of the students will be wearing the brand-name shoes that are advertised by Michael Jordan or Marion Jones. The students conclude that those shoes are the best and everyone will be wearing them. After this cognitive process, the individual has made a faulty inference from the data collected. Ask the learners to "think about their thinking." Was enough evidence gathered? Was the evidence reliable and adequate? Who else could be polled? What other information may help you know what to look for in athletic shoes?

Students should be given guidance and time in planning a research project. Ask the students to keep a journal where they can capture and reflect on questions, ideas, and information. There are three main areas of metacognitive activity and questions to ask oneself (Beyer, 1987, as cited in Feldhusen, 1994a) when planning, monitoring progress, and assessing performance:

1. Task analysis and planning
   - What is the goal?
   - What do I need to do to reach the goal?
   - What should I do first? Second? Third?
   - What do I already know that can help me?
   - What more do I need to know?
   - What obstacles must be overcome?
   - How can I fix potential errors?
   - What will the solution look like?
2. Monitoring progress
   - Am I progressing toward my goal?
   - What is my next step?
   - Have I reached all necessary subgoals?
   - Am I ready for the next steps?
   - Does this strategy seem to be working?
   - Are there any other strategies I could use?
   - Have I made any mistakes?
   - How can I fix any of my mistakes?
3. Assessing performance
   - Did I reach my goal?
   - Does my solution fit my prediction?
   - Did I do what I planned to do?
   - Did I fix all my mistakes?
   - Did I use my time well?
   - How could I do better next time?

Students should continually monitor their progress—where is there room for improvement, what needs to be changed, what needs to be added? Teachers should also encourage learners to evaluate their own project work. Before planning research projects, students should be provided with the criteria by which processes and products will be judged. Figure 3.8 is an example of a rubric appropriate for research project assessment.

One of the most important steps in the research process is engaging students in thinking about their thinking, or metacognition. Through this process, students can monitor the clarity, accuracy, logic, and fairness of their thinking. Metacognition also assists students in checking the quality of their work, and it infuses an inner voice that is a guide to better planning and reasoning.

Directions: Rate student project according to the list elements by the following scale:

3 = Strong   2 = Adequate   1 = Needs Improvement

Issue and problem are clearly defined.	1	2	3
Sources are diverse.	1	2	3
Literature sources are summarized.	1	2	3
Interview, survey, or document analysis questions are included.	1	2	3
Interviews, surveys, or document analysis are summarized.	1	2	3
Results are reported appropriately.	1	2	3
Interpretation of data was appropriate.	1	2	3
Implications of the data were noted.	1	2	3
Given the data, reasonable conclusions were stated.	1	2	3
The project paper was mechanically competent.	1	2	3

Figure 3.8
Research Project Rubric

Note. From *A Guide to Teaching Research Skills and Strategies for Grades 4–12* (p. 97), by L. N. Boyce, 1997, Williamsburg, VA: Center for Gifted Education, College of William and Mary. Copyright © 1997 by the Center for Gifted Education. Reprinted with permission.

Conclusion

Engaging gifted learners in higher order process skills is an important element in the ICM and in implementing effective curricula for gifted and high-ability learners. Gifted students need to become proficient in thinking and problem-solving strategies that examine concepts central to specific disciplines, but are also common to different fields of study. Incorporating specific models such as Socratic questioning, Paul's Elements of Reasoning, or the Center for Gifted Education's research model into a framework for teaching can only heighten the potential for student learning well beyond current levels.

Key Points Summary

❑ Higher order processes incorporate both critical and creative thinking skills; problem solving, including creative problem solving; decision making; research; reasoning; and metacognition.

❑ Bloom's taxonomy is not a framework for teaching higher order process skills, but rather a tool for teachers to categorize objectives and activities and write student outcomes.

❑ Socratic questioning engages gifted learners in deep and broad discussions about an issue, idea, or statement.

❑ Paul's Elements of Reasoning represent a model designed for individuals to draw justifiable conclusions based on evidence or data about an issue, question, or problem. This model is based on the principles that all reasoning has a purpose; is an attempt to figure something out, settle a question, or solve a problem; is rooted in assumptions; is grounded in some point of view; is based on data and evidence; is expressed through concepts and ideas; contains inferences on which we draw conclusions and give meaning to data; and leads to implications and consequences.

❑ Creative problem solving (CPS) provides a process to develop both convergent and divergent thinking abilities.

❑ The Center for Gifted Education's research model incorporates several thinking skills models into a framework for the exploration of the intellectual and implementation stages of a research study.

References

Adler, M. J. (1982). *The Paideia proposal: An educational manifesto.* New York: Macmillan.

Adler, M. J. (1983). *Paideia problems and possibilities: A consideration of questions raised by the Paideia proposal.* New York: Macmillan.

Archiving Early America. (1996). The Boston massacre: A behind-the-scenes look at Paul Revere's most famous engraving. *The Early America Review, 1.* Retrieved October 31, 2001, from http://earlyamerica.com/review/winter96/massacre.html

Beyer, B. K. (1987). *Practical strategies for the teaching of thinking.* Boston: Allyn and Bacon.

Bloom, B. S. (Ed.). (1956). *Taxonomy of educational objectives. Handbook 1: Cognitive domain.* New York: McKay.

Boyce, L. N. (1997). *A guide to teaching research skills and strategies for grades 4–12.* Williamsburg, VA: Center for Gifted Education, College of William and Mary.

Center for Gifted Education. (1999). *Guide to teaching a language arts curriculum for high-ability learners.* Dubuque, IA: Kendall/Hunt.

Cohen, D. K., & Spillane, J. P. (1993). Policy and practice: The relations between governance and instruction. In S. H. Fuhrman (Ed.), *Designing coherent education policy: Improving the system* (pp. 35–95). San Francisco: Jossey-Bass.

Daupert, D. (1996). *The Osborne-Parnes creative problem solving process manual.* Retrieved June 4, 2001 from http://www.ideastream.com/create.

Dewey, J. (1938). *Experience and education.* New York: Macmillan.

Eisner, E. (1988). The celebration of thinking. *National Forum: Phi Kappa Phi Journal, 68,* 30–33.

Ennis, R. H. (1985). Goals for a critical thinking curriculum. In A. Costa (Ed.), *Developing minds: A resource book for teaching thinking* (pp. 54–57). Alexandria, VA: Association for Supervision and Curriculum Development.

Feldhusen, J. F. (1994a). Strategies for teaching the gifted. In J. VanTassel-Baska (Ed.), *Comprehensive curriculum for gifted learners* (2nd ed. pp. 366–378). Boston: Allyn and Bacon.

Feldhusen, J. F. (1994b). Thinking skills and curriculum development. In J. VanTassel-Baska (Ed.), *Comprehensive curriculum for gifted learners* (2nd ed. pp. 301–324). Boston: Allyn and Bacon.

Foundation for Critical Thinking. (1996). *Critical thinking workshop handbook.* Rohnert Park, CA: Center for Critical Thinking.

Gronlund, N. E. (1998). *Assessment of student achievement* (6th ed.). Boston: Allyn and Bacon.

Halpern, D. F. (1984). *Thought and knowledge: An introduction to critical thinking.* Hillsdale, NJ: Erlbaum.

Horn, C. (2001, March). *Socratic seminar: A dynamic search for understanding.* Presentation at the National Curriculum Network Conference, Center for Gifted Education, College of William and Mary, Williamsburg, VA.

Juster, N. (1961). *The phantom tollbooth.* New York: Random House.

Maker, C. J. (1982). *Curriculum development for the gifted.* Rockville, MD: Aspen.

Marzano, R. J., Brandt, R. S. Hughes, C. S., Jones, B. F., Presseisen, B. Z., Rankin, S. C., & Suhor, C. (1988). *Dimensions of thinking: A framework for curriculum and instruction.* Alexandria, VA: Association for Supervision and Curriculum Development.

National Commission on Excellence in Education. (1983). *A nation at risk: The imperative for educational reform.* Washington, DC: U.S. Department of Education.

Parnes, S. J. (1967). *Creative behavior guidebook.* New York: Scribners.

Paul, R. (1992). *Critical thinking: What every person needs to survive in a rapidly changing world.* Rohnert Park, CA: Foundation for Critical Thinking.

Paul, R., & Elder, L. (1999). *The miniature guide to critical thinking concepts and tools.* Dillon Beach, CA: Foundation for Critical Thinking.

Paul, R., & Elder, L. (2001). *Critical thinking: Tools for taking charge of your learning and your life.* Upper Saddle River, NJ: Prentice Hall.

Seiger-Ehrenberg, S. (1985). Educational outcomes for a K–12 curriculum. In A. Costa (Ed.), *Developing minds: A resource book for teaching thinking* (pp. 7–10). Alexandria, VA: Association for Supervision and Curriculum Development.

U.S. Department of Education, Office of Educational Research and Improvement. (1993). *National excellence: A case for developing America's talent.* Washington, DC: U.S. Government Printing Office.

VanTassel-Baska, J. (1992). *Planning effective curriculum for gifted learners.* Denver: Love.

Developing Creative Student Products

by
Janine M. Lehane

You are a language arts teacher who is familiar with national and state standards that require the simultaneous development of students' ability to understand, respond to, critically analyze, and evaluate literary works, and to express these areas of learning through the development of high-quality products. These same standards demand a learner-centered curriculum that will prepare students for various roles within the community. You are committed to the education of the whole person; however, you constantly worry about finding sufficient time to help your students achieve required learning goals and objectives. Therefore, you urgently seek ways of maximizing instructional time by creating challenging interdisciplinary curricular experiences that will effectively meet the intellectual and emotional needs of your students, as well as the demands of the system for core skill development.

This chapter constitutes an exploration of the educational concept of quality, which is fundamental to both developing appropriate student products and understanding the arts and humanities. An examination of the effects of quality artwork upon the viewer and of the criteria for determining quality in the arts and humanities will be followed by a description of its centrality to the contemporary educational problem of enabling gifted students to develop quality products.

An excellent work of art arrests and sustains our attention, moves us to depths of feeling, prompts a re-evaluation of that which we have previously held to be true, and thus enlivens us in a manner that is generally believed to reside firmly in the realm of the mysterious.

> An artist—even a painter, even a musician—tells. He tells of the ineffable. An artwork prolongs, and goes beyond, common perception. What common perception trivializes and misses, an artwork apprehends in its irreducible essence. . . . Where common language abdicates, a poem or a painting speaks. (Levinas, 1987/1948, as cited in Hand, 1989, p. 130)

The value of an excellent work of art, including the literary work, is that it provides, as Smith (1991) has acknowledged, "a perpetual reminder of the possibility of transcending the ordinary; excellent art constantly calls us away from a pedestrian existence" (p. 213). The "freshness and immediacy" of the experience it affords "returns us to ourselves" (Warren, 1975, as cited in Smith, p. 213). Arnheim (1966) proposed that the especial value of art lies in its power "to enlighten and enrich . . . life through seeing and hearing" (p. 15), an emphasis that, he believed, should dominate the study of great works. The task of enabling students to grow and make sense of their world requires, in effect, making the world "visible" once more, yet Arnheim's assertion of more than three decades ago is no less true today:

> How to make the world visible is so much of a problem today because that world, being the world of man, must necessarily be one of ideas. Ideas, however, are precariously weak in a culture given essentially to the amusement of the body and the distraction of the mind. (p. 360)

Smith and Simpson (1991) articulated the primary goal of aesthetic education as "the development of a capacity to appreciate excellence in art for the sake of the worthwhile experience that art at its best is capable of affording" (p. 199). Aesthetic pleasure—the encounter with beauty—may result from an artist's rendering of form and content (DeLong, Egner, & Thomas, 1966), and, as Abbs (1991) has pointed out, its educative power relies on heightened faculties:

> All aesthetic activity as it is developed through the manifold forms of the arts is simultaneously perceptive, affective, and cognitive; it can offer an education, therefore, of the highest order not through the analytical intellect but through the engaged sensibility. (p. 247)

Of vital importance to the education of gifted learners is Arnheim's (1966) insight that "human beings cannot live below their level of capacity without disturbance. You may call it a matter of conscience; for conscience is the instinct of self-preservation applied to the mind" (p. 360). Stimulation of students' ability to produce quality products is therefore a worthy undertaking for educators who may, by these means, as Buber (1965/1947) believed, enable young people to approach personal unity and awaken in them "the courage to shoulder life again" (p. 115).

Judging the Quality of an Artwork

Criteria for judging the quality of a work of art have been variously articulated by different scholars. Lord Kenneth Clark believed that excellence in art was dependent on "inspired virtuosity, supreme compositional power, intensity of feeling, masterful design, uncompromising artistic integrity, imaginative power, originality of vision, and [a] profound sense of human values" (Smith, 1991, p. 205). Reimer (1991) identified four criteria against which judgments regarding the quality of a work of art may be made: craftsmanship, sensitivity, imagination, and authenticity. *Craftsmanship* refers to mastery of the expressive potential of the chosen medium; *sensitivity* refers to the degree of subtlety with which depth and quality of feeling are caught within the form of the work; *imagination* refers to the vividness, the level of challenge posed by an art object; and *authenticity* concerns the refusal to compromise in the handling of one's materials. In the interaction between the artist and his or her material, artistic control "includes a giving way to the demands of the material," rather than the imposition of the artist's will upon the material (Reimer, p. 336).

Within a great work, formal devices are submerged in the statement that is made by the artist, and the quality of the work is usually attributed to its form or design and to its content or depth of statement (DeLong et al., 1966). The power of these attributes in determining degree of quality emerges more fully when comparisons are made.

The encounter with works of art activates three major dispositions: historical awareness, aesthetic appreciation, and critical judgment (Smith, 1991, p. 206). The refinement and strengthening of these dispositions, Smith argued, occurs through engagement in creative activities.

Fostering Students' Ability to Develop Quality Products

Buber (1965/1947) believed that "art is then only the province in which a faculty of production, which is common to all, reaches completion. Everyone is elementally endowed with the basic powers of the arts" (p. 84). These faculties need "only the right cultivation" and are, in fact, the natural activities of the self that form the basis for "the education of the whole person" (p. 84). This conception of education rests on what Buber identified as an autonomous "originator instinct," which is found within all people, for

> what the child desires is its own share in this becoming of things: it wants to be the subject of this event of production. . . .What is important is that by one's own intensively experienced action something arises that was not there before. (pp. 84–85)

Arnheim (1966) maintained that the experience of perception is supported by a natural sense of proportion that, "like all other perceptual properties . . . is dynamic."

> Rightness is seen not as dead immobility but as the active equipoise of concerted forces while wrongness is seen as a struggle to get away from an unsatisfactory state of affairs. Well-balanced shape is a main source both of the harmony found in

many products of nature and man and of the pleasure given by that harmony. (p. 102)

The importance of fostering the capacity for the ready discernment of quality in the arts cannot be overstated when attempting to free gifted learners to produce quality products. Although, as Arnheim (1966) reminded us, it is difficult to penetrate and so to analyze the "secret" of great works of art, it is nevertheless the case that talented individuals throughout history have benefited at the hands of teachers who have been able to do so and who have encouraged and guided them in their pursuit of excellence. The appreciation of quality in art requires contexts

> in which students learn to perceive art, to understand it histori-cally, to appreciate it aesthetically, to make it, and to reflect about it critically. Such contexts imply a range of teaching meth-ods which include the direct imparting of information, the guiding of problem solving, and the coaching of perceptual and critical skills. (Smith, 1991, p. 205)

Gardner (1991) has argued that the capacity to discriminate the distinctive features of a work is essential to competence in produc-tion, along with the ability to "reflect upon the arts, upon one's own goals and methods in artistic production, and upon the means and aims of other artistic practitioners" (pp. 281–282). Beardsley (1991) also identified the emotional response occasioned by "insight into connections and organizations—the elation that comes from the apparent opening up of intelligibility" (p. 78) to be crucial to the development of artistic competence.

The student must be encouraged to attend to the unified manner in which the senses, the intellect, and the emotions are engaged as they encounter great works. The prompting of this movement from the student's current level of understanding and sensitivity "*towards* some-thing more discriminating, finer, richer, fuller, more complex" is the work of the educator (Reid, 1973, as cited in Redfern, 1991, p. 265). It allows refinement of perception to occur by providing students with "a glimpse of what lies beyond the presently fashionable, the hack-neyed, the trivial, and the obvious—beyond that which lacks subtlety and complexity" (p. 265).

Aesthetic literacy must be achieved not prior to, but simultaneous with the development of products in the arts and humanities (Smith, 1991). As Gardner (1991) has argued,

> the heart of any arts-educational process must be the capacity to handle, to use, to transform different artistic symbol systems—to think with and in the materials of an artistic medium. Such processes can occur only if artistic creation remains the cornerstone of all pedagogical efforts. (p. 281)

Refinement of the sensibilities does not occur in a void or in an a historical and isolated transaction between the observer and the great work. In reality, this heightening of discernment may occur as affinity develops between the learner and the author or artist through an act of interpretation, which is one means by which "tradition is 'affirmed, embraced, cultivated,' and passed on" (Louth, 1983, p. 35).

The simultaneous promotion of the intellectual, affective, and moral growth of gifted students through open-ended, interdisciplinary inquiry is possible via the Integrated Curriculum Model (ICM). This model reflects the multidimensionality that is characteristic not only of the learners themselves, but also of the mode in which people learn and of the disciplines within which learning will take place. Learning outcomes that are consistent with standards of excellence in education are deliberately and thoughtfully matched to standards of excellence that underpin the structure of the disciplines within which study will occur. Outcomes are also carefully matched with age-old standards of quality that are naturally accessible by human beings. The educator will lead students toward these designated outcomes in order to enable them to produce works that are in good standing with those criteria of excellence.

Discipline-Based Product Development

Any attempt to enable students to develop quality products must be founded on their grasp of the underlying structures of the discipline in question. Each discipline relies on multiple structures, many of which are shared amongst disciplines. Analysis of these structures yields knowledge about the specific character of the discipline, the types of thinking employed by scholars and practitioners within the discipline, the representative ideas on which the discipline is founded, and the methods of inquiry that are typically used to gain understanding of these ideas (Phenix, 1964).

Apart from the tenets of quality held by artists or practitioners within the discipline, a firm understanding of the type of knowledge that may be available through their study is required. If we presuppose that the education of gifted learners is at heart an education for personal unity, as Buber (1965/1947) has suggested, then the opportunities for the refinement of the perceptive, affective, and cognitive faculties (Abbs, 1991) of these students through analysis and interpretation of great literature, art, and music must be guided by a principle of coherence. Encounters with great works in the arts and humanities, therefore, involve working with this principle of unity in such a way that "we are not imposing an interpretation on the phenomena, but tracing their own inherent structure" (Louth, 1983, p. 23). Students, then, must be introduced not only to the structure of a discipline, but also to the tradition within which this structure is lodged.

Louth (1983) has laid out the process according to which understanding is achieved in the humanities:

> one learns a language by seeing how it is used, from examples of its use. And the same is true, in another way, of any particular literary work: only when we understand the whole can we understand its parts, and only as we understand its parts can we understand the whole. (pp. 23–24)

This principle of coherence that governs understanding in the humanities is distinct from the type of knowledge available through the study of the natural sciences (Hodges, 1944, as cited in Louth). Louth argued that

> our understanding of nature, though objective, is external, in contrast to the understanding possible to us in the humanities, an understanding from "inside." . . . The method of science is logical and rational; the method of the humanities is one of imagination, sympathetic understanding, "indwelling." (p. 26)

The essence of the humanities is, therefore, "an engagement between persons—including, indeed especially, the men and women of the past" (Louth, p. 145).

Judging Quality Via Assessment

The tenets of quality and the primary attitude required for the study of the arts and humanities, which is the starting point for an aesthetic literacy, may be presaged quite deliberately by the teacher through preassessment. This instructional tool may at once determine existing levels of aesthetic sensitivity, understanding of the concept in question, skill in communicating this understanding, and ability to apply conceptual understanding to the task at hand and to one's personal life. Current levels of ability with respect to all of the intended learning objectives (e.g., interpretation and analysis of literary or artistic subject matter and facility in persuasive writing) may be simultaneously ascertained through the careful selection of a single literary or artistic work as a preassessment of student learning. How do the students in one's care initially differ in their understanding and skill level with respect to intended learning outcomes of the unit to be studied? Answers to this question enable appropriate differentiation of curricular content for even widely dissimilar ability levels in a given classroom.

Writing Preassessment

And if only we arrange our life in accordance with the principle which tells us that we must always trust in the difficult, then what now appears to us as the most alien will become our most intimate and trusted experience. How could we forget those ancient myths that stand at the beginning of all races, the myths about dragons that at the last moment are transformed into princesses? Perhaps all the dragons in our lives are princesses who are only waiting to see us act, just once, with beauty and courage. Perhaps everything that frightens us is, in its deepest essence, something helpless that wants our love. (p. 92)[1]

What is the author's central assumption regarding difficult or fearful experiences?

Write a paragraph to answer the question. State your opinion, include three reasons for your opinion, and write a conclusion to your paragraph.

 Figure 4.1
Sample Student Writing Preassessment

Note. Adapted from *Persuasion* (p. 27), by the Center for Gifted Education, 1998, Dubuque, IA: Kendall/Hunt. Copyright © 1998 by the Center for Gifted Education.

1. Excerpt from *Letters to a Young Poet*, by R. M. Rilke (S. Mitchell, Trans.), 1984, New York: Random House. Copyright © 1984 by Stephen Mitchell. Reprinted with permission.

The writing preassessment in Figure 4.1 is adapted from the work of the Center for Gifted Education at the College of William and Mary (1998) and is drawn from two units of study in the language arts that have been designed by the author for highly gifted students in grades 10–12, *Morality: The Mystery in the Everyday* (Lehane, in press) and *Conversations in Aesthetics and Morality* (Lehane, 2000). The preassessment demonstrates the principle of choosing exemplars that are not only appropriate with respect to specific educational objectives, but encompass "the prior criterion of intrinsic quality" (Reimer, 1991, p. 337).

Use of this example is also consistent with the principle that "in regard to such matters as beauty in life the artist often functions as a teacher. He can remind young and old alike of many special kinds of beauty" (DeLong et al., 1966, p. 37). The purposeful selection of this example attends to the fact that "the artist teaches us to see, but through different eyes [and that] enriched by the personal interpretations of many individualized artists, our understandings of the beautiful may be multi-valued and multi-leveled" (DeLong et al., 1966, p. 38).

The Role of the Teacher in Creative Production

Just as the creator must be freed from faulty preconceptions regarding art, ability, and quality, the teacher too must be freed from expectations that cripple the unique, creative instinct in another who is in his or her care. The capacity for both the appreciation and rendering of quality artistic creations is available to all (Buber, 1965/1947; Edwards, 1992)—a latent capability—requiring attention, attunement, discrimination, and, above all, the freeing of the capacity for wonder (Louth, 1983).

The ability to shepherd another through this process of "undeception" is available to all teachers. In essence, it consists of allowing students to discern the figure from the ground, the significant from the peripheral, and involves a relaxation of the belief that the teacher must be solely responsible for generating the conditions within which this may occur. Artists themselves have spoken not only through their works, but also through their autobiographies. The combined usage of these forms of art in the classroom affords students the opportunity for direct engagement with the person of the artist who may then assume the role of teacher.

Autobiographical writings and secondary sources that illuminate the often arduous path of creative productivity are underused classroom resources. Both teacher and student may gain wisdom from such sources. The rigor and discipline of the creative process, the exultation, the emotional tension and release, the confusion and sometimes momentary reprieve from it—all of these states that make up the life of creative production may be communicated directly by the artist through his artistic creations and through the records available on the nature of the process involved. That there is a discernible form and flow, a process involving time and thought and feeling and dissatisfaction and desire, is information that is invaluable to the gifted learner. The unchallenging nature of much of the curriculum to which he or she has typically been exposed—and perhaps a false notion that success is achieved hastily or not at all—may not have equipped such students with an understanding of the nature of the process of artistic creation, and this may readily be communicated by current and past exponents of the arts.

By granting opportunities for students to establish affinity with artists who have gone before them, students may then more willingly submit to the creative process. An important limitation with respect to aiding gifted learners in the production of quality products may be overcome when it is realized that, for some gifted learners, each and every engagement with curricular content in the classroom will be construed by them to be a creative act.

Application to Literature

The simple act of selecting, for instance, a poem for interpretation and analysis that adheres to the requirement of advanced content for gifted learners and the criterion of quality and communicates the difficulties the artist often undergoes in the pursuit of his or her work becomes an extremely powerful and effective learning experience for gifted students. The following excerpt from T. S. Eliot's "East Coker" from *Four Quartets* (1971/1943) illustrates this technique:

> So here I am, in the middle way, having had twenty years—
> Twenty years largely wasted, the years of *l'entre deux guerres*
> Trying to learn to use words, and every attempt
> Is a wholly new start, and a different kind of failure
> Because one has only learnt to get the better of words
> For the thing one no longer has to say, or the way in which
> One is no longer disposed to say it. And so each venture
> Is a new beginning, a raid on the inarticulate

With shabby equipment always deteriorating
In the general mess of imprecision of feeling,
Undisciplined squads of emotion. And what there is to
    conquer
By strength and submission, has already been discovered
Once or twice, or several times, by men whom one cannot
    hope
To emulate—but there is no competition—
There is only the fight to recover what has been lost
And found and lost again and again: and now, under
    conditions
That seem unpropitious. But perhaps neither gain nor loss.
For us, there is only the trying. The rest is not our business.
(pp. 30–31)[1]

Students' interpretation and analysis of this work may be framed initially through the use of the following questions, derived from the Literature Web (Center for Gifted Education, 1999; see Chapter 6):

- Which words in the poem stimulated you most? In what way did they appeal to you? What specifically did you find particularly exciting or unusual about them?
- What feelings did the poem generate within you? Did you experience a range of emotions or a single emotion? What feelings do you believe motivated the poet as he wrote this piece?
- What were the major ideas or concepts contained in the piece? What do you believe to be the purpose of their articulation through the poem?
- What were the dominant images or symbols contained in the poem? In your opinion, how effectively did the poet use them?
- How do you think the structure the poet selected to communicate his message enhanced its delivery?

After students have successfully analyzed this poem, they should be encouraged to write their own, hopefully having internalized the standards of word choice, creation of emotional response in the reader, communication of ideas, development of images and symbols, and use of structure to convey meaning. The students' experience and skill in

---

1. Reprinted with permission.

interpretation and analysis may then be extended through the further use of higher order questions. Exemplars such as this communicate that the student's own tension is real and to be expected and that perseverance will see the creation through to completion, even if the completed product is far removed from the original conception.

Sensitivity to Gifted Students' Perfectionism

Teaching gifted students to develop quality products is an iterative process during which fundamental reassurance regarding their own capacities must be continually articulated in a variety of ways, as such students are often prone to self-criticism and discounting of their creative products. It is wise to remind gifted students that they characteristically learn with great rapidity so that consistent progress toward mastery can be expected as intuitive, emotional, and technical capacities are exercised in a disciplined and systematic manner.

Gifted learners exhibit a propensity to strive for perfection and a similarly strong tendency toward disparagement of personal products due to perceived failure to attain internal standards of excellence. Redfern (1991) acknowledged that "the capacity to respond to mature works and performances usually far outruns the capacity to create and perform mature works" (p. 270). She added, "What seems to be dissatisfaction with an activity is frequently, in fact, dissatisfaction with themselves, their own amateurish and perhaps rather pedestrian achievements, as their horizons expand and change" (pp. 270–271). The virtue of the initial attempt and tolerance for the preparatory stage of development, the ebb and flow pattern that characterizes the creative process, and the particularities of the student's own learning style must be brought to the student's attention. This aspect of a teacher's methodology is completely in alignment with the nature and needs of students who are precocious, intense, and complex, and therefore consistent with the underpinnings of the ICM (VanTassel-Baska, 1994).

Shaping Quality Products

Structured opportunities for aesthetic development in the classroom allow the experience of tangible achievement through the exercise of one's perceptive skills (Wolff, 1970), the development of trust in one's intuitive judgment, reinforcement of "the validity of individual outlook," and affirmation of the significance of direct experience and personal response (Arnheim, 1969).

The honing of talent requires exposure to works of quality, the discovery of personal potential, and opportunities to learn by example at the hands of teachers who drill and explain and permit increasingly acute and independent observation of the accomplishments of others. Ability, competence, and identification with the task form the dispositions necessary for creative productivity within a discipline (Gardner, 1991).

Patterns of meaning within the arts and humanities may be understood more readily by students as they engage in the process of creative production. When fostering students' understanding, a teacher should first provide learning opportunities that direct their awareness and appreciation of the ways in which the artist has used the materials of his or her craft. A focus on the elements that comprise the work and the relationships among them leads to a more refined appreciation of the composition. Students may then execute their own compositions with growing discernment and, ultimately, with greater skill. The elements and relationships in focus may then form the basis for the development of rubrics according to which the relative success of student products may be determined. The following examples illustrate this procedure.

Upon presenting students with an artwork—for example, Matisse's stencil *The Clown* (Jazz, 1943; in Néret, 1995, p. 27) or Picasso's oil painting *Two Children* (1952; in Jaffé, 1970, p. 39)—the teacher many ask them to comment on the emotional appeal of the work and then to discuss its elements and their arrangement. Discussion would focus, therefore, on concepts of line, color, light and shade, perspective, balance, subject, theme, and the unity of these elements. The students may then be asked to use one of these images as inspiration for the creation of a story, and then later invited to experiment with the media employed by the artist to enhance their grasp of the qualities of the work. Students' own renderings would then be studied by means of a rubric that allows teacher, peer, and self-assessment (see Figure 4.2). This type of product assessment is consistent with the understanding to be gained by students within the discipline while simultaneously allowing for continued growth toward standards of quality. As students grow in confidence and skill, wider audiences for their creative products may be sought.

Artistic Self-Assessment, Teacher Assessment, and Peer Assessment

Name _____

Activity _____

Directions: Use the following rating scale to evaluate each quality.

3 = Excellent   2 = Satisfactory   1 = Needs Improvement

	Needs Improvement	Satisfactory	Excellent
1. Appropriate use of line			
color			
light and shade			
perspective			
balance			
subject			
theme			
2. Unity of the elements			
3. Emotional appeal			

Particular strengths:

_____

_____

_____

Suggestions for improvement:

_____

_____

_____

 Figure 4.2
Sample Rubric for Assessing Artistic Products

Note. Adapted from *A Guide to Teaching Research Skills and Strategies for Grades 4–12* (p. 94), by L. N. Boyce, 1997, Williamsburg, VA: Center for Gifted Education, College of William and Mary. Copyright © 1997 by the Center for Gifted Education. Reprinted with permission.

A similar type of process may be applied when prompting the development of students' understanding, appreciation, and skill as musicians. Knowledge of music theory and the ability to analyze and apply the elements of rhythm, melody, harmony, and tone with accuracy, sensitivity, and imagination constitute defensible curricular objectives. Measurement of students' progress toward these objectives may likewise be ascertained by rating their current levels of achievement with respect to the use of these elements in isolation and in combination.

The sample lesson *Learning From Experience* (Lehane, 2000) demonstrates the interweaving of art, music, and literature. Assessment of students' understanding takes on a variety of forms and is embedded in classroom and homework activities.

Judgments About Student Products

The assignment of worthwhile projects that maximize student learning is key to the continued development of students' creative abilities. Determination of the type of student product to be assigned is made according to the intended learning outcomes, which reflect the structure of the relevant discipline and the nature of the learner. Decisions as to the assignment of individual or group products, the duration for completion of products, and the modality of projects to be completed are also reflective of intended learning outcomes.

Assessment is intended as a learning tool for promoting the continued development of students' ability to produce quality products. Assessment of student products in the arts and humanities must be based on accepted criteria of excellence in the relevant discipline and on criteria that reflect current exemplary assessment practices in education. Within the framework for judgment of aesthetic works in general (i.e., according to its craftsmanship, sensitivity, imagination, and authenticity [Reimer, 1991]), student products may be assessed against specific elements of expert practice in the discipline using a teacher-designed rubric. These criteria for assessment are consistent with intended student learning outcomes and would, for example, apply to the task in Figure 4.3.

Judgment of student products may be undertaken by a range of individuals or groups provided that those enlisted for the task have the necessary expertise for determining the quality of the works.

Sample Lesson
Learning From Experience

Instructional Purposes:

- Compare and contrast literature selections.
- Promote critical analysis and synthesis within and across domains of learning.
- Promote creativity.

Activities and Questions:

1. Distribute the poems "To Narcissus" by Martin Buber and "Narcissus" by Rilke. Ask students to read the poems and to respond to the following questions independently, followed by small-group and whole-group debriefing. (Note: Literature Web organizer [see Chapter 6] should be used for responses and discussion.)

   - *Vocabulary:* What words did you find interesting, exciting, or unusual? Why? How did the poet use them?
   - *Reader Response:* What feelings did the poem evoke in you? How do you think the poet created such a response in the reader?
   - *Theme:* What main ideas(s) did the poem convey to you? Where in the text are these ideas located?
   - *Images and Symbols:* What were some of the images and symbols you found in the poem? What do you think they represent or mean? Why do you think the poet uses them?
   - *Literary Form and Related Devices:* How does the structure of the poem contribute to its meaning? Why do you think the poet employs these techniques?

2. Ask students to respond to the following questions in their response logs:

   - What are the essential features of the narcissistic life as contained in the poems? Which of the generalizations about morality appear to be at odds with this way of living?

- In what ways do the central characters in the novels you have read appear to lead narcissistic lives?
- In what ways do their lives appear to diverge from narcissistic leanings?
- Cite modern-day examples of narcissism.

3. Play a recording of Bach's suite for violon cello No. 2 in D minor, BWV 1088.

4. Ask students to create a response to this music (e.g., poetic, prose, visual image).

5. Invite students to discuss their creative interpretations with the class.

Homework:

From Mark Salzman's *The Soloist,* read pp. 260–266 and 272–275 and answer the following questions in a three-paragraph essay:

- What was the essential understanding that the cellist derived from his experience?
- How did this understanding afford Renne freedom from past frustrations and a renewed sense of purpose?
- What and who were the formative influences in his life?
- What does Renne now believe he must do with his life?
- How does Renne's behavior demonstrate the generalization that morality is impervious to attack?

Note. From *Conversations in Aesthetics and Morality: A Secondary Language Arts Unit for Grades 10–12* (pp. 58–59), by J. M. Lehane, 2000, Unpublished curricular unit, Center for Gifted Education, Williamsburg, VA. Reprinted with permission.

Directions:

1. Present the following art works to students:
   - Delaunay - Rhythm, joie de vivre (Hoog, 1976, p.115)
   - Van Gogh - *Prisoner's Round* (after Doré), Saint-Rémy, February 1890, Oil on canvas, 80 x 64 cm, Pushkin State Museum of Fine Arts, Moscow (Charles, 1997, p. 137).
   - Hugo, Charles - *Victor Hugo Among the Rocks on Jersey*, photograph, Paris, Maison de Victor Hugo. (Rodari, Georgel, Sante, Prévost, 1998, Half-title page).
   - Hugo, Victor - *Planet* ca. 1854, Pen, brown-ink wash and black ink over rubbed charcoal with highlights of gouache on paper 12 ⅜ x 14 ⅝" (310 x 372 mm; Rodari, Georgel, Sante, Prévost, 1998, p. 63).
   - Messiaen recording - *Quartet for the End of Time.*

2. Ask students to select one of the pieces and to match it with one of the generalizations about morality. Ask students to write three paragraphs on the piece they have chosen and their reasons for choosing it in relation to the generalization.

 Figure 4.3
Sample Assessment Activity

Note. From *Conversations in Aesthetics and Morality: A Secondary Language Arts Unit for Grades 10–12* (p. 135), by J. M. Lehane, 2000, Unpublished curricular unit, Center for Gifted Education, Williamsburg, VA. Reprinted with permission.

Conclusion

As high-ability learners engage in product development, their capacity to absorb ideas and methodologies rapidly yet deeply allows them not only to create, but to develop an understanding of the disciplinary process of creating. Thus, they assimilate the behaviors associated with a creative discipline and begin to discover how their own creative voice can be at once grounded in established methods and demonstrative of their individual talents and imagination. This process is often fraught with difficulties that are both peculiar to the individual engaged in the process and have been shared by many people who have produced great works. By teaching gifted learners about the nature of being gifted and about the nature of the creative process, both directly and through the voices and works of gifted men and women, the unexpected, the dreadful, and the sublime then become expected and somehow natural. Students may then gain hope in their own powers of discernment and artistry and in their ability to produce what is peculiarly their own art, confident that this art may in time approach the quality of great works. The vital gift to students in this mode of teaching is "a sense of being an integral factor in a larger human drama, of having, as it were, an extended historical companionship" (Edmonson, 1981, as cited in Smith, 1991, p. 210).

Key Points Summary

❑ Exposure to high-quality literary, artistic, and musical works and teaching/coaching as to the use and formal arrangement of their elements refines students' ability to appreciate and produce creative products.

❑ Perception, emotion, and intellect are united in discerning the worth and beauty of works of art.

❑ Students must be familiar with criteria for determining the quality of an artwork in order to produce their own.

❑ Assignment of worthwhile projects that maximize student learning is key to the continued development of students' creative abilities.

❑ Assessment of creative products may at once determine existing levels of aesthetic sensitivity, the understanding of relevant concepts, skill in communicating this understanding, and the ability to apply and transfer conceptual understanding.

❑ Assessment of student products in the arts and humanities must be based on accepted criteria of excellence in the relevant discipline and on criteria that reflect current exemplary assessment practices in education.

❑ Fostering the development of quality student products is an iterative process that requires much reassurance regarding students' progress toward standards of excellence.

References

Abbs, P. (1991). Defining the aesthetic field. In R. A. Smith & A. Simpson (Eds.), *Aesthetics and arts education* (pp. 245–255). Urbana: University of Illinois Press.

Arnheim, R. (1966). *Toward a psychology of art.* Berkeley: University of California Press.

Arnheim, R. (1969). *Visual thinking.* Berkeley: University of California Press.

Bach, J. S. (1997). Suite for violoncello no. 2 in D minor, BWV 1008 [Recorded by Jaap Ter Linden]. On *Suites, violoncello, BWV 1007–1012* [CD]. Los Angeles: Harmonia Mundi.

Beardsley, M. C. (1991). Aesthetic experience. In R. A. Smith & A. Simpson (Eds.), *Aesthetics and arts education* (pp. 72–84). Urbana: University of Illinois Press.

Boyce, L. N. (1997). *A guide to teaching research skills and strategies for grades 4–12.* Williamsburg, VA: Center for Gifted Education, College of William and Mary.

Buber, M. (1965). *Between man and man* (R. G. Smith, Trans.). London: Macmillan. (Original work published 1947)

Charles, V. (1997). *Van Gogh.* Bournemouth, England: Parkstone Press.

Center for Gifted Education. (1998). *Persuasion.* Dubuque, IA: Kendall/Hunt.

Center for Gifted Education. (1999). *A guide to teaching a language arts curriculum for high-ability learners.* Dubuque, IA: Kendall/Hunt.

DeLong, P. D., Egner, R. E., & Thomas, R. (1966). *Art and music in the humanities.* Englewood Cliffs, NJ: Prentice-Hall.

Edmonson, N. (1981, October). An agnostic response to Christian art. *Journal of Aesthetic Education, 15*(4), 34.

Edwards, B. (1992). *Drawing on the right side of the brain: How to unlock your hidden artistic talent.* London: HarperCollins.

Eliot, T. S. (1971). *Four quartets.* New York: Harcourt Brace. (Original work published 1943)

Friedman, M. (1982). *Martin Buber's life and work.* London: Search Press.

Gardner, H. (1991). Toward more effective arts education. In R. A. Smith & A. Simpson (Eds), *Aesthetics and arts education* (pp. 274–285). Urbana: University of Illinois Press.

Hand, S. (Ed.). (1989). *The Levinas reader.* Oxford, England: Blackwell.

Hodges, H. A. (1944). *William Dilthey: An introduction.* London: Routledge & Kegan Paul.

Hoog, M. (1976). *Robert Delaunay 1885–1941.* Paris: Musées Nationaux.

Jaffé, H. (1970). *Picasso.* London: Hamlyn.

Lehane, J. M. (2000). *Conversations in aesthetics and morality: A secondary language arts unit for grades 10–12.* Unpublished curricular unit,

Center for Gifted Education, College of William and Mary, Williamsburg, VA.

Lehane, J. M. (in press). *Morality: The mystery in the everyday: A secondary English unit for grades 10–12*. Sydney, Australia: Gifted Education Research, Resource, and Information Centre, University of New South Wales.

Levinas, E. (1987). Reality and its shadow. In A. Lingis (Ed.) *Collected philosophical papers* (pp. 1–13). Dordrecht, The Netherlands: Martinus Nijhoff. (Original work published 1948)

Louth, A. (1983). *Discerning the mystery: An essay on the nature of theology.* Oxford: Clarendon Press.

Messiaen, O. (1987). *Quartet for the end of time.* [Recorded by D. Shifrin, I-H. Bae, W. Lash, & W. Doppmann]. [CD]. Santa Monica, CA: Delos.

Néret, G. (1995). *Henri Matisse: Cut-outs.* New York: Barnes & Noble.

Phenix, P. H. (1964). *Realms of meaning: A philosophy of the curriculum for general education.* New York: McGraw-Hill.

Redfern, H. B. (1991). Developing and checking aesthetic understanding. In R. A. Smith & A. Simpson (Eds.), *Aesthetics and arts education* (pp. 264–273). Urbana: University of Illinois Press.

Reid, L. A. (1973). Knowledge, aesthetic insight, and education. *Proceedings of the Philosophy of Education Society of Great Britain, 7*(1), 1.

Reimer, B. (1991). Criteria for quality in music. In R. A. Smith & A. Simpson (Eds.), *Aesthetics and arts education* (pp. 330–338). Urbana: University of Illinois Press.

Rilke, R. M. (1984). *Letters to a young poet* (S. Mitchell, Trans.). New York: Random House.

Rilke, R. M. (1981). *An unofficial Rilke: Poems 1912–1926.* (M. Hamburger, Trans.). London: Anvil Press Poetry.

Rodari, F., Georgel, P., Sante, L., & Prévost, M. (1998). *Shadows of a hand: The drawings of Victor Hugo.* New York: Merrell Holberton.

Salzman, M. (1995). *The soloist.* London: Bloomsbury.

Smith, R. A. (1991). An excellence curriculum for arts education. In R. A. Smith & A. Simpson (Eds.), *Aesthetics and arts education* (pp. 245–255). Urbana: University of Illinois Press.

Smith, R. A. & Simpson, A. (Eds). (1991). *Aesthetics and arts education.* Urbana: University of Illinois Press.

VanTassel-Baska, J. (1994). *Comprehensive curriculum for gifted learners* (2nd ed.). Boston: Allyn and Bacon.

Warren, R. P. (1975). *Democracy and poetry*. Cambridge, MA: Harvard University Press.

Wolff, R. J. (1970). *Essays on art and learning*. New York: Grossman.

Concept Development and Learning

by
Linda D. Avery
and
Catherine A. Little

The Constitutional Convention. Converting fractions to decimals. The solar system. The Secret Garden, Bridge to Terabithia, A Wrinkle in Time. *The discrete stimuli and content elements that fill your plan book have begun to seem alarmingly disconnected, and you recognize from their behavior that your students are learning information for tests and promptly forgetting it. You are searching for ways to provide a curriculum that connects—not only across subject areas or segments of the school year, but also to students' lives and experiences in ways that will help them more readily retain what they learn in school. Plus, you are searching for ways to deepen your curriculum so that it becomes more engaging and more challenging for your gifted students. What can you do?*

In the middle of the last century, scholars gathered together the texts that comprised the Western world's traditional literary canon into a collection they titled *The Great Ideas: A Syntopicon of Great Books of the Western World* (Adler, 1952). Within this collection, the editor presented a list of central concepts fundamental to the literature and, indeed, to the history of the Western world. A review of these concepts today, even in a more globally conscious society, demonstrates that many or most of the ideas can be generalized beyond *The Great Ideas* to fit the human condition, although their definitions and specific structures may vary from culture to culture and time to time. Among these common concepts are *family, authority, faith, love, change, causality, truth,* and *wisdom.*

The concepts fundamental to the human condition are also fundamental to human learning, to our understanding of the world around us and within us. Consequently, such ideas can and should be fundamental to the educational process, as well. The Integrated Curriculum Model (ICM; VanTassel-Baska, 1986, 1995), outlined in Chapter 1 and discussed throughout this book, places concept learning as one of its three primary dimensions, with the recognition that concept learning is crucial to the understanding of any discipline and the relationships among disciplines.

This chapter will focus on the use of concepts in curriculum development and in instruction. After discussing further the rationale for concept teaching, the chapter introduces a specific model for concept development that provides an entrée to concept study in any discipline. The chapter then explores various ways of embedding concept study within the curriculum. As with other chapters throughout the book, the emphasis here is on how to use concepts as a means to differentiate curricula for gifted students even as they are used as a foundation for strong curricula in general.

The Importance of Concept Learning

Many architects of curricula for the gifted have recognized the importance of concepts as central to the organization and content of units of instruction. In one of his principles of differential education, Ward (1961) advocated that "the content of the curriculum should be organized in a manner which reduces to generic areas the concepts undertaken for instruction" (p. 148). Feldhusen (1988) described an ideal program for the gifted as one that "involves them in ideational challenges and activity as a vehicle to learn subject matter and as stimulus for their cognitive development" (p. 119). Perkins (1993) recommended an education organized around "generative knowledge," which is "a powerful conceptual system that yields insight and implications in many circumstances" (p. 91). VanTassel-Baska (1995), as noted previously, identified concept learning as one of the three key dimensions of her ICM. Moreover, she emphasized that learning fewer concepts in greater depth is advisable over trying to address too many concepts at a surface level. This reflects the position of the American Association for the Advancement of Science (AAAS; 1990), which identified six central concepts for science learning across K–12 education (see Chapter 8 for further discussion).

Concepts are, by definition, abstractions, and they require higher levels of thought to absorb, understand, and extend. Concept learning is fundamental to knowledge acquisition in every discipline and in everyday living, and our comprehension of abstract ideas affects our behavior from kindergarten to the corporation. We cannot function effectively in society without understanding concepts such as *justice*, *authority*, *responsibility*, and *honor*. Concepts such as *change* and *systems* may first be introduced in the elementary curriculum, but continue to be studied through advanced graduate work. Fullan (1991, 1993) made his reputation in the field of education by synthesizing the research on change in relation to school systems, while graduate programs in educational leadership have incorporated a systems perspective in conceptualizing the function of administration.

Our knowledge of concepts of such breadth is always evolving and paradigmatic, requiring that we revisit these ideas over and over to understand them fully. Concept learning is also instrumental in facilitating various types of reasoning processes. We use concept learning to negotiate the application of deductive and inductive thinking. Inferring from the specific to the general or deducing from the general to the specific involves understanding the nature of generalities, and generalities are conceptual understandings. The ability to execute analogical reasoning and related problem-solving tasks also relies heavily on concept learning, as in the popular analogy problem relating the destruction of a tumor surrounded by healthy tissue to the destruction of a fortified city (Gick & Holyoak, 1980, 1983, as cited in Goswami, 1991).

VanTassel-Baska (1998) noted that concepts and themes provide "important pathways between the disciplines so that separate aspects of knowledge are understood as being integrated" (p. 347). Schack (1994) recognized the power of concepts to draw students and teachers alike more deeply into the material, provoking curiosity and inquiry. Because concepts are truly relevant to our lives, our ability to identify and connect with them infuses them with vitality and dynamism. Thus, concepts not only link disciplines together, they also link the learner to the content.

What is a Concept?

One of the difficulties inherent in defining *concept* is that the term itself names a concept. Language (also a concept) relies upon common understandings of concept labels and of the defining characteristics that group objects or ideas under these labels. Ehrenberg (1981) described some of the key features of concepts. First, all concepts are abstract because a concept "constitutes a generalized mental image of the characteristics that make items examples" (p. 37). Concept labels are terms that are used to describe any and all examples of a concept. For instance, the label *fruit* refers to the characteristic part of a plant that contains the seeds. In fact, the concepts (or sets of attributes or characteristics) are used interchangeably with the labels.

Although concepts themselves are abstract, the individual characteristics that define an item as belonging to the concept may be concrete, abstract, or a combination of both. For example, the characteristics that designate an apple as a fruit are more concrete than the characteristics that define an action as just or moral. When we speak of concept learning in curriculum development, especially with regard to interdisciplinary concepts, we are generally referring to those concepts with characteristics that are more abstract in nature—the "big ideas" discussed at the start of this chapter.

A second feature of concepts is that they cannot be verified, like facts, as being "right" or "wrong." Their meaning is socially constructed. This means that our understanding of concepts must be dynamic. Ehrenberg (1981) used the concept of *family* to illustrate this point, exploring changing definitions of the term across time and place to encompass nuclear, extended, blended, and other forms of the family.

In addition to understanding the dynamic social construction of concepts, it is also important to recognize that individual understanding of concepts is also a constructive process. Learning involves the establishment of conceptual understandings based on experiences of

Table 5.1
Sample Concepts Useful in Curriculum Development

Change	Life and death	Scale
Constancy	Models	Signs and symbols
Evolution	Origins	Systems
Family	Patterns	Time
Good and evil	Patterns of change	Truth
Knowledge	Power	Wisdom

Note. List compiled from Adler, 1952; AAAS, 1990; and VanTassel-Baska, 1998.

the world; a child's initial conception of *dog* may be related to the characteristics of his or her own pet until experiences with other dogs in person or through books and pictures broadens and solidifies the concept. Similarly, experiences with literature, history, and real-world interactions can broaden a child's conceptions of truth, change, patterns, and wisdom. Moreover, discussions of the varying individual and social constructions of various concepts as expressed through behaviors and writings of individuals and groups across time periods and cultures can bring to consciousness the reasoning processes that underlie concept construction.

Ehrenberg's (1981) third key point about concepts is the idea that concepts are hierarchical: "some classes include other classes" (p. 39). The example of *fruit* as a concept was given above; *apple* is a concept within the larger concept of *fruit*, but *fruit* is also a part of the larger concept of *plant*, which falls under the class of *living things*. Encouraging recognition of classes of concepts supports students in reasoning about connections between them, as well as distinguishing among them. Moreover, a curriculum developer's careful consideration of conceptual hierarchies also ensures that central concepts selected for study are sufficiently broad to encourage such deep reasoning and opportunities for comparison and contrast. Several broad concepts useful in curriculum development are illustrated in Table 5.1. These concepts, because of their universality and relevance to specific disciplines, can form the centerpiece of a curriculum that encourages students to explore and deepen their understanding by analyzing instances of the concept in discipline-relevant materials and questions.

The Center for Gifted Education at the College of William and Mary has developed several series of curricular units that are organized around key concepts. The language arts curriculum focuses on the concept of *change*, with the various units delving into some of the nuances of change, such as cyclical change and social versus individual change. The science curriculum and a portion of the social studies curriculum focus on the concept of *systems*, again exploring different nuances of the concept as it relates to the specific content under study. Other social studies curricula focus on additional concepts, such as *cause and effect*, *nationalism*, and *perspective*.

The development of each of these concepts into foundations for a curriculum involved the development of examples and generalizations, to be discussed below, and also a review of discussions of the concepts as they applied to various disciplines. Such a review of previous theory and treatment of the concept assists the curriculum developer in ensuring that the treatment of the concept within the curriculum reflects the principles and practices of the related content disciplines. In the Center for Gifted Education's curriculum development projects, concept papers have been written to demonstrate these connections as a support to the curriculum developers and to teachers wishing to implement the curriculum successfully (e.g., Boyce, 1992; Pence, 1999; Sher, 1991). Concept papers at this level of detail are certainly useful to the curriculum developer; however, more abbreviated concept maps can be developed to support smaller curricular efforts from the practitioner.

Supporting Student Concept Development

Concepts, as discussed above, underscore all human thought and communication, and individuals develop conceptual understandings as a part of the natural learning process (Ehrenberg, 1981). However, this does not mean that a more structured process of concept development cannot be guided and supported by a teacher's intervention. On the contrary, teachers can provide excellent contexts in which students may undergo a process of concept development that is well organized and leads step-by-step to deeper understandings. The concept development model to be explained here is based on the work of Taba (1962), a major theorist in the area of curriculum development. The process is a constructivist one that asks students to take what they already know about a concept, organize and reflect upon it, develop generalizations, and then apply those generalizations back to previous knowledge. The use of the concept development model as applied to a particular idea is outlined in the sample lesson *The Concept of Change* (Center for Gifted Education, 1998a).

Change is used as the central organizer in the Center for Gifted Education's series of language arts units (Center for Gifted Education, 1999). In these units, students progress through the stages of this activity in an early lesson, at the conclusion of which they are presented with a list of the following generalizations about the concept:

- Change is everywhere.
- Change is linked to time.
- Change may be positive or negative.
- Change may happen naturally or be caused by people.
- Change may be perceived as orderly or random.

These generalizations were developed based on a review of literature in various disciplines about change, with central ideas organized into these five statements accessible to student understanding. In using the concept development model in organizing curricula and in instruction, such a prepared list is useful to ensure that the concept has been addressed comprehensively; however, students' own generalizations should be aligned with this list and validated through discussion and activities throughout a related unit.

Curriculum developers may also want to add essential questions as a further tool for stimulating student thinking about the concept. Some essential questions based on the generalizations might be as follows:

- How has the idea of change evolved differently in different cultures and time periods?
- Why are some societal changes judged to be good and others bad?
- What patterns of change are all around us?

Adding essential questions helps students focus their thinking on broad aspects of the generalizations and provides teachers with a basis for further lesson planning and development.

As a concluding step to the concept development model, students are asked to re-examine their examples with the generalizations in

Sample Lesson
The Concept of Change

Instructional Purpose:

- To develop understanding of the concept of *change*.

Activities and Questions:

1. Divide students into groups of four or five. Give each group several large sheets of paper for recording ideas. Each section of the activity that follows should incorporate small-group work followed by whole-class debriefing.

2. Students generate examples of the concept of *change* that are derived from their own understanding and experiences with changes in the world. Encourage students to provide at least 25 examples.

   Guiding questions:
   - What words come to mind when you think about change?
   - What kinds of things change?
   - What is it about them that changes?
   - How do you know when something has changed?
   - What evidence do you look for to determine whether change has occurred?

3. Once an adequate number of examples has been generated, students then group examples together into categories. This process allows students to search for interrelatedness and to organize materials. Students should be able to explain their reasoning for given categories and seek clarification from each other as a whole class. Teachers should ensure that students have accounted for all of their examples through the categories established.

   Guiding questions:
   - How would you categorize these ideas into groups?
   - What would you call each group? Why?

- Do all of your changes fall into groups?
- Might some of them belong in more than one group?
- Is there a different way you might categorize your ideas?
- What other categories might you use?
- What are some of the characteristics of change, based on the ideas you wrote?

4. Next, ask students to think of nonexamples of the concept of *change*. Begin the brainstorming process with the direction, "Now list examples of things that *do not change*." Encourage students to think carefully about nonexamples and discuss ideas within their groups. Each group should list six to eight nonexamples.

    Guiding questions:
    - What are some things that do not change?
    - What are some things that always seem the same or always happen the same way?
    - What evidence or proof do you have that these things do not change?
    - How might you group the things that do not change?
    - What can you call each of these groups?
    - How are the groups of things that do not change similar to or different from the groups of things that do change?
    - Think about the following ideas and whether they show change: routines or habits, rules and regulations, table manners, laws, customs of cultures. Explain your answers. If they show change, where would they fit into your categories of changes? If they do not, where would they fit into your categories of things that do not change?

5. The students now determine generalizations about the concept of *change*, using their lists of examples, categories, and nonexamples to help them. Then, present a list of prepared generalizations developed from a review of literature

related to the concept and essential for the discipline under study. Student generalizations should be aligned with the prepared generalizations and posted for use throughout a unit of study.

Guiding questions:
- A generalization is something that is always or almost always true. What generalizations can you make about change?
- Use your examples and categories to guide your thinking and write several statements that are generalizations about change.

---

mind, demonstrating how particular examples support the generalizations. Figure 5.1 illustrates how this portion of the activity may be presented in graphic form.

This versatile model is applicable to almost any concept, although sometimes it requires additional instruction prior to the activity to orient students toward an understanding of the term used as the concept label. One feature to note is the difference between the *concept development* or *concept formation model* as outlined above (Taba, 1962) and a *concept attainment model* (Bruner, Goodnow, & Austin, 1967). Concept attainment bears some similarity to the model described above, but the order and orientation of the procedures are quite different. In a concept attainment model, students are given a list of examples and nonexamples and asked to figure out to what concept these lists refer. The concept development model used above is somewhat more open-ended in its orientation and encourages divergent contributions from students' own experiences and ways of thinking.

The two student examples in Figures 5.2 and 5.3 illustrate the power of an open-ended stimulus to capture student understanding of key generalizations about concepts. The first illustration was crafted by a fourth-grade girl when asked to choose one of the generalizations about the concept of *change* and show its relevance to her life. She chose to focus on how change relates to time. The second illustration was developed by a fourth-grade boy who decided to focus on the generalization that "Change is everywhere."

Directions: Write 3–5 examples to illustrate each of the generalizations.

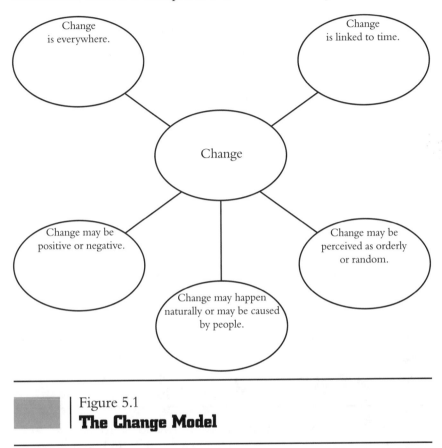

Figure 5.1
The Change Model

Each example illustrates the student's capacity to find personal relevance in studying the concept and to deepen his or her understanding of his or her own life as a result. The girl recognized the power of reading in her life as a developmental progression, while the boy gained insight into how his writing had become more sophisticated.

Ehrenberg (1981) identified several key points that summarize the benefits of the concept development lesson for encouraging student thinking:

- Students must focus on several examples and nonexamples of the concept.

My Reading Change

This story is all about how I developed reading skills. Before I learned to read from the time I was about 9 months old, to when I was about 4 years old, I liked books. When I was about 3, I would always want to hear the same books—Pee Wee Scouts books and Oz books, both of which, in fact, are series.

The process of learning to read started when I was about 4. I don't remember too much about starting, but I have a few scraps of memory. One memory picture about preschool and kindergarten reading is of me reading a beginner book and having trouble with some of the words. It was a rectangle-shaped book. Another vivid memory is, in kindergarten, the class was reading a book together and I was reading ahead a little because I already knew how to read. In first grade, I must have completed the beginner book stage, though I have no memories of first-grade reading. In second grade I liked to read an awful lot. One of the books I read in second grade was *Aliens Don't Wear Braces*. In third grade, I was almost as much of a reader as I am now. I even had a reputation for being a major reader! This year I can read at least one book a day. One day this year, I read 123 pages of small print in a few hours.

Each year I get a little faster at reading and the stuff I read changes. Reading has become an enormous part of my life, so this was a monumental change for me. I can't remember a time when books were not part of my life. And it's no wonder. It all started before I was even a year old!

—9-year-old girl

Figure 5.2
Student Example 1

- Students must gather and verify information as to the *concept-relevant characteristics* of each individual example and nonexample.
- Students must note how the examples vary and yet are still examples of the concept.
- Students must note what is alike about all the examples of the concept.
- Students must generalize that what is alike about all the examples they've examined is also true of all other examples of the concept.
- Students must note how the nonexamples resemble examples, but, particularly, how they differ from them.
- Students must generalize about the characteristics that distinguish all examples of the concept from any item that might resemble them in some way.

Change is Everywhere

I think that the generalization about change, "Change is everywhere," is most true. You don't have to agree with me, but I do think that, if you listen closely, you will understand my point. My opinion is supported by the following three reasons.

My first reason is that a large part of change is natural, and there is no place where nature is absent. Some examples of natural change are orbits, plant growth, animal evolution, and erosion. Two important examples of natural change are continental drift and seasons. Continental drift is definitely everywhere. Wherever there are continents, there is continental drift. Seasons are also everywhere, though they may differ in different places. Some examples of seasonal change are the changing of the leaves and having snow fall.

My second reason is that cultural change is a part of change and it is everywhere. Wherever there are groups of people, there is cultural change. There are lots of cultural things that occasionally change. Some change frequently. Here are some examples of cultural change: holidays (change dates and the way they are celebrated), politics, technology, human knowledge, languages, religions, industrial product crazes, customs, and styles. One cultural change that happened very recently was the Presidential election.

My third reason is that personal change is an aspect of change, and it is definitely everywhere. Wherever there are individuals, there is personal change. Some things that fit into the personal category of change are interests, ages, feelings, opinions, and so forth. An example of personal change that happened to me very recently was that I moved from third grade, to summer vacation, to fourth grade. Now I have different ideas and opinions, and I think that some of the pieces I wrote in third grade that are supposed to be funny are a little too outward. That means that my idea of subtlety is changing.

For the above three reasons, I think that the statement, "Change is everywhere" is most true. I hope that now you understand my opinion.

—9-year-old boy

Figure 5.3
Student Example 2

Moving From a Lesson to a Curriculum

Within the framework of a curricular unit, the concept development activities described above can serve as an explicit introduction to a concept that is then embedded throughout a content-based unit of study. The generalizations developed in the initial lesson, along with details of the definition, examples, and categories related to the con-

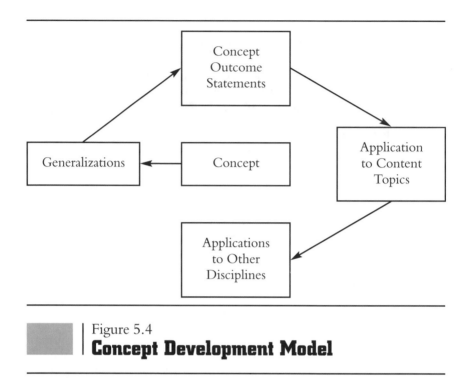

Figure 5.4

Concept Development Model

Note. From *A Guide to Teaching a Problem-Based Science Curriculum* (p. 25), by the Center for Gifted Education, 1997, Dubuque, IA: Kendall/Hunt. Copyright © 1997 by the Center for Gifted Education. Adapted with permission.

cept, provide guidelines for student outcomes and for questions and activities that reinforce student understanding and ability to apply the concept within and across disciplines for deeper understanding of content. This curricular process of developing generalizations, outcomes, and applications is illustrated graphically in Figure 5.4.

The outcomes related to the concept represent the most critical element of this process for the curriculum developer because these outcomes and the curricular framework of which they are a part serve as the foundation for whatever degree of instructional guidance follows. Applications of the concept within and across disciplines should refer back to these outcomes such that teachers can understand and demonstrate how the activities in which they engage with students relate to the larger framework.

Possible applications of concepts may vary considerably from one unit to another, depending on the concept, the developmental level of the students, and the discipline under study. However, one general application that relates across disciplines and across concepts is the development and implementation of core questions. Questions that encourage students to recognize and define examples and nonexamples of the concept or to apply the concept generalizations to specific instances support students in developing a deeper understanding of the concept. A set of such questions should be prepared in advance of teaching a given lesson to ensure that the discussion is maintained at a higher level, although the need for additional probing questions will undoubtedly arise during the course of the implementation of the discussion.

For example, in a Center for Gifted Education language arts unit focusing on the concept of *change*, students are asked to explain how a story by Edgar Allen Poe illustrates human and natural control over change or how a Nathaniel Hawthorne story utilizes changing times of day to symbolize larger implications of the links between change and time (Center for Gifted Education, 1998c). In a social studies unit exploring the concept of *cause and effect* within the context of a study of the American Revolution, students are asked to analyze the chain of related effects resulting from the taxes instituted by Parliament in the 1760s, as well as the causes of these taxes in the first place; they are also asked to consider how a generalization addressing the predictability of effects relates to the debates of the Continental Congress in early 1776 (Center for Gifted Education, 2001). In a science unit utilizing the concept of *systems* to explore acid-base chemistry, students are asked to analyze how organisms within an ecosystem represent interdependent systems and how this interdependency is affected by the introduction of an acidic input (Center for Gifted Education, 1997). In a math unit utilizing the concept of *models* to explore populations, students examine existing mathematical models and create new ones to represent real-world phenomena; for example, students are asked to determine the accuracy of $y = 3^x$ as a predictor of population size for a bacteria culture (Johnson & Sher, 1997).

Another way in which a concept may be embedded into the curriculum is to encourage students to see connections across selections of readings throughout a unit related to the concept. Figure 5.5 is an example of how students record reflections about *change* throughout the course of a unit, allowing for a closing discussion that incorporates the concept, as well as the literature selections and students' own personal responses.

In addition to the overall conceptual organization of the curriculum under one concept, curricula for the gifted should also encourage students to develop their awareness of multiple concepts affecting what

Literature Selection	Changes in relation-ships	Changes that can be perceived as positive	Changes that can be perceived as negative	Changes in you as a result of reading
"Autobiographia Literaria"				
"Ghost Cat"				
"Literary Lessons" from *Little Women*				
"All Summer in a Day"				
"Ode to my Library"				
"Charles"				
Your own story				

Figure 5.5
Change Matrix

Note. From *Autobiographies* (p. 61), by the Center for Gifted Education, 1998, Dubuque, IA: Kendall/Hunt. Copyright © 1998 by the Center for Gifted Education. Reprinted with permission.

they read, hear, discuss, and understand. Consequently, questioning strategies should encourage students to identify other ideas underscoring literature. Students should be encouraged to recognize themes and ideas that appear frequently within given selections, and also across selections, and to demonstrate their understanding of how these concepts are elaborated. The development of concept maps is also an effective tool for encouraging students to develop their understanding of a concept. For example, the illustration in Figure 5.6 may serve as the

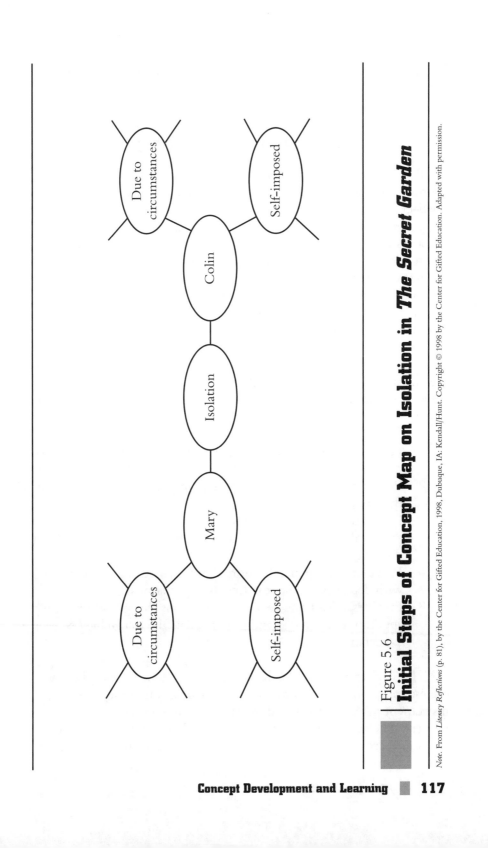

Figure 5.6
Initial Steps of Concept Map on Isolation in *The Secret Garden*

Note. From *Literacy Reflections* (p. 81), by the Center for Gifted Education, 1998, Dubuque, IA: Kendall/Hunt. Copyright © 1998 by the Center for Gifted Education. Adapted with permission.

beginning steps of a concept map about isolation in the novel *The Secret Garden*.

Assessing Concept Learning

Because concepts are a critical dimension in the ICM, concept learning must be assessed routinely. Strategies that encourage more open-ended responses allow students to demonstrate their understanding of concepts through illustration and application. We have used several assessment approaches in our curriculum development work at the Center for Gifted Education. One strategy is to use a pretest and posttest design that allows the teacher to assess growth.

In the Center for Gifted Education's language arts units, a concept question is embedded in the pretest and posttest on literary analysis and interpretation. This question typically asks students to infer what a passage of text (from a poem, story, etc.) tells us about the concept of *change* and to support what is said with details from the text. Because the question is open-ended with more than one "right" answer, a rubric is used to score the response. The latest edition of the rubric has five points on the scale arranged as follows:

0 – Provides no response or a response inappropriate to the task demand.

2 – Provides limited, vague, inaccurate response; only quotes from the story.

4 – Provides literal description of change occurring in the story or a generalization about the concept made without support from the text.

6 – Provides valid generalization about change that is supported with details from the text (meets expectations).

8 – Provides at least one generalization about change with multiple applications from text and/or with analogies to real life (exceeds expectations).

The Center for Gifted Education's social studies units also use a pretest and posttest design for concept learning, but a more expanded instrument has been developed to focus on different aspects of concept mastery. The same instrument is used for both the pretest and posttests, but three versions of the instrument have been developed, one for primary students (grades 2 and 3), one for intermediate students (grades 4 and 5), and one for middle school students (grades 6–8). A sample item on this instrument gives students a list of objects and asks them to code whether or not each object represents a system. Then, they are to select one object from the list that they have indicated is a system and explain why it is a system. The instructions for this item contain preteaching that explains why a bicycle is a system. The degree to which students employ the different aspects of a system in their illustration (boundaries, elements, inputs, interactions, and outputs) determines their mastery of the concept. Since this instrument is still in development, the specific items and rubrics are not described in their entirety here.

Another strategy for measuring concept learning is through embedded assessment activities. An example of such a strategy is found in the Center for Gifted Education's problem-based science units, which also focus heavily on the concept of *systems*. This example involves having students complete and label the elements in a fish bowl. By comparing and contrasting student responses to this exercise, the teacher is able to illustrate that system boundaries are fluid and established by social construction and that the relationship of inputs, interactions, and outputs is often governed by where these boundaries are established. The fish bowl exercise can be included in a student's portfolio of work as an illustration of his or her understanding of the concept at a given point in time.

The big ideas by which we come to know and understand our reality provide ample opportunity for depth and complexity in curricular design and implementation. Because they are such an essential part of our instructional focus, we need to have sufficient tools to measure whether students' understanding of the concepts grows and deepens over time. Both pretest and posttest instruments, as well as embedded assessment strategies, afford us insights into ascertaining the level of concept acquisition by students.

Using Concepts to Design Interdisciplinary Curricula

Our discussion thus far has focused largely on discipline-specific applications of concept learning. But, in reality, concepts transcend artificial disciplinary boundaries and enable us to make important connections across bodies of knowledge. The model previously presented in Figure 5.4 shows that, once generalizations have been translated into student outcomes, these outcomes can be embedded across

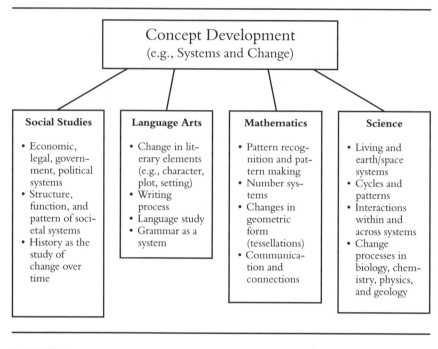

Figure 5.7
Disciplinary Applications of Concepts

Note. From *Curriculum Planning and Instructional Design for Gifted Learners*, by J. VanTassel-Baska, in press, Denver: Love. Copyright © 2001 by Love. Reprinted with permission.

fields of inquiry. In fact, most of the national and state standards of learning require that higher order concepts, such as *change, systems, models,* and *scale* be addressed within most subject matter areas. Figure 5.7 takes the concepts of *systems* and *change* and shows sample applications within the major disciplines as seen in the Virginia Standards of Learning (Commonwealth of Virginia Department of Education, 1995).

At the elementary level, it is relatively easy for teachers to elicit applications of the same concept as the subject under study progresses from math, to language arts, to social studies, to science, to art and music. Seasonal changes addressed in science from summer, to fall, to winter, to spring may be related to symbolism in literature. Why did the protagonist have his or her crisis in winter? Why did the epiphany occur in spring? Such parallels can be extended to psychology with questions about seasonal affective disorder (SAD), where light deprivation appears to trigger depression in some individuals. The savvy teacher can use such interdisciplinary connections to help students appreciate the connectedness of the world.

At the middle school and high school levels, curricular planning by multiple teachers is necessary for higher order concepts to be addressed simultaneously across subject areas within the larger curricular scope and sequence. Although multiple concepts will always be embedded within content and thus represent potential for in-depth study and exploration, collaborative decision making around how to focus the curriculum and instruction provides students with a more targeted learning experience across disciplines.

It is an interesting paradox of modern life that, as progress demands increasing areas of specialization, these areas often represent the intersection of multiple disciplines. For instance, beyond training biologists generally, we train sociobiologists and psychobiologists. Such descriptors demonstrate how we have come to blend science and social science orientations in particular fields. These connections across fields often afford new professional vistas for human development. It is particularly important that our high-ability students come to grasp the interdependence of disciplines in understanding life and carving out a meaningful experience of it. By incorporating a focus on concept learning, we can create scaffolds for ensuring that these connections are addressed within and across classrooms.

Conclusion

Concept learning enables students to make connections across the disciplines and to forge a deeper understanding and appreciation of the complexity of the world we inhabit and shape to our own ends. By focusing acutely on the concept dimension of learning, the teacher elevates the level of learning from the concrete to the abstract, from the particular to the general. A theoretical model for understanding how to teach concepts both within and across the disciplines is useful for teachers and curriculum developers in supporting authentic concept learning. Taba's (1962) ideas, as operationalized in the Center for Gifted Education's curricular units, provide a template for moving from concepts, to generalizations, to outcomes, to applications in the classroom, thus supporting teachers in their guidance of student understanding of the ideas that underscore all that they learn and experience.

Key Points Summary

❑ Concept development requires student manipulation of abstract thought and higher level thinking within and across areas of learning.

❑ All disciplines of learning are organized by powerful ideas that help shape our understanding of these areas.

❑ Curricula that are organized and taught by concepts deepen and enhance student learning over time.

❑ While concepts are useful for curricular organization, their real power rests in their being effective within units of study across lessons.

❑ Developing curricula that are concept-based requires the formation of generalizations and the transformation of those into student outcomes, followed by relevant content applications.

❑ Assessment of concept learning engages students in demonstrating deep understanding of relevant generalizations.

References

Adler, M. J. (Ed.). (1952). *The great ideas: A Synopticon of great books of the Western world*. Chicago: Encyclopedia Britannica.

American Association for the Advancement of Science (AAAS). (1990). *Science for all Americans*. New York: Oxford University Press.

Boyce, L. N. (1992). *The concept of change*. Williamsburg, VA: Center for Gifted Education, College of William and Mary.

Bruner, J. E., Goodnow, J. J., & Austin, G. A. (1967). *A study of thinking*. New York: Science Editions.

Center for Gifted Education. (1997a). *Acid, acid everywhere*. Dubuque, IA: Kendall/Hunt.

Center for Gifted Education. (1997b). *Guide to teaching a problem-based science curriculum*. Dubuque, IA: Kendall/Hunt.

Center for Gifted Education. (1998a). *Autobiographies*. Dubuque, IA: Kendall/Hunt.

Center for Gifted Education. (1998b). *Literary reflections*. Dubuque, IA: Kendall/Hunt.

Center for Gifted Education. (1998c). *Threads of change in 19th century American literature*. Dubuque, IA: Kendall/Hunt.

Center for Gifted Education. (1999). *Guide to teaching a language arts curriculum for high-ability learners.* Dubuque, IA: Kendall/Hunt.

Center for Gifted Education. (2001). *The world turned upside down: The American revolution.* Williamsburg, VA: Author.

Commonwealth of Virginia Department of Education. (1995). *Standards of learning for Virginia public schools.* Richmond, VA: Author.

Ehrenberg, S. D. (1981). Concept learning: How to make it happen in the classroom. *Educational Leadership, 39*(1), 63–43.

Feldhusen, J. (1988). Developing units of instruction. In J. VanTassel-Baska, J. Feldhusen, K. Seeley, G. Wheatley, L. Silverman, & W. Foster (Eds.), *Comprehensive curriculum for gifted learners* (pp. 112–150). Boston: Allyn and Bacon.

Fullan, M. (1991). *The new meaning of educational change.* New York: Teachers College Press.

Fullan, M. (1993). *Change forces: Probing the depths of educational reform.* Bristol, PA: The Falmer Press.

Gick, M. L., & Holyoak, K. J. (1980). Analogical problem solving. *Cognitive Psychology, 12,* 306–355.

Gick, M. L., & Holyoak, K. J. (1983). Schema induction and analogical transfer. *Cognitive Psychology, 15,* 1–38.

Goswami, U. (1991). Analogical reasoning: What develops? Review of research and theory. *Child Development, 62,* 1–22.

Johnson, D. T., & Sher, B. T. (1997). *Models: A study of animal populations.* Williamsburg, VA: Center for Gifted Education, College of William and Mary.

Pence, M. (1999). *The concept of systems.* Williamsburg, VA: Center for Gifted Education, College of William and Mary.

Perkins, D. (1993, October). The connected curriculum. *Educational Leadership 51*(2), 90–91.

Schack, G. (1994, November). *Designing integrated units.* Presentation at the annual meeting of the National Association for Gifted Children, Salt Lake City, UT.

Sher, B. (1991). *A guide to key science concepts.* Williamsburg, VA: Center for Gifted Education, College of William and Mary.

Taba, H. (1962). *Curriculum development, theory, and practice.* New York: Harcourt, Brace, and World.

VanTassel-Baska, J. (1986). Effective curriculum and instructional models for the gifted. *Gifted Child Quarterly, 30,* 164–169.

VanTassel-Baska, J. (1995). The development of talent through curriculum. *Roeper Review, 18,* 98–102.

VanTassel–Baska, J. (Ed.). (1998). *Excellence in educating gifted and talented learners* (3rd ed.). Denver: Love.

Ward, V. S. (1961). *Differential education for the gifted.* Los Angeles: National/State Leadership Training Institute for the Gifted and Talented.

Section II

Introduction

The emphasis of Section II is on the major adaptation of core content area curricula for gifted and high-ability learners. Each chapter uses the reform elements as a basis to describe these adaptations, along with ICM connections. Research-based best practices are also noted where they differ from the models employed. Sample lesson plans and key teaching models are included to highlight their use in differentiating instruction for the populations of interest.

The language arts chapter focuses strongly on the use of key strategies to teach reading, writing, and vocabulary to high-ability learners, highlighting the embedding of these models in selected content lessons. Careful attention is paid to the role of selecting resources appropriate for advanced readers, as well as choosing selections that honor multicultural writing talent in the United States and abroad.

The mathematics chapter emphasizes the dual role of acceleration and enrichment in serving mathematically able students effectively in schools and details the relationship of the standards to good practice with such learners. Sample lesson segments are included to highlight the principles shared in regard to differentiation of mathematics learning. Useful resources for incorporating technology into mathematics instruction are also explicated.

The science chapter establishes early on the relationship of high-quality curricular emphases for gifted learners and the emphasis of both national sets of science standards, demonstrating a goodness of fit in most areas. This chapter also delineates the importance of teacher thought to lesson planning, demonstrating what such plans reveal about teacher understanding of differentiation. The chapter is especially helpful in annotating several resources in science that gifted students will enjoy and schools would be well advised to purchase.

The social studies chapter focuses strong attention on professionals' developmental habits in the social science disciplines and how these may be internalized by high-ability learners as they master the skills of history, geography, economics, and political science. This chapter also puts a strong focus on teaching historical analysis skills and the use of primary sources to understand periods of history from multiple and multicultural perspectives. Sample models and lessons are included to guide teachers in implementing advanced social studies learning.

Taken as a group, these chapters represent an important step forward in the integration of core content with gifted pedagogy and reform principles. As such, they serve as an explication of the curricular units that have been developed by the Center for Gifted Education at the College of William and Mary and are used as exemplary curricula across this country and abroad.

Adapting Language Arts Curricula for High-Ability Learners

by
Catherine A. Little

You are a fifth-grade teacher. Your school has decided to regroup students by ability for language arts and mathematics in the next school year to serve all students' needs more effectively. You will be working with the top and above-average groups of students for language arts. Your principal has encouraged you to seek and develop curricula that will challenge these students who are already reading above grade level and excelling on their state-mandated reading comprehension tests. What will you do to work with these students effectively?

As a unified group, the language arts represent one of the four core content areas in the school curriculum. Indeed, in elementary school, this area is generally given priority over all other subjects in terms of the time and resources devoted to it, and even into the secondary years it never loses its prominence as the centerpiece of schooling. As a result of this heavy emphasis on language arts instruction in schools, students who are gifted and talented in the verbal areas may find language arts class to be either a saving grace or a source of boredom and anguish in school. Verbally talented students often read voraciously and enjoy opportunities to interact with literature and to write. However, if classroom literature selections, the activities designed to relate to them, and the opportunities for writing and language development are not sufficiently challenging and interesting, then the extensive time spent on language arts instruction in school may be a great source of tedium to these students.

How, then, can language arts curricula and instruction be made challenging and motivating for high-end learners? What steps can teachers and curriculum developers take to ensure that students are progressing in their learning and actively engaged in processes that will support their lifelong involvement with the language arts? A central element of achieving this level of challenge and student interest comes from the literature selections chosen for instructional purposes; another element is the type and level of questions asked for discussion and writing purposes. In addition, the language arts curriculum should encourage students to develop habits of inquiry and critical reading, and it should provide them with opportunities to delve deeply into their language and all its complexities. These and other key elements of a challenging language arts curriculum will be discussed in the following pages.

This chapter is organized around the major elements of curricular reform discussed in Chapter 1, with emphasis on how each may be realized in strong language arts curricula and instruction for the gifted. First, the key elements of significant learner outcomes and authentic assessment are addressed, with the idea that a well-grounded curricular framework that is systematically assessed throughout the instructional process is the foundation of a strong curriculum. Following these elements, the three dimensions of the Integrated Curriculum Model (ICM; VanTassel-Baska, 1986, 1994) are discussed as they specifically relate to the language arts. The chapter then focuses specifically on constructing meaning as the centerpiece of a language arts curriculum, followed by a discussion of strategies and resources that are especially relevant to language arts curricula and instruction, as well as the importance of interdisciplinary connections from the language arts to the other core content areas. Each section will draw upon sample lessons from the Center for Gifted Education's award-winning and research-based language arts curriculum for examples of how the elements of reform may be applied to enhance curricular appropriateness for verbally talented learners. Relevant sections from these lessons are included.

Learner Outcomes of Significance

Outcomes in the language arts content area should reflect the four primary language arts themselves—reading, writing, listening, and speaking—as well as the structure and organization of the language itself, which underscores all of these functions. The National Council of Teachers of English (NCTE) and the International Reading Association (IRA), in their *Standards for the English Language Arts* (1996), emphasized three major categories of learning opportunities for students: (a) to read and interact with a wide range of literature selections, (b) to communicate effectively in writing and speaking in a variety of genres and for a variety of purposes, and (c) to develop a strong sense of language structure and to use this as a starting point for understanding various types of communication. In developing outcomes of significance in the language arts for gifted students, these standards may be used as a starting point for developing higher levels of expectation—a floor from which to begin, not a ceiling for which to strive. In addition, the outcomes of significance should take into account the teaching of embedded skills and concepts above facts and knowledge, and they should have relevance to other disciplines and to the world of work.

The ICM is grounded in an understanding that outcomes for gifted students should represent a higher level of expectation than outcomes for students who are not so advanced. Such outcomes do not eliminate the expectation for performance of more basic skills; rather, they implicitly require that such skills be utilized as foundations for performance of more complex tasks. For example, decoding and comprehension of texts are presumed under the outcome of developing critical reading behaviors.

The Center for Gifted Education at the College of William and Mary has developed a series of curricular units in the language arts, all organized around the ICM and incorporating six central goals common across multiple units and grade levels (Center for Gifted Education, 1999). Four of these are content goals, representing reading, writing, language study, and oral communication; one goal represents a focus on process; and one represents the conceptual organization of the curriculum. Several learner outcomes—specific enough for measurement, but general enough to apply across a range of developmental levels—were also developed for each goal. Samples of these goals and outcomes are given in Table 6.1 and will be discussed in more detail throughout the chapter. The third column of the table illustrates how specific goals and outcomes of the curricular units align with aspects of the *Standards for the English Language Arts* (NCTE & IRA, 1996). In addition, the Appendix at the end of the book demonstrates how the curriculum aligns with the overall vision of the national standards.

Note that both the curricular goals and the related national standards are broad in scope, while the outcomes are more specific; also, note that the curricular goals and outcomes reflect attention to the advanced verbal skills and behaviors characteristic of gifted students.

Habits of Mind

Developing learner outcomes of significance for language arts curricula must incorporate attention to the desired habits of mind of the disciplines it reflects; moreover, a disciplinary orientation toward curricula and instruction represents a more challenging and complex approach, thus supporting the notion of differentiation for gifted learners. The fundamental goal of language arts education is to develop literacy for the language tasks of everyday life (NCTE/IRA, 1996). Building upon and beyond this, however, language arts education must also encourage in students habits related to critical reading, the iterative processes of writing, and the exploration of language as the foundation for the aesthetic and intellectual experience of communication. Langer (1995) defined two types of experiences that characterize interactions with literature: the literary experience, in which the primary goal is "exploring horizons of possibilities" (p. 26), and the discursive experience, that which focuses on gaining or sharing ideas or information, in which the primary goal is maintaining a point of reference with which we develop agreements or disagreements. Recognizing the purpose of reading a given text and identifying how the experience reflects one of these goals represent an important part of developing critical reading behaviors; moreover, the same goal directions apply in developing pieces of writing. Related to this, another important aspect of literate behavior, and thus a key habit of mind to promote in language arts edu-

Table 6.1
Goals and Outcomes of Significance

Goals	Sample Related Outcomes	Related National Standard (NCTE & IRA, 1999)
Students will be able to:		
Develop analytical and interpretive skills in literature.	Cite similarities and differences in meaning among selected works of literature. Make inferences based on information in given passages.	Apply a wide range of strategies to comprehend, interpret, evaluate, and appreciate texts.
To develop persuasive writing skills.	Develop a written persuasive essay, given a topic. Complete various pieces of writing using a three-phase revision process.	Employ a wide range of strategies as they write and use different writing process elements appropriately.
Develop linguistic competency.	Analyze the form and function of words in a given context. Develop vocabulary power commensurate with reading.	Apply knowledge of language structure [and] language conventions to create, critique, and discuss print and nonprint texts.
Develop listening/oral communication skills.	Evaluate an oral persuasive message according to main idea and arguments cited to support it. Develop skills of argument formulation.	Use spoken language to accomplish their own purposes.
Develop reasoning skills in the language arts (process goal).	Apply aspects of the Paul reasoning model through specific examples. Define a problem, given ill-structured, complex, or technical information.	Conduct research on issues and interests by generating ideas and questions and by posing problems.
Understand the concept of *change* in the language arts (concept goal).	Interpret change as positive or negative in selected works. Analyze social and individual change in a piece of literature.	Read a wide range of literature from many periods in many genres to build an understanding of the many dimensions of human experience.

Note. "Goals" and "Sample Related Outcomes" from *A Guide to Teaching a Language Arts Curriculum for High-Ability Learners* (pp. 63–64), by the Center for Gifted Education, 1999, Dubuque, IA: Kendall/Hunt. Copyright © 1999 by the Center for Gifted Education. Adapted with permission. "Related National Standard" from *Standards for the English Language Arts*, by the National Council for Teachers of English (NCTE), & International Reading Association (IRA), 1996, Urbana, IL: Author. Copyright © 1996 by NCTE & IRA. Reprinted with permission. See Appendix for the complete standards.

cation, is the ability to make good choices about what one will read and write (Zemelman, Daniels, & Hyde, 1993). Thus, students should be given opportunities to choose literature pieces and writing topics and to reflect upon their reasoning for and effectiveness of their choices.

Emphasis on all the steps of the writing process in schools offers support to students in developing the habits of mind of the professional writer. However, within the structured steps of prewriting, drafting, revising, and editing fall the diverse and idiosyncratic behaviors of the individual writer; almost paradoxically, an important writing habit of mind is to define one's own writing process—such elements as favorite format for prewriting, degree of revision that occurs during drafting, and how writing time is allotted to the different steps. Students need to have opportunities to find themselves as writers and to discover their own most effective habits for writing, with instruction in the writing process used as a flexible foundation, not a source of rigid rules. Beyond the processes of writing, students must also work to develop their own style as writers, which involves not only practice in writing, but practice in analyzing the writing styles of others through critical reading and literature study.

The study of language also encourages the habits of mind of the critical reader and the practiced writer; the meaning we create when reading or when expressing ourselves in writing or speech is constructed on a frame of words and their combinations into grammatical structures. Thompson (1996a) emphasized the importance of formal language study focused on grammar, vocabulary, and poetics because language is both "a medium for the mind" and "a manifestation of the mind" and thus not only a habit, but a very definition of the mind (p. 151). Study of the structures of language, moreover, not only provides students with the tools for understanding and analyzing the texts they read, but also deepens their aesthetic appreciation for linguistic expression as an art form.

Authentic Assessment

Authentic assessment in the language arts involves students in the actual processes of interacting with language in both classroom instruction and in the real world. Reading and response, writing and speaking tasks, and appropriate language-use tasks can all be examples of authentic assessment in this area, with care taken in how the tasks are presented and assessed. Assessment in the language arts should be ongoing—formative, as well as summative—an opportunity for student learning in itself and a tool not only for evaluating students for accountability purposes, but also for planning and organizing instruction (Marzano, 1992). In order to accomplish this, clear goals and outcomes and embedded opportunities for assessment should appear throughout a curricular document.

An example of an authentic literary response and interpretation assessment would be to have students read a selection of literature and then respond in writing to a series of targeted questions. Ideally, a literary response assessment task such as this engages students with a new piece of literature and requires that they demonstrate their own capacity for responding to and interpreting new literature—not their ability to remember and repeat someone else's interpretation. Again, this also allows the assessment task to be an opportunity for learning, as well as for demonstration and mastery of key processes and critical reading behaviors.

In writing, assessment tasks should, simply enough, require students to write. However, in order for assessment tasks to be useful to teachers as diagnostic tools and manageable for scoring purposes, the tasks should be clearly stated in terms of expectations for student performance. In addition, rubrics should be shared with students, along with writing models, so as to demonstrate to them what level of performance is expected.

Another key component of assessment in the language arts is the development of challenging products. Writing assignments in the language arts should involve not only short, power-writing pieces, but also longer term products that require students to draft and then revise and edit their work. Professional writers engage in these types of practices, so likewise students should be asked to do so in order to represent the types of real-world experiences for which language arts instruction is supposed to be preparing them. Furthermore, to make such product development even more real-world-oriented, students should be encouraged to prepare their writing products for real audiences in order to promote the key outcome of awareness of intended audience in writing. One central aspect of developing audience awareness is the use of peer-review techniques in the preparation of writing products. Students should be encouraged to read one another's work with a critical eye and according to a specific set of guidelines, with emphasis on the need for objective review and objective response to constructive criticism.

Naturally, audience awareness is also a key feature of effective speaking, and emphasis on audience should infuse oral communication tasks and assessments, as well (Chaney, 1996). Presentation of the content of written products in an oral format is one way of integrating product assignments and creating opportunities for assessment in both areas. Such presentations allow for not only assessment of the oral language skills of the presenter, but also of the listening skills of other students through peer-assessment tools and through questioning and discussion. Moreover, such economy of assessment through tasks that address multiple outcomes at once is an important consideration in planning a curriculum.

Conceptually Oriented Curricula

The Taba (1962) concept development model discussed in Chapter 5 encourages students to delve deeply into their understanding of an abstract concept and then to apply a renewed understanding of that concept in the form of generalizations. In the language arts, the options for appropriate concepts to use as curricular organizers are extensive and rich. Literature is a common ground from which the concepts fundamental to the human experience are explored, explained, and passed down from generation to generation and culture to culture, as the list of fundamental concepts found in *The Great Ideas* (Adler, 1952) demonstrates. The selection of a concept for a language arts curriculum, then, is more a question of narrowing a field of appropriate options than seeking possibilities. Selection depends primarily on ease of application across subjects and upon the types of literature to be employed. The broader the concept, the more applicable it will be to multiple units and multiple selections of literature.

In the language arts units developed at the Center for Gifted Education, *change* was selected as the central concept for discussion and development (Center for Gifted Education, 1999). The concept of *change* is an extremely versatile one because it is familiar to every individual's experience of life and of the world and because it applies to virtually every aspect of life. It also applies to literature in a variety of ways. For example, movement of a plot requires change of some kind to be occurring; character development through the course of a literature selection involves change; and, moreover, the fundamental purpose of many literature selections is to change the mind of the reader in some way, as Downs (1978) demonstrated in a discussion of revolutionary literature throughout history.

Chapter 5 has already provided some suggestions regarding curriculum development around the concept of *change* and its generalizations. The sample lesson *Reflections on Change in Poetry* (Center for Gifted Education, 1998c) specifically demonstrates the embedding of the concept and its generalizations within a language arts activity. In this lesson, designed for upper elementary gifted students, an in-depth discussion of several short poems by Emily Dickinson is organized around the concept of *change*. The opening journal activity is meant to focus students on the occurrences of change in nature as they relate to changes in human emotion, as well as to demonstrate the cyclical nature of change and the fact that some changes are positive and some are negative. The bulk of the lesson then involves students in discussing how Dickinson's poetry demonstrates the generalizations about change.

In this lesson, students are interacting with literature and seeking specific ways in which the central concept of the curriculum is demonstrated in poetry, with connections to students' own lives. Key elements of this lesson to note in considering curriculum development are the selection of literature pieces that demonstrate important features of the concept and the preparation of specific questions in advance to promote student thinking around the concept.

Higher Order Reasoning

As discussed in Chapter 3, one of the keys to encouraging higher order thinking in students is to select a strong thinking model, teach it to students directly, and then apply aspects of that same model systematically in various contexts. In the language arts, such a thinking model makes an effective tool for teachers and for students, serving as a support structure for questioning, analyzing literature, writing and revising, and conducting research.

Paul's (1992) Elements of Reasoning, detailed in Chapter 3, represent a comprehensive model for reasoning around issues and also serves as a versatile framework for supporting critical thinking in the language arts. In literature discussions, the reasoning model provides a scaffold for the development of higher level questions around a given literature selection. For example, in the unit *Autobiographies* (Center for Gifted Education, 1998b), students are asked to read a chapter called "Literary Lessons" from Louisa May Alcott's *Little Women* and

Sample Lesson
Reflections on Change in Poetry

Instructional Purpose:

- To develop reasoning and interpretive skills in literature through discussing poetry.
- To develop understanding of the concept of *change*.

Activities and Questions:

1. Ask students to respond to the following question in their response journals: "How do the changing seasons affect your emotions?" Invite students to discuss their responses.

2. Divide the class into five groups. Assign each group an Emily Dickinson poem, using the selections beginning with the following lines:

    - *"Presentiment is that long shadow on the lawn"*
    - *"Funny to be"*
    - *"The morns are meeker than they were"*
    - *"It sifts from leaden sieves"*
    - *"Dear March, come in!"*

    Ask each group to read the poem silently and aloud within the group and then to discuss how the poem shows that change is linked to time.

3. As a class, discuss the group of poems using the following questions as a guide:

    Literary Response and Interpretation Questions
    - What is personification? How did Emily Dickinson use personification in each of these poems? Why might a poet choose to use this poetic device?
    - What does the word *it* refer to at the beginning of many lines of "It sifts from leaden sieves"? How do you know?

- What are the secrets a century keeps?
- What is meant by the words, *"The morns are meeker than they were"*? What words might you use to describe summer mornings?
- Why is the speaker in *"Dear March"* happy to see March but not April?
- If you do not know the meaning of the word *presentiment* in *"Presentiment is that long shadow . . . ,"* what context clues in the poem give you an idea of what it means?

Reasoning Questions
- What is the feeling the poet is trying to express in each poem? What evidence from the poem supports your response?
- What assumptions does the poet make about the century's secrets in *"Funny to be a century"*?
- How is the concept of *time* important in these poems?

Change Questions
- These poems demonstrate in several ways that change is linked to time. How do the other generalizations about change relate to the poems?
- What other signs of changing times and changing seasons did the poet not include in these pieces?

Note. From *Literary Reflections* (p. 169–172), by the Center for Gifted Education, 1998, Dubuque, IA: Kendall/Hunt. Copyright © 1998 by the Center for Gifted Education. Adapted with permission.

then to respond to the following reasoning questions in discussion (reasoning elements are given in italics):

- How important are a writer's powers of observation? What does the *evidence* in the chapter suggest about Jo's powers of observation?
- How is the *concept* of unselfishness played out in this chapter? In what ways did different characters display selfishness?
- Compare the descriptions of the writing Jo did for the contest with the writing she did for her novel. How did the *purposes* for each change the style of the writing?
- What is the difficult *issue* Jo must face with regard to her writing? What circumstances help her resolve the issue?
- What were the *implications* or *consequences* for Jo's novel when she tried to please all of her critics?

In the area of writing, the reasoning model forms an effective complement to the persuasive writing emphasis in language arts curricula. Persuasive writing involves the presentation of a point of view on a given issue with evidence to support it, thus reflecting key elements of reasoning. Although this type of writing is an important skill in everyday life and a foundational component of thesis development throughout education, studies of persuasive writing have demonstrated weak student performance (Gentile, 1992). Therefore, persuasive writing is an important emphasis for language arts curricula, and its complexity when coupled with intensive exploration of connections to the reasoning model makes it particularly appropriate for gifted students. The Hamburger Model for Persuasive Writing (see Figure 6.1) demonstrates the basic format of a persuasive piece as presented to students in the Center for Gifted Education's language arts units, with a more complex version found in the Dagwood Essay Model for older students (see Figure 6.2; Center for Gifted Education, 1999).

Teaching a writing model through a deliberate strategy and targeted feedback has been found effective in previous writing research with gifted students (Schunk & Swartz, 1992); similarly, the Center for Gifted Education's units utilizing the Hamburger Model have been found effective in improving gifted students' persuasive writing skills (VanTassel-Baska, Zuo, Avery, & Little, 2002). The writing models also provide a concrete framework within which students may explore to what degree their persuasion is based on strong inferences versus

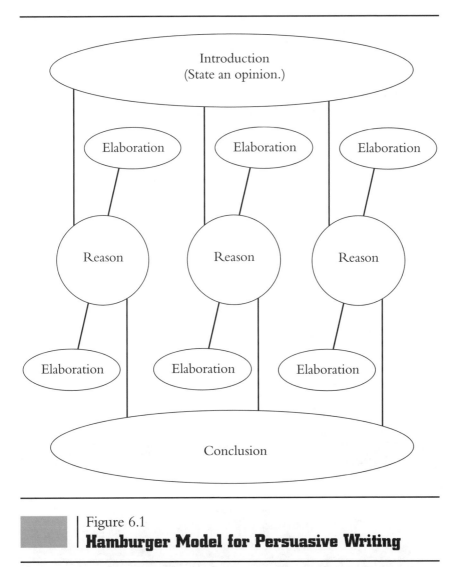

Figure 6.1
Hamburger Model for Persuasive Writing

Note. From *A Guide to Teaching a Language Arts Curriculum for High-Ability Learners* (p. 53), by the Center for Gifted Education, 1999, Dubuque, IA: Kendall/Hunt. Copyright © 1999 by the Center for Gifted Education. Reprinted with permission.

weak data or inappropriate assumptions. Moreover, the standards of reasoning (Paul, 1992) and the elements together provide a framework within which students may understand and assess their own writing and that of others, including their peers' work and persuasive selections drawn from the media, literature, and historical documents. Issue-based research, also a key process skill incorporating many related lan-

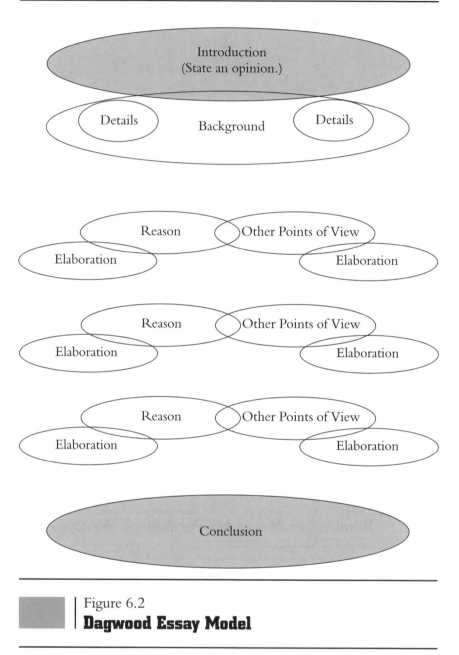

Figure 6.2
Dagwood Essay Model

Note. From *A Guide to Teaching a Language Arts Curriculum for High-Ability Learners* (p. 54), by the Center for Gifted Education, 1999, Dubuque, IA: Kendall/Hunt. Copyright © 1999 by the Center for Gifted Education. Reprinted with permission.

guage arts competencies, is closely linked to the reasoning mode,1 as well. This correspondence among persuasive writing, reasoning, and research provides a seamless set of outcomes to be addressed together within a comprehensive language arts curriculum for gifted learners.

Substantive Content

The content of the language arts curriculum draws upon several sources for its challenge and substance; fundamentally, however, the most important foundation for the content of the language arts is in literature. Strong literature pieces, selected on the basis of their literary value, applicability to the lives and experiences of gifted students, degree of challenge, and relationship to the concepts central to the curriculum, are key to establishing substantive content (VanTassel-Baska, Johnson, & Boyce, 1996). The content of the curriculum then grows from the literature—through specific questions developed to encourage deep thinking about the pieces, through writing assignments that require reflection about the literature and creation of connections to other literature and to life, and through other types of projects and discussions. Moreover, the other key piece of content in the language arts—the study of language itself, its vocabulary and usage—may also be drawn from literature pieces selected for study on the basis of linguistic, as well as literary, value (see Thompson, 1996a, 1996b).

Language arts curricula for the gifted should be deeply grounded in the study of literature and language. Thus, crucial elements of developing an appropriate language arts curriculum include the selection of rich and rigorous reading materials and the development of objectives and tasks that engage the students in high-level inquiry and interpretation experiences related to those reading materials (VanTassel-Baska, 1995). In order to ensure that the content is both advanced and substantive, the literature selected should be at least two reading levels above the grade for which the curriculum is intended, and, at least by middle school, students should be reading world literature not necessarily aimed at young readers. In addition, the vocabulary contained in this literature should be rich, varied, and advanced to encourage students to develop their abilities in this area of language arts content (Baskin & Harris, 1980). A strong language arts curriculum for the gifted should give students opportunities to explore given literature selections in depth and then to engage in analysis and synthesis at a conceptual level across literature selections, thus involving them in advanced levels of literary criticism, rather than mere comprehension of given pieces. In the area of language study, rather than teaching students parts of speech, spelling, and rules of usage, teachers may instead teach grammar as a complex system of thought. Vocabulary study should reach beyond definitions of specific words and into stems and etymology and the fundamental structure of language at the morphological and grammatical levels. These types of approaches to literature and language study engage students in challenging, substantive content and encourage involvement and discussion. They also support integration of the language arts, which makes the content at once richer, more real world, and more interesting for students (Tschudi, 1991). Moreover, through the emphases described here, the language arts curriculum for gifted students can fulfill several of the aspects of differentiation discussed in Chapter 1 of this text, namely providing experiences at an advanced level through instructional strategies that promote thinking and utilize appropriate materials that challenge and engage students.

Constructing Meaning

At the center of all language arts curricula and instruction is the element of constructing meaning. As we read, listen, write, or speak, we are constantly constructing our own understanding of the words, sentences, paragraphs, and books we encounter and create; the very learning of language itself requires the construction of meaning. In language arts curricula and instruction, educators should support students in efforts to construct their own meaning and understanding of the texts they encounter, providing strategies for exploring literature both analytically and holistically. Moreover, teachers should provide ongoing opportunities for students to express themselves in writing and speech, refining their skill at constructing and communicating meaning.

We accomplish the task of supporting students in constructing meaning by providing scaffolds that allow them to explore their understanding in an organized way. The Literature Web, for example, serves as an effective scaffold for exploring literature and the constructions placed upon it by the active mind. Figure 6.3 demonstrates sample responses to the web based on Robert Frost's poem "The Road Not Taken." The Literature Web is based on the notion that literary understanding is found in a combination of the contributions of the text and

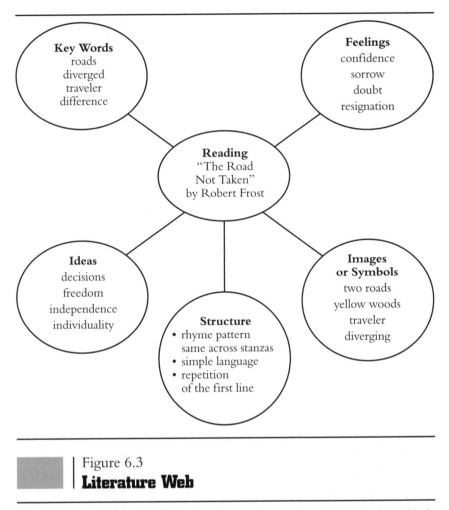

Figure 6.3
Literature Web

the reader (Rosenblatt, 1991). It asks students to work with the text directly and with their own responses to delve deeper into their conceptions of the piece. Independently, students work to identify key words, feelings, ideas, images and symbols, and structural elements of a given piece; then, in discussion, they share their personal reflections and the specific aspects of the text that inspired their responses. Moreover, small-group discussions of the web also strengthen students' construction of meaning because the comments shared by others may offer new insights about the selection.

Preplanned, higher level questions following upon the Literature Web also add to the development of understanding because they represent guided probing of specific and important issues by the teacher. Finally, when students are given opportunities to reflect further on their understanding through journal responses and activities and questions that encourage comparison across multiple texts, they strengthen not only their construction of a given text's meaning, but also their ability to apply techniques of analysis to multiple contexts.

Another factor in encouraging in-depth construction of meaning is the frequent use of short literature passages in classroom discussions. When students are given opportunities in one sitting to read, analyze, and discuss a text, the holistic process is more effectively reinforced. In addition, shorter pieces allow for more in-depth discussions of a greater percentage of the literary elements in a text. Although longer pieces, such as novels, should certainly be incorporated into a language arts curriculum, teachers and curricular developers should give careful consideration to the use of shorter pieces as the primary focus of classroom instruction in literary analysis and interpretation.

If the intent or goal of the curriculum and, consequently, the instructional processes focus on constructing meaning, then the assessments must also focus on constructing meaning. It is for this reason that new pieces of literature are presented for assessment in the Center for Gifted Education's language arts units, with questions that require students to demonstrate that they are using their practiced processes to construct meaning of these new texts.

All the processes involved with developing written products involve students in the act of constructing meaning. Spivey (1995, 1996) noted that, throughout the process of composition, the writer is engaged in organizing and selecting content and making connections among ideas in order to create a coherent presentation of his or her own meaning and to provide a context within which readers may bring their own perspectives and thus construct meaning again. The necessity of considering context, content, and audience, as well as features of style and mechanics, makes the writing process a complex and challenging one and a key part of the substantive content of a language arts curriculum.

Multicultural/Global Emphasis

In today's society, a gradually broadening awareness of our complex human heritage and the contributions of multiple cultures and individuals to the present world has created a demand in the schools for a more representative study of many cultures in the curriculum. In addition, the growing diversity of American society has made it imperative to acknowledge and respect the diverse backgrounds of our students in both the materials presented to them and the ways in which they are presented. The *Standards for the English Language Arts* (NCTE & IRA, 1996) emphasize multicultural literature and study, as do state and local standards for schools across the country.

One important way of establishing and maintaining a multicultural emphasis in a language arts curriculum is through the selection of literature. Many excellent and challenging literature selections are available that represent authors from and portray cultures across the world. However, many less-than-exemplary selections also exist. Careful selection of multicultural literature is necessary in order to represent cultures accurately and also to ensure that a balance is struck among the cultures represented in the curriculum.

Several texts exploring multicultural literature are available to provide guidance to educators seeking strong texts from varied cultures. Miller-Lachman (1992) suggested the following criteria to consider in making text selections:

- general accuracy;
- avoidance of stereotypes;
- authentic, up-to-date, and age-appropriate language;
- attention to author's perspective;
- currency of facts and interpretations;
- concept of audience;
- integration of cultural information;
- balance and multidimensionality; and
- accurate and appropriate illustrations.

Ladson-Billings (1995) emphasized that, in developing curricula to represent and respond to diversity, the key issues to consider are multiculturalism and relevance—first, that the curriculum incorporate content and materials reflecting many cultures and accurate representations of their characteristics and interactions; and, second, that the curriculum be designed in such a way that it is made relevant and comprehensible to students, with deep connections to their own diverse lives and backgrounds. These issues of multiculturalism and relevance are significant for both the curriculum development process and instructional planning, with regard to the types of grouping models, activities, and expectations used with students (some of these issues will be discussed further in Chapter 11).

Related to the issue of a multicultural emphasis in language arts is the idea of studying foreign language. Incorporating foreign language into the curriculum, both as its own subject and as an aspect of English study, allows students to develop a deeper understanding of the structures and history of their own language and also to expand their cultural understandings (Adler, 1984; Thompson & Thompson, 1996). Moreover, adding some degree of foreign language exploration to the study of English can raise the complexity level of the language arts curriculum for students, thus making it more challenging and engaging for verbally talented learners.

Intradisciplinary and Interdisciplinary Connections

Chapters 2–5 discussed the elements of the ICM in depth and its versatility in terms of supporting intradisciplinary and interdisciplinary connections. Curricula for gifted students, in particular, should incorporate such connections in order to develop and encourage students' capacity for recognizing the complex, interdisciplinary nature of abstract concepts. Intradisciplinary connections in the language arts are natural and actually allow for smoother instruction than separating the divisions of reading, writing, listening, speaking, and language study. These elements should be interwoven in the curriculum in such a way that students naturally come to appreciate and utilize the connections that exist.

Similarly, interdisciplinary connections may be made naturally from the language arts to a range of other disciplines, both in terms of content and the processes and habits of mind involved. Literature of a period necessarily reflects the social and cultural values of that period, as well as historical events. Consequently, effective study of literature should incorporate social science connections. For example, a lesson from a unit drawing on the literature and culture of the 1940s includes the following elements:

- discussion of a news article from *The New York Times,* December 8, 1941, about steps taken in major cities with regard to Japanese American populations following Pearl Harbor ("Entire City," 1941);

- reading and discussion of the picture book *The Journey* (Hamanaka, 1990), giving background on the internment of Japanese Americans;
- reading and discussion of several poems written by an interned Japanese American woman; and
- persuasive essay assignment regarding whether or not a similar situation could happen in the United States today (Center for Gifted Education, 1998a).

The background information provided and the critical analysis of the historical situation from multiple perspectives encourage a deeper understanding of the literature selections for students, even as the literature of a period can provide a broader and deeper understanding of historical events.

Other important interdisciplinary connections may be made with the "sister arts" of the visual arts and music. One example of how such connections may be promoted is found in an exploration of how artists of various types express their own identities in their work. In *Autobiographies*, students spend much of the unit exploring themselves as writers and reading autobiographies of authors, thus developing an understanding of how life experiences affect expression in writing. In one lesson of this unit, students explore self-expression in the visual arts and in music by examining self-portraits of various artists and musical selections that reflect specific events and experiences in the lives of their composers. Students are then asked to respond to a global question: "How is every work of art in some way a reflection of the artist?"

In addition to these specific examples of potential intradisciplinary and interdisciplinary connections, the other most viable foundation for such connections is the abstract concept underscoring the curriculum. In the case of *change*, the concept is central to understanding the major strands of the language arts since change is a universal theme in all great literature, is central to understanding the writing process, and defines key approaches to teaching language study.

Beyond the language arts, change is also a central concept in almost every other discipline; thus, it provides a bridge for making connections across subject areas in school and to the larger world. For example, students may explore how changes in the plot of a short story or novel are symbolic of historical events; how changes in the writing styles of novelists across their lifespans reflect changes in their societies; or how the style of one's writing changes depending on whether the writing is narrative, technical, or descriptive and what such changes reveal about the intended audience. Thus, the concept serves as an effective basis for thought-provoking connections across the disciplines.

Materials and Resources

Very often in education, the materials *become* the curriculum instead of being the foundation for it (Apple, 1991). Materials are a key part of developing and implementing strong curricula, and, in the language arts, the choices made about literature and support materials are key to making the curriculum strong.

Literature to support a language arts curriculum for gifted students must be carefully selected to challenge students appropriately. As mentioned previously, one strong criterion for literature selection is to select works at least two grade levels above the target group of students. Along with challenge and complexity, teachers and curriculum developers should also emphasize variety in their choices of literature in terms of author, topic, culture, time period, length, and genre. Classic literature—reflecting the best of literary accomplishment across times and cultures—should be incorporated in the curriculum throughout the school years to encourage deep and aesthetic literary experiences.

Several texts recommending literature for gifted students have been published in the last several decades, including both lists of books and lists of criteria (Baskin & Harris, 1980; Halsted, 1994; Hauser & Nelson, 1988). Such criteria are a valuable resource for the curriculum developer. One set found particularly useful in the development of the Center's language arts curriculum came from the work of Baskin and Harris, who recommended that books for the gifted be selected according to the following criteria:

- The language used in books for the gifted should be rich, varied, precise, complex, and exciting, for language is the instrument for the reception and expression of thought.
- Books should be chosen with an eye to their open-endedness and their capacity to inspire contemplative behavior, such as

through techniques of judging time sequences, shifting narrators, and unusual speech patterns of characters.

- Books for the gifted should be complex enough to allow interpretive and evaluative behaviors from readers.
- Books for the gifted should help them to build problem-solving skills and develop methods of productive thinking.
- Books should provide role models for emulation.
- Books should be broad-based in form, from picture books, to folk tale and myths, to nonfiction, to biography, to poetry, to fiction.

Beyond selection of literature for classroom lessons, discussions, and independent reading activities, curriculum developers should also have a strong sense of support materials available to supplement the curriculum. Additional discussion of criteria for evaluating materials, along with a list of some suggested titles, may be found in Chapter 10.

Technology Relevant

Every area of the curriculum and, seemingly, every area of life today is inextricably tied in with the technology explosion. People rely more and more each day on their technological tools to accomplish daily goals, and our children will grow up into a world of technological dependency and growth that we can barely begin to imagine. For this reason, all curricula today should be technology relevant, both for the benefits of technological resources in the core subject areas and to promote technological literacy as a key aspect of students' development in and of itself (Dugger, 2001). In the language arts, several natural connections to technology are possible that promote student learning in both areas.

Technology provides three major areas of support for the language arts curriculum for gifted students. The first and most obvious is in terms of how writing is accomplished today. Although there are some authors who tell us in interviews that they still write longhand on legal pads as they compose their literary masterworks, more and more writers in all fields are developing skills at composing, revising, editing, and publishing on desktop computers. Students today need to be familiar with and competent in using word-processing and desktop-publishing programs; encouraging students to do at least some of the steps of their writing process on a computer instead of longhand is a reflection of our time. However, this may also encourage more and more well-developed writing because of student interest in using the computer tools and because of potential time saved in the revision process. Furthermore, by incorporating a technological emphasis into the revision and editing stage of the writing process, teachers can support students in developing good habits around writing and editing, perhaps offsetting some of the sloppier habits often developed through unstructured e-mail communication (Leibowitz, 1999).

The second technological support for the curriculum is the one that is the most quickly changing and, in some ways, the most dangerous and controversial in schools: the use of the Internet for research activities. The Internet has provided the world with unimaginable volumes of research and resources at our fingertips, giving access to far-off places and authentic materials and texts that otherwise might be difficult or even impossible to bring to students. However, the difficulties inherent in this wonderful resource are that access is always dependent on how many computers are available at a given time for use by students. The National Center for Education Statistics (2001) reported great progress with regard to computer and Internet access in schools since 1994; increased access to technology and increased teacher understanding of its use can contribute to a more effective and efficient use of Internet resources for classroom research.

A concomitant problem, of course, with the wealth of information available online is the issue of determining quality and reliability of sources. Although the issue of inappropriate or inaccurate materials on the Internet is a problem, it also may be turned into an opportunity for students. Part of the reasoning model they use should include assessing inferences based on evidence provided and recognizing assumptions and points of view. These elements and other considerations of bias, credibility, and careful selection may be incorporated into lessons encouraging questioning of sources. The goal, then, is for students to develop into critical reasoners who analyze and reason about what they read and view, which consequently equips them with lifelong tools for how they handle the technology available at their fingertips.

Another area of support from technology in the language arts curriculum is the reinforcement, exploration, and learning extensions it can provide for students. Among the quality sites on the Internet are a number of literature-, language-, and writing-related sites that are useful to both students and teachers. The National Endowment for the Humanities lists a number of literature sites at EDSITEment (http://edsitement.neh.gov/tab_lesson.asp?subjectArea=4), which includes both generalized sites and places for investigation of particular authors or poets, such as Shakespeare (http://shakespeare.palomar.edu) and Mark Twain (http://etext.virginia.edu/railton). The Academy of American Poets site (http://www.poets.org/index.cfm) includes biographies and works of a wide range of poets, as well as topical poetry exhibits. Several sites provide "word of the day" options for vocabulary development, as well as etymological information, word games, and question-and-answer sections: Wordsmith.org (http://www.wordsmith.org) incorporates word of the day and anagram studies; Vocabulary University (http://www.vocabulary.com) contains vocabulary activities for kids and adults; The Grammar Lady Online (http://www.grammarlady.com) explores rules of English grammar and discusses common confusions and questions; and World Wide Words (http://www.quinion.com/words) explores international English from a British perspective.

One other key feature related to the integration of technology in a curriculum involves differentiating for levels of technological competency. As with any other skill or discipline, technological competency involves a combination of students' past experiences and talent in a given area, and some students will be more adept at completing technological assignments and activities than others. The growing awareness of the need for technological literacy (Dugger, 2001) suggests that emphasis on developing technological competency as it relates to every subject area will continue to grow in schools, and the incorporation of best practices regarding learner outcomes, authentic assessment, and substantive content must also be considered as they relate to student learning in the area of technology.

Inquiry-Based Learning and Other Models

An inquiry-based orientation to learning in the language arts involves active participation from students, as well as skilled guidance from the teacher and carefully prepared questions as a framework. Questioning strategies important in analyzing and interpreting literature involve encouraging students to ask questions, as well as answer them, using Socratic techniques.

The Literature Web model, as previously discussed, provides a strong example of a foundational structure that takes students deeply into their understanding of a literature selection and then lends itself to further discussion and inquiry. Carefully prepared interpretive questions that guide students deeply into an understanding of a work of literature are a hallmark of both the Center for Gifted Education's language arts units and the shared inquiry model that is the basis for the Junior Great Books program (Great Books Foundation, 1990). In both cases, the goal of the literature discussion is to encourage students to develop the habits of mind of the critical reader, including the ability to focus on central ideas and fundamental messages and to connect texts to their own lives and to their understanding of the larger world. The teacher's ability to facilitate such discussions and to follow up on student responses through probing questions and utilization of Socratic techniques is a key element of supporting inquiry-based learning for students in the language arts (Cawley & Corbett, 1996; see Chapter 3 for further discussion of Socratic questioning).

Another model for taking students deeper into their own understanding of content in the language arts is the Vocabulary Web. Again, this model uses a graphic organizer approach; it encourages students to begin with advanced vocabulary they encounter in their reading and to explore words at an etymological and connective level, thus increasing their own vocabulary by the in-depth study of specific words. An example of a completed Vocabulary Web is found in Figure 6.4.

A research model encourages students in developing habits of inquiry by its very nature; authentic research requires that the researcher ask questions, not only find out answers to the questions posed by others. The Center for Gifted Education research model (Boyce, 1997), outlined in Chapter 3, provides opportunities for such development of habits of inquiry. Research is central to all the disciplines; but, in schools, the language arts curriculum generally bears particular responsibility for teaching the skills of questioning, data collecting, and writing. Thus, appropriately challenging research should be a part of curriculum development in this area.

Metacognition

The final curricular reform element that is key to developing an effective language arts curriculum for gifted students is a concentration on metacognition. All of the processes and the disciplinary and conceptual emphases described in this chapter can become even richer and more meaningful for students if concerted efforts are made to have students

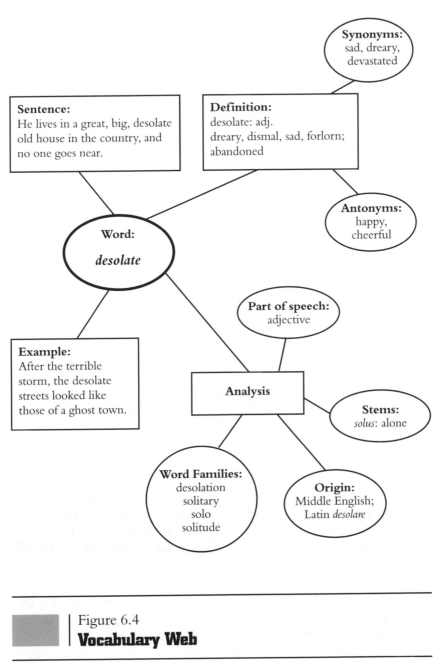

Figure 6.4
Vocabulary Web

Note. From *Literacy Reflections* (p. 65), by the Center for Gifted Education, 1998, Dubuque, IA: Kendall/Hunt. Copyright © 1998 by the Center for Gifted Education. Reprinted with permission.

reflect upon their work systematically, including acknowledgement of their learning goals, monitoring of progress, and evaluating accomplishments. As students reflect upon themselves as readers, writers, speakers, listeners, and thinkers, they become aware of their own strengths and areas for improvement, thus encouraging growth and progress.

One natural vehicle for such reflection in the language arts is the use of journals. Student journals provide a forum for reflecting on connections between the literature they read and their own lives, both in terms of how they resonate to the pieces and how reading and reflecting on the pieces changed them in various ways. Again, as has been illustrated with so many of the sections above, careful planning for attention to metacognition should be incorporated into the curricular documentation, including specific questions for journal writing, self-evaluation around given products, and other types of reflection. Moreover, metacognition should be modeled for students by the teacher. Teachers can take opportunities to share reflections on their own thinking processes, discussions of the way their thoughts or actions were changed by given events or encounters with literature, and the ways in which monitoring and evaluating progress has contributed to personal development as a reader, writer, speaker, and thinker.

In using journals as a metacognitive tool, teachers can design specific questions that require students to reflect on their own thinking and how it connects to their experiences in the language arts classroom. For example, the following question appears as a follow-up to the discussion of the selection from *Little Women* mentioned earlier in this chapter:

> This chapter describes Jo's preferred conditions for writing—where she liked to be, what she wore, etc. Beverly Cleary wrote in "The Platoon System" how she liked to write when it was raining. What conditions do you prefer for writing? Describe your best writing environment and explain why you think this environment works for you. (Center for Gifted Education, 1998b, p. 113)

On a larger scale, beyond the metacognitive possibilities inherent in individual lessons, students should be encouraged to maintain records of their progress and to reflect on their learning throughout a unit. This should also be developed within a context, however, and a conceptually based curricular unit provides such a context. For example, in each language arts unit, students may reflect on how the generalizations regarding change are exemplified in each literature selection they read. However, from another vantage point, they are asked to examine how each selection changed *them* and, at the end of the unit, to review their portfolio of accomplishments and to discuss how they changed as writers during the course of the unit. Students should also maintain logs of their progress across long-term assignments, such as extended research activities.

Conclusion

Teaching language arts to high-ability learners represents a worthy challenge to teachers who must find ways to differentiate effectively for the needs of those learners. The ICM and the elements of curricular reform addressed here provide teachers and curriculum developers with a foundation upon which to build goals and units of study that are appropriately challenging for their gifted students. Across all of the elements, the differentiation features of advanced level materials and tasks that add depth and challenge to the curriculum, as well as utilization of instructional strategies and project work that promote higher order processes and complex thinking, ensure that the curriculum will support gifted students in their growth as readers, writers, and overall learners.

Key Points Summary

❏ Teaching the language arts to high-ability learners requires differentiation in all the major strands: literature, writing, language study, and oral communication.

❏ Selection of readings that are intellectually challenging is a cornerstone of an effective language arts curriculum for high-ability learners.

❏ Using short and complex reading selections for analysis and interpretation assesses student capability to handle difficult texts and allows in-depth classroom discussion of texts holistically.

❏ Using models to teach writing allows for greater student growth.

❏ Diversity in types of activity, as well as depth and complexity, characterizes a well-differentiated language arts curriculum.

❏ Performance-based assessment models are essential in gauging students' deep understanding of the language arts.

References

Adler, M. J. (1952). *Great ideas: A syntopicon of great books of the Western world*. Chicago: Encyclopedia Britannica.

Adler, M. J. (1984). *The Paideia program*. New York: Collier.

Apple, M. W. (1991). The culture and commerce of the textbook. In M. W. Apple & L. K. Christian-Smith (Eds.), *The politics of the textbook* (pp. 22–40). New York: Routledge.

Baskin, B. H., & Harris, K. H., (1980). *Books for the gifted child*. New York: Bowker.

Boyce, L. N. (1997). *A guide to teaching research skills and strategies for grades 4–12*. Williamsburg, VA: Center for Gifted Education, College of William and Mary.

Cawley, C., & Corbett, J. (1996). Constructing meaning through shared inquiry. In J. VanTassel-Baska, D. T. Johnson, & L. N. Boyce (Eds.), *Developing verbal talent: Ideas and strategies for teachers of elementary and middle school students* (pp. 333–356). Boston: Allyn and Bacon.

Center for Gifted Education. (1998a). *The 1940s: A decade of change*. Dubuque, IA: Kendall/Hunt.

Center for Gifted Education. (1998b). *Autobiographies*. Dubuque, IA: Kendall/Hunt.

Center for Gifted Education. (1998c). *Literary reflections*. Dubuque, IA: Kendall/Hunt.

Center for Gifted Education. (1998d). *Persuasion*. Dubuque, IA: Kendall/Hunt.

Center for Gifted Education. (1999). *Guide to teaching a language arts curriculum for high-ability learners*. Dubuque, IA: Kendall/Hunt.

Chaney, A. (1996). Oral communication: Thinking in action. In J. VanTassel-Baska, D. T. Johnson, & L. N. Boyce (Eds.), *Developing verbal talent: Ideas and strategies for teachers of elementary and middle school students* (pp. 115–132). Boston: Allyn and Bacon.

Downs, R. B. (1978). *Books that changed the world* (2nd ed.). Chicago: American Library Association.

Dugger, W. E., Jr. (2001). Standards for technological literacy. *Phi Delta Kappan, 82,* 513–517.

Entire city put on war footing. (1941, December 8). *The New York Times*, pp. 1, 3.

Gentile, C. (1992). *Exploring new methods for collecting students' school based writing: NAEP's 1990 portfolio study*. Washington, DC: National Center for Education Statistics.

Great Books Foundation. (1990). *Junior Great Books teacher's edition.* Chicago: Author.

Halsted, J. W. (1994). *Some of my best friends are books.* Dayton: Ohio Psychology Press.

Hamanaka, S. (1990). *The journey.* New York: Orchard Books.

Hauser, P., & Nelson, G. A. (1988). *Books for the gifted child* (Vol. 2). New York: Bowker.

Ladson-Billings, G. (1995). Challenging customs, canons, and content: Developing relevant curriculum for diversity. In C. A. Grant (Ed.), *Educating for diversity: An anthology of multicultural voices* (pp. 327–340). Boston: Allyn and Bacon.

Langer, J. A. (1995). *Envisioning literature: Literary understanding and literature instruction.* New York: Teachers College Press.

Leibowitz, W. R. (1999, November 26). Technology transforms writing and the teaching of writing. *The Chronicle of Higher Education,* p. A67.

Marzano, R. (1992). *Cultivating thinking in English.* Urbana, IL: National Council for Teachers of English.

Miller-Lachman, L. (1992). *Our family our friends our world: An annotated guide to significant multicultural books for children and teenagers.* New Providence, NJ: Bowker.

National Center for Education Statistics. (2001). *Statistics in brief: Internet access in U.S. public schools and classrooms, 1994–2000.* Retrieved October 30, 2001, from http://nces.ed.gov/pubs2001/2001071.pdf

National Council for Teachers of English, & International Reading Association. (1996). *Standards for the English language arts.* Urbana, IL: Author.

Paul, R. (1992). *Critical thinking: What every thinking person needs to survive in a rapidly changing world.* Rohnert Park, CA: Foundation for Critical Thinking.

Rosenblatt, L. M. (1991). Literary theory. In J. Flood, J. M. Jensen, D. Lapp, & J. R. Squire (Eds.), *Handbook of research on teaching the English language arts* (pp. 57–62). New York: Macmillan.

Schunk, D., & Swartz, C. (1992, April). *Goal and feedback during writing strategy instruction with gifted students.* Presentation at the annual meeting of the American Educational Research Association, San Francisco.

Spivey, N. N. (1995). Written discourse: A constructivist perspective. In L. P. Steffe & J. Gale (Eds.), *Constructivism in education* (pp. 313–329). Hillsdale, NJ: Erlbaum.

Spivey, N. N. (1996). Reading, writing, and the construction of meaning. In J. VanTassel-Baska, D. T. Johnson, & L. N. Boyce (Eds.), *Developing verbal talent: Ideas and strategies for teachers of elementary and middle school students* (pp. 34–55). Boston: Allyn and Bacon.

Taba, H. (1962). *Curriculum development, theory, and practice.* New York: Harcourt, Brace, & World.

Thompson, M. C. (1996a). Formal language study for gifted students. In J. VanTassel-Baska, D. T. Johnson, & L. N. Boyce (Eds.), *Developing verbal talent: Ideas and strategies for teachers of elementary and middle school students* (pp. 149–173). Boston: Allyn and Bacon.

Thompson, M. C. (1996b). Mentors on paper: How classics develop verbal ability. In J. VanTassel-Baska, D. T. Johnson, & L. N. Boyce (Eds.). *Developing verbal talent: Ideas and strategies for teachers of elementary and middle school students* (pp. 56–74). Boston: Allyn and Bacon.

Thompson, M. C., & Thompson, M. B. (1996). Reflections on foreign language study for highly able learners. In J. VanTassel-Baska, D. T. Johnson, & L. N. Boyce (Eds.), *Developing verbal talent: Ideas and strategies for teachers of elementary and middle school students* (pp. 174–188). Boston: Allyn and Bacon.

Tschudi, S. (1991). *Planning and assessing the curriculum in English language arts.* Alexandria, VA: Association for Supervision and Curriculum Development

VanTassel-Baska, J. (1986). Effective curriculum and instructional models for talented students. *Gifted Child Quarterly, 30,* 164–169.

VanTassel-Baska, J. (1994). *Comprehensive curriculum for gifted learners* (2nd ed.). Boston: Allyn and Bacon.

VanTassel-Baska, J. (1995). Talent development through curriculum: The Integrated Curriculum Model (ICM). *Roeper Review, 18,* 98–103.

VanTassel-Baska, J., Johnson, D. T., & Boyce, L. N. (1993). *A curriculum framework for the language arts.* Williamsburg, VA: Center for Gifted Education, College of William and Mary.

VanTassel-Baska, J., Johnson, D. T., & Boyce, L. N. (Eds.). (1996). *Developing verbal talent: Ideas and strategies for teachers of elementary and middle school students.* Boston: Allyn and Bacon.

VanTassel-Baska, J., Zuo, L., Avery, L. D., & Little, C. A. (2002). A curriculum study of gifted student learning in the language arts. *Gifted Child Quarterly, 46,* 30–44.

Zemelman, S., Daniels, H., & Hyde, A. (1993). *Best practice: New standards for teaching and learning in America's schools.* Portsmouth, NH: Heinemann.

Adapting Mathematics Curricula for High-Ability Learners

by
Dana T. Johnson

You are a middle school mathematics teacher who is responsible for a class of sixth graders. In your class you have both students of average ability and a cluster group of students who are mathematically gifted. The school district is pressuring you to make sure that all of your students pass the state performance tests in May, so you have been pushing hard on skills listed in the state standards for sixth grade. It is October. One of your students comes to you and complains that she already knows the material because most of the topics were covered in previous years, and even the new material is covered painfully slow. What can you do to meet her instructional needs while covering the bases with the rest of the class?

Many changes have come about in recent years with the publication of national standards documents in the content areas. *Principles and Standards for School Mathematics* (National Council of Teachers of Mathematics [NCTM], 2000) does not mention gifted students explicitly, but it clearly acknowledges that students are not all the same. For all students, the standards place a greater emphasis on areas that traditionally have been emphasized for the gifted. All students are now expected to complete a core curriculum that has shifted its emphasis away from computation and routine problem practice toward real-world problem solving, communication, and connections to other disciplines and the real world. Reasoning is now a major emphasis for all students. "Mathematical thinking and reasoning skills, including making conjectures and developing sound deductive arguments, are important because they serve as a basis for developing new insights and promoting further study" (NCTM, 2000, p. 15).

Research supports the practices advocated in the NCTM *Principles and Standards*. Grouws and Cebulla (1999) included the following among research-based best practices in mathematics curricula and instruction:

- *Opportunity to learn*. When students are exposed to new material, achievement increases. Teachers must ensure that students are given the opportunity to learn important content that is new to them.
- *Focus on meaning*. Student learning increases when instruction is focused on meaningful development of important mathematical ideas. Instruction should build on student intuition and make connections to other subjects, student interests, and students' past knowledge and experience.
- *Learning new concepts and skills in the context of solving problems*. Students can develop understanding of important mathematical ideas when given nonroutine problems to solve. It is not necessary to begin with skill development; in fact, if students are drilled too much initially on isolated skills, they may have a harder time making sense of them later.
- *Opportunities for discovery*. Research suggests that students benefit from a balance of practice and invention. Frequent use of nonroutine problems can help students build new knowledge.
- *Openness of student solution methods*. When students develop their own solution methods, they are better able to apply mathematical knowledge to new problems.
- *Use of small groups*. Working with others can enhance achievement. The tasks chosen should be appropriate for group work and should involve important concepts and ideas, not just skill

work. By "putting their heads together," students can learn more than they might have learned on their own.

- *Whole-class discussion following individual and group work.* Students should present solutions to problems and discuss each other's methods and reasoning. In this context, teachers may identify misconceptions and seize opportunities for guiding understanding.
- *Teaching mathematics with a focus on number sense.* This involves being able to compute mentally, to estimate, to move between various representations of numbers, to judge the relative magnitude of numbers, and to judge the reasonableness of numerical results. An integrated approach seems preferable to focusing on a single skill.
- *Long-term use of concrete materials by students.* The "hands-on" approach can improve student concept development and improve attitudes toward mathematics.
- *Student use of calculators.* Studies show calculator use enhances understanding of arithmetical concepts and problem-solving skills, as well as improving student attitudes toward mathematics (Hembree & Dessart, 1986). Calculators can be used as a tool for mathematical discovery.

These approaches are integrally linked and supportive of each other. Many of these practices are exemplified in the excellent eighth-grade Japanese geometry class shown on the videotape of the *Eighth-Grade Mathematics Lessons* produced as part of the Third International Mathematics and Science Study (Office of Educational Research and Improvement, 1999).

Current trends in mathematics curricula and instruction for all students seem to be moving toward what has traditionally been advocated for gifted learners. In light of this trend in which all students should engage in higher level processes, how should mathematics curricula look different for mathematically gifted students?

This chapter will explore the ICM and the elements of curricular reform as they apply to strong curricula for mathematically gifted students. It will particularly emphasize several specific content-related issues, including attention to acceleration and pacing along with depth and complexity, as well as the need for independent work and conceptual organization. Sample lessons will be used to illustrate key ideas, and specific suggestions for adaptation of existing lessons will be offered at the end of the chapter.

Learner Outcomes of Significance

The development of appropriate learner outcomes for gifted students in mathematics requires attention to the standards and best practices addressed above, as well as special consideration of the issues of pacing, depth, and complexity. The three dimensions of the ICM—content, process, and concept—provide a context for exploring ways to differentiate the standards and adapt the curriculum and instruction for gifted students' learning needs. Table 7.1 provides some examples for grade 7 of goals and outcomes linked to the three dimensions of the ICM and to the national mathematics standards.

The sequential nature of the mathematics curriculum and the tendency of mathematics textbooks to incorporate a considerable amount of review (Flanders, 1987), particularly at the elementary level, underscore the importance of developing appropriate learner outcomes in mathematics for gifted students across a range of years and courses instead of within only one school year or unit of study. Within and across courses, developing curricular goals and activities for gifted learners requires careful attention to the process by which a student is placed into a particular mathematics course, to degree of review, and to pacing. These issues will be discussed further in the sections that follow.

Placement and Assessment

Acceleration has a long tradition as a method for successfully serving the needs of gifted students in mathematics (Stanley, Keating, & Fox, 1974; Swiatek, 1993). However, effective use of acceleration practice in mathematics requires careful assessment of student achievement and determination of areas of need. Thus, diagnostic testing for placement is a key consideration in developing and implementing mathematics programs for gifted students. Beyond such diagnostic testing for placement, authentic assessment of student learning, including both formative and summative assessment techniques, is also a central feature to incorporate into curriculum development and implementation.

Placement
Educators should determine the best curricular placement for students using a diagnostic-prescriptive approach. The learners in any

Table 7.1

Outcomes of Significance

Dimension	Goal	Outcome	Link to *Principles and Standards*
Concept	Develop an understanding of what constitutes proof and how to show that proof.	Prove that the diagonals of a rectangle divide the rectangle into four triangles of equal area.	Recognize reasoning and proof as fundamental aspects of mathematics; Make and investigate mathematical conjectures; Develop and evaluate mathematical arguments and proofs; and Select and use various types of reasoning and methods of proof.
Process	Improve problem-solving skills.	Solve problems presented on the Math Forum "Problem of the Week" and submit a clear and accurate solution to the Forum by e-mail.	Build new mathematical knowledge through problem solving; Solve problems that arise in mathematics and in other contexts; Apply and adapt a variety of appropriate strategies to solve problems; and Monitor and reflect on the process of mathematical problem solving.
Content	Analyze the behavior of numerical sequences.	Write the next three terms of a given sequence; write a symbolic expression for the nth term; and determine whether the sequence converges; and, if it does, show what the limit is.	Use symbolic forms, including iterative and recursive forms, to represent relationships arising from various contexts.

given grade level or content area are diverse in their needs, but the diversity can be more extreme in the area of mathematics because of the sequential nature of the skills required. Precocious students who are required to proceed at the average pace for their grade level can become negative toward the subject due to boredom. It is imperative that a diagnostic–prescriptive mechanism be in place to identify appropriate placement for students who have already achieved mastery of math skills. In elementary and middle grades, this can be accomplished by giving a version of an end-of-year test to see how much students already know. Those who have mastered 80% or more of the desired objectives should be placed in a more advanced class along with a plan to address any apparent knowledge gaps that were uncovered in the pretest. If more than a small group of such students exists in a given school at a given grade level, the school might offer a course that is based on the next year's math content. If the numbers do not warrant a special class, a few students may be included with the next grade's math class, especially if there is a cluster group or a whole class of gifted math students in that group. For students who are accelerated in mathematics classes, advanced performance in later coursework is supported by research (Sowell, 1993; Swiatek, 1993). For the top 1% of students, the appropriate level of challenge (depending on interest and learning style) may be an independent-study approach such as Stanford University's Education Program for Gifted Youth (EPGY), in which students work independently from a CD or textbook and are in e-mail contact with a tutor (Ravaglia, Suppes, Stillinger, & Alper, 1995).

Two cautions are in order with regard to special arrangements. Whenever possible, students should work at least some of the time in a setting in which they are able to interact with others of their ability level and readiness for advanced content, rather than only working independently. An extracurricular activity, such as participation in the mathematics coaching and competition opportunities provided by a MathCounts team (MathCounts Foundation, 2000), might be the way to accomplish this for the student who is not in a class with his or her peers. Also, long-term planning needs to take place to make sure that students do not discontinue taking mathematics just because they have exhausted the available courses in high school. Additional courses such as Advanced Placement (AP) statistics may be added to the high school curriculum, or students may be scheduled to attend courses at a local college or university, where there are likely to be other gifted students also participating in coursework.

Consider the following problem:

> There are water hyacinths growing in a pond on your farm. On March 1st, there is one hyacinth in the pond. The number of water hyacinths in the pond doubles every week and none die.

1. Make a table showing the numbers of water hyacinths in the pond from March 1st to June 28th.

2. Sketch a graph of your data on graph paper. (Remember that the input or independent variable corresponds to the horizontal axis.)

3. Can the pond sustain this growth forever? Explain.

Figure 7.1
Hyacinths in the Pond

Note. From *Models: A Problem-Based Study of Animal Populations* (p. 71), by D. T. Johnson & B. T. Sher, 1997, Williamsburg, VA: Center for Gifted Education, College of William and Mary. Copyright © 1997 by the Center for Gifted Education. Reprinted with permission.

Authentic Assessment

One thing gifted students can do well (even without instruction) is solve math problems. In order to document real growth and understanding, multiple means of assessment are important for gifted students. If the teacher asks, "How can I give these students the opportunity to show what they know and can do?," this should generate assessment ideas that go beyond the typical test situation. Authentic performance-based tasks in the mathematics classroom might include a math journal that asks students to explain their problem-solving methodologies and choices and their understanding of concepts; presentations of problem solutions to the class; or independent and small-group project work. Performance-based tasks should be embedded within units of study to allow for ongoing assessment; for example, the problem in Figure 7.1 is drawn from a lesson on exponential growth within a unit focused on the concept of *models* as it relates to populations (Johnson & Sher, 1997).

Authentic assessment tasks may also be presented in lieu of some more traditional tests. The following example might appear as a summative assessment of a unit on surface area and volume:

Use the next 50 minutes to write an organized explanation of the big ideas that you have learned during this unit on surface area and volume of three-dimensional figures. This should include not only formulas for all solids we encountered in class, but also explanations of where the formulas came from and examples of applications of these formulas in solving problems.

Or, another example on the same content might be a "take-home" assessment that asks the following:

You are a city planner who is tasked with making a recommendation for building a water storage tank for 100,000 gallons of water. Analyze all of the three-dimensional solids we have studied by showing (a) the dimensions of each that would be needed to contain the 100,000 gallons and (b) how much surface area each has (as the tower needs to be painted every 10 years). Make your recommendation based on which structure would require the least amount of paint. Your work will be evaluated based on completeness, clarity, accuracy, and organization.

Each of these examples gives students a chance to show what they know. Unlike a multiple-choice test, they require students to demonstrate real understanding, not just good guesses.

Habits of Mind

Learner outcomes of significance in any content area and the assessments used to measure achievement of these outcomes should reflect an emphasis on encouraging students to develop the habits of mind of the related disciplines. The standard mathematics curriculum gives students standard problems that are usually solvable by the methods that are taught by example. This is fine for building a repertoire of mathematical skills, but it is not enough to build the mathematical habits of mind that mathematicians typically employ. These include creativity, tenacity, skepticism, and collaboration.

Mathematically gifted students need to experience the open-ended exploration that is the essence of what mathematicians do. They should be encouraged to both create problems and solve them, to think of questions that have not been asked of them, and to wonder if things are always true and then attempt to find out. If their only assignments are drill problems on one section of the textbook that are due the next day, students are not experiencing and developing the tenacity required for a problem that takes weeks or months to solve. Collaboration with others is important in the real problem-solving world, as reflected in the joint authorship by several mathematicians of many articles appearing in mathematical journals. Skepticism is an important quality of mathematical reasoning, as one should not be too accepting of any result until one can see the reason that it is true or disprove it with a counterexample.

Consider this question that I heard discussed by a math professor and an honors thesis student here at the College of William and Mary: *If two positive integers are selected at random, what is the probability that they will be relatively prime (that the largest common factor is one)?* One needs to have some content background in probability and a small amount of number theory to think about this, but it is a question that should be accessible to middle school students. The process of posing questions like this one, studying the patterns, and providing solutions (often collaboratively and over an extended period of time) is what mathematicians do. It is higher order thinking at its best and should be experienced by gifted students as much as possible in their school life.

Substantive Content

A curriculum based on substantive content in mathematics that supports the development of mathematical habits of mind should reflect consideration of both depth and breadth, as well as careful attention to pacing. Again, pretests and ongoing formative assessments support the integration of these considerations in working to challenge mathematically gifted students.

Pacing

Because of the sequential nature of a mathematics curriculum, the pace of instruction is especially important. Once a student is placed at the appropriate level, the instruction should proceed at a faster pace than that of an average class. Therefore, moving a student to a higher grade level is not sufficient differentiation if the new class is not paced with gifted math students in mind. The most precocious may be able to handle a compressed course, such as summer classes offered by talent search programs, in which students can master as much as a year's worth of material in 3 weeks. Various studies report the success of these programs in preparing students for more advanced courses (Mills, Ablard, & Lynch, 1992; Miller, Mills, & Tangherlini, 1995). In the time gained by faster pacing, more depth and breadth of content can be addressed.

Depth Considerations

The abilities of the mathematically gifted require that the treatment of topics be at a deeper level than would be provided for average students. For example, in the primary grades, students spend a large amount of time learning addition facts. The gifted should, instead, be engaged with questions that go beyond the skill level, such as looking for patterns in addition. They should grapple with open-ended situations, such as the nature of various sums of odd and even integers, addressing questions such as the following:

- Why is the sum of two odds always even?
- What can you say about the sum of three odd integers?
- What is true about the sum of any number of odd integers?
- Why is that result always true?

In the sample lesson *Patterning*, fourth-grade students engage in an investigation of a toothpick pattern. All fourth graders should be expected to fill out the table through the 10th term. Some may need to form all the squares with the toothpicks so they can count them. Others may be able to determine the answer for 100 terms. In addition, gifted students should be asked to write a formula for the general term, *n*. This is a more abstract task demand, taking the activity to a higher level of complexity and abstraction that is appropriate for these students. They should also be given further examples of function tables without manipulatives so that they have practice in determining general patterns from abstract data.

At the secondary level, the choice of textbooks for gifted students makes a big difference in terms of availability of challenging problems and applications. Within these texts, teachers should not merely require correct answers, but should also emphasize detailed and careful explication of thought processes used. Alternative and creative solutions to problems should be shared and discussed.

Sample Lesson
Patterning

Directions:

If one square is made of four toothpicks and two squares are made from seven toothpicks as shown in the pattern below, how many toothpicks would be needed to build 10 squares, 100 squares, and one other number of squares? What pattern did you find? Explain.

Assessment:

Students create a table of values, such as the one below.

Number of squares	Number of toothpicks
1	4
2	7
3	10
4	13
10	?
100	?
n	?

Breadth Considerations

With the extra time gained by moving more quickly through the core curricular material, it is possible to include some extra content that will benefit and interest strong students. This might be thought of as analogous to the difference between (a) getting on the interstate and driving from point A to point B as fast as possible and (b) taking a few exits along the way to explore museums, historical sights, natural phenomena, and so forth. The enrichments may be either within a topic already under study, or they may be topics that are not usually included.

An example of the first type might be the inclusion of a module of activities from *The Challenge of the Unknown* (Maddux, 1986), a set of supplementary materials developed under the auspices of the American Association for the Advancement of Science (AAAS) that illustrates how real-world problem solving can be incorporated within the study of estimation at elementary and middle school levels. The video from the materials shows a marine biologist estimating shark populations and also discusses issues of accuracy in carrying out a census in China. Students should be asked to create a model for the tag-and-recapture process and analyze its accuracy.

An example of the second "breadth" type (new topics) might include the study of number bases other than base 10 in the elementary school. This would include counting in the new base, representation of numbers in various bases, addition and subtraction within a new base, and the study of place value in early civilizations, such as base 20 in Mayan culture and base 60 in Babylonian culture.

As a cautionary note, however, both types of breadth considerations must be tailored to the gifted population. If the activity is one that would benefit all students, it is not sufficiently differentiated for the gifted. For example, if students are shown how to create an Escher-like tessellation, which they make and then color in, this should be considered enrichment for all students. To differentiate it, gifted students might use the tessellations of M.C. Escher in the following tasks:

- analyze the types of symmetry in the drawings;
- compare photos of the tile tessellations in the Alhambra Palace to Escher's drawings and make conjectures about which palace tiles inspired the artist; or
- learn about mathematical mosaics, then compare and contrast them with Escher's tessellations (see Figure 7.2).

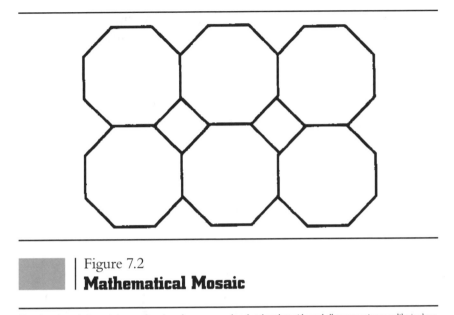

Figure 7.2
Mathematical Mosaic

Note. A mathematical mosaic is a set of regular polygons arranged so that they share sides and all corner points are alike in shape and number.

Math games and puzzles are also a good source of enrichment. Rather than just playing the game or solving the puzzles, students should analyze their own strategies to maximize the benefit of the activities. Again, the expectations for such activities should be differentiated to challenge students at different levels appropriately.

Conceptually Oriented Curricula

In mathematics, one might organize learning around a theme such as problem solving, as is done in *The Challenge of the Unknown* (Maddux, 1986). This more abstract way of approaching curricula prompts students to look beyond skills and discrete facts, again reflecting the complexity and practices of the discipline of mathematics. The ideas presented are taken from a Center for Gifted Education unit for middle school students, *Models: A Study of Animal Populations* (Johnson & Sher, 1997). This is a problem-based learning unit inspired by the problem of the overpopulation of deer in a suburban community. Mathematics and science are integrated in the unit so that the mathematics arises naturally as needed to support solutions to the problem. The unit is built around the concept of *models*, including physical, conceptual, and mathematical examples. It uses models to study population growth through activities such as examining deer data, growing bacteria, and studying a hypothetical set of data regarding plant growth that assumes doubling every day. An example of this is included in the sample lesson *Exponential Growth* (Johnson & Sher, 1997).

Another example of conceptual organization of content is the sample lesson *Properties and Operations,* from a prealgebra unit developed by the South Carolina Consortium for Gifted Education (Peeples, 1994). In this lesson, mathematical concepts such as inverses and identities are studied as properties of an abstract number system, instead of in terms of how they apply to multiplication and addition in the set of whole numbers.

A third example of a conceptual organization of content can be found in the sample lesson *Patterns of Rational Numbers.* This also represents a comprehensive example of "deeper treatment" in an extended lesson that would be part of a unit on rational numbers and number systems (broader concepts), rather than fractions (the topical approach). The lesson requires students to investigate patterns of the decimal forms of rational numbers and ask them to discover the reasons why some terminate while others repeat.

Higher Order Reasoning

Higher order questions can bring about the type of reasoning required to explore the depth and breadth of mathematical content and concepts indicated in the sections above. A study by Friedman and Lee (1996) showed that higher cognitive levels of teacher questions elicited higher cognitive levels of student responses.

By emphasizing induction, deduction, analysis, and synthesis, teachers can guarantee higher level reasoning opportunities in the classroom. Both inductive and deductive reasoning are used in mathematics. Inductive reasoning is used when one makes a generalization about what usually happens based on particular examples (e.g., examining a set of ordered pairs and then writing a function based on them). Reasoning from known principles to particular situations uses deductive reasoning (e.g., concluding that a square is a rectangle by reasoning from the definition of a rectangle. A rectangle is a parallelogram

Sample Lesson
Exponential Growth

Instructional Purpose:

- To investigate long-term growth rates in various populations and write mathematical models to represent them.

Activities:

1. Lesson to be taught as part of a math/science unit on populations and the concept of *models*. Give students the following hypothetical situation and encourage them to create a mathematical model to help solve the problem:

   Suppose that you start with a pair of rabbits (one male and one female) that are born on January 1. Assume that all months have equal length and that rabbits begin to produce their own young 2 months after their own birth. After reaching the age of 2 months, each pair produces a mixed pair (one male and one female) and then another pair each month thereafter. Assume no rabbits die. How many pairs of rabbits will there be after 1 year?

2. Discuss the problem with students. Ask the following questions:

   a. Do you think this reflects what happens in the real world?
   b. Why or why not?
   c. What can we do to find out how real populations change over time?

3. Work with students to explore patterns in different organisms to see what they can find out about population growth. Some possible examples include the following:

   a. Contact the game department to get some data on deer populations in your area or state over a number of years. Graph the data.

b. Try the problem "Hyacinths in the Pond" (see Figure 7.1).

c. Talk to someone who has raised mice or guppies. Ask him or her what patterns of population growth he or she noticed.

d. Design a way to measure the growth of yeast or bacteria. Graph the data.

4. After doing at least one of these activities, ask students, "What are the patterns you noticed in each of the examples?" Explain the term *exponential growth*, used to indicate this kind of pattern. Explain that a mathematical model for the hyacinth problem would be $y = 2^x$. Have students complete the handout on Graphing Exponential Models.

5. Show students a graph of the human population on planet Earth over human history. How do the patterns compare to the patterns studied in this lesson? How can you account for the tiny valleys in the graph of world population?

6. Have students write responses to the following questions for homework:

a. Examine existing deer population data from city or county agencies, the extension service, or another source. Is it similar to any of the patterns we have looked at? If so, how?

b. Explain any differences between real deer data and the growth models. What does this say about your assumptions?

c. What are the factors that could keep any population from continuing to grow exponentially?

d. What are some ways that growth is kept under control
   1) for deer?
   2) for towns or suburbs?
   3) for mosquitoes?

Note. From *Models: A Problem-Based Study of Animal Populations* (p. 68–74), by D. T. Johnson, & B. T. Sher, 1997, Williamsburg, VA: Center for Gifted Education, College of William and Mary. Copyright © 1998 by the Center for Gifted Education. Adapted with permission.

Handout
Graphing Exponential Models

1. The hyacinth problem uses an exponential growth model that looks like this: $y = 2^X$. Graph this function on a graphing calculator with the window settings as follows:

    xmin = -1
    xmax = 20
    ymin = -1
    ymax = 20

2. On the same set of axes, graph the following function: $y = (1.5)^X$ How does it compare to the first function?

3. Predict the shape and placement of the following functions. Then, graph them on the same set of axes as the others.

    a. $y = (1.1)^X$
       Prediction:
       Were you right?

    b. $y = 3^X$
       Prediction:
       Were you right?

4. Clear the graphs except for the graph of $y = 2^X$. Predict the placement and shape of this function and then graph it on the calculator:

    $y = (\frac{1}{2})^X$
    Prediction:
    Were you right?

    Place the cursor near the y-axis and zoom in to get a closer look. How do the two graphs compare? What do you think explains the difference?

Sample Lesson
Properties and Operations

Activity:

1. Operation ⋆ (call it "star") is defined in the table below. It gives the result of combining two elements from set A where A = {R, S, T, U} by using operation ⋆. To read the table, locate the first element in the left column and the second element in the top row. The result is found where the row of the first element intersects the column of the second element.

Example: T ⋆ U = T

⋆	R	S	T	U
R	S	R	T	U
S	U	T	R	S
T	R	S	U	T
U	T	U	S	R

⋆	R	S	T	U
R	S	R	T	U
S	U	T	R	S
T	R	S	U	T
U	T	U	S	R

a. Find S ⋆ T
b. Find U ⋆ U
c. Find T ⋆ S
d. Find R ⋆ T
e. Is operation ⋆ commutative? How do you know?
f. Is there an identity element for operation ⋆ ? Explain.

Note. From *Ideas for Algebra: Operations, Variables, Properties* (p. 12), by S. Peeples, 1994, Columbia: South Carolina Council for Gifted Education. Copyright © 1994 by the South Carolina Council for Gifted Education. Adapted with permission.

Sample Lesson
Patterns of Rational Numbers

Instructional Purpose:

- To determine (without dividing) whether a given proper fraction will yield a repeating or terminating decimal form and to explain how the underlying principles determine the structure of the decimal form.

Activities:

1. [This lesson would be preceded by a lesson that teaches the concept of *rational numbers* through examining examples and nonexamples. This lesson requires knowledge of prime numbers, how to determine the prime factorization of a composite number, and how to change fractions to decimals (with and without a calculator).] Review the concept of rational numbers. Ask students what we mean by a rational number. Be sure they see the link between the words *ratio* and *rational*. Then, ask them to distinguish between fractions and rational numbers. (All rational numbers can be written in fraction form. For example, 0.3 is a rational number. It has several possible representations, among which is $\frac{3}{10}$, the fractional form.) Have students find the decimal form of $\frac{1}{43}$ on a calculator. Ask: Is this the exact value or a rounded value? How can you tell? Allow discussion.

2. Use the following list of fractions for gathering data. Have students write the decimal form for each fraction. They may use a calculator. $\frac{1}{2}$ $\frac{1}{3}$ $\frac{3}{4}$ $\frac{8}{9}$ $\frac{5}{8}$ $\frac{1}{11}$

3. Make a two-column table on the board and separate the fractions from the list above into two lists:

Fractions that convert to repeating decimals	Fractions that convert to terminating decimals

4. Use the following questions as the basis of a discussion about the nature of fractions: If we choose any fraction and divide the numerator by the denominator to generate a decimal form, will the resulting decimal form always fall into one of the two categories above? Or, could the decimal form be a nonrepeating, nonterminating decimal? Why?

> *Answer:* All fractions *will* convert to either a repeating or terminating form. If students are having trouble, have them examine the process of long division used in changing fraction form to decimal form. They should see that they will eventually run out of different possibilities for remainders so that either the remainder will be zero or they will re-encounter the original dividend, thus revisiting the previous cycle of divisors.)

5. Ask students to go back to the table and study the entries. In small groups, they should see if they can form a conjecture that will predict to which category a given fraction belongs. Have them write down their findings, but they will not share them yet.

6. Call the attention of all groups to the list of fractions below. Ask them to use their conjectures to assign these fractions to the table. (No actual division should be allowed until after they have made a decision. Then, they can check on the calculator.)

$$\frac{6}{7} \qquad \frac{17}{125} \qquad \frac{199}{200} \qquad \frac{5}{13} \qquad \frac{9}{80} \qquad \frac{15}{24} \qquad \frac{11}{24}$$

If they were not right, they can revise the conjecture and choose some more fractions to guess and check. (Note: You may suspect that a group has discovered the rule if they are consistently placing fractions in the right group. Do not let them give away the rule to other students if they have discovered it.)

7. If the students are having trouble, prompt their thinking with questions such as these:

a. *Does the outcome depend on the numerator? How can you find out?* (Gently nudge them, but do not tell them directly. Write the list of *simplified* fractions with the same denominator but different numerators and study their placement in the two groups. Do another list using another common denominator. This incorporates elements of good experimental design—holding one variable constant [the denominator] and repeated trials.)

b. *Does it depend on the denominator? How can you find out?* (You can use a similar method as in part a.)

[Note. A fraction (in simplest form/lowest terms) terminates in its decimal form if the prime factors of the denominator are only 2s or a combination of 2s and 5s. Otherwise, it repeats.]

8. Have each group report their findings and, through discussion, make sure all have discovered the rule. Then ask about $\frac{3}{12}$. It is a terminating decimal—but the prime factorization of the denominator is 2 x 2 x 3, so shouldn't it repeat? Encourage discussion.

   Answer: $\frac{3}{12}$ is not in lowest terms. The rule only applies to fractions that are completely simplified.

9. Have students write in their math journals using a prompt such as this: Explain why the decimal form of $\frac{3}{11}$ is repeating and the decimal form of $\frac{3}{40}$ terminates.

10. Lead a whole class discussion using questions such as the following:

    - Is our reasoning in this problem an example of *inductive* or *deductive* reasoning? Why?
    - How do we know this "rule" that we have conjectured is always true?
    - Is it sufficient to show it works for 10 examples? 100? 1,000? (inductive reasoning)

- What can you see about the structure of our number system that makes this work?

  Answer: Ours is a *decimal* system! This means that each digit represents a group of some power of 10. Since 10 = 2 x 5, you can convert each fraction whose denominator contains only factors of 2s and 5s into an equivalent fraction whose denominator is some power of 10. When the denominator is a power of 10, the decimal form terminates.

  Example: $\frac{4}{25} = \frac{16}{100} = 0.16$

  This is deductive reasoning, as we are reasoning from known facts and relationships and applying them to this particular situation.

11. Have students complete the following in their math journals to wrap up the lesson:

    a. Which of the following fractions terminate in their decimal form?

    $\frac{3}{8}$ $\frac{4}{15}$ $\frac{7}{9}$ $\frac{7}{50}$ $\frac{1}{40}$

    $\frac{9}{36}$ $\frac{7}{99}$ $\frac{55}{56}$ $\frac{3}{20}$ $\frac{1}{14}$

    Write a short paragraph telling how you made those decisions.

    b. Explain the underlying principles of our number system that make these "fraction-to-decimal patterns" work.

with four right angles, therefore, the square is a particular instance of a rectangle). Both types of reasoning should be understood and discussed as underlying processes in mathematical thought, as illustrated in the sample lesson *Patterns of Rational Numbers*. Moreover, analysis and synthesis should be emphasized in mathematical learning as part of the effort to move away from discrete facts and skills.

Inquiry-Based Learning

A discovery approach to seeking and finding patterns works well in mathematics, but it takes more careful planning of activities. Such an approach requires "nudging" students toward results, rather than telling them. For example, rather than being told, elementary students should be expected to develop the rules for addition of fractions. High school geometry students should figure out the conditions under which two triangles are congruent and then prove why. By posing questions, teachers can push students toward the habits of mind of mathematicians instead of merely training them in algorithmic skills and problem-solving strategies. Manipulative materials should be part of this approach; just because students are gifted does not mean that they do not need, or cannot benefit from, concrete representations of ideas. However, they may move more quickly than other students from the concrete to the abstract. For instance, students might use cubes to model volume and surface-area problems when the ideas are being introduced, but they would not continue to use them every time they work a problem.

Encouraging habits of mathematical inquiry also requires that students engage in individual and small-group problem solving and projects. Gifted students are capable of working on substantive math tasks independently. Self-pacing activities, such as Techniques of Problem Solving (TOPS, 1980) cards or Visual Thinking cards (Seymour, 1983), can provide such an experience. However, rather than working toward answers only, students should document their solutions in a math journal so that the process of solving problems is emphasized, rather than the answers themselves. The solutions become products, rather than accumulated points. These kinds of tasks can be a good basis for group problem solving and discussion.

Gifted students should also be engaged in some longer term student-directed projects in which they can work independently or in groups. One such project might be the planning and building of 3-D fractal structures, such as a Sierpinski pyramid (a self-replicating structure made of tetrahedra) or Menger's Sponge (similar to the pyramid, but cubic in nature). This should entail a presentation that explains the fractal principles that are used in the design of the structure.

Principles of depth and breadth that were discussed earlier also apply to the implementation of projects. An example from arithmetic that seems deceptively trivial on the surface is the following problem: Arrange the digits 1–9 so that they form a correct sum in the form XXX + XXX = XXX (where each X represents a different number). The typical expectation in a regular classroom would be to have students find one solution. However, there are somewhere in the neighborhood of 300 solutions. Finding and cataloging solutions and making generalizations about patterns would make a wonderful group project.

Materials and Resources

Relying on standard math textbooks is not always adequate for providing the necessary depth and breadth of content. Multiple resources, including the Internet, print sources, and communication with experts, need to be used for both teacher planning and student investigations.

Examples of new areas of study are fractals, topology, and logic. An inspirational source for problems in these areas and others that could be independently carried out is *Mathematics: A Human Endeavor* (Jacobs, 1994). Web sites such as Megamath (http://www.c3.lanl.gov/mega-math/workbk/contents.html) and The Math Forum (http://mathforum.org) are filled with ideas for extensions in the classrooms or use as independent projects. Both depth and breadth can be incorporated in high-level applications of mathematical ideas, such as those found in *The Challenge of the Unknown* (Maddux, 1986). This program portrays adult problem solvers tackling issues and topics, such as how to minimize waste when cutting stones to build a cathedral, creating mathematical models for determining the running speed of ostriches (and, indirectly, dinosaurs), and refining the flight path of a boomerang.

Interdisciplinary and Intradisciplinary Connections

According to Galileo, mathematics is the language of the universe. There are unlimited ways of applying it to other content areas and real-world problems. These applications should be important and well integrated, not just word problems that disguise skills in sentences. One such example is given in the sample lesson *Exponential Growth* (Johnson & Sher, 1997), in which mathematical models are studied in the context of animal populations. Mathematical analyses can lend support to the research work in other content areas. It can be the glue for the data and evidence part of a persuasive argument in other disciplines. Moreover, real-world connections to the concepts and principles of mathematics may be explored as part of, or extensions to, lessons in the mathematics classroom. For example, the following two questions might be used to extend the sample lesson *Patterns of Rational Numbers*:

- Until recently, stock prices on the New York Stock Exchange were given in rational form, rounding prices to the nearest eighth of a dollar. Now, the prices are given in decimal form. What are the advantages and disadvantages of each system of reporting and bookkeeping?
- Fabric is measured to the nearest ⅛ of a yard in fabric stores. Why do you think eighths are the fraction of choice?

Constructing Meaning and Metacognition

The inquiry-based and higher order reasoning elements that are discussed above are the main tools used to guide students toward building meaning about the relationships and significance of mathematical ideas. Students should be asked to share the process they used in solving problems. If the teacher models thinking and questions students for deep understanding and processes, students will be better prepared for further study at the college or university level. A math journal is a good tool in encouraging and documenting thinking. The following example, a possible extension to the sample lesson *Patterns of Rational Numbers*, demonstrates an opportunity for students to develop their understanding of the key concepts further and to reflect upon their thinking process:

Think about the following question:
What is the maximum number of decimal places necessary before the decimal representation of a fraction will either repeat or terminate?

- Make a plan for finding out.
- Carry out the plan.
- Use your hypothesis to predict the number of places required in the cycle of repeating digits in the decimal expansion of ¼₇.

- Write a description of what you decided and how you found out.
- Discuss with the whole class and see if all reached the same conclusion. If you did not, argue for your point of view or acknowledge that your result was flawed.

Follow-up to this activity:

Assume that you are Dr. Math at the Math Forum (http://mathforum.org) and a student sends you the following question. Write a response to the student in your math journal.

Dear Dr. Math,

A section about rational and irrational numbers in our algebra textbook has the following question: A student who used long division to find the repeating decimal form for 1/7 claimed that there were 20 digits in the repeating block of digits. Is this correct? Explain.

The textbook answer says that there can be no more than 16 digits in the repeating block. Do you have to divide it out to figure this out, or can you predict the number of digits without dividing?

Technology Relevant

Technological resources, such as spreadsheets, graphing calculators, specialized software, and the Internet, are wonderful tools for student exploration and discovery in mathematics. If self-paced acceleration is desired, the mathematics portion of the EPGY is worth considering. It covers content from kindergarten to college. Students must be able to work independently, but they have access to an online tutor (see http://epgy.stanford.edu).

By middle school, gifted students should be exposed to a graphing calculator as a powerful tool for making mathematical discoveries. The function tables and statistical lists allow data to be examined for numerical patterns, while the graphing capabilities expose the geometry of the patterns. Any scientific calculator is a treasure trove of examples of inverse functions—from addition and subtraction, to the exponential and logarithmic functions—so students can carry out multitudes of calculations to see how inverse functions "undo" each other. They can then make generalizations based on the patterns observed.

Programming is an important skill for students who are interested in mathematics and science. Elementary students can learn a lot about programming by using a Logo program. Logo is a user-friendly programming language that incorporates spatial reasoning along with programming; students give commands to the Logo turtle, telling it how far to go and in what direction. The graphing calculator is a good tool for teaching programming to middle and high school students. Middle school students should be able to write simple programs, such as one that will prompt the user to enter numbers and then calculate the average of those numbers and the median. High school students should be able to write a program for solving quadratic equations.

The Internet is a rich source of enrichment, as many powerful mathematical ideas that are not included or barely mentioned in textbooks are presented here. For example, at Mega Mathematics (http://www.c3.lanl.gov/mega-math/index.html), a project of the Computer Research and Applications Group of Los Alamos National Laboratory, students can explore the concept of *infinity* at the Infinity Hotel, learn about knot theory, or find out about graph theory. They can interact with Sierpinski triangles while discovering the patterns that unfold within them at http://www.best.com/˜ejad/java/ fractals/sierpinski.shtml.

There are many challenging problems presented on the Internet for students to solve. For example, they might go to the Math Forum (http://mathforum.org) and choose "Problems of the Week," where they will find problem categories of elementary, middle school, geometry, algebra, discrete math, and trigonometry and calculus. They can submit their solutions (not merely answers, but detailed descriptions of the steps they took and why) and perhaps have them published on the Web site. Students with advanced skills and abilities will not feel so different or isolated when they see the interesting solutions to hard problems that other students have submitted to sites such as this.

Conclusion

Once gifted students are placed in a grade level or course that is appropriate for their level of mathematical maturity and content knowledge, teachers are faced with the question of whether or not the curriculum of the operative classroom is challenging and rewarding. How can teachers of mathematics make their lessons more in line with some of the elements that have been addressed in this chapter?

1. Begin with the best curricular materials possible that reflect multiple characteristics of appropriate resources for gifted learners as discussed in this chapter and in Chapter 10. Draw from specialized resources and not just the basal textbook.
2. Reorganize the content under larger concepts such as patterns, systems, or proof.
3. Pretest students before each chapter or unit so that the needs of the students are clear and time is not wasted on material they already know.
4. Redesign some of the lessons you already teach by telling less and giving students more opportunities to explore ideas and make discoveries.
5. Craft higher level questions that probe student thinking so that facts and algorithms are not the only end-product of learning.
6. Make assessment opportunities more open-ended, not just traditional skill-based tests. Presentations of solutions to challenging problems, projects, group problem solving, and math journals can be included.
7. Give opportunities for independent exploration with clear guidelines about process and product expectations.
8. Include some topics that go beyond the required content of your course. The Internet can be a good resource for this. See Chapter 10 for some resources that will help you.
9. Require all students in your gifted program to learn some computer programming or use a graphing calculator. Both are excellent environments for higher level thinking.
10. Have students keep a math journal in which they document problem-solving processes and results.
11. Focus on challenging problem solving, not just skill building concepts.
12. Seek help from experts in mathematics if the interests and needs of your students go beyond your level of expertise.

The key question teachers should ask themselves in a planning mathematics curriculum is: Where is the thinking? If it is not there, it is not an appropriate curriculum for the gifted.

Key Points Summary

❑ A mathematics curriculum has to be accelerated before it can be effectively enriched.
❑ Treating mathematics as conceptual, rather than topical, raises the level of thinking for high-ability learners.
❑ Emphasis on problems that are nonalgorithmic enhances mathematical challenge.
❑ The use of computer programming and graphing calculators provides powerful learning enhancements for the gifted.
❑ Use of math manipulatives deepens the understanding of mathematics concepts for all learners, including the gifted.
❑ Mathematics curricula can be diversified through effective use of puzzles, games, activities, challenging problems, and selected Web sites.

References

Flanders, J. R. (1987). How much of the content in mathematics textbooks is new? *Arithmetic Teacher, 35*, 18–23.

Friedman, R. C., & Lee, S. W. (1996). Differentiating instruction for high-achieving/gifted children in regular classrooms: A field test of three gifted-education models. *Journal for the Education of the Gifted, 19*, 405–436.

Hembree, R., & Dessart, D. J. (1986). Effects of hand-held calculators in pre-college mathematics education: A meta-analysis. *Journal for Research in Mathematics Education, 17*, 83–99.

Grouws, D. A., & Cebulla, K. (1999). Fostering effective mathematics instruction: Implications from research. In G. Cawelti (Ed.), *Handbook of research on student achievement* (pp. 117–134). Arlington, VA: Educational Research Service.

Jacobs, H. R. (1994). *Mathematics: A human endeavor*. New York: Freeman.

Johnson, D. T., & Sher, B. T. (1997). *Models: A problem-based study of animal populations*. Williamsburg, VA: Center for Gifted Education, College of William and Mary.

Maddux, H. X. C. (Ed.). (1986). *The challenge of the unknown: Teaching guide*. New York: Norton.

MathCounts Foundation. (2000). *MathCounts in a nutshell*. Retrieved October 8, 2001, from http://www.mathcounts.org/Program/nutshell.html

Mills, C. J., Ablard, K. E., & Lynch, S. J. (1992). Academically talented students' preparation for advanced-level coursework after individually paced precalculus class. *Journal for the Education of the Gifted, 16,* 3–17.

Miller, R., Mills, C., & Tangherlini, A. (1995). The Appalachia model mathematics program for gifted students. *Roeper Review, 18,* 138–141.

National Council of Teachers of Mathematics (NCTM). (2000). *Principles and standards for school mathematics*. Reston, VA: Author.

Office of Educational Research and Improvement. (1999). *Attaining excellence: A TIMSS resource kit: Third International Mathematics and Science Study* [Multimedia kit]. (Available from the National Center for Education Statistics, U.S. Department of Education, 555 New Jersey Ave. NW, Washington, DC 20208-5574.)

Peeples, S. (1994). *Ideas from algebra: Operations, variables, properties*. Columbia: South Carolina Council for Gifted Education.

Ravaglia, R., Suppes, P., Stillinger, C., & Alper, T. (1995). Computer-based mathematics and physics for gifted students. *Gifted Child Quarterly, 39,* 7–13.

Seymour, D. (1983). *Visual thinking*. Palo Alto, CA: Seymour.

Sowell, E. J. (1993). Programs for mathematically gifted students: A review of empirical research. *Gifted Child Quarterly, 37,* 124–132.

Stanley, J., Keating, D., & Fox, L. (1974). *Mathematical talent*. Baltimore: Johns Hopkins University Press.

Swiatek, M. A. (1993). A decade of longitudinal research of academic acceleration through the study of mathematically precocious youth. *Roeper Review, 15,* 120–123.

Techniques of problem solving. (1980). Palo Alto, CA: Seymour.

Adapting Science Curricula for High-Ability Learners

by
Beverly T. Sher

You are a middle school teacher, teaching four 30-student sections of sixth-grade science in a suburban public school. Your students are heterogeneously grouped, and you know that you have everything from developmentally delayed at-risk students, to students who have been identified as gifted. You have been provided with a basal textbook from the series that is used throughout the district and a long list of topics that must be covered by the time the students take the state performance assessments in the spring. Your school's accreditation depends upon having at least 70% of your students pass the test. You know that some of the identified gifted students already know all of the material you're trying to teach; some of them even question the accuracy of the book. "But, Mrs. Hollis, I went to the planetarium, and the scientists there said that Pluto's not a planet!" The textbook asserts unequivocally that Pluto is, indeed, a planet. How can you meet the needs of the gifted students, teach the content needed for the state tests to the rest, and stay sane?

iven the movement to ensure accountability through high-stakes testing, it can be difficult for pressured teachers and administrators to find the time and energy needed to cope with the challenges posed by the needs of high-ability learners. Addressing the needs of the majority of the class is central to achieving an acceptable passing rate, an urgent priority for schools facing challenges to their accreditation. Meeting the needs of high-ability students for advanced content, greater depth, and a faster pace will not increase the passing rate on the tests—after all, many of these students already know most of the material before it is covered in class. Subjecting these students solely to the regular curriculum, though, can result in alienation, underachievement, and a loss of interest in learning.

Carefully chosen curricula, used wisely, can help. The science curriculum reform movement has encouraged the development of many high-quality science curricular materials that can be used effectively with gifted students. Compacting and accelerating, based on careful assessment of student performance, can help to ensure an appropriate match between students and the curriculum. This chapter will explore how the dimensions of the Integrated Curriculum Model (ICM; VanTassel-Baska, 1986, 1995) and the elements of curricular reform addressed throughout this text can be used to guide curriculum development and decision making in the area of science, with examples including discussion of the science curriculum for high-ability learners developed by the Center for Gifted Education at the College of William and Mary (Center for Gifted Education, 1997b). Because of the wealth of quality curricular materials available in this content area, this chapter will also explore some characteristics and examples of high-quality materials and suggest ways in which they can be successfully adapted and implemented with high-ability learners.

Learner Outcomes of Significance

Among the elements of curricular reform identified in Chapter 1, the element of learner outcomes of significance offers perhaps the greatest potential for capturing the overall "puzzle" holistically because it implies a focus on what we as educators want students to know and be able to do in each given content area. The relationship between this element (and, by extension, the whole puzzle) and the science curriculum reform movement can be explored through discussion of the best-known products of the science movement: the national standards for science education.

State-specific science standards now dictate the curriculum for growing numbers of K–12 students in the United States. This development has been controversial, as many of the state standards have been criticized as inadequate (Lerner, 1998, 2000). For this reason, this chapter will focus on the national science education standards produced by two eminent scientific groups. The National Science Education Standards were developed by the National Research Council (NRC), whose members are drawn from the National Academy of Sciences, the National Academy of Engineering, and the Institute of Medicine (NRC, 1996). The American Association for the Advancement of Science (AAAS), the largest professional association in the United States, has also produced a set of science education standards, the Benchmarks for Science Literacy, as a part of its science education reform initiative, Project 2061 (AAAS, 1995). Both sets of standards reflect the collaboration of some of the nation's best scientists and educators.

The NRC has set standards for six different areas: science teaching, professional development for science teachers, assessment, science content, K–12 science programs, and educational systems. Three of these areas—science teaching, assessment, and science content—are immediately relevant to the development of science curricula; the other three areas support the delivery. The NRC standards includes sections entitled "Changing Emphases" at the end of the discussion of the standards for each area; these sections, taken together, illuminate the NRC's approach to science curricular reform.

The science education reform movement seeks to improve science literacy by enhancing science instruction for all students, placing emphasis on conceptual understanding and scientific habits of mind. In developing science curricula for gifted students, educators must combine the best ideas of the science reform movement with an understanding of the special needs of advanced learners. Thus, learner outcomes should reflect attention to advanced content and a higher degree of complexity and intensity for this population. Developing outcomes within the three dimensions of the ICM supports this combination of emphases. Moreover, diagnostic assessment of students' science abilities and knowledge is also critical to ensure that the curriculum is sufficiently challenging for each individual learner. Table 8.1 illustrates the alignment of learner outcomes from a problem-based unit on acid-base chemistry (Center for Gifted Education, 1997a) with emphases in the NRC standards and the Benchmarks.

Table 8.1

Alignment of Learner Outcomes

ICM Emphasis	Sample Student Outcomes (from Center for Gifted Education, 1997a)	Related Emphases in National Science Education Standards (NRC, 1996)	Related Emphases in Benchmarks for Science Literacy (AAAS, 1995)
Concepts	*Students will be able to …* 1. analyze systems; 2. use systems language; 3. analyze systems interactions; 4. do predictions based on systems thinking; and 5. transfer systems concept to new system.	• A system is an organized group of related objects or components that form a whole. • Systems have boundaries, components, resources flow (input and output), and feedback. The goal of this standard is to think and analyze in terms of systems. • Prediction is the use of knowledge to identify and explain observations, or changes, in advance.	*Systems:* 1. Something that consists of many parts, and the parts usually influence one another. 2. Something may not work as well if a part of it is missing, broken, worn out, mismatched, or misconnected.
Content Topics	*Students will be able to …* 1. draw and interpret the pH scale; 2. identify common acids and bases;	*Physical Science:* • Students will develop an understanding of properties of objects and materials.	*Nature of Mathematics:* • Mathematical ideas can be represented graphically. *Technology and Science:* • Measuring instruments can be

Life Science:
- Students will develop understandings of organisms and environments.

Science in Personal and Social Perspectives:
- Students will develop understanding of science and technology in local challenges.

Students will be able to …
1. ask a question about objects, organisms, and events in the environment;
2. plan and conduct a simple investigation;
3. employ simple equipment and tools to gather data and extend the senses;
4. use data to construct a reasonable explanation; and
5. communicate investigations and explanations.

used to gather accurate scientific comparisons.

Structure of Matter:
- When a new material is made by combining two or more materials, it has different properties.

Interdependence of Life:
- Changes in an organism's habitat are sometimes beneficial and sometimes harmful.

Students should know that …
1. Scientific investigations may take many different forms.
2. Results of similar investigations seldom turn out the same.
3. Scientists' explanations come from observation and thinking.
4. Claims must be backed up with evidence.
5. Clear communication is an essential part of doing science.

3. devise safe method for determination of pH of unknown;
4. neutralize an acid safely;
5. construct and use a titration curve;
6. analyze the effect of water dilution on acid; and
7. analyze the effects of acids and bases on living organisms.

Scientific Processes

Students will be able to …
1. design, perform, and report on the results of experiments;
   - demonstrate data handling,
   - analyze experimental data;
   - make predictions to similar problems; and
   - communicate understanding to others.
2. identify meaningful scientific problems for investigation.

Note. "Sample Student Outcomes" from *A Guide to Teaching a Problem-Based Science Curriculum for High-Ability Learners* (p. 18), by the Center for Gifted Education, 1997, Dubuque, IA: Kendall/Hunt. Copyright © 1997 by the Center for Gifted Education. Reprinted with permission. "Related Emphases in National Science Education Standards" from *National Science Education Standards* (pp. 122, 127, 138), by the National Research Council, 1996, Washington, DC: National Academy Press. Copyright © 1996 by the National Academy of Sciences. Reprinted with permission. "Related Emphases in Benchmarks for Science Literacy" from *Science for All Americans: Project 2061*, 1990, New York: Oxford University Press. Copyright © 1990 by the American Association for the Advancement of Science (AAAS), 1990, New York: Oxford University Press. Copyright © 1990 by the American Association for the Advancement of Science.

Substantive Content

The science curriculum reform movement has placed heavy emphasis on integrating science content with science process, encouraging the development of habits of inquiry. As a part of this effort, science curricula should provide opportunities for students to develop questions and seek answers beyond the summaries provided in their textbooks. Moreover, gifted students should be encouraged both to develop questions that are more complex and to seek answers from a wider range of sources and experiences.

Consider Mrs. Hollis' dilemma in the scenario at the beginning of this chapter. She is teaching students with a wide range of abilities. The content she must cover includes the planets, as required by the NRC Science Content Standards for grades 5–8 (NRC, 1996). A gifted child in the group has been to the planetarium at the American Museum of Natural History in New York City and has brought back the idea that Pluto isn't really a planet. Mrs. Hollis could handle this in several different ways:

Scenario 1:

Mrs. Hollis: "The Earth is the third planet from the Sun, and there
(*lecturing*)   are nine planets in the solar system."

Tommy: "Mrs. Hollis, I went to the planetarium in New York, and they said that Pluto's not a planet!"

Mrs. Hollis: "You must have misheard them, Tommy. Everybody knows that Pluto's a planet. See, it says so right here in the book."

Tommy: "But, Mrs. Hollis . . ."

Mrs. Hollis: "You'd better remember that there are nine planets in the solar system, or you'll fail the state test next month. Now, class, let's make our solar system mobiles. Did everyone remember to bring coat hangers and cardboard? I have string and crayons and scissors here on my desk. Remember, Mars is red, Venus is orange, and you need to put a big red spot on Jupiter. Copy the pictures in the book."

Scenario 2:

Mrs. Hollis: "The Earth is the third planet from the Sun, and there
(*lecturing*) are nine planets in the solar system."

Tommy: "Mrs. Hollis, I went to the planetarium in New York,
and they said that Pluto's not a planet!"

Mrs. Hollis: "Really? Why did they say that?"

Tommy: "I don't remember exactly. It's too small, or something."

Mrs. Hollis: "Why don't you go to the library and see if you can learn
more about this for your astronomy project. Use the list
of astronomy Web sites you found yesterday to start with,
and see if you can find the Web site for the planetarium
in New York, too."

Tommy: "Okay."

*Tommy goes to the library; Mrs. Hollis continues her lecture, well aware that
Tommy already knows everything that she's going to say. Two days later . . .*

Tommy: "Mrs. Hollis, look what I found online! See? This article in
The New York Times says that some astronomers think we
should still call Pluto a planet, but other scientists don't, and
that's why the planetarium changed its solar system display."

Mrs. Hollis: "Good for you, Tommy! Would you like to tell the rest of
the class about this?"

Tommy: "Yes, and I'll add it to the poster I'm making for my
astronomy project. I have pictures of the planets from the
Jet Propulsion Laboratory Web site, and I'll add this to
the text I'm putting in underneath them."

Mrs. Hollis: "Remember that the developers of the state test agree
with the scientists who think that Pluto's a planet: That'll
be the right answer on the test next month."

Tommy: "Okay."

Clearly, Mrs. Hollis is more open to the needs of her gifted students in the second scenario. Fortunately for those students, and the other students, as well, she's also working with a different curriculum. The lesson plans, student activity instructions, and grading rubrics for each scenario are included in Table 8.2 to illustrate the curricular indications of Mrs. Hollis' differentiated response.

In both scenarios, Mrs. Hollis is using the district-recommended basal textbook and covering the content needed for the state assessments. In Scenario 2, though, she also uses supplementary curricular materials and reliable outside sources of information. In this scenario, she has chosen to spend the time that her teacher's manual allocates to textbook-supplied hands-on activities on a worthier project that encourages all students to explore science content beyond the textbook, and she has addressed the needs of her gifted students in the process.

Problem-Based Learning: Integrating Content, Process, and Concepts

As noted in the Scenario 2 options given above, substantive science content should incorporate opportunities to explore findings of science research and to conduct experiments, supporting a view of inextricable integration of science content and science process. Furthermore, connections between the science of the classroom and lab and their implications for the "real world" should also be emphasized in the science curriculum. One way of approaching this integration of emphases is the use of problem-based learning (PBL). PBL, the approach utilized in the Center for Gifted Education's science units (1997b), was chosen because of its potential to increase student motivation, deliver high-level content, and facilitate differentiation for the gifted. PBL arose in the education and training of medical students as an alternative to the traditional, lecture-based medical curriculum (Barrows, 1998). In problem-based learning, the focus is on "the problem," a complex, ill-defined, real-world situation that gradually unfolds and changes direction as the students learn more about it. In PBL-based courses, individual patients are the basis for the problem; medical students learn the basic science they would otherwise have learned in lecture as they attempt to solve the real-world problem posed by the patient's condition. This approach is highly motivational for students. PBL is not a complete substitute for the traditional curriculum, however. Patel and Kaufman (2001) found significant differences in the clinical reasoning skills of PBL and traditionally trained students, with traditionally trained students being more likely to display an expert style of clinical reasoning than students from pure PBL-trained programs. Nevertheless, in combination with other teaching methods, PBL enhances medical education. Many medical schools now combine problem-based learning experiences with more traditional coursework.

Over the last decade and a half, PBL has gradually diffused into other parts of education. In the late 1980s and early 1990s, staff members at the Illinois Math and Science Academy (IMSA), a residential high school for gifted high school students, implemented several successful problem-based science and social studies courses (Stepien, Gallagher, & Workman, 1993). Research findings from IMSA and related programs provide support for adding PBL to the menu of curricular choices available to gifted students. Students exposed to PBL social studies courses acquired the content they would have acquired in a traditional course, but performed better on fact finding, problem finding, and solution finding (Gallagher & Stepien, 1996; Gallagher, Stepien, & Rosenthal, 1992). Students in a PBL-based biochemistry course acquired in-depth understanding of concepts, although content coverage was promoted by lecture, rather than by PBL (Dods, 1997).

The success of the IMSA courses was part of the basis for developing problem-based science units for younger gifted students at the Center for Gifted Education (1997b). Reflecting the ICM and the science reform principles, the units were designed around a central concept and intended to help students understand the scientific process and to convey significant scientific content. The concept of *systems* was the organizer for the series of units, based on one of the early recommendations of the AAAS (1990).

To illustrate the integration of the ICM and the PBL approach, a closer examination of one of the Center for Gifted Education's units is helpful. In *Acid, Acid Everywhere* (Center for Gifted Education, 1997a), a unit for fourth, fifth, and sixth graders, the first thing students see when they begin the unit is a localized version of the following problem statement:

You are the supervisor of the day shift of the State Highway Patrol. It is six a.m. on a cool autumn morning. You are sleeping when the phone rings. You answer and hear, "Come to the

| Table 8.2

Curricular Indications of Mrs. Hollis' Differentiated Response

Lesson Plan, Student Activity Instructions, and Grading Rubric for Scenario 1

Lesson Plan:

1. Have the students read pages 47–49 in the textbook.
2. Give the solar system lecture. Points to include: The Earth is the third planet from the Sun; there are nine planets; Saturn has rings; Jupiter has a big red spot.
3. Students will make their solar system mobiles. Follow the "Activity: Solar System Mobile" instructions on page 50 of the book.

Student Activity: Solar System Mobile

1. Cut out 10 cardboard circles. Three of them should be big; the rest should be smaller.

Lesson Plan, Student Activity Instructions, and Grading Rubric for Scenario 2

Lesson Plan:

1. Have the students read pages 47–49 in the textbook.
2. Give the solar system lecture. Points to include: The Earth is the third planet from the Sun; there are nine planets; Saturn has the biggest rings of any planet in the Solar System; some of the other planets have smaller rings, although the textbook only mentions Saturn's; Jupiter has a big red spot, which is a gigantic storm in the planet's atmosphere; right now, Pluto is the outermost planet, just as it says in the book, although sometimes, Neptune is farther from the Sun than Pluto is.
3. Allow students to work on their astronomy projects.

Instructions for Fall Quarter Science Project: Astronomy

You may work alone or in a small group for this project and choose one of the following:

2. Color the circles to match the pictures of the planets on page 47. Label each of your circles on the back with the name of the planet. Jupiter and Saturn should be on the big circles. Use pipe cleaners for Saturn's rings.
3. Cut nine 10-inch pieces of string. Tape one end of each piece to the back of one of your cardboard planets. Tie the other end to the long part of the coat hanger. Make sure that you have your planets in the same order as the planets are from the Sun. Mercury should be at one end of the coat hanger and Pluto should be at the other end.
4. Label the last big circle "The Sun." Color it yellow and attach it to the top of the coat hanger.

Grading Rubric for the Solar System Mobile

This activity is worth 100 points:

- 25 points for neatness;
- 25 points for planets being in the right order;
- 25 points for the planets matching the pictures in the book; and
- 25 points for all of the models being labeled and the planets' names being spelled correctly.

- library research on some aspect of astronomy;
- an astronomy experiment from the resource materials in the back of the room; or
- an astronomy experiment or observation project of your own design.

You may present your work in one of these ways:

- an oral presentation with visual aids and a bibliography listing your information sources and a written outline of your presentation;
- an informative poster with illustrations and text and a bibliography listing your information sources; or
- a written report with illustrations and a bibliography.

Grading Rubric for the Astronomy Science Project

This project will be worth 100 points, given as follows:

- 25 points for the bibliography (you must use at least three high-quality information sources);
- 15 points for the quality of your visual aids or illustrations;
- 40 points for the accuracy and completeness of your information; and
- 25 points for oral presentation/poster/writing criteria.

[Clear Creek Bridge on Route 15]. There has been a major accident and you are needed." Quickly you dress and get on the road to hurry to the site of the emergency. As you approach the bridge, you see an overturned truck that has apparently crashed through the metal guardrail. It has lost one wheel and is perched on its front axle. You see "corrosive" written on a small sign on the rear of the truck. There is a huge gash in the side of the truck and from the gash a liquid is running down the side of the truck, onto the road, and down the hill into a creek. Steam is rising from the creek. All traffic has been stopped, and everyone has been told to remain in their cars. Many of the motorists trapped in the traffic jam appear to be angry and frustrated. Police officers, firemen, and rescue squad workers are at the scene. They are all wearing coveralls and masks. The rescue squad is putting the unconscious driver of the truck onto a stretcher. Everyone seems hurried and anxious. (p. 17)

This problem statement has three key features reflecting the principles of PBL. First, it is ill-defined: The elements needed to solve the problem are not present in the problem statement; indeed, it is not entirely clear what the problem is. Second, the problem is a real-world problem: Accidents such as this one occur all the time, as a quick newspaper database search will reveal. As indicated by the brackets in the problem statement above, teachers localize the problem by choosing a site in their area that combines a major thoroughfare, a bridge, and a creek, stream, or river. Localizing the problem makes it more compelling to the students and allows the teacher to use local resources as the problem develops. Finally, the students are given a stakeholder's role in the situation: As a highway patrol supervisor, they have both the authority and the responsibility needed to be a part of the problem's solution.

After students have read the problem statement, they discuss it as a group. The teacher, acting as a metacognitive coach, facilitates their discussion with questions such as "What's going on at the bridge?," "What are our responsibilities as Highway Patrol supervisor?," "What are the key pieces of information?," "What is the main problem?," and "Where can we find out more?" A class Need to Know board, a metacognitive organizer, is used to help students organize their thoughts and the tasks they need to complete in order to make progress on the problem. The generic format for the Need to Know board is

What do we know?	What do we need to know?	How can we find out?

Figure 8.1
Need to Know Board

Note. From *Acid, Acid Everywhere* (p. 19), by the Center for Gifted Education, 1997, Dubuque, IA: Kendall/Hunt. Copyright © 1997 by the Center for Gifted Education. Reprinted with permission.

shown in Figure 8.1. Students return to the Need to Know board repeatedly throughout the problem and modify it with new information and new questions. A second metacognitive organizer, the problem log, is used to help individual students work through their ideas about the problem; each lesson in the unit includes questions for students to answer in their problem logs.

As the students work through the problem, they complete a series of preplanned lessons that are given when they have come to appropriate questions about the problem. The lessons ensure that the students' science content, science process, and science concept outcomes for the unit are achieved. New information about the problem, supplied by the teacher, and new information acquired from outside sources, such as the Internet, help move the problem along.

The specific science content focus of the unit emerges when students learn that the spill contains concentrated hydrochloric acid. They learn about the pH scale and use relevant technology (pH paper and a pH meter) to determine the pH of safe, everyday liquids. They design experiments to answer questions about the effects of acids on living and nonliving things and discover different ways to clean up an acid spill. They use local maps to determine the likely effects of the spill on the surrounding community and invite local experts to the classroom to share their expertise.

In the final lesson of the unit, students are forced (by a weather forecast indicating that thunderstorms will arrive in the area shortly) to come to a consensus about the best way to clean up the acid spill. They then present their solutions to a panel of community members, including local hazardous materials experts who have served as consultants during the problem.

Assessment opportunities include teacher observations, the students' problem logs, and experimental design worksheets. Final unit assessment activities include a systems assessment, a scientific process assessment, and a science content assessment. The U.S. Department of Education's Office of Educational Research and Improvement (2001) report discussing the Center for Gifted Education's science curriculum included the comment that

> [t]he program's focus on unifying concepts and processes, important science content, and scientific inquiry serves as an exceptional model for program developers as they make the transition to reform-driven curricula and for teachers as they look for guidance in meeting rigorous state and national science standards. (¶ 7)

As the unit summary above illustrates, the PBL approach allows teachers to develop a curriculum that integrates content, process, and concepts in science into an engaging whole that involves students in inquiry learning and scientific experimentation. The science content found in standards and textbooks is folded in with a real-world problem situation that requires students not only to engage in developing and carrying out science experiments, but also to reason about how those experiments are relevant for understanding and responding to contemporary issues. Moreover, the conceptual emphasis helps students to understand the complexity of the problem and the interdependence of systems in society and in the natural world, thus also providing opportunities for authentic interdisciplinary and intradisciplinary connections.

The potential benefits of the PBL approach are numerous, particularly in terms of engaging gifted students in open-ended, complex science study. Teachers and curriculum developers should note, however, that the process of developing and implementing units utilizing the PBL approach is a complicated one that requires a considerable investment of time and effort—although, in the end, the result can be a highly satisfying experience for all involved.

Scientific Habits of Mind and Inquiry-Based Learning

Because of its requirement that students define and investigate an ill-structured problem PBL is one example of inquiry-based learning in science curricula and instruction. However, other forms of inquiry-based learning should also appear throughout science curricula and in every science classroom because the nature of science itself involves inquiry and exploration. Thus, science education should encourage habits of curiosity, observation, and logic, along with the communication skills to share ideas.

Science projects can be the ultimate inquiry learning experience and can result in the ultimate advanced product: a scientific paper, poster, or presentation. A student formulates a scientific question, does the intellectual work required to decide how to solve it (whether through observation, experimentation, or calculation), and then does the real work needed to arrive at a solution. The student then writes up the results and communicates them to others. These steps are exactly the same as the steps a working scientist goes through when doing research; a successful science project, then, teaches the student how science is actually done.

Science projects meet many of the needs of gifted students. They allow students to explore an area of interest in a deep, complex way. They are potentially open-ended, in that most experiments generate more new questions than answers. They are individually paced, allowing gifted students to learn much more rapidly than their age peers. They can be either collaborative, allowing the student to work with someone he or she enjoys, or solitary, allowing the student to follow his or her own muse. Science projects can be used as enrichment, allowing a student who has compacted out of his or her science course to spend science time doing something meaningful. They can also be accelerative, in that they may require the student to learn advanced concepts and work with resources, such as scientific journal articles, normally used by older students or adults. In the early grades, science projects can be simple and guided by the teacher. For teachers with no background in experimental design, the book *Students and Research: Practical Strategies for Science Classrooms and Competitions* (Cothron, Giese, & Rezba, 2000) can serve as a useful guide in providing strategies and activities for rigorously teaching the components of experimental design in the classroom.

More advanced students benefit from mentoring as they proceed through their science projects. Mentors can be anyone from a high school science teacher, to a working scientist, and they should be chosen based on the specific interests of the student. The Johns Hopkins publication *Imagine* frequently runs stories describing mentored student projects and students and teachers thinking about doing such projects will find such examples valuable. For subscription information or to read a sample issue, visit the Center for Talented Youth's publications Web site at http://www.jhu.edu/~gifted/pubres/pubres.html.

National science competitions, such as the Intel competition, are available to the most talented and advanced high school science students. These competitions reward students for completing deep, careful, insightful science projects. Most competitive projects submitted to these contests have been completed under the guidance of a professional scientist or mathematician. Competitions provide opportunities for students to present their work in public, interact with like-minded students, and earn scholarship money and recognition. The Johns Hopkins University Study of Exceptional Talent (SET) Web page has a comprehensive list of science competitions for middle school and high school students at http://www.jhu.edu/~gifted/set.

Constructing Meaning and Metacognition

Much of the scientific enterprise is an effort to observe and understand the natural world more fully; consequently, science itself is largely about constructing understanding. Students should be encouraged to see science as a process of exploring what is already known about a topic, framing new questions, gathering and interpreting data, and framing conclusions and even more new questions, thus appreciating the active role of the scientist in constructing meaning from observation and experimentation. Such a view of science is far more interesting and complex, as well as more representative of the discipline, than viewing science as the information contained in a textbook.

The metacognitive behaviors of planning, monitoring, and evaluating one's progress on a project, along with reflection on thought and performance in general, are critical elements to incorporate into a science curriculum. Several examples of effective metacognitive tools have been noted earlier in this chapter; in PBL units, the Need to Know board and problem log help students to monitor and reflect on their ongoing work, and the development of good science projects requires careful planning, monitoring, and evaluating throughout. Indeed, outlining and following an experimental design requires metacognitive reflection at every stage. Moreover, teacher questioning strategies can support metacognitive behaviors through both formally developed discussions and informal conversations during activities involving scientific processes.

Materials and Resources

Creating new curricula takes a great deal of time, and there are few commercially available science curricular materials specifically designed for gifted students. Inevitably, then, it is necessary to adapt existing materials to the needs of the gifted. Thus, an exploration of existing materials and their quality in terms of science content and the learning opportunities they provide is useful as a starting place for selecting resources worth adapting for use with gifted students.

The following pages discuss three categories of curricular materials: (1) basal/stand-alone texts designed to be the basis of a student's total science program for a whole year; (2) modular curricula packaged in independent units organized around a single large concept or content area, which can sometimes be used in place of a basal text; and (3) supplementary curricular materials with a narrower focus that can be used to enrich existing curricula. High-quality examples of each of these will be discussed below, along with commentary regarding appropriateness and adaptations for gifted students.

Basal Textbooks

Basal textbooks produced by large educational publishers are the most commonly used curricular materials in science classrooms in the United States. In recent years, there have been changes in the appearance, if not necessarily the substance, of basal textbooks. These changes appear to have occurred in response to the science reform movement, as well as to the adoption of state-specific science standards. Many basal textbook series now look more like modular curricula: comprehensive textbooks, meant to be used for a whole school year, have been divided into short, quasi-modular units. Publishers have incorporated references to broad concepts, such as *models* and *change*, into the teacher's guides. The content of basic science chapters is related to the real world by boxed discussions of current problems such as pollution and global warming. Hands-on activities are suggested, in a nod to inquiry-based learning, although they often are not truly required for a student to progress through the curriculum. Extension activities that reach out to math, literature, and even music are suggested in an attempt to build interdisciplinary connections.

Despite the popularity of basal textbooks, serious complaints about their quality have persisted for at least 40 years. In the best-selling book, *Surely You're Joking, Mr. Feynman* (Hutchings, Leighton, Feynman, & Hibbs, 1997), Nobel-prize-winning physicist Richard Feynman described his experience as a textbook reviewer for California in the 1960s:

> Finally I come to a book that says, "Mathematics is used in science in many ways. We will give you an example from astronomy, which is the science of stars." I turn the page, and it says, "Red stars have a temperature of four thousand degrees, yellow stars have a temperature of five thousand degrees, . . ."—so far, so good. It continues: "Green stars have a temperature of seven thousand degrees, blue stars have a temperature of ten thousand degrees, and violet stars have a temperature of . . . (some big number)." There are no green or violet stars, but the figures for the others are roughly correct. It's *vaguely* right—but, already, trouble! That's the way everything was: Everything was written by somebody who didn't know what the hell he was talking about, so it was a little bit wrong, always! And how we are going to teach well by using books written by people who don't *quite* understand what they're talking about, I cannot understand. I don't know why, but the books are lousy; UNIVERSALLY LOUSY!
>
> Anyway, I'm *happy* with this book, because it's the first example of applying arithmetic to science. I'm a *bit* unhappy when I read about the stars' temperatures, but I'm not *very*

unhappy because it's more or less right—it's just an example of error. Then comes the list of problems. It says, "John and his father go out to look at the stars. John sees two blue stars and a red star. His father sees a green star, a violet star, and two yellow stars. What is the total temperature of the stars seen by John and his father?"—and I would explode in horror. (p. 267)

The authors of a recent study of middle school physics textbooks echo Feynman's criticisms (Holden, 2001). The study, headed by physicist John Hubisz, concluded that they are plagued with "a very large number of errors, many irrelevant photographs, complicated illustrations, experiments that could not possibly work, and diagrams and drawings that represented impossible situations" (p. 587).

Although many basal science textbooks have serious accuracy problems, there are exceptions. The Biological Sciences Curriculum Study (BSCS), for example, offers outstanding high school biology textbooks with strong research evidence of effectiveness (Boyce et al., 1992). One of their texts, the *BSCS Blue Version* (BSCS, 1996), was specifically designed for gifted high school students and has been widely used in honors biology classes. Although the first edition of this textbook was written long before the most recent science curriculum reform movement, it incorporated many of the elements desired by the reformers, and its structure has been maintained in subsequent editions. The authors use the broad theme of evolution to organize the book's treatment of biology. The text begins with molecular evolution and the origin of life; biochemistry, physiology, and taxonomy follow naturally within the evolutionary framework. The laboratory activities teach important concepts, as well as scientific process skills. The extension activities are worthwhile and add depth. The book's coverage of biology is advanced and complex enough to meet the needs of gifted students.

Even in well-constructed textbooks, some errors are inevitable because science changes so rapidly. Information in textbooks is, necessarily, old compared to information available in the most current issues of scientific journals. This can be turned into a teaching opportunity: Teachers of the gifted can take advantage of inaccuracies or outdated information in the textbook to teach critical thinking and scientific process skills. *The New York Times* Tuesday science section, magazines such as *Scientific American*, scientific journals such as *Science* and *Nature*, the PBS series *NOVA*, and the National Public Radio program *Science Friday* can be used to bring new scientific ideas into the classroom. When information from a reliable, independent source contradicts information presented in the textbook, fruitful class discussions can result.

Spiraling, a fundamental structural principle of K–8 basal science textbook series design, poses a particularly challenging problem for gifted students. Within a spiraled science curriculum, topics are repeated from grade to grade with only marginally deeper coverage at higher levels than at lower levels. This curricular structure may be helpful for students who forget significant amounts of material from year to year or may not have understood the material when it was first presented. For gifted students, however, covering a concept once, in depth, is preferable to seeing it over and over again, year after year. Too much repetition results in loss of interest and motivation.

Subject acceleration can be used to minimize the repetition created by spiraling and meet the gifted student's need for faster pace and greater depth. Side-by-side comparison of seventh-grade life science and high school biology textbooks, for example, reveals that the high school textbooks cover the same material, but more accurately and comprehensively. Allowing gifted middle school students to take high school biology in place of middle school life science can help provide the deeper content and greater complexity they require.

Accelerating gifted middle school students into high school physics and chemistry is more complicated than accelerating them into high school biology because the math background required is greater. Fortunately, many schools are now allowing subject acceleration in mathematics in elementary school. This creates a pool of gifted middle school students who have the mathematical skills needed to take high school science courses early. Students who complete the introductory high school science courses in middle school will be ready to move on to Advanced Placement courses or concurrent college science courses when they enter high school. These accelerated science students will have a strong foundation for participation in high school science competitions such as Intel's Science Talent Search. Chapter 2 of this book, as well as the Johns Hopkins University's Center for Talented Youth's (CTY) *Acceleration: Knowing Your Options* (CTY, 1995), are useful resources when deciding how and when to use subject acceleration.

Bringing advanced textbooks down to lower grade levels for gifted students has been successful in a variety of settings. The *Blue Version* has been used successfully with gifted seventh graders (BSCS, 1996) and also has been used by CTY's Fast-Paced High School Biology summer course. Many of the summer talent search programs for gifted middle school and high school students use higher level science textbooks. Syllabi for CTY's program, Duke University's Talent Identification Program (TIP), Northwestern University's Center for Talent Development (CTD) program, and Denver University's Rocky Mountain Talent Search (RMTS) program are available online; some include the names of the textbooks used in the courses. Textbooks used in the summer programs might also be appropriate for gifted students in their regular schools. Research evidence indicates that not only can academically talented students complete a 1-year course in biology, chemistry, or physics in 3 weeks in such summer programs, but they master the subject and do well in subsequent science courses (Lynch, 1992). Clearly, the textbooks used by these programs are adequate even for academically talented students moving at a very rapid pace.

Modular Curricula

Modular curricula are made up of independent units that, taken together, can substitute for a basal textbook series or, taken individually, can be used to enrich a science program. Individual modules cover a single scientific topic in depth, rather than skimming lightly over the surface of many topics, as basal textbooks frequently do. Many take a significant amount of class time. The order in which modules are presented can vary, allowing a school to rotate individual modules through its science classrooms, rather than buying a full set for each classroom. These modular programs are frequently developed by university- or museum-based curriculum development programs, rather than by textbook publishers, and such consortia often produce the best modular materials (Boyce et al., 1992, 1993; Johnson et al., 1995).

The curriculum developers at the Lawrence Hall of Science (LHS) in Berkeley, CA, have created a number of high-quality science curricular packages. The most comprehensive LHS program is the Full Option Science System (FOSS). FOSS can be used in place of a basal textbook series for students in grades K–6; new modules for use in middle school are available, and FOSS will eventually be useful as a substitute for basal textbooks at the middle school level. Each module includes a teacher's manual and a kit containing all of the materials necessary for the module's activities.

FOSS is an inquiry-based and activity-rich program. The science content and process aspects of FOSS are of exceptionally high quality, and concepts are presented in significant depth (Boyce et al., 1992). The teacher's manuals include unusually interesting extension activities that might have special appeal for gifted students. FOSS was designed as a "developmentally appropriate" curriculum, thus its developers made assumptions about the cognitive skills and learning abilities of students at different ages that may not be accurate for gifted students. Its inquiry-based approach and depth, however, compensate for this potential flaw, as do the high-level extension activities suggested in each module. Acceleration is possible with FOSS; gifted students can move more quickly through the modules than suggested by the developers, or modules can be brought down from higher grades for use by groups of gifted students. FOSS has an excellent Web site, with sample activities and a detailed explanation of the curriculum, at http://www.lhs.berkeley.edu/FOSS/FOSS.html.

The University of Hawaii's Curriculum Research and Development Group's Foundational Approaches in Science Teaching (FAST) is another excellent modular program. FAST was recently identified as an exemplary science program by the U.S. Department of Education's Expert Panel on Mathematics and Science Education, based on its quality and on the research evidence available for its effectiveness (OERI, 2000). An inquiry-based program designed to address the needs of students aged 12–15, FAST offers three courses organized around three strands: ecology, physical science, and "relational study," a strand focusing on the connections between scientific disciplines and real-world problems. Laboratory work and field work are integral to each module, and the scientific process aspects of the curriculum are exceptionally strong. While FAST, like FOSS, is a "developmentally appropriate" curriculum, acceleration should be possible.

Other excellent modular curricula include Science and Technology for Children (STC, 1991–present), produced by the National Science Resources Center, and the modular materials produced by 1960s curriculum development projects such as Elementary Science Study (ESS, 1966–1986) and Science Curriculum Improvement Study (SCIS, SCIIS, 1961–1988). These inquiry-based modular programs are excellent in terms of scientific process and content, and they are flexible enough to allow acceleration of gifted learners. Some of the modular curricula, such as FOSS, have been adopted as basal textbook equivalents by a number of states. Replacing basal textbooks with well-designed modular programs would improve science instruction at the K–8 level for all students, as well as enhance the education of gifted students.

Supplementary Curricula

The best supplementary curricular materials, like the best modular materials, allow students to focus on a single scientific topic in depth. Unlike modular materials, supplementary materials are only used to enrich an existing science program, rather than serving as the basis for a science program. There is a much higher degree of variability in style, content, and quality among supplementary materials than there is among modular materials; while this allows teachers of the gifted to match materials to the needs and interests of individual gifted students, it also makes choosing appropriate curricular materials more complicated.

Some of the commercial materials, while superficially attractive to students and teachers, are scientifically shallow or, worse, rife with error. One lesson from a popular teacher-produced supplementary science activity series, for example, asks students to weigh a stick of gum, chew it, and then weigh it again; students are then told to infer that the difference is the weight of the sugar initially present in the gum. For a thinking student, this "experiment" raises more questions than it answers:

- Was sugar the only ingredient that chewing the gum removed?
- The package lists flavoring and other ingredients. Don't they get removed by chewing the gum, too?
- Doesn't the saliva added to the gum during chewing weigh something?

In the lesson, there is no provision for allowing students to question the (flawed) assumption that underlies the activity; critical questioning of this assumption would be a useful exercise for developing scientific habits of mind. The instructional purpose of this activity appears to be to convince students that gum contains lots of sugar and therefore chewing it could be bad for their teeth. Requiring students to chew gum in class, though, defeats even this simple health message.

Other supplementary activities lack a scientific purpose. Writing a friendly letter from a plant to the Sun when studying photosynthesis may look like "writing across the curriculum" if students are simultaneously learning how to write friendly letters in their English class, but it has no scientific value. The student learns nothing new about science from the experience. Writing a lab report on a photosynthesis experiment, on the other hand, both enhances the student's writing skills and strengthens his or her understanding of photosynthesis and the scientific process. Lab reports have significant metacognitive value. Interdisciplinary extension activities need to have a significant instructional purpose for all disciplines involved, not just the nonscience disciplines.

Simulation activities are popular in supplementary science materials, although many of these are less useful to students than they seem at first glance. In a second activity from the teacher-produced science activity series mentioned above, students spend a class period observing the attributes of Gummi worms and creating a classification system based on these attributes. While learning about scientific classification is valuable, this activity takes a shallow, dead-end approach to the topic. Students would be better off, for example, creating a classification system based on leaves they collect on the playground and then comparing it with the scientific classification system found in a field guide to trees. Leaves are more complex and interesting than Gummi worms, and students can hone their observation skills better on these irregular, natural materials. They can also compare their observations and classification systems with those of professional scientists by using the field guide, an activity with metacognitive value. Students who classify Gummi worms, on the other hand, learn nothing new about the natural world or about scientific classification techniques.

The rapid expansion of the Internet has resulted in the availability of Web-based science investigations that provide simulated experiments. Like the Gummi worm example, though, many of these simulations offer less-authentic scientific inquiry opportunities than they appear to on the surface. Kitchen chemistry with safe, real materials is open-ended and more satisfying than any simulated explosion—and mixing baking soda and vinegar is a memorable experience. Gifted students need the depth and complexity that doing inquiry-based science with natural materials provides.

Fortunately, there are many excellent supplementary science materials that can be used to provide the deep, complex, rapid-paced learning opportunities that gifted students need. As was true for the modular materials described above, many of the best supplementary curricular materials are produced by university- or museum-based curriculum developers. The Lawrence Hall of Science, in particular, has produced several excellent supplementary science curricular packages.

Great Explorations in Math and Science (GEMS) originated as a series of museum activities at the Lawrence Hall of Science, and each GEMS unit has undergone extensive testing. GEMS units are available for preschoolers through middle school students. Many of these units can be used with a wide range of ages, although gifted students will be ready for a given GEMS unit before their age peers and probably before they reach the age range suggested by the unit developers. The topics that are covered range from animal behavior, to kitchen chemistry, to geology, allowing a teacher to match GEMS activities to the interests of small groups of students. For each GEMS unit, there is a short, inexpensive teacher's guide that contains instructions for a series of well-integrated activities that allow students to explore a topic in depth. The teacher's guide also contains background information and suggests extension activities. Material kits for GEMS units are now available, although most of the materials needed are easily obtained consumer items.

Teaching Integrated Math and Science (TIMS) is another excellent supplementary curriculum, produced by a team working at the University of Illinois at Chicago and available on CD-ROM. TIMS activities are mathematically rigorous and do an excellent job of teaching experimental design and data analysis. Most TIMS activities are physics experiments, although there are some chemistry and biology activities, as well. Each TIMS activity focuses on an experiment. The same four-step process is used in each unit:

1. draw a picture of the experiment;
2. collect data and organize it into a data table;
3. make a graph of the data; and
4. answer a series of rigorous comprehension questions.

TIMS activities could be used to strengthen an existing physical science program or to allow gifted students who have compacted out of their science classes to work on their scientific process skills. The activities are designed for students in grades 1–9; again, gifted students might be able to succeed in TIMS activities well ahead of their age peers. This curriculum would be particularly useful for students who are preparing for their first meaningful independent science project, since the experimental-design and data-analysis components of the curriculum are so strong.

Conclusion

Matching existing curricular materials to the needs of individual gifted students can be a challenge, but it is both manageable and worthwhile. When used to support significant instructional objectives and chosen with the learning needs of individual gifted students in mind, good materials can help even the most gifted students learn something new in science class every day.

It's the last day of May, and the state science tests have been over for 2 months. Susie, the fourth grader who was accelerated into your sixth-grade science class, was one of the highest scorers on the state science exam. Jamal and Ben, after a rocky start, worked well together on their science project and went to the district science fair, where their solar energy project won a third-place ribbon. You haven't seen Gloria for 3 weeks because she compacted out of the last quarter's instruction and has been doing a botany project with the greenhouse manager at the local nursery, but the G/T resource teacher reports that she is doing well. Rosa, Jennifer, and Susie enjoyed doing the GEMS convection unit with the G/T resource teacher, and their weather poster has been donated to your classroom for the benefit of next year's students. While you wish that Sam had passed the state assessment, you know that you were able to help him work around his learning disability well enough to come close to passing. It's been a good year and, thanks to Tommy, you know that there are solid arguments on both sides for whether Pluto can be considered a planet.

Key Points Summary

❑ Science reform recommendations and adaptations needed for gifted and high-ability learners converge well in high-quality curricular materials.
❑ Problem-based learning and other inquiry-based approaches model how real scientists practice their craft.
❑ Meaningful science projects and competitions can serve as powerful learning tools for gifted students.

❑ Selecting high-quality science curricular materials for core and supplementary use is vital to serving the needs of high-ability learners.

❑ In general, modular materials are superior to basal texts for use with high-ability learners, while supplementary materials vary in quality.

References

American Association for the Advancement of Science (AAAS). (1990). *Science for all Americans: Project 2061.* New York: Oxford University Press.

American Association for the Advancement of Science (AAAS). (1995). *Benchmarks for science literacy on disk* (Version 1.0 for Apple Macintosh) [Computer software]. New York: Oxford University Press.

Barrows, H. S. (1998). *The tutorial process.* Springfield: Southern Illinois University School of Medicine.

Biological Sciences Curriculum Study (BSCS). (1996). *Biological science: A molecular approach* (BSCS Blue version, 7th ed.). Lexington, VA: Heath.

Boyce, L. N., Bailey, J. M., Sher, B. T., Johnson, D. T., Gallagher, S. A., & VanTassel-Baska, J. (1992). *Consumer's guide to science curriculum.* Williamsburg, VA: Center for Gifted Education, College of William and Mary.

Boyce, L., Bailey, J., Sher, B., Johnson, D., VanTassel-Baska, J., & Gallagher, S. (1993). *Curriculum assessment guide.* Williamsburg, VA: Center for Gifted Education, College of William and Mary.

Center for Gifted Education. (1997a). *Acid, acid everywhere: A problem-based unit.* Dubuque, IA: Kendall/Hunt.

Center for Gifted Education. (1997b). *Guide to teaching a problem-based science curriculum.* Dubuque, IA: Kendall/Hunt.

Center for Talented Youth. (1995). *Academic acceleration: Knowing your options.* Baltimore: Center for Talented Youth, Johns Hopkins University.

Cothron, J., Giese, R., & Rezba, R. (2000). *Students and research: Practical strategies for science classrooms and competitions* (3rd ed.). Dubuque, IA: Kendall/Hunt.

Dods, R. F. (1997). An action research study of the effectiveness of problem-based learning in promoting the acquisition and retention of knowledge. *Journal for the Education of the Gifted, 20,* 423–437.

Gallagher, S. A., & Stepien, W. (1996). Content acquisition in problem-based learning: Depth versus breadth in American studies. *Journal for the Education of the Gifted, 19*, 257–275.

Gallagher, S. A., Stepien, W., & Rosenthal, H. (1992). The effects of problem-based learning on problem solving. *Gifted Child Quarterly, 36*, 195–200.

Holden, C. (2001). Physics texts found wanting. *Science, 291*, 587.

Hutchings, E. (Ed.), Leighton, R., Feynman, R. P., & Hibbs, A. (1997). *Surely you're joking, Mr. Feynman!* New York: Norton.

Johnson, D. T., Boyce, L. N., & VanTassel-Baska, J. (1995). Science curriculum review: Evaluating materials for high-ability learners. *Gifted Child Quarterly, 39*, 36–43.

Lerner, L. S. (1998, March). State science standards: An appraisal of science standards in 36 states. *The Fordham Report, 2*. Retrieved May 25, 2001 from http://www.edexcellence.net/standards/science/science.htm

Lerner, L. S. (2000). Good science, bad science: Teaching evolution in the states. *The Fordham Foundation*. Retrieved May 25, 2001 from http://www.edexcellence.net/library/lerner/gsbsteits.html

Lynch, S. J. (1992). Fast-paced high school science for the academically talented: A six-year perspective. *Gifted Child Quarterly, 36*, 147–154.

National Research Council. (1996). *National science education standards*. Washington, DC: National Academy Press.

Patel, V. L. & Kaufman, D. R. (2001, February 2). Medical education isn't just about solving problems. *The Chronicle of Higher Education, 47*, B12.

Stepien, W. J., Gallagher, S. A., & Workman, D. (1993). Problem-based learning for traditional and interdisciplinary classrooms. *Journal for the Education of the Gifted, 16*, 5–17.

U.S. Department of Education, Office of Educational Research and Improvement. (2001, January 8). *National science curriculum for high ability learners project*. Retrieved May 25, 2001 from http://www.ed.gov/offices/OERI/ORAD/KAD/expert_panel/highabilityproj.html

VanTassel-Baska, J. (1986). Effective curriculum and instructional models for the gifted. *Gifted Child Quarterly, 30*, 164–169.

VanTassel-Baska, J. (1995). The development of talent through curriculum. *Roeper Review, 18*, 98–102.

Adapting Social Studies Curricula for High-Ability Learners

by
Molly M. Sandling

As a high school social studies teacher, you teach three 90-minute blocks of freshman world history. The scope of the course is 1000 A.D. to the present, but your textbook ends with the French Revolution in 1789. This leaves more than 200 years of history for which you, the classroom teacher, are the sole source of information. This requires you to locate resources around which to construct all classroom activities and assignments. The tasks of identifying resources and planning goals and activities are further complicated by the heterogeneous grouping of your classes. While many, if not most, of your students have little or no prior knowledge of the material, some gifted students have such extensive knowledge of given topics that they seek a level of complexity and detail that would overwhelm those encountering the information for the first time. Given the time-consuming and complex task of finding and organizing materials and activities to meet your goals, how do you adapt your curriculum and instruction to challenge the gifted learner effectively?

The task of teaching social studies is complicated by the great number of disciplines comprised by the term—history, geography, economics, and political science, to name just a few—and the vast body of content, process, and concept knowledge. Complicating the teacher's task still further, particularly in the elementary grades, is the relatively limited amount of time allocated to social studies during the school day.

Moreover, limited curricular materials make it difficult for a teacher to provide sufficient resources for a diverse group of students to explore topics adequately. Even given the vast resources on the Internet, a teacher can spend hours searching for appropriate materials to supplement, or substitute for, a textbook's presentation of information. Once the materials are located, the teacher must then construct meaningful activities in which to use them. In addition, lessons must introduce the ideas and processes of the social sciences to an increasingly uninformed majority of students while challenging gifted students with greater depth and advanced content.

This chapter attempts to provide teachers with ideas about how to differentiate in social studies by exploring each of the elements of curricular reform from Chapter 1 as they apply in this domain. As in previous chapters, this discussion utilizes examples from existing social studies curricular materials to demonstrate the reform elements at work.

Learner Outcomes of Significance and Habits of Mind

An overarching goal of social studies curricula and instruction in general as stated by Bragaw (1996), is to "help young people develop the ability to make informed and reasoned decisions for the public good as citizens of a culturally diverse, democratic society in an interdependent world" (p. 12). Despite the diversity of disciplines covered by "social studies" in schools, the habits of mind required to achieve this goal are similar. Students become good citizens by understanding the problems of the world, and these problems are more deeply understood when approached from the multiple perspectives of the various disciplines. By studying the world's various cultures in anthropology, the interaction of places and peoples in geography, the sequence of events in history, or the social causes and consequences of human behavior in sociology, a student gains a deeper understanding of what is happening in the world, allowing him or her to make reasoned decisions more effectively. Furthermore, such reasoning ability is achieved not by memorizing a series of facts in a textbook, but by developing the habits of mind utilized by practitioners of the social science disciplines:

- analyze documents of all sorts to detect bias, weigh evidence, and evaluate arguments;
- distinguish between fact and conjecture and between the trivial and the consequential;
- view human subjects nonjudgmentally and with empathy instead of present-mindedness;
- recognize and analyze the interplay of change and continuity;
- recognize the complexity of causality and avoid easy generalizations and stereotypes while analyzing how change occurs;
- recognize that not all problems have solutions;
- understand how people and cultures differ and what they share; and
- analyze how the actions of others, past and present, influence our own lives and society.

Developing these habits of mind in our students requires teachers to teach inclusiveness and complexity through active learning and critical inquiry. Students must study the many people whose actions and interactions with others have shaped world events. Students must also be repeatedly confronted with the reality that what they are studying was not inevitable—different choices made by many different people could have led to dramatically different outcomes. Learner outcomes reflecting this level of complexity are important for all students, but especially for the high-ability student, whose cognitive capacity necessitates such challenge for new learning to occur. An example of a key goal and related learner outcomes reflecting essential habits of mind in history for high-ability learners is demonstrated in Table 9.1 with alignment to national standards for history (National Center for History in the Schools, 1996).

Beyond the goal and outcome level, every lesson should incorporate behaviors requiring the use of significant social science habits of mind and should also encourage critical inquiry. A basic geography lesson on maps can have students question why a map is drawn a certain way, rather than merely accepting the map: Why is the world map centered on the U.S. or on the Atlantic? How else could it be drawn? How

Table 9.1
Key Goal and Related Learner Outcomes

Goal	Sample Student Outcomes	Related National Standards
Develop skills in historical analysis and primary source interpretation.	Define the context in which a primary source document was produced and the implications of context for understanding the document.	*Historical Research Capabilities* • Marshal contextual knowledge and perspectives of the time and place and construct a sound historical interpretation. *Historical Issue -Analysis and Decision Making* • Marshal evidence of antecedent circumstances and contemporary factors contributing to problems and alternative courses of action.
	Analyze a document to define problem, argument, assumptions, and expected outcomes.	*Historical Comprehension* • Reconstruct the literal meaning of a historical passage. • Identify the central questions the historical narrative addresses.
	Evaluate the influence of author and audience bias in a given document. Describe an author's intent in producing a given document based on understanding of text and context.	*Historical Analysis and Interpretation* • Identify the author or source of the historical document or narrative. • Compare and contrast differing sets of ideas, values, personalities, behaviors, and institutions.
	Validate a source as to its authenticity, authority, and representativeness.	*Historical Research Capabilities* • Interrogate historical data.
	Research short- and long-term consequences of a given document.	*Historical Analysis and Interpretation* • Challenge arguments of historical inevitability. • Hypothesize the influence of the past.
	Analyze effects of given sources on interpretation of historical events.	*Historical Analysis and Interpretation* • Analyze cause-and-effect relationships and multiple causation, including the importance of the individual, the influence of ideas, and the role of chance.

Note. "Goal" and "Sample Student Outcomes" from *Defining Nations: Cultural Identity and Political Tensions* (p. 5), by M. M. Sandling, 2000, Williamsburg, VA: Center for Gifted Education, College of William and Mary. Copyright © 2000 by the Center for Gifted Education. Reprinted with permission. "Related National Standards" from *National Standards for History* (pp. 18–19), by the National Center for History in Schools, 1996, Los Angeles: Author. Copyright © 1996 by the National Center for History in Schools. Reprinted with permission.

does its focus reveal the point of view of the cartographer?

These habits of mind can also be developed through the use of specific strategies that students may employ in a variety of contexts. For example, "Reasoning About a Situation or Event" (see Figure 9.1) is an application of Paul's (1992) Elements of Reasoning that helps students to identify the many people who are involved in a given circumstance and their points of view and then to evaluate the implications of the coexistence of these diverse positions. This approach could be used across social studies courses to focus on the complexity of world events and to develop an awareness of the possibilities for alternative outcomes. In addition, every one of the social science disciplines incorporates analysis of documents, written and otherwise, and relies upon this analysis to understand the perspectives of people and events. By emphasizing strategies for primary source analysis in the curriculum, teachers provide challenging reading materials, as well as complex interpretive tasks, that support students in developing the habits of critical inquiry that they can then use every day in confronting the enormous amount of information they receive from the newspaper, television, Internet, and other sources.

Beyond general strategies, certain content lends itself better to teaching specific habits of mind. In the sample lesson *Tensions in the Former Yugoslavia* (Sandling, 2000), the situation in the Balkans following the break-up of the former Yugoslavia provides an opportunity for students to grapple with the idea that people and cultures differ, but share a common humanity; to explore the complexity of cause; and to consider the possibility that not all problems have workable solutions. Court cases, such as the Sacco and Vanzetti case in the 1920s (see the sample lesson *Sacco and Vanzetti* [Center for Gifted Education, 2001a]), can be presented to students first without their outcomes, thus allowing students to weigh evidence and evaluate arguments while stressing historical empathy as they attempt to understand the values and views of the historical actors. Engagement in real-world issues, with emphasis on the complexity of circumstances, encourages critical reasoning even as it helps students develop a knowledge base of social science content, thus representing several significant areas of learner outcomes in this subject.

Higher Order Reasoning

In order to develop the habits of mind of the social sciences and to achieve significant outcomes, students must move beyond the memoriza-

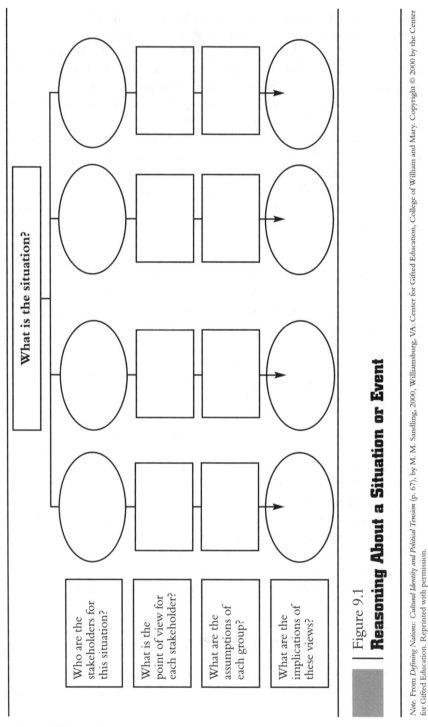

What is the situation?

Who are the stakeholders for this situation?

What is the point of view for each stakeholder?

What are the assumptions of each group?

What are the implications of these views?

Figure 9.1
Reasoning About a Situation or Event

Note. From *Defining Nations: Cultural Identity and Political Tension* (p. 67), by M. M. Sandling, 2000, Williamsburg, VA: Center for Gifted Education, College of William and Mary. Copyright © 2000 by the Center for Gifted Education. Reprinted with permission.

Sample Lesson
Tensions in the Former Yugoslavia

Instructional Purpose:

- To identify cross-cutting and overlapping cleavages in populations.
- To use maps to examine the ethnic divisions in the former Yugoslavia.
- To write a persuasive paragraph using evidence.

Activities and Questions:

1. Simulate the process of group formation. Tell students to form groups with other students in the classroom based on shared elements of their identity (e.g., aspects of family, race, ethnicity, beliefs, values, nationality, social aspects, class, time, and place). Give them no further directions.

2. Have each group report on what elements of identity unite the group. Then, ask questions that will require students to question the way they grouped themselves:

   - All of you are students in this school and in this class, so why didn't you all group together?
   - In what ways are you different from others in your group? In what ways are you like students in the other groups? Why did you choose the particular elements you did for grouping purposes?
   - What other ways could you form yourselves into groups? On which elements of identity might you base those decisions? How would the makeup of the groups change?
   - What can we learn about how people identify and group themselves based on this activity?

3. Point out to students that, depending on what elements of identity they stressed, they may find themselves in different groups with different people; that, in some way or another, they share an element of their identity with every

other student. Explain that they have divided themselves based on *cross-cutting cleavages*. Draw a circle on the board and demonstrate that, if the students divide on religion, it may divide them according to this line (draw a line through the circle), but if they divide based on something else, it will divide them differently (draw a different line). Explain that some societies are like this. Ask what the benefits would be of having a society that is divided by cross-cutting cleavages. What would be the drawbacks? What other ways can a society be divided besides cross-cutting?

4. Explain that the other division discussed by geographers is *overlapping cleavages*. What do you think this means? Draw another circle with one line through it and say that, in some groups, the people are divided by religion, by nationality, and by economic status and that all the lines fall in the same place, so the group is always divided into the same subgroups no matter what element of identity you look at. What are the benefits of a society's being divided by overlapping cleavages? The drawbacks? Can you think of a place in the world where this is the case?

5. Tell students that they are going to look more closely at the effect of the collapse of communism by studying the area of the former Yugoslavia. With the end of a common political identity, people in former communist areas searched to identify themselves as countries and political boundaries shifted. Today, students will look at cleavages in those areas and discuss why there has been such tension in the region since the early 1990s. Explain that the divisions in this region have existed for many, many years, and it is necessary to examine the history of the area in order to understand the present.

6. Break students into small groups and have each group represent either the Serbians, Bosnians, or Croatians of the former Yugoslavia. Provide each group with relevant documents to read and encourage them to identify the groups in conflict in their region and the issues that divide these groups.[1] Give the students the form for Reasoning About

a Situation or Event (see Figure 9.1) and have them identify the central issue and major stakeholders. Then, have each group complete the point of view, assumptions, and implications for one stakeholder, followed by a large-group sharing and discussion of the overall chart based on the following questions:

- What are the implications of the interactions of these various assumptions?
- What has caused these very different points of view to develop?
- Are the cleavages in this society overlapping or cross-cutting?
- What are potential areas of conflict in this situation?
- What are potential areas of compromise in this situation?
- What are the possible resolutions for this situation?
- What would have to happen for those resolutions to be possible?
- What might be obstacles to achieving a resolution in this situation?
- What elements of identity are being stressed?
- How is identity influencing the tensions and the possibilities of resolution?
- Is it possible for these people to continue living together in one country? What would have to happen for that to work?

7. Share with students accounts of experiences in Kosovo from Mertus' (1999) *Kosovo: How Myths and Truths Started a War*. Ask students to consider the following questions: Who is stirring up the divisions? How is identity being used to make people act?

8. Give students a map depicting the ethnic groups of Serbia. Ask students how they would draw political boundaries in this region to best resolve the situation. Have them present their solution to the class along with a justification for it. (To facilitate this process, you could give groups of students a map on an overhead transparency that they could

then put up for the class to see, or use one overhead and erase the lines between groups.) Ask:

- How small of a group should an individual country be?
- In general, where should political boundaries be drawn in the world and according to which elements of identity?
- What other issues are at stake when drawing political boundaries?

9. Ask students to write individually an answer to the following scenario:

> You are a Department of State official. Write a memo to the President about what the United States' role should be in the former Yugoslavia. What potential conflicts might you encounter and what possible compromises can be reached?

---

1. Suggested documents: Serbia: excerpts from speeches given by Radovan Karadzic to key Serb Democratic Party [SDS] activities in the fall of 1991, available online at http://www.barnsdle.demon.co.uk/bosnia/kara.html; Bosnia: excerpts from a 1994 speech by Alija Izetbegovic, available at http://www.bosnia.org.uk/bosrep/jan95/address.htm; Croatia: Excerpts from letter from the Deputy Prime Minister and Minister for Foreign Affairs of Croatia, 29 January 1994; letter from the Permanent Representative of Croatia to the UN 15 September 1994; letter from the President of the Republic of Croatia [Franjo Tudjman] to the UN Secretary-General 12 January 1995. All reprinted in Trifunovska (1999).

Note. From *Defining Nations: Cultural Identity and Political Tension* (pp. 50–64), by M. M. Sandling, 2000, Williamsburg, VA: Center for Gifted Education, College of William and Mary. Copyright © 2000 by the Center for Gifted Education. Adapted with permission.

Sample Lesson
Sacco and Vanzetti

Instructional Purpose:

- Describe both sides taken in the Sacco and Vanzetti trial.
- Examine primary sources (e.g., speeches, court records), and construct the positions of the prosecution and the defense.

Activities and Questions:

1. Lesson to be taught in the context of studying the period of the 1920s in the United States and the Red Scare of that time. Give students a brief overview of the events surrounding the arrest of Sacco and Vanzetti from background information. Then, divide students into small groups and share documents on the case, including details of the arrest and evidence and the defendants' final statements to the court (from Monk, *Ordinary Americans*). Assign half of the groups to be the prosecution, and the other half of the group to be the defense. Briefly establish the position of each side: The prosecution believes the men are guilty and wants them convicted, while the defense feels they are innocent and unjustly accused.

2. Give students the "Assessing an Issue" handout and have them complete their side's influences on point of view and evidence based on their role. Then, bring students together in a large group and discuss the two sides. Once the evidence is established, discuss and further develop the position statements for each side.

3. Ask:

   - Why did the two groups have different reactions to Sacco and Vanzetti when they were examining the same incident and the same evidence?
   - Do some factors influence the decision more than others do? Which ones and why? Give examples and explain (*bias* or *point of view*, *beliefs*).

Have students discuss what were influences on the prosecution's and defense's viewpoints and add to their sheets. If all that was different was your point of view, what does that tell you? What does this mean for us when we look at documents, listen to someone speak, or encounter information? (*We need to be careful—they could be twisting the truth or seeing it differently because it is their point of view. The information may be wrong because of how someone saw it.*)

- What are some ways we can prevent our point of view from making us misinterpret information we receive? (*Be aware of our point of view, try to take other points of view.*)

4. Ask students to weigh both sides and hypothesize or guess what they think the jury decided. Encourage healthy mini-debate. Explain the jury's actual decision, reiterating the Red Scare social and political context.

- What does this case reflect about the workings of the political system during this time?
- How did the inputs of the Red Scare affect the processes of the political system?

Close with the 1977 decision to reopen the case and reverse the 1921 decision as described in the background information.

Background Information:

Red Scare:
Following World War I and the rise of communism in the Soviet Union, socialist ideologies spread around the world. The majority of U.S. citizens were alarmed by the rise of socialism, and, in May 1919, mobs in a dozen U.S. cities broke up socialist parades, injured hundreds, and killed three people. Americans believed they were under attack and that their political system was going to be overthrown because communist ideology talks of a worldwide revolution. In addition, postwar demobilization led to inflation, unemployment, and waves of strikes—3,600 strikes in

1919. People and Congress blamed the Bolsheviks for the unrest. This fear led to government-led raids of homes, meeting halls, and social places where people were arrested without warrant, beaten, and sometimes deported.

Sacco and Vanzetti:

On April 15, 1920, two payroll guards from a shoe factory in South Braintree, MA, were shot and killed by two men. The culprits escaped with the payroll and $16,000 in a get-away car with several other men. Several days later, the car was found abandoned in the woods several miles away from the crime. Eyewitnesses said they believed the criminals were Italians. On May 5th, the police arrested two Italian immigrants, Nicola Sacco and Bartolomeo Vanzetti. The two men had no police records, but both were carrying loaded pistols.

1921 Decision in Commonwealth of Massachusetts vs. Sacco and Vanzetti:

After 5 hours of deliberation, the jury declared Sacco and Vanzetti guilty of murder in the first degree. The penalty was death in the electric chair. For 6 years there were appeals, and public support for Sacco and Vanzetti grew as millions around the world demonstrated on their behalf. A police captain later stated that the bullet did not necessarily come from Sacco's gun, and a man named Celestino Madeiros confessed that he was a member of the gang that killed the guards, but the judge did not believe him. On August 22, 1927, the two men were electrocuted.

1977 Decision:

In 1977, Massachusetts Governor Michael Dukakis commissioned a study of the case. After the report was finished, Dukakis signed a proclamation that stated in part that Sacco and Vanzetti had received an unfair trial. "The very real possibility exists that a grievous miscarriage of justice occurred with Sacco and Vanzetti's deaths."

Issue:

Prosecution's Position:

Defense's Position:

What are the possible influences on their particular viewpoints?

Influences on Prosecution's Viewpoint:

Influences on Defense's Viewpoint:

Supporting Arguments

	Prosecution	Defense
Evidence:	1.	1.
(Key points of support)	2.	2.
	3.	3.
	4.	4.
	5.	5.

tion and repetition of facts to active analysis and higher order thinking. In the social sciences, each discipline seeks to answer a set of questions that students should also attempt to answer. Anthropologists attempt to understand human development while recognizing the value of all cultures. Economists analyze how the choices people make about resources then affect public policy and international interactions. Geographers examine where things are located and why and how the interactions among these locations shape the world. Historians study human activity and thinking in past societies and try to construct an understanding of the effects of past actions on the contemporary world. Political scientists focus on how public choices are made, by whom, for what purposes, and with what consequences, both locally and globally. Sociologists study the pattern and organization of human behavior and the causes and consequences of that behavior. These questions have no answer that students can look up in a book and memorize; instead, students must be taught to examine sources of information and draw conclusions.

Students need a structure to guide their reasoning and to help them identify the questions to be asked. Once such a method has been taught to students, they can use it in any discipline and in their daily lives. Paul's (1992) reasoning model, outlined in Chapter 3, serves as a useful and versatile tool in social studies courses. As they use and reflect upon the Elements of Reasoning, students should recognize possibilities for varied interpretations and conclusions about issues, and they should attempt to identify and examine the various perspectives and sources of evidence that can affect their inferences. The graphic organizer, Reasoning About a Situation or Event (Figure 9.1), provides a framework within which students may identify different points of view in a situation and then examine the reasons for each point of view and the possible outcomes related to each perspective. Thus, it helps students avoid thinking of historical events as inevitable. Moreover, the Elements of Reasoning also provide foundations for strong questions for discussion and writing about historical events and documents. Their alignment to key elements of persuasive writing (discussed in Chapter 6) is relevant for writing in social studies, as well.

Conceptually Oriented Curricula

As discussed in Chapter 5, the use of concepts promotes higher order thinking. Identifying and organizing information under an "umbrella" concept helps to generate questions of data and aids in analyzing new experiences or evidence (Beyer, 1971). In addition, concept development is a tool that enables students to evaluate evidence and construct chains of causality. It is impossible to do advanced reasoning and real-world problem solving without knowledge of important concepts and how they function within and across disciplines.

A conceptual framework for organizing and understanding information is critical in all of the disciplines, including the social sciences. Social science content, whether government, history, economics, or geography, consists of large amounts of factual knowledge, much of which is rather abstract in nature (e.g., the concepts of supply and demand in economics). Also, many aspects of the social sciences are comparative in nature, and students are repeatedly called upon to compare familiar events and processes with other places, circumstances, and historical periods (Schecter & Weil, 1996). For example, students may be asked to analyze the similarities and differences between the Revolutionary War and the Civil War in the United States. A concept-based instruction in social studies is crucial in making this volume of information meaningful; without the concepts, students get lost in the isolated facts and cannot perceive the whole or make useful comparisons (Kneip, 1989; Wesley & Wronski, 1973). Thus, incorporation of concept development activities represents one of the central best practices in social studies instruction (Shaver, 1991).

Because social sciences are concerned with so many aspects of the human condition, many of the universal concepts discussed in Chapter 5 apply well to this subject area. Moreover, each of the specific social science disciplines includes numerous concepts specific to themselves that students must understand as foundations of those disciplines. Figure 9.2 lists some of the major concepts across all the social sciences, along with some of the discipline-specific concepts that can be used to inform instruction in each of these areas.

When concepts are to be used as a focus for instruction, it is important that students first receive instruction on the concept and are then given many opportunities to practice using that concept within the content. By varying the approach to the concept throughout a unit of instruction, a teacher can alter the degree of complexity and help students to develop a better understanding of the concept. The sample lesson *Sacco and Vanzetti* (Center for Gifted Education, 2001a) does not ask students to analyze a specific system fully; instead, students focus only on the influence of one major event on a political system, with acknowledgement of other influences in the larger context. The sample lesson

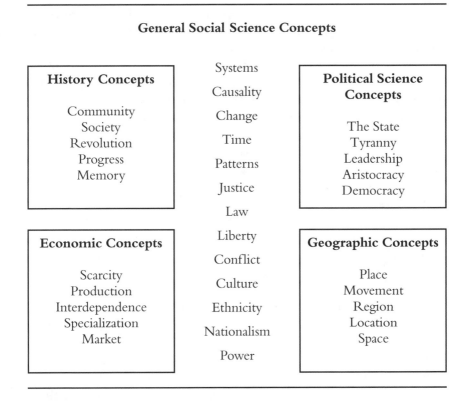

Figure 9.2
Concepts in the Social Sciences

Tensions in the Former Yugoslavia (Sandling, 2000) addresses the concept of *nationalism* with an added level of complexity by asking students to look at how nationalism shapes and is shaped by the concept of *identity*. By such variation and yet consistency in the treatment of central concepts, the curriculum supports students in deep reflection upon the place of those concepts within their understanding of the world.

Substantive Content

Inextricably linked with conceptual learning is substantive content—drawing upon the complex knowledge, principles, and questions that represent the essence of the social sciences disciplines. High-ability students can quickly grasp the vocabulary and basic facts presented in class. To be challenged and successful, these students need to go deeper, engaging in the habits of mind of the discipline. In order to move beyond simplistic, rote memorization, such students need rich sources of information from which to draw conclusions. One key element of achieving this goal is to make heavy use of primary source documents in social studies education. Using primary sources as central reading materials and textbooks only as supplements can greatly increase the complexity of the learning process for students. Primary sources engage them in the historian's task of trying to construct an understanding of past people and events instead of reading and digesting someone else's summary; such sources allow a more direct exploration of the perspectives, biases, and emotions of the stakeholders, and they are not influenced by the degree of hindsight that affects secondary source accounts. Figure 9.3 is a model for analyzing primary sources that helps students explore key aspects of a source's *context*, the text of the source itself, and critical analysis elements of reliability, authenticity, and potential and actual consequences.

Secondary sources are, of course, useful and important for students to review for background knowledge and wider perspectives; indeed, many of the questions on the analysis chart in Figure 9.3 are generally best answered from a review of related secondary sources. Secondary sources are also useful for teacher reference and for content coverage across the span of a course because of the great volume of information generally included. Nevertheless, teachers of high-ability learners should consider how much of the secondary material students can cover on their own, leaving class time for in-depth analysis of primary sources and the writings of great thinkers in the social sciences. For example, instead of memorizing a list of causes of World War I, students can read documents and study events of the time to develop their own tentative understandings of key issues, followed by a guided debriefing with the teacher. Rather than just reading that Thomas Paine's *Common Sense* influenced the patriots in the Revolutionary period, students can read from *Common Sense* itself and compare its concepts and rhetoric to those of the Declaration of Independence. Similarly, students studying government or economics should explore the actual writings of political theorists and economists and work with teacher guidance to understand the attempts to realize the theories of these thinkers.

In addition to the use of primary source documents to support the notion of substantive content, students should also engage in exploration of the tools and concepts of the disciplines as a component of

Document Title:

Establishing a context and intent for the source:

Author:
Time/When was it written?
Briefly describe the culture of the time and list related events of the time:
Purpose (Why was the document created?)
Audience (For whom was the document created?)

Understanding the Source:

What problems/issues/events does the source address?
What are the main points/ideas/arguments?
What assumptions/values/feelings does the author reflect?
What actions/outcomes does the author expect? From whom?

Evaluating/Interpreting the Source:

Authenticity/Reliability. (Could the source be invented, edited, or mistranslated? What corroborating evidence do you have about the source? Does the author know enough about the topic to discuss it?)

Representative. (How typical is the source of others of the same period? What other information might you need to find this out?)

What could the consequences of this document be? (What would happen if the author's plans were carried out? What could happen to the author when people read this? How might this document affect or change public opinions?)

What were the actual consequences? What really happened as a result of this document? Short-term? Long-term?

What new or different interpretation does this source provide about the historical period?

Figure 9.3
Analyzing Primary Sources

Note. From *The Road to the White House* (pp. 192–193), by the Center for Gifted Education, 2000, Williamsburg, VA: Author. Copyright © 2000 by the Center for Gifted Education. Reprinted with permission.

substantive content, thus connecting the three dimensions of the ICM and encouraging development of disciplinary habits of mind. For example, instead of merely learning how to *use* scale to measure distance on a map. From an elementary school on, students should develop an understanding of *what scale is* and how cartographers use it as they study geography. Students of economics and sociology should learn about the predictive and descriptive models used in these disciplines and practice their use. Simulations of political and societal situations also allow students to utilize authentic tools and concepts within content study.

Content can be made more substantial by broadening the scope of information covered, making it more multicultural or global in focus, and by providing materials that allow students to explore and draw conclusions. The sample lesson *Chinese Thought and Education* (Center for Gifted Education, 2001b) is an example of substantive content for primary students. This lesson not only teaches students who Confucius was, but has them analyze and interpret some of his sayings. The sample lesson *Tensions in the Former Yugoslavia* (Sandling, 2000) does not *tell* students the causes of conflict; rather, the students explore documents to build an understanding of the tensions. Students analyze multiple perspectives in the conflict, allowing them to appreciate the difficulty in resolving the issues. Similarly, a discussion of the Stamp Act crisis during the Revolutionary period in American history may be enhanced by reading the actual documents written at the time and discussing the fundamental assumptions about political authority that existed on all sides of the conflict. An entire unit's content can take on a greater degree of complexity by focusing on a theme or concept. Instead of just teaching about the Presidency, have students learn about the Presidency while using the concept of *leadership*. Thus, substantive content is supported by integration with the other two dimensions of the ICM—process and concept—and also justifies them more thoroughly by providing worthwhile material for wrestling with these dimensions.

Multicultural/Global Emphasis

One way rich content and a realistic paradigm of the world can be achieved in social studies education is by expanding one's view to incorporate a greater number of human actors. A broader understanding emerges when students examine the multiple perspectives and

Sample Lesson
Chinese Thought and Education

Instructional Purposes:

- To explore the ancient Chinese system of education and civil service examinations.
- To introduce the Chinese philosopher Confucius and his teachings.
- To recognize the importance of following rules for behavior.

Activities and Questions:

1. [Lesson presented in the context of a study of ancient China.] Tell students that, in ancient Chinese societal structure, most people were peasants; generally, they were poor farmers. There were some merchants who sold and traded goods; the merchants were higher in the societal structure than the peasants and usually were wealthier. Above these were the group known as the scholar-gentry, who held important positions in the government. Have students think about how people who work for the government get to their positions. Ask them to imagine being locked into a small, closet-size room for several days to take a very hard test. Explain that this was how the Chinese tested people who wanted to work for the government or in the "civil service." The exams tested people's knowledge of books of history, poetry, and philosophy, including the teachings of an influential Chinese philosopher called Confucius.

2. Distribute a handout of the following text and read with students.

    Confucius was a great philosopher, or thinker, of ancient China. He was born about 2,500 years ago, in about 551 B.C. (help students find and label this date on their timelines).

    The dynasty ruling in China at that time was called the Chou or Zhou dynasty, but many other powerful families had control over different areas of the country, and these families and their armies fought many battles with one another.

Confucius was very interested in learning when he was young, but not everyone in his time was allowed to have a formal education, only the children of the royalty and nobility. Confucius' father had a job in the government, so Confucius was able to study with tutors. He loved to learn and tried to learn everything he could. He hoped someday he could be a government official who advised the rulers on wise decisions, but he had trouble finding such a position and getting rulers to listen to him. Many other students listened to Confucius, though, and soon he started teaching others what he had learned and was learning. He traveled around the country and taught anyone who wanted to learn from him. He had many ideas about how people could get along with each other by following certain rules and customs. He also thought the government should always be trying to make life better and safer for the people. Even though Confucius never found the kind of job helping rulers that he wanted, he had many followers throughout his life who learned from him and tried to follow his teachings.

We do not have any of Confucius's own writings, but his students wrote down many of his important ideas after he died. These teachings were collected in a book called the Analects. *An example of Confucius's teaching is in the statement,*

"Do not do unto others, what you would not want others to do to you."

Write this statement on the board and ask students to explain what they think the statement means and if they have heard similar statements before.

3. Divide students into small groups. Give each group one of the quotes listed below. Ask each group to read the quote, discuss the meaning of the quote, and then choose a way to share the teaching with the class. They may choose to draw a picture of an event the quote might apply to, act out a situation, or write a group story relating to the quote. Invite students to share what their groups have done.

- I hear and I forget. I see and I remember. I do and I understand.
- Our greatest glory is not in never falling, but in rising every time we fall.
- If you make a mistake and do not correct it, this is called a mistake.
- Learn as if you were following someone with whom you could not catch up, as though it were someone you were frightened of losing.
- Put me in the company of any two people at random—they will invariably have something to teach me.

4. Wrap up the discussion by explaining to students that the influence of Confucius was strong and long-lasting in Chinese society and the value he placed on learning was a value that has been shared by many in Chinese society throughout history. Remind students of the comment earlier in the lesson that those who took the civil service exams had to know of Confucius' teachings. Also discuss with students the idea of working hard to learn and how that relates to the idea of working hard in general; remind them of the readings on Chinese farming they studied previously and the value placed on hard work by the Chinese people. Do you think Confucius valued hard work? Why or why not?

Note. From *Ancient China: The Middle Kingdom* (pp. 96–103), by the Center for Gifted Education, 2001, Williamsburg, VA: Author. Copyright © 2001 by the Center for Gifted Education. Adapted with permission.

experiences of a given event or situation, whether that is a historical event, a current economic trend, or the distribution of natural resources. Students should be exposed to the perspectives of diverse ethnic and cultural groups and should attempt to view issues, events, and concepts from the viewpoints of these groups. Incorporating these multicultural perspectives especially benefits high-ability students by enabling them to confront the complexity of society.

Only in recent years has the focus of history instruction started to shift away from being the history of "winners." Textbooks and instruction have long focused on the powerful and the successful, as well as the perspective of the present, examining the viewpoints and actions of the individuals and groups who have most obviously created the world we live in today. Little time has been spent on people, ideas, and cultures that "failed or were overwhelmed by others." The problem with this approach is that those who "failed" still shaped the world in which we live; in their interactions with the "winners," ideas were exchanged and the winners were affected by the act of overwhelming or replacing the less successful. Expanding one's view beyond the "winners" also means looking at the voices of ethnic, racial, religious, and ideological minorities. Their ideas were not the ones the majority followed, but society was influenced by their existence and had to respond to them. For example, the sample lesson *Sacco and Vanzetti* (Center for Gifted Education, 2001a) looks at two Italian immigrant anarchists who were part of a radical fringe group in the United States in the early 20th century. While these two men and those who shared their ideas were not successful in achieving their goals, U.S. citizens at the time responded strongly to them, altering U.S. behavior and views. Today, American memory and thought have been shaped by the treatment and deaths of these two men. By expanding social studies instruction to include the perspectives of multiple cultures, students can more clearly see the contingency of events and how the decisions, actions, and interactions of many individuals, rather than an inevitable sequence of events, shaped our world. This awareness of the possibilities for change can then lead students to take social action now and in the future. With solid instruction in the habits of mind of the social sciences, students can develop informed opinions on important issues and work to address those issues, thus exemplifying the civic education desired (Banks, 1995; Bragaw, 1996).

Beyond focusing on individuals and specific events, a balanced multicultural emphasis in the social studies curriculum also requires examining situations in their larger global context over extended periods of time to explore the world's complexity and its interconnectedness. For example, the Great Depression, or any economic trend, was not solely dependent on conditions in the United States, but was a result of decisions and conditions around the world. The sample lesson *Tensions in the Former Yugoslavia* (Sandling, 2000) looks at multiple perspectives within a context and then has students look at the event in its larger global setting. Students first analyze the multiple ethnic groups at odds in the former Yugoslavia and then analyze the larger repercussions of this ethnic division by examining how the tension shapes U.S. actions. Politics, economics, history, and geography do not happen in a vacuum; they are all shaped by national and international forces. By confronting events in their larger global setting, students gain a deeper understanding of why things happen as they do, which enables them to address today's important issues more knowledgeably and effectively.

Interdisciplinary and Intradisciplinary Connections

People are not only influenced by the actions of other individuals and political and social organizations; they are also affected by things such as religion, music, art, and literature. In turn, the cultural products of a people are influenced by political, economic, and military events. Therefore, studying these other disciplines can shed light on what motivates and influences human actions. Gifted learners can make connections at abstract levels and benefit from a more holistic approach, rather than compartmentalizing history, government, literature, and music. The resulting instruction does not just involve reading a piece of literature and identifying how the time period is reflected in it; instead, students examine the interplay between literature and reality and increase their understanding of both.

The title of "social studies" reflects important connections across disciplines, as it combines into one school subject multiple social science disciplines. Within social studies, various fields of study can enrich one another. The geography of the Balkans helps explain the historic and current events in that region; an understanding of politics sheds greater light on the significance of Sacco and Vanzetti; and geographic regions and boundaries in the U.S. influence the process of electing a President. Interdisciplinary connections can also enrich and inform the social studies. Literature lends itself easily to enhancing history instruction, through both the study of literature written in a given place and time for its ability to capture and demonstrate culture and the study of high-quality historical fiction that deliberately provides insights into the past. Music, art, and architecture may also be used to teach about cultures, demonstrating the values and visions of creators and the effects of their work, from Gregorian chant to rock'n'roll, from the Italian Renaissance to the Harlem Renaissance, from the ancient Egyptian pyramids to the skyscrapers of the modern metropolis. Understanding physical science concepts makes geographic features and environmental issues such as the Dust

Bowl crisis of the 1930s more meaningful, and math can be used to increase an understanding of the electoral college system or the effect of immigration quotas.

Technology Relevant

The use of technology in the classroom can help provide advanced content and also assist in developing social science habits of mind in students. Television and video can be used to provide students with visual images of the people, conditions, or events being studied, adding complexity to basic facts and statistics by showing details about people, places, and ways of life. Used effectively, documentary footage of the past or of other cultures can make material more meaningful and help students to construct a more complete understanding of it. For example, geography students can discuss population growth around the world, but watching the Zero Population Growth (2000) video and seeing dots appear and start to fill the continents to demonstrate population growth makes the statistics more powerful. Video can also be a tool for authentic assessment of students. Students can create TV advertisements, talk shows, or newscasts; recreate historic events; film documentaries; or create other projects to demonstrate their learning in a real-world task. In all of these cases, however, technology used instructionally or for assessment needs to be incorporated as a tool to support the learning endeavor, not as a substitute for teaching or a time-filler.

As with video, computers enable students to demonstrate learning. Students can use word-processing and desktop publishing to type papers, make newspapers or advertisements, or generate surveys. They can make PowerPoint presentations of research or to make a persuasive argument. Students can also use spreadsheets to analyze data or make Web pages with information, images, and links to other relevant sites. The computer provides a wide range of possibilities that can be adapted to meet the technological abilities of the students.

Computers also enable students to use resources that are not otherwise easily accessible. The Internet and CD-ROMs allow students to do research, explore their interests, and extend the lesson. Many primary source documents are available on the Internet, including things such as World War II propaganda from various countries or posters from Mao Zedong's China, and many of these sites also provide historical commentary and contextual information. Often, it is difficult for students or teachers to find primary source material in school libraries, but the Internet makes it much more accessible. At other Web sites, students can take virtual tours of places like Ellis Island (http://www.ellisisland.com/indexInfo.html) or the Palace of Versailles (http://www.chateauversailles.fr). Students can also use the computer to look at maps, zooming in and out on specific areas, or to check the current world population. Useful map-related sites include the University of Texas' Perry-Castañeda Library Map Collection (http://www.lib.utexas.edu/maps/index.html) and the National Geographic Society's site (http://www.nationalgeographic.com). Thus, technology allows students to explore topics with more depth, viewing images and obtaining information that helps them build a more complex understanding of the material being studied.

Using the Internet does have its pitfalls; sometimes there is no control over Internet sites, so the accuracy or reliability of some sites may be questionable. Students, therefore, need to be taught to be critical users of the Internet so they will know how to analyze a Web site for bias and reliability and to check facts obtained from the Internet with other sources. Developing these habits in students not only reduces the potential problems of using the Internet, but it helps strengthen critical thinking skills. Technology is a powerful tool for students as they construct an understanding of material, explore their own interests, and demonstrate their learning in meaningful ways, and it does all this in a way that is fun and engaging.

Additional important Web sites for every social studies teacher's bookmark list include the National Archives and Records Administration at http://www.nara.gov and the Smithsonian Institution at http://www.si.edu. Many universities and museums also have online exhibits covering a vast array of social science topics; investigation using search engines provides access to many of these sites.

Inquiry-Based Learning

Inquiry teaching was introduced formally to social studies education in the early 1970s. The main goal of this approach was not to provide students with a particular amount of predetermined content; rather, the focus was on teaching children how to learn, acquire information, make meaning from experiences, and find solutions on their own, as well as formulate their own attitudes and values based on these experiences

(Beyer, 1971; Brown, 1996). To achieve these goals, inquiry teaching stressed the development of concepts, generalizations, and intellectual skills instead of presentation of information and memorization.

By stressing the skills for gaining knowledge and examining assumptions and conclusions, the core of inquiry teaching is useful and valid no matter how students' or society's perspectives change. In inquiry teaching, students follow a series of steps. The process begins as teachers allow students to generate and define problems to be solved without limiting the questions to a specific syllabus. In order for students to define a problem, they must become aware of the problem and its immediacy and relevance to their own experience (Beyer, 1971). Teachers can initiate this process by presenting an argument with which the teacher knows students will strongly disagree or that contradicts student biases. Teachers may also introduce conflicting opinions on a topic that will raise questions for students concerning how both sides can exist. These will evoke student concerns and responses and, therefore, a desire to pursue the problem. Whatever the initial approach, inquiry teaching encourages questions that grow out of students' own experiences and beliefs (Beyer; Brown, 1996).

Once the students have chosen and defined a problem to be studied, they must examine their existing knowledge and data, draw logical inferences, and develop a hypothesis, or tentative response to the problem. The hypothesis is crucial, as it guides the investigation of the data and establishes a goal for the inquiry process. The students then gather relevant evidence that supports and possibly contradicts the hypothesis, evaluate the evidence for credibility, and analyze the data for trends, similarities, and differences. They then look for relationships between the evidence and their hypothesis, testing their assumptions against the facts. The process ends as students draw a conclusion based on the experience and generalize that conclusion to new data or experiences. Throughout the process, the teacher piques student curiosity, guides students through the process, and models the use of skills, but does not supply information concerning the content (Brown, 1996). In order to facilitate inquiry, teachers need a considerable knowledge of whatever content the students choose to pursue, and the open-endedness of the process makes it difficult for teachers to assemble resources and plan ahead of time. These methods emphasize the authenticity of tasks and the real-life contexts of students instead of topics and units designed by scholars (Beyer, 1994). In its emphasis on analytical and evaluative skills, inquiry instruction also provides scaffolding for students as they develop the abilities required for critical evaluation of data sources. Considering the many information sources inundating contemporary society, these skills are crucial for student development (Beyer; Wheeler, 1996).

Similar to inquiry instruction in its open-ended aspects and focus on real-world problems, problem-based learning is also an effective model for supporting complex learning in social studies (Stepien, Gallagher, & Workman, 1996). Problem-based learning, discussed in more detail in Chapter 8 as it relates to science instruction, engages students in the exploration of a real-world, ill-structured problem. Both of these models encourage not only the habits of inquiry in the disciplines, but also the habit of recognizing the complexity of problems in the real world and the need for a balanced and multifaceted approach to solving them.

The reasoning model (Paul, 1992) outlined in Chapter 3 and discussed earlier in this chapter also reflects an inquiry-oriented notion that students need to be taught how to think, not just what to think (Paul, Binker, Martin, Vetrano, & Kreklau, 1995). Under this perspective on education, teachers are questioners, not transmitters of knowledge, and they encourage students' metacognitive awareness. In addition, teachers must encourage another dimension of inquiry: the "traits of the reasoning mind," such as intellectual empathy, courage, and humility (Paul; Paul & Elder, 2001). Education must not foster the development of thinking skills while "ignoring the ultimate use to which the learner puts them" (Paul et al., p. 5). This emphasis on the consequences of inquiry teaching for society is particularly significant in social studies, in which society itself is the focus of the content. Through emphasis on responsibility within inquiry, teachers can underscore the importance of empathy for the perspectives of others, the need to clarify issues and justify judgments based on evidence, and the habit of considering the implications and possible contradictions of one's own thinking (Paul et al.).

Constructing Meaning

The integration of substantive content, the reasoning taught in inquiry methods, and the concepts that organize information enable students to construct meaning from the facts they encounter. This is the task of social scientists: to take facts, analyze them, and use the pieces of information to draw conclusions about the people they are studying. For example, historians use photographs, letters, court records, title records, and artifacts to create a narrative of what happened in the past, how, and why.

Therefore, if we are to develop the social science habits of mind and obtain significant outcomes from students, the students must be able to construct meaning from facts and classroom materials. To allow students to construct meaning, teachers must not teach to receive specific student answers or to give students the information to be learned. Instead, students should analyze, synthesize, and evaluate data. As with inquiry, teaching the process of constructing meaning requires scaffolding by teaching students strategies and tools to use while they work to understand the content.

The framework for analyzing primary sources, illustrated in Figure 9.2, is an example of an organizer that helps students construct meaning from a document. The organizer provides a series of questions that guide the student through the process of analyzing and evaluating a source, but the answers to the questions are not directly provided in the text. In the "Understanding a Source" section, the student first identifies the focus of the document, then he or she has to draw conclusions based on reasoning elements about the author's values and assumptions, as well as outcomes the author desires. The final series of questions requires the student to evaluate the document and make connections among the document, its consequences, and the historical period of the text. Answering these questions takes the student beyond reading comprehension and memorization of facts to constructing a more complex understanding of the text and the time period. The same goal can be accomplished in a class discussion through a well-constructed questioning sequence.

Materials and Resources

Providing students with substantive content that reflects multiple perspectives and allows them to construct meaning depends largely upon the materials and resources made available in the classroom. Moreover, given that research in many of the social science disciplines relies largely on interpretation of documents, artifacts, and other resources, supporting student learning through the use of strong sources encourages essential social science habits of mind. Consequently, the selection of appropriate resources is an important element of good social studies teaching. In working with gifted students in particular, issues of providing challenge and complexity arise in both materials selection and in the development of activities around them.

Students should read a variety of sources that reflect various points of view and provide insight into the topic or issues. Resources should be diverse enough to enable students to examine both the "big picture" and the complex details that comprise it. Both teacher and students should have access to general and specific resources that not only achieve the purpose of the lesson or unit, but also support extensions. Sufficient resources will provide the means for students to pursue their interests and go beyond the classroom activities. However, a potential danger arises with the tendency to amass too large a selection of materials. Today, with the Internet, teachers have easy access to a greater wealth of information than ever before. This can make it tempting to provide students with large amounts of resources to "just have a look at," which overwhelms students and makes a lesson too difficult. Moreover, many of the resources available on the Internet are not of high quality, as discussed previously. Careful selection and parsimony are as important as breadth when choosing materials for classroom use.

Variety is a central issue in considering materials selection, with several dimensions to address. A variety of resources will be necessary to obtain a multicultural perspective, but some groups do not have written sources, or their writings and views have not been preserved. Teachers need to try to find other materials that might provide insights into the experiences of these people in order to have a more authentic multiple-perspective emphasis. There should also be a variety of primary and secondary sources. Primary sources will provide insights into individual feelings and experiences, helping illuminate the details that shaped events. Secondary sources will be useful in providing more general knowledge on a topic and provide a summary of multiple people's experiences, helping students to make sense of the details they encounter.

The *length* of a selection is also important to consider when planning for use of given sources. Even for students who are advanced readers, use of short selections is often advisable. Short but substantive reading selections enable teachers to provide lessons in which students can quickly read and comprehend the material, thus allowing more time for in-depth discussion of the issues and concepts contained in the document. If a desired document is fairly lengthy, it may be more beneficial to provide the excerpts that relate most directly to the lesson.

When choosing any source, first consider the *reliability* and *representativeness* of that source. Primary sources reflect the ideas of individuals. If students are going to be drawing conclusions and making generalizations from the documents, then the sources must be reflective of the ideas of a large percentage of the population. If students use documents that reflect the views of one person or a few people, then the conclusions about society the students make will be inaccurate. These documents are still useful and can provide students with important information, but their limited nature needs to be kept in mind. In addition, take into account the purpose of the document. The author's purpose can shape the way information is conveyed, possibly leading to inaccuracies that will affect student conclusions.

Secondary sources are also susceptible to bias. When choosing secondary sources, consider the sources and perspective of the author. No secondary source is purely objective, but some are more agenda-driven than others. Also consider the reliability of a secondary source: Is the author speaking knowledgeably on the topic, or is it ill-informed opinion? Reliability is of even greater importance with the Internet; it is important to know who has supplied the information because there are rarely identifiable editors or publishers that control Web sites. Students should be encouraged to identify the reliability and bias of a source because this is a skill that will be useful to them. While students benefit from critiquing their sources, the classroom teacher has to choose sources responsibly for use in classroom activities.

Authentic Assessment and Products

If teachers are striving to have their students engage in the habits of mind of practitioners of particular disciplines, constructing meaning of the content they encounter, then assessment of students must go beyond reading and answering comprehension questions and tests must not be limited to multiple-choice tasks. Students should be assessed on their performance of the tasks required of historians, geographers, economists, or political scientists. Activities that can be used in any of the disciplines include debates on key issues, designing museum exhibits on a particular event or group, or developing policy statements for a given country about what actions it should take locally and globally. Such activities require not only content learning, but also an emphasis on strong reasoning skills and deep understanding of values, assumptions, and concepts, as well as facts.

Assessment in social studies, as in any of the content areas, should be an ongoing process, occurring not only as the culmination of a unit of study, but within each lesson in which students are engaged. Again, such assessment should be based at least partially on tasks that engage students in the practices of the disciplines they are studying. Geography students can construct maps, create and justify regions in a country, or decide how to draw political boundaries. History classes can evaluate primary sources for authenticity and how representative of the time they are, put historic figures on trial, and discuss issues from the perspectives of various people. Such tasks require students to demonstrate their understanding of the documents and the context in which events occurred; consequently, they also provide opportunities to assess students on multiple goals beyond knowledge of the facts.

Teachers can also assess students by having them create products related to the discipline under study. They may create original artwork that incorporates the themes and values of the Harlem Renaissance of the 1920s or the Renaissance of the 15th and 16th centuries. In political science classes, students can draft legislation and have mock Congresses or simulate an election campaign by writing campaign speeches, developing platforms, and lobbying for changes. Sociology students can create questionnaires, poll students or community members, and analyze their data to draw conclusions about human behavior. All of these methods force students to utilize the skills and information they have gained in the classroom to construct an original expression of what they have learned. Some of the products students develop should be short-term in nature, completed in a single class period or homework assignment, while others should be longer term not only to deepen students' understanding of issues in depth, but also to encourage their metacognition and project-management skills.

One other key issue related to assessment in social studies is the consideration of prior and prerequisite knowledge. Many social studies teachers face the challenge of presenting students with volumes of facts in order to achieve established standards. However, when considering gifted students in particular, pretesting prior knowledge is essential to ensuring that students' class time will not be wasted. By assessing students early in a year or a unit of study on the prerequisite content, or by allowing them to read some background information and then to complete an assessment on that information, teachers free up time from content presentation for these students and expand the time available for engaging in more in-depth, issue-based research and product development.

In order to accomplish all of the assessment goals discussed here, then, assessment in social studies should incorporate pretesting and posttesting, performance-based tasks in addition to more traditional tests, and ongoing formative assessment through lesson activities.

Metacognition

The goal of social studies curricula and instruction is not just to teach students social studies material, but also to develop in them the skills necessary to be responsible citizens. Moreover, professionals in the disciplines recognize that a key element of research is the ability to explicate the research process practiced and to support the validity of findings and conclusions. Therefore, not only should students be taught how to construct meaning from information, but they should also be able to articulate how they accomplished this task. Students should be given long-term assignments in which they must plan how to fulfill the requirements, monitor their progress, and then evaluate their products. These assignments can be tied to classroom activities such as model congresses or simulated campaigns, or they can be individual projects such as research papers, mini-museums, or travel journals. In addition to providing structure to guide students through long-term projects, teachers should actively model metacognition in the classroom and encourage students to do the same. Students should then be assessed not only by the teacher, but also by their own self-evaluation of their performance.

Conclusion

Adapting social studies curricula for high-ability learners depends upon students using the analytical skills of practitioners and having access to primary sources that provide depth in understanding. In order to use the resources, students must have a sufficient background in the content, aided by the use of concepts, and be given instruction and scaffolding in the process of critical thinking. Through the selection of materials at various levels for different students and varying degrees of scaffolding and flexible grouping, teachers can appropriately challenge gifted students within a heterogeneously grouped classroom. Being successful in this endeavor requires a teacher not only to have a good knowledge of the content, but also to be willing to ferret out a variety of engaging and appropriate resources and develop contacts with fellow teachers and practitioners of social science disciplines. Classroom teaching does not, and should not, happen in a vacuum. Constant collaboration with other teachers and social science practitioners will allow a teacher to continually gain new insights and ideas for the benefit of the students.

Key Points Summary

❏ Active learning and critical inquiry are central tenets in teaching gifted students the social science habits of mind.

❏ The use of specific thinking models and tools over time can enhance student understanding of important aspects of social studies learning.

❏ Teaching universal concepts in the social sciences serves to bind together disparate strands of the curriculum while encouraging high-level inquiry.

❏ Concepts in the social sciences may be general, such as systems or causality, or specific to the subdisciplines, such as leadership and tyranny in a study of political science.

❏ Use of extensive primary source material that students must analyze, synthesize, and evaluate emphasizes higher order thinking and problem solving more than the use of survey-like secondary sources.

❏ Incorporating multicultural points of view on history is essential to a broader understanding of significant events and eras.

❏ Use of technology can expose student to multiple perspectives on current issues and lead to a stronger emphasis on assessing credibility of sources.

References

Banks, J. (1995). Multicultural education: Historical development, dimensions, and practice. In J. A. Banks & C. A. M. Banks (Eds.), *Handbook of research on multicultural education* (pp. 3–24). New York: Macmillan.

Beyer, B. K. (1971). *Inquiry in the social studies classroom: A strategy for teaching.* Columbus, OH: Merrill.

Beyer, B. K. (1994). Gone but not forgotten—reflections on the new social studies movement. *The Social Studies, 85,* 251–255.

Bragaw, D. (1996). The social studies: The civic process. In Social Science Education Consortium (Ed.), *Teaching the social sciences and history in secondary schools: A methods book* (pp. 10–36). Belmont, CA: Wadsworth.

Brown, R. H. (1996). Learning how to learn: The Amherst project and history education in the schools. *The Social Studies, 87,* 267–273.

Center for Gifted Education. (2001a). *The 1920s: A system of tensions.* Williamsburg, VA: Author.

Center for Gifted Education. (2001b). *Ancient China: The middle kingdom.*Williamsburg, VA: Author.

Kneip, W. (1989). Social studies within a global education. *Social Education, 53,* 399–403.

Mertus, J. A. (1999). *Kosovo: How myths and truths started a war.* Berkeley: University of California Press.

Monk, L. R. (Ed.). (1994). *Ordinary Americans: U.S. history through the eyes of everyday people.* Alexandria, VA: Close Up.

National Center for History in the Schools. (1996). *National standards for history.* Los Angeles: Author.

Paul, R. (1992). *Critical thinking: What every person needs to survive in a rapidly changing world.* Rohnert Park, CA: Foundation for Critical Thinking.

Paul, R., Binker, A. J. A., Martin, D., Vetrano, C., & Kreklau, H. (1995). *Critical thinking handbook: 6th–9th grades: A guide for remodeling lesson plans in language arts, social studies, and science.* Santa Rosa, CA: Foundation for Critical Thinking.

Paul, R., & Elder, L. (2001). Critical thinking: Nine strategies for everyday life: Part 1. *Journal of Developmental Education, 24,* 40–41.

Sandling, M. M. (2000). *Defining nations: Cultural identity and political tension.* Williamsburg, VA: Center for Gifted Education, College of William and Mary.

Schecter, S. L., & Weil, J. (1996). Studying and teaching political science. In Social Science Education Consortium (Ed.), *Teaching the social sciences and history in secondary schools: A methods book* (pp. 137–170). Belmont, CA: Wadsworth.

Shaver, J. P. (Ed.). (1991). *Handbook of research on social studies teaching and learning.* New York: Macmillan.

Stepien, W. J., Gallagher, S. A., & Workman, D. (1993). Problem-based learning for traditional and interdisciplinary classrooms. *Journal for the Education of the Gifted, 16,* 5–17.

Trifunovska, S. (1999). *Former Yugoslavia through documents: From its dissolution to the peace settlement.* The Hauge, Amsterdam: Martinus Nijhoff.

Wesley, E. B., & Wronski, S. P. (1973). *Teaching secondary social studies in a world society* (6th ed.). Lexington, MA: Heath.

Wheeler, R. (1996). Rx for social studies. *Social Education, 60,* 313–314.

Zero Population Growth (Producer). (2000). *World population* [Video]. (Available from Zero Population Growth, Inc., 1400 Sixteenth St. NW, Ste. 320, Washington, DC 20036)

■| Section III

Introduction

This final section of the book explores in more detail some of the issues surrounding the implementation of curricula and the partner concepts of instruction and assessment. Each of the issues addressed as chapter topics in this section has been touched upon in previous chapters, but is here discussed with additional depth in order to provide practical guidelines for actualizing content-based curricular innovation in schools.

Avery and Zuo explore a process for curricular review and selection of materials and resources that has been utilized in each major content area to

255

examine available resources for appropriateness for high-ability learners. In addition to discussing the steps of the process, the chapter also provides lists of criteria for use in reviewing materials and a listing of recommended resources in each content area, based on prior reviews of existing materials.

Struck and Little focus on the instructional decisions of the teacher still to be made beyond the preparation of a good curriculum. The chapter explores the various influences of the content to be taught, the students who participate, the characteristics of the teacher, and other details of the instructional context that all affect how a curriculum is implemented and what it looks like in action. The critical issue of grouping is also addressed.

Assessment is an essential part of the teaching-learning process, ideally inseparable from curricula and instruction and used to evaluate and inform both. Zuo and VanTassel-Baska address the issue of assessment, exploring the special considerations surrounding the assessment of high-ability students' learning. The chapter also explains technical details of assessment construction, such as reliability, validity, fairness, and test ceiling. Sample assessments are used to illustrate the concepts discussed and to serve as exemplars of assessments for high-ability learners.

Little and Ellis expand the scope of curricula to address issues of alignment, focusing on how curricula developed or selected based on the principles addressed throughout this book may be aligned with other existing curricula and standards to create a more unified approach to learning across the vertical and horizontal spectra in schools. The chapter includes discussion of the exemplary high school programs of Advanced Placement and International Baccalaureate, addressing vertical alignment mechanisms already in place for these programs, as well as methods of considering the goals of these programs in planning scope and sequence for students earlier in their educational progress.

VanTassel-Baska's final chapter continues to explore implementation issues, addressing assessment, staff development, and leadership considerations as central to the implementation of curricular innovation in schools. The chapter utilizes data collected on the Center for Gifted Education's units in science and language arts to demonstrate the importance of systematic curricular assessment, as well as to provide support for the use of curricula developed under the ICM in promoting gifted student learning. It then includes a discussion of research-based practices in staff development, providing a model for staff development designed to support and sustain innovative practice. The issue of leadership is addressed from a theoretical and a practical perspective, exploring the principles and research-based practices that promote learning and change in schools.

These last five chapters utilize the reform principles and research-based practices discussed throughout this book to ground recommendations for implementation in real-world situations. They represent some answers to the practical questions surrounding implementation of curricular innovation, recognizing the essential contextual considerations that must be made in order for curricular change to be actualized. As a group, they serve as a reminder that curricula, instruction, and assessment are an inseparable triad, existing within the real world of schools, and they provide guidance for developing this triad effectively to provide high-quality learning experiences for students.

Selecting Resources and Materials for High-Ability Learners

by
Linda D. Avery
and
Li Zuo

You are a newly hired teacher, assigned to work as a gifted resource teacher. Your new boss is sending you to a conference on gifted education and has given you a purchase order for selecting and purchasing new curricular materials for use in the gifted program. You arrive at the conference exhibit hall and see dozens of booths with materials for teaching gifted students. You want to take advantage of your time browsing to make the best decisions possible about what to buy. However, there are so many materials with different features that you feel a little overwhelmed.

Much of this book has addressed the issue of how to design curricula for the gifted and how to adapt curricula already in place. However, it is not always necessary—or practical—to reinvent the wheel when it comes to finding appropriate curricula to use in teaching gifted students. Many existing resources are of a high quality and include features specifically appropriate to meeting the needs of gifted students or to addressing a given content area at an appropriately high level. However, other existing resources, even those purportedly designed for gifted students, may not actually demonstrate such appropriateness.

A good core curriculum is an essential foundation for exemplary instruction in any content area. In selecting or creating curricular materials, it has become increasingly important to attempt to achieve several goals simultaneously:

- delivery of content that is substantive, up-to-date, and essential to an understanding of major concepts in the field;
- demonstration of practices and "habits of mind" that give students experience in the behavior and thinking of experts in the content field;
- opportunity for students to make connections within and between content areas; and
- encouragement of inquiry and high levels of student engagement in the process of constructing meaning.

These goals are, in some respects, more reflective of instructional practice than of the curriculum per se. However, since written curricular materials are the foundation for implementing such instruction, it is critical for educators to consider the degree to which the written materials demonstrate attention to the features given above in terms of goals, outcomes, and activities.

This chapter will address specific guidelines for selecting curricular resources for classroom use with gifted students by using a curriculum assessment checklist that has been employed in the review of curricula in each of the major content areas (Aldrich & McKim, 1992; Center for Gifted Education, 1999; Gregory, 2000; Johnson, Boyce, & VanTassel-Baska, 1995; Johnson & Sher, 1997). This checklist includes three phases: a review of general curricular design features, a review of specific content area emphases, and a review of features reflecting essential elements for high-ability learners. This chapter includes an explanation of each of these phases, followed by the specific criteria employed, as well as a list of some key resources that are suitable for gifted learners in each of the four major content areas.

Curricular Selection Process

Curricular selection decisions cannot be made lightly, as they impact the expenditure of limited resources and are expected to last over multiple academic years. As a result, it is important to utilize a review and decision-making process that is defensible and wise. A collaborative process that capitalizes on the knowledge and expertise of a number of professionals (teachers, media specialists, consultants, and administrators) helps to bring a balanced perspective to the choices that are made. The process should also be dynamic in that it is revisited annually to incorporate research advances and evolving technology. Like all systemic processes, curricular review is never complete, but is always in a stage of recycling.

Figure 10.1 presents a model of the curricular review process undertaken by the Center for Gifted Education (1997) in reviewing curricular materials to supplement or supplant basal texts. This review process is based on four key steps, starting with the development of criteria to use in the review process. This process of developing criteria requires careful consideration of the ultimate goals of the curricular review, central principles of curricula in general and of the content under study, and influential characteristics of the learners in question. Step 2 involves the identification and acquisition of materials to be reviewed, and Step 3 requires the implementation of the critiquing process. Step 4 involves the comparative analysis across individual units, texts, or resources in order to make the final decision as to how best to deploy funds.

It is our belief that, in order for educators to make informed decisions about instruction, they must first become informed consumers (Center for Gifted Education, 1997). Since textbooks are the curriculum in over 95% of U.S. public schools (Lockwood, 1992), the selection of materials and resources has powerful instructional consequences. Based on the Center for Gifted Education's findings in conducting curricular reviews across the four content areas, no single program will meet the needs of all students at a given grade level. Basal texts, in particular, have been found to be particularly lacking in their capacity to meet the needs of the high-ability learner. Supplementary materials should not "automatically be equated with enrichment," but should instead be examined with an eye toward alignment with curricular standards and instructional objectives (Johnson, Boyce, & VanTassel-Baska, 1995).

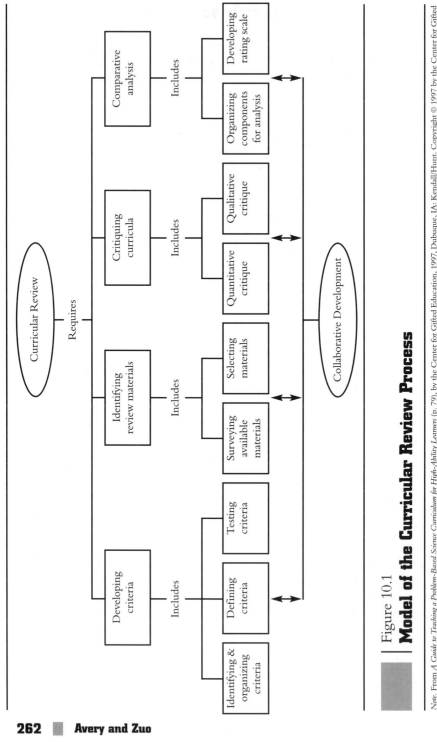

Figure 10.1

Model of the Curricular Review Process

Note. From *A Guide to Teaching a Problem-Based Science Curriculum for High-Ability Learners* (p. 79), by the Center for Gifted Education, 1997, Dubuque, IA: Kendall/Hunt. Copyright © 1997 by the Center for Gifted Education. Reprinted with permission.

The next section of this chapter presents the criteria that were developed by the Center for Gifted Education for use in reviewing materials for high-ability learners. These criteria are presented to educators to help expedite the first step in the curricular review and selection process.

Phase 1: General Curricular Design Features

The first phase of curricular review, incorporating the first set of criteria for consumers to consider in selecting materials, concerns features of general curricular design. This phase acknowledges that a strong curriculum has certain key elements no matter who its intended student audience may be. Although these features may seem at first glance to reflect the foundations of introductory education coursework, they nevertheless do not always appear in useful or fully developed form in many curricular resources.

Phase 1 includes eight categories of criteria to review, including aspects that appear in broad curricular frameworks, as well as within specific lesson plans (Center for Gifted Education, 1997, 1999; Gregory, 2000; Johnson & Sher, 1997). The eight categories, with their specific criteria and brief descriptions, appear below.

1. Rationale and Purpose: This feature addresses the reasons for developing a particular unit of study for use with a given group of learners at a particular stage of development. It provides the reader with a sense of the importance of the topic under study and why it is being taught.
   a. Substantive and worthy: Content is important and valuable; publishers/authors provide reasons why content was selected or the value is self-evident.
   b. Clear and understandable: Teachers can easily tell why the selected content is important. Rationale and purpose are written in meaningful and clear language, rather than in educational or content-specific jargon.
   c. Logical order and integrated structure to scope and sequence: The suggested order for presentation of topics and concepts makes sense both within and between grade levels.
   d. Identified outcomes consonant with purpose: The content and processes identified as desired goals of learning are consistent with the stated reasons to learn.

2. Lesson Objectives
    a. Clear and understandable
    b. Measurable
    c. Related to overall rationale and purpose

3. Activities
    a. Used to explore, reinforce, clarify, and extend content
    b. Use of concrete experiences/manipulatives
    c. Balance of teacher facilitation and student direction
    d. Possibilities for flexible grouping to allow independent, cooperative, or collaborative learning

4. Instructional Strategies
    a. Varied to include lecture, inquiry activities, group and independent work, and engagement with core teaching/learning models
    b. Opportunities for students to discover ideas and concepts
    c. Opportunities for open inquiry through problem finding, problem solving, and decision making
    d. Use of various types of questions, such as convergent, divergent, and evaluative
    e. Opportunities for students to reflect upon and evaluate their own thinking

5. Assessment Procedures
    a. Use of well-designed pretests and posttests linked to core goals and outcomes
    b. Use of authentic modes of assessments for significant student outcomes aligned with unit objectives
    c. Use of multiple means of assessment, including observation and self-assessment
    d. Opportunities for extending learning embedded throughout the lessons
    e. Clearly stated criteria for assessment

6. Materials and Resources
    a. Engaging style of presenting information
    b. Well-aligned with national and state standards of learning
    c. Evidence of attention to multiculturalism or cultural diversity

    d. Evidence of attention to multiple perspectives
    e. Background material for teachers incorporated
    f. Bibliography for teacher support and student extensions
    g. Supportive handouts to enhance learning
    h. Use of print and nonprint resources
    i. Opportunities for students to learn how to use multiple resources

7. Technology
    a. Reasonably up-to-date
    b. Appropriate for age and task
    c. Enhances and complements instruction and learning
    d. Opportunities to assess student technology competence and to teach necessary skills

8. Extensions
    a. Worthwhile and related activities and resources for students to pursue beyond the classroom
    b. Quality homework assignments
    c. Orientation to parents on how to help students' extended learning

Phase 2: Content Area Emphases

Although the features outlined above can be generalized across content areas to represent essential curricular features no matter what the subject, each discipline has its own principles, practices, and habits of mind that are key to support in student learning. Moreover, the treatment of content varies significantly from one subject area to another, with major differences in processes and conceptual elements. Consequently, a curricular review should take into account specific criteria related to the content area under study, and an interdisciplinary curriculum should be reviewed according to as many of the criteria as are relevant.

A first step in the review of a curriculum in relation to the content dimension is to consider the alignment of the materials with national, state, and local content standards. Standards-based reform has had a profound effect on curricular, instructional, and assessment practices and serves as the linchpin of educational accountability initiatives. In our experience, there is substantial convergence between national and state standards in the disciplines of mathematics and language arts, but less in the areas of science and social studies. Nevertheless, this issue of alignment of content with discipline-specific standards should be a first step in the review of all the content areas. The following pages outline additional key criteria in each of the four major content areas.

Language Arts. The language arts standards at both the national and state levels are largely focused on the development and mastery of communication skills (National Council of Teachers of English & International Reading Association, 1996). In a sense, the "process" skills associated with reading, writing, listening, and speaking form the basis of the "content" standards in the discipline of language arts. The standards have become more challenging as a result of an increased emphasis on literary analysis and interpretation, higher order thinking skills, interdisciplinary study, and sensitivity to cultural diversity. The eight criteria detailed below focus on the key features of educational reform that have influenced this discipline:

- integration of the language arts of reading, writing, listening, speaking, and language study;
- emphasis on developing critical reading behaviors;
- incorporation of high-quality multicultural literature and cultural study opportunities;
- choice of literature reflecting cognitive and affective considerations;
- evidence of balanced perspectives presented;
- employment of interdisciplinary approaches to connect language arts to other disciplines;
- incorporation of techniques for enhancing thinking skills; and
- use of questions for discussion that emphasize high-level thinking (VanTassel-Baska, 1998).

Mathematics. In the discipline of mathematics, the introduction of the content standards (National Council of Teachers of Mathematics, 2000) has dramatically impacted the threshold expectations for all students, with many states requiring competency in Algebra I as a condition for matriculation. Furthermore, international comparisons in mathematics and science made available through the Third International Mathematics and Sciences Study (National Center for Educational Statistics, 1996, 1997, 1998) have shown the relatively poor performance of U.S. students in comparison with students in other technologically advanced countries. This impetus to keep our country economically competitive in a global marketplace has led to mathematics standards that emphasize concept learning and reasoning skills. The nine criteria set forth below will help educators evaluate the mathematics content of curricular materials and resources in the wake of these tougher standards:

- organization of content around major mathematical ideas;
- depth in coverage of important mathematical concepts;
- progression from the concrete to the abstract presented in an understandable manner;
- inclusion of the history of mathematical ideas, concepts, and mathematicians;
- opportunities for both inductive and deductive reasoning;
- encouragement of divergent thinking and multiple solutions;
- emphasis on communicating ideas using various modes, including oral, written, and visual forms;
- connection of mathematics to real-world and other disciplines; and
- opportunities for students to develop habits of mind of mathematicians, such as curiosity, tenacity, skepticism, and respect for evidence (Johnson & Sher, 1997).

Science. The proliferation of advances in science and technology have become so commonplace in the last century that we often fail to appreciate the scope and magnitude of the changes that have taken place. Many of the fascinating questions with which we wrestle in modern society are grounded in scientific developments. Dilemmas such as balancing ecological protections with energy demands, deciding to what extent cloning and genetic engineering should be regulated, finding an optimal match between military might and world peace, and deciding what constitutes the initiation and cessation of life are endlessly recast in the wake of scientific and technological progress. Responses to such issues are increasingly complex and sophisticated and require a citizenry that values accuracy, precision, and parsimony in assessing information and has the capacity to identify and reason through alternative choices and consequences. The impact of educational reform in science has been to emphasize the "big picture" through concept development and higher order thinking skills as well as to balance knowledge of science with scientific habits of mind. The following 12 criteria address these emphases:

- coverage of important science concepts in depth;
- accurate and understandable presentation of science;
- linking of topics to broad scientific concepts (intradisciplinary connections);
- linking of topics to ideas outside of science (interdisciplinary connections);
- balance of qualitative and quantitative information;
- balance of theoretical and practical science;
- presence of moral, ethical, and historical dimensions of science and technology;
- opportunities for open-ended scientific investigation (not simply verification exercises);
- laboratory and field work integral to, and integrated with, the curriculum;
- opportunities for students to work together to investigate real-world scientific technological problems;
- inclusion of instruction on building and testing hypotheses; and
- allowance for questioning of assumptions and presentation/ exploration of diverse opinions on scientific issues (Center for Gifted Education, 1997; Johnson, Boyce, & VanTassel-Baska, 1995).

Social Studies. The development of national standards in the various subjects of the social studies (e.g., Center for Civic Education, 1994; National Center for History in the Schools, 1992) has been met with some controversy and debate. Critics have suggested that the standards cover too much material and are burdensome to teachers (Saunders, 1996), praise native cultures while sanctioning European achievements (Saxe, 1995), and undermine the importance of plurality as a seminal tenet in understanding history (Whelan, 1995). There is also a great deal of support for the standards. Evans and Pang (1995) defended the standards as an excellent and inclusive guide to the broad topics and themes appropriate to the study of history, and Mirel and Angus (1994) indicated that the standards benefit U.S. education by equalizing quality and access to challenging programs and courses (cited in Gregory, 2000). Perhaps more than in any other discipline, the articulation of standards has catalyzed discussions about the substance, scope, and nature of social studies education in the U.S. Aspects of educational reform reflected in the social studies standards echo many of the same concerns and themes as the other discipline areas: the importance of critical inquiry and conceptual learning, an emphasis on problem solving and reasoning, recognition of cultural diversity, and connections to current events and real-world issues. The following 12 criteria will help frame these dimensions of a curricular review process for this subject area:

- use of critical inquiry as an analytical tool by students;
- emphasis on the meaning and the process of history;
- use of simulations or scenarios that involve students directly in problem solving;
- use of multiple perspectives in viewing issues or events;
- strong focus on the well-organized essay as a grading tool;
- engagement of students with primary source material;
- provisions for direct field experience;
- adequate components of values education;
- evidence of attention to multiculturalism or cultural diversity in the selection of reading material;
- instruction in problem finding, problem solving, and addressing real-world issues and current events;
- provision of opportunities for linking content to current events so that relevance is established; and
- emphasis on depth, rather than breadth (Gregory, 2000).

Phase 3: Essential Features for Gifted Learners

The third phase in the curricular review and selection process focuses on the specific needs of high-ability students. These students' abilities are accelerated in relation to the general population, and their academic or intellectual precocity often manifests itself in rate, degree, and depth of learning behavior. Such learning needs require that the curriculum be sufficiently differentiated to optimize cognitive and affective development. The 12 criteria that we have found useful in reviewing materials for high-ability students are listed below:

- selected activities, resources, and materials are sufficiently challenging for advanced learners;
- organizing concept is treated in sufficient depth;

- opportunities are provided for creative production;
- opportunities are provided for integrating higher order thought processes;
- issues, problems, and themes are sufficiently complex;
- ample opportunities are provided through unit activities for students to construct meaning for themselves;
- both content and instruction provide for a sufficiently high level of abstraction;
- reading material is sufficiently advanced;
- different levels of ability are provided for by the unit;
- open-ended questions that encourage multiple or divergent responses are identified for the teacher;
- opportunities are provided for independent learning; and
- opportunities are provided for meaningful project work (Center for Gifted Education, 1997, 1999; Gregory, 2000; Johnson & Sher, 1997).

The five essential factors that one should keep in mind in assessing the appropriateness of curricula for gifted learners deal with complexity, depth, challenge, creativity, and acceleration (VanTassel-Baska, in press). Materials that successfully respond to these factors are able to address multiple instructional goals simultaneously. In addition, they provide sufficient opportunities for student work that promotes integration and synthesis of learning. In some cases, this requires the selection of alternative texts and resources; in other cases, the issue is one of supplementation. It is important to keep in mind how the different pieces of a curriculum work together to ensure that instruction is both at a high level and on target. This holistic orientation is achieved by looking at the frequency and distribution of the criteria that are met by each resource reviewed.

Curricular Resources for High-Ability Learners

As a component of our curriculum development work at the Center for Gifted Education at the College of William and Mary, we have reviewed a wide variety of materials within each major subject area. On the basis of the criteria outlined in this chapter, we have identified a number of resources appropriate for use with high-ability learners, as well as teacher resources that are particularly helpful in framing curricula for these students. Teachers will need to make selections from these lists based on their instructional objectives and the level of student development.

Language Arts

American Heritage Dictionary of the English Language (4th ed.). (2000). Boston: Houghton-Mifflin.

The American reader: Words that moved a nation. (1990). Edited by D. Ravitch. New York: Harper Perennial.

Art of the forties. (1991). Edited by R. Castleman. New York: Museum of Modern Art and Abrams.

The arts: A history of expression in the 20th century. (1991). By R. Tamplin. New York: Oxford University Press.

Audiences and intentions: A book of arguments. (1991). By N. M. Bradbury & A. Quinn. New York: Macmillan.

Children in the Holocaust and World War II: Their secret diaries. (1992). Edited by L. Holliday. New York: Pocket Books.

Children of promise: African American literature and art for young people. (1991). Selected by C. Sullivan. New York: Abrams.

Conversations: Readings for writing. (1991). By J. Seizer. New York: Macmillan.

The democracy reader: Classic and modern speeches, essays, poems, declarations, and documents on freedom and human rights worldwide. (1992). Edited by D. Ravitch & A. Thernstrom. New York: HarperPerennial.

Educating for diversity: An anthology of multicultural voices. (1995). Edited by C. A. Grant. Boston: Allyn and Bacon.

Here is my kingdom: Hispanic American literature and art for young people. (1994). Selected by C. Sullivan. New York: Abrams.

Hispanic, female, and young: An anthology. (1994). Edited by P. Tashlik. Houston, TX: Pinata Books.

Merriam Webster's Collegiate Dictionary (10th ed.). (1993). Springfield, MA: Merriam-Webster.

One world, many cultures. (1992). Selected by S. Hirschberg. New York: Macmillan.

Our family our friends our world: An annotated guide to significant multicultural books for children and teenagers. (1992). By L. Miller-Lachmann. New Providence, NJ: Bowker.

Talking to the sun. (1985). Edited by K. Koch & K. Farrell. New York: New York Metropolitan Museum of Art and Henry Holt.

Writing: The story of alphabets and scripts. (1992). By G. Jean. (Jenny Oates, Trans.). New York: Abrams.

Mathematics

Challenge of the unknown. (1986). Produced by A. M. Derry & D. A. Hudson. Wilkes Barre, PA: Karol Media.

Discovering geometry: An inductive approach (2nd ed.). (1997). By M. Serra. Berkeley, CA: Key Curriculum Press.

EPGY (Education Program for Gifted Youth). Stanford University continuing education program. Online: http://www–csli–stanford. edu/epgy

Jane and Johnny love math: Recognizing and encouraging mathematical talent in elementary students: A guidebook for educators and parents. By A. E. Lupkowski & S. G. Assouline. Unionville, NY: Royal Fireworks Press.

Krypto. [Card game]. Palo Alto, CA: Pearson Learning.

Terrapin logo. (2000). [Computer Software]. Cambridge, MA: Terrapin Software.

Mathematics: A human endeavor. (1994, 3rd ed.). By H. Jacobs. New York: W. H. Freeman.

Maya Math. (1995). [Computer software]. By Maya Math: Bank Street College Project in Science and Mathematics. Pleasantville, NY: Sunburst/WINGS for Learning.

SET. [Card game]. Fountain Hills, AZ: SET Enterprises. Online: http://www.setgame.com

Techniques of problem solving (TOPS). Palo Alto, CA: Seymour.

Teaching integrated math and science (TIMS). By the Institute for Mathematics and Science Education. Chicago: University of Illinois at Chicago.

Teaching mathematics. A sourcebook of aids, activities, and strategies. (1988). By M. Sobel & E. Maletsky. New York: Prentice Hall.

Transition mathematics (2nd ed.). (1995). By Z. Usiskin, J. Flanders, C. Hynes, L. Polonsky, S. Porter, & S. Viktoria. Glenview, IL: Scott, Foresman.

Twists and turns and tangles in math and physics. By S. Katzoff. Baltimore: IAAY Publications and Resources, Johns Hopkins University.

The National Council of Teachers of Mathematics publishes numerous resources for teachers of mathematics. A catalog can be obtained from NCTM at (800) 235-7566.

Science

Biological science: A molecular approach (BSCS Blue Version). (1990). Developed by Biological Sciences Curriculum Study. Lexington, MA: D. C. Heath.

Challenge of the unknown. (1986). Produced by A. M. Derry & D. A. Hudson. Wilkes-Barre, PA: Karol Media.

Chemical education for public understanding program (CEPUP). (1990–present). Developed by Lawrence Hall of Science. Menlo Park, CA: Addison-Wesley.

Elementary science study (ESS). (1966–1986). Developed by Education Development Center. Hudson, NH: Delta Education.

Foundational approaches in science teaching (FAST). (1990) Honolulu: University of Hawaii: Curriculum Research and Development Group.

Full option science system (FOSS). (1990–present). Developed by Lawrence Hall of Science. Chicago, IL: Encyclopedia Britannica.

Great explorations in math and science (GEMS). (1990–present). Developed by Lawrence Hall of Science. Berkeley, CA: University of California.

Insights: A hands-on elementary science curriculum. (1991–present). Developed by Education Development Center. Warren, NJ: Optical Data.

LEGO® TC logo. (1989). [Computer Software]. Enfield, CT: Lego Systems.

Middle school of life science. (1991). Developed by Jefferson County, Colorado, Public Schools. Dubuque, IA: Kendall/Hunt.

National Geographic Kids network. (1990–present). Washington, DC: National Geographic Society.

Science—A process approach (SAPA, SAPA II). (1960–1974). Developed by American Association for the Advancement of Science. Hudson, NH: Delta Education.

Science and technology for children (STC). (1991–present). Developed by National Science Resources Center. Burlington, NC: Carolina Biological Supply.

Science curriculum improvement study. (1961-1988). Hudson, NH: Delta Education.

Science for life and living. (1989–present). Developed by Biological Sciences Curriculum Study. Dubuque, IA: Kendall/Hunt.

Search for solutions. (1980). By H. F. Judson. Wilkes-Barre, PA: Karol Media.

Students and research: Practical strategies for science classrooms and competitions. (1989). By J. H. Cothron, R. N. Giese, & R. J. Rezba. Dubuque, IA: Kendall/Hunt.

Teaching integrated mathematics and science (TIMS). (1992–present). Developed by H. Goldberg & P. Wagreich. Chicago: The University of Illinois at Chicago.

Voyage of the Mimi. (1985). Edited by L. A. Driggs. Scotts Valley, CA: WINGS for Learning.

Windows on science. (1990). Warren, NJ: Optical Data.

Social Studies

The American reader: Words that moved a nation. (1990). Edited by D. Ravitch. New York: Harper Perennial.

The ascent of man. (1973). By J. Bronowski. Boston: Little, Brown.

Civilization. (1969). By K. Clark. New York: Harper & Row.

The democracy reader: Classic and modern speeches, essays, poems, declarations, and documents on freedom and human rights worldwide. (1992). Edited by D. Ravitch & A. Thernstrom. New York: HarperPerennial.

History of the idea of progress. (1980). By R. Nisbet. New York: Basic Books.

Immigration: Opposing viewpoints. (1992). Edited by B. Leone & T. O'Neill. San Diego: Greenhaven Press.

Legacy: Challenging lessons in civics and citizenship. (1989). Edited by J. P. Hardin. Winston-Salem, NC: Center for Research and Development in Law-Related Education.

Man: A course of study (MACOS). (1968). By J. S. Bruner. Washington, DC: Education Development Center.

The second voyage of the Mimi. (1989). Edited by L. A. Driggs. Scotts Valley, CA: WINGS for Learning.

Voyage of the Mimi. (1985). Edited by L. A. Driggs. Scotts Valley, CA: WINGS for Learning.

Conclusion

Sound curriculum development requires incredible investments of time, energy, and expertise. Furthermore, curricular units that are created by individual teachers are often underdeveloped and idiosyncratic to the extent that they cannot be used effectively by other teachers. It is our firm belief that it should not be necessary to reinvent the curriculum wheel, particularly for every academic bandwagon that rolls down the road. In fact, it is often a more efficient use of resources to select and integrate materials that have been successfully reviewed and selected by district staff.

Having a prescribed set of criteria to use in curricular review facilitates the implementation of the process. Furthermore, the phasing in of the use of these criteria over three stages allows staff to discard materials that fail to meet the criteria in the early stages of the process. Even as an aid to individual teachers charged with purchasing materials while attending conferences and exhibits, these criteria can help focus one's thinking about important elements of appropriate resources and materials for high-ability learners.

The criteria shared in this chapter can help educators examine resources and justify selection decisions. However, there is an additional question that should underscore this resource identification process: What evidence exists that these materials are effective with high-ability learners? In our experience, very few curricular materials or units have empirical evidence that documents learning gains tied to the use of the curriculum. Every year, the National Association for Gifted Children hosts a competition to identify curricula for gifted learners that meet similar criteria to those cited in this chapter. Although they do not designate any curricular unit as exemplary unless it has evidence of learning effectiveness, the quality of the research undertaken to investigate student impact has been uneven at best. In order to strengthen the quality of curricular interventions with high-ability learners, more teachers and administrators must assume responsibility for testing the efficacy of the materials that are used. This requires focusing on evidence of student learning as a way to measure curricular and instructional effectiveness and a deeper understanding of performance-based methodology to collect relevant empirical data. The adoption of challenging content standards not only raises the stakes on the selection of thoughtful, relevant, and powerful curricular materials and resources, it also propels us to create or tailor student assessment practices to higher levels of sophistication and complexity.

Key Points Summary

❏ It often makes more sense to select materials that have already been developed and tested than to create curricular materials from scratch.

- ❑ The use of a structured checklist can aid both in examining materials and in making decisions about materials and resources.
- ❑ Three phases have been suggested for conducting such a review. Phase 1 focuses on general curricular design features, Phase 2 on exemplary content area emphases, and Phase 3 on essential elements for high-ability learners.
- ❑ While the review process is sequenced so that time is allocated to the most promising materials, a holistic perspective should be taken when choosing among potential texts or resources.
- ❑ We must continue to ask publishers for data on curriculum effectiveness, in spite of their historical absence, in order to stay focused on the right questions in making resource decisions.

References

Aldrich, P., & McKim, G. (1992). *The consumer's guide to English-language arts curriculum.* New York: Saratoga–Warren Board of Cooperative Educational Services.

Center for Civic Education. (1994). *National standards for civics and government.* Calabasas, CA: Author.

Center for Gifted Education. (1997). *Guide to teaching a problem-based science curriculum.* Dubuque, IA: Kendall/Hunt.

Center for Gifted Education. (1999). *Guide to teaching a language arts curriculum for high-ability learners.* Dubuque, IA: Kendall/Hunt.

Evans, R. W., & Pang, V. (1995). National standards for United States history: The storm of controversy continues. *Social Studies, 86,* 270–274.

Gregory, T. (2000). *Social studies curricula for gifted learners in elementary and middle school.* Unpublished master's thesis, College of William and Mary, Williamsburg, VA.

Johnson, D., Boyce, L. N., & VanTassel-Baska, J. (1995). Science curriculum review: Evaluating materials for high-ability learners. *Gifted Child Quarterly, 39,* 36–43.

Johnson, D. T., & Sher, B. T. (1997). *Resource guide to mathematics curriculum materials for high-ability learners in grades K–8.* Williamsburg, VA: Center for Gifted Education, College of William and Mary.

Lockwood, A. (1992). Whose knowledge do we teach? *Focus on Change, 6,* 3–7.

Mirel, J., & Angus, D. (1994). High standards for all? The struggle for equality in the American high school curriculum, 1890–1990. *American Educator, 18,* 4–9, 40–42.

National Center for Education Statistics. (1996). *Pursuing excellence: A study of U.S. eighth-grade mathematics and science teaching, learning, curriculum, and achievement in international context* (NCES 97–198). Washington, DC: U.S. Government Printing Office.

National Center for Education Statistics. (1997). *Pursuing excellence: A study of U.S. fourth-grade mathematics and science achievement in international context* (NCES 97–255). Washington, DC: U.S. Government Printing Office.

National Center for Education Statistics. (1998). *Pursuing excellence: A study of U. S. twelfth-grade mathematics and science achievement in international context* (NCES 98–049). Washington, DC: U.S. Government Printing Office.

National Center for History in the Schools. (1992). *Lessons from history: Essential understandings and historical perspectives students should acquire.* Los Angeles: Author.

National Council of Teachers of English & International Reading Association. (1996). *Standards for the English language arts.* Urbana, IL: Authors.

National Council of Teachers of Mathematics. (2000). *Principles and standards for school mathematics.* Reston, VA: Author.

Saunders, R. M. (1996). National standards for United States history. *Social Studies, 87,* 63–67.

Saxe, D. W. (1995). The national history standards: Time for common sense. *Social Education, 60,* 44–48.

VanTassel-Baska, J. (Ed.). (1998). *Excellence in educating gifted and talented learners* (3rd ed.). Denver: Love.

VanTassel-Baska, J. (in press). *Curriculum planning and instructional design for gifted learners.* Denver: Love.

Whelan, M. (1995). Right for the wrong reasons: National history standards. *Social Education, 60,* 55–57.

Chapter 11

Making Appropriate Instructional Choices

by
Jeanne M. Struck
and
Catherine A. Little

The school district has established mandatory policy around how many hours per day are to be spent on specific aspects of language arts instruction in the primary grades. You are a first-grade teacher with a heterogeneous group of students who are very diverse in terms of their experiential backgrounds and demonstrated ability and achievement in the verbal areas. Your available language arts curricular materials include a wide range of literature selections and teaching ideas, but you are concerned about how to organize your instruction to meet the needs of all your students, as well as the district requirements concerning time spent on various aspects of your language arts teaching.

Teaching, at its fundamental level, is a task focused on the creation of environments in which students are able to interact and learn how to learn (Dewey, 1916; Joyce, Weil, & Calhoun, 2000). The curriculum, naturally, is an element of the teaching-learning environment, as are the instructional processes employed, the teacher, the learners, and the physical context in which they interact.

However, there often is a lack of clarity as to the line that exists between curriculum and instruction. These two concepts are inextricably connected, yet the distinctions between them are important to consider in examining how teachers are able to meet the needs of their students most effectively. In simplest terms, the *curriculum* is the "what" and *instruction* is the "how"; the curriculum is the content and intended outcome, and instruction is the process used to achieve it. No matter how well intended, clearly written, and creatively designed a curricular resource may be, it is not given life until enabled by quality instruction in a classroom setting.

Curricular resources vary in the degree of instructional guidance they give to teachers. Some resources provide detailed guidelines for the instructional strategies and specific questions to be utilized in implementing lessons and activities, while others provide only goals and objectives and brief suggestions regarding specific instruction. Whether the curriculum provides limited or extensive detail, the teacher must still make important choices regarding the instructional process—decisions about how to enact the intended curriculum within his or her classroom with a specific group of students. These choices and the actions following them represent the true artistry of teaching: the power of the teacher to recognize the ideal match between curriculum and context, to pull together the related threads of the worlds inside and outside the classroom to create a learning environment.

The list of variables that affect a teacher's instructional decision making is long and complex, involving the consideration of human and material elements, short- and long-term goals and outcomes, and other factors over which the teacher has varying levels of control. The most salient elements to consider, perhaps, are the role of the teacher, the characteristics of the students, and the content to be addressed (Eggen & Kauchak, 1996; Tomlinson, 1999). Clearly, since two of these central elements vary considerably from classroom to classroom no matter how similar the content required of them, packaged curricular documents cannot fully prescribe the instructional decisions to be made. Also, beyond the individuals participating in the instructional process as teacher and students, other features of the specific classroom context affect how the instructional process is to be carried out. Finally, instructional decisions must consider not only short-term influences, but also long-term implications related to what students will need to learn over a period of time and how they are expected to demonstrate that learning.

This chapter will consider several major factors that influence instructional decision making, focusing specifically on the special considerations that affect decisions in the teaching-learning contexts of gifted students. The discussion begins with a focus on the influence of content, looking at how different subject areas or aspects of them affect instructional choices. Then, the chapter examines the human variables in instructional decision making, exploring the influence of students and their characteristics and of the teacher's aptitudes, interests, and skills. Finally, the chapter explores how classroom-based variables affect instructional issues. Within each of these areas of focus, specific elements that affect the instructional endeavor and influence the choices teachers make are outlined, along with guiding questions teachers may use as they approach their instructional decisions.

The Influence of Content

The discussion of the influence of content on instructional decision making includes two major subcategories. The first important consideration is the issue of instructional alignment—the connection of learning activities undertaken in the classroom to curricular goals and outcomes (Cohen, 1987; Eggen & Kauchak, 1996). The second consideration is the issue of balance—the need to manage activities in such a way that appropriate attention is given to both variety and consistency in developing the activities in which students will engage.

Instructional Alignment

In considering content, instructional choices are integrally tied to curricular goals and outcomes. Strong curricular design involves careful selection of content with an eye to both goals to be addressed and the optimal match between students and the subjects under study. Moreover, good curricular planning also involves organization of content into a written format that outlines how it may best be presented to the diverse group of students in a given classroom, including suggested teaching models, instructional strategies, and assessments to support and measure effective learning. However, as teachers select, develop, and personalize a curriculum, the degree to which their enacted activities align with intended goals becomes central to determining the effectiveness of the instruction.

Thus, instructional decision making commences with examination of curricular goals and learner outcomes. Every instructional decision should be rooted in the intended outcome for students, with consideration of both the content addressed in the outcome and the process either explicitly or implicitly suggested. Moreover, the instructional choices made should also align with appropriate assessment strategies that correspond with the goals and follow seamlessly from the instructional activity.

For example, an outcome stating that students will understand and apply the elements of experimental design would not be well met by a lecture covering definitions of hypothesis, procedure, and so forth, followed by an assessment consisting of matching the definitions to the terms. Rather, such an outcome might be addressed through instruction that involves modeling an experiment, followed by engaging students in a hands-on experimental design activity around their own question, thus also incorporating possibilities for performance-based assessment.

As Dewey (1916) and many contemporary educators have suggested, the primary purpose of the instructional endeavor and education in general should be to equip children with tools for learning, not merely with static factual knowledge from a textbook. Consequently, instructional decisions must consider how the content framed in the outcome fits within the habits of mind of the discipline under study and how it may reveal to students the underlying connections across disciplines, times, places, and cultures.

If, then, such instructional decisions represent what would be denoted as *good practice* for all students, what is different about making appropriate instructional choices for gifted students? As chapters throughout this book have emphasized, several key principles form the foundation of effective differentiation of a curriculum and, by extension, of instruction. Some of the key elements to consider as fundamental elements of instruction with gifted students are as follows:

- accelerating basic content experiences;
- constructing meaning as the central goal;
- use of higher order process models;
- exploration of substantive content at a conceptual and abstract level;

- inquiry as a fundamental tool for encouraging learning;
- open-ended activities and questions that encourage further exploration or social action;
- development of creative products to stimulate use of higher level thinking and problem-solving processes; and
- extensions to pique interest around substantive content (Feldhusen, 1998; Gallagher & Gallagher, 1994; Maker & Nielson, 1996; Passow, 1982; Stanley, Keating, & Fox, 1974; VanTassel-Baska, 1998).

With these elements in mind, the process of implementing appropriate instruction requires the use of carefully selected strategies and models chosen to align with content goals and outcomes and the specific needs of learners. The distinction between models and strategies in instruction is a fine one, and the terms are often used interchangeably. However, it is important to understand and maintain a distinction. In general, *models* are more prescriptive and more closely aligned to particular goals and outcomes than teaching strategies (Eggen & Kauchak, 1996). Models work at a more conceptual level to define and frame a way of thinking, reasoning, problem solving, or evaluating. *Strategies* are more process-oriented, representing not process *goals,* as the process dimension of the ICM addresses and requires of students, but rather the classroom processes that are undertaken to achieve goals in the areas of process, content, and concept. Each of these two tools may be effective or ineffective, valuable or wasteful in the hands of the teacher, depending on both the teacher's skill with them and the optimal match of model or strategy to content and students.

Within the context of instructional decision making, perhaps the greatest danger is to allow the instructional strategy to supersede the content in the learning process. For example, a teacher might develop six questions—one at each of the six levels of Bloom's taxonomy (1956)—relating to a specific topic in history and have students create paper cubes, each side of which represents a response to one of the questions. This strategy may work if appropriate emphasis is given to answering the questions. However, if excessive time is given to how to create the paper cubes—an unrelated geometric and motor task—or to teaching students the designations of the levels of the taxonomy—a teacher resource, not relevant to the goals for students—then the strategy has wasted valuable learning time. Well-designed models, because of their more direct link to content and process goals, are less likely to result in this situation, though they can also be problematic for the teacher who does not apply them appropriately. Tomlinson (1999) noted that "there's nothing inherently good or bad about instructional strategies . . . [they] can be used artfully or clumsily as part of well-conceived, or poorly conceived, lesson plans and delivery" (p. 61). Thus, as teachers make instructional decisions, they must review their repertoire of strategies in conjunction with their curricular goals and outcomes and select strategies that are the most appropriate tools for the situation.

The following set of questions may be utilized as a guideline for making appropriate instructional choices with regard to content in the instructional context of educating gifted learners:

- What aspects of the content, as outlined in the goals, outcomes, and activities of the curricular document, can be eliminated based on the pretest performance of students?
- What foundational content is necessary for students to have as a prerequisite before they are able to engage in an in-depth study of the content outlined in the curriculum?
- What aspects of the content can most efficiently be presented in an independent learning activity, leaving time for teacher-student interaction around more complex issues?
- What questioning techniques will best encourage depth and breadth of thinking about this content?
- What strategies and models will allow students to recognize and explore genuine connections to the organizing concepts critical to the curriculum and to the discipline?
- Are the strategies I am considering going to enhance student understanding of content, or are they going to distract from content because of their own complexity? In other words, will students remember the content or the strategies?

Balance

The section above addressed the need for careful selection of instructional strategies and models for given segments of the content included in the curriculum. However, another key issue to consider is the choice of appropriate instructional strategies and models across time and across the disciplines. This requires attention to the need for balance—providing consistency through repeated use of a core set of powerful models and strategies, while, at the same time, providing sufficient variety to maintain student interest. This section will suggest questions to consider in trying to achieve that balance.

Once again, the differences between instructional strategies and models are important to consider. A core set of strong conceptual models is a valuable tool for the teacher and students because each model has the potential to maintain consistency in terms of ways of thinking and also in encouraging students to develop habits of mind and recognize abstract connections. For example, the Elements of Reasoning (Paul, 1992) outlined in Chapter 3 and the Taba (1962) concept development model discussed in Chapter 5 are versatile, solid models for thinking about concepts and issues across the disciplines, and they can be used effectively multiple times in each subject area to support general reasoning abilities. Similarly, a discipline-specific model such as the Literature Web addressed in Chapter 6 or the primary source analysis model outlined in Chapter 9, designed to reflect principles of the discipline under study, supports students in practicing disciplinary habits of mind. Thus, a teacher should continually use a core set of strong models in as many ways as possible, rather than presenting a smorgasbord of models that may distract focus from the content. The purpose of using such models is to promote automatic application of ways of reasoning in daily issues, as well as in the classroom setting; thus, some parsimony in model choice emphasizes the automaticity of the few chosen.

On the other hand, the teacher who always teaches in the exact same way may lose students' attention and be unable to promote any such automatic application. Thus, a variety of instructional strategies closely linked to underlying conceptual models should be applied in the classroom. Most teachers have many strategies in their "bag of tricks," but the key to effective implementation of instructional strategies and models is the link between the two and between the instructional plan and the students. Strategies are as effective as the planning behind them and the thinking they require.

One of the difficulties teachers face in making instructional choices around content is that students may need more time to engage with the content, but not in a traditional teacher-student engagement pattern. Consequently, among the instructional strategies to be considered are those that ask the students to take primary responsibility for learning, with the teacher as facilitator or background. For example, learning centers provide good opportunities for students to develop content understanding and to apply some strong conceptual models independently or in small groups.

Several questions for consideration around the issue of balance follow:

- What is the cost-benefit ratio in terms of time of the variety of strategies I am using? (Is the time taken to teach new strategies worth the time taken away from content?)
- Which of my strategies has staying power? Which is worth using many times?
- What is a set of strategies that will link to each of my conceptual models? To my goals for student learning?
- Which models promote connections across multiple disciplines and may be used in classroom activities in more than one subject area?
- Which models most effectively support students in developing discipline-based habits of mind and higher order reasoning skills while also being sufficiently engaging for repeated use?

The Influence of Students

When making instructional decisions, teachers must carefully reflect upon the population of the class and the particular needs, interests, and abilities that characterize the students. Students enter the educational system from many varying backgrounds, with diverse experiences and different levels of prior knowledge. Teachers will want to consider the following when making appropriate instructional choices for students.

Prior Knowledge

Instructors compensate for diverse knowledge levels by performing "on-the-spot" monitoring of what learners know. With all states adopting learning standards, an effective practice is for teachers to "unpack" each standard. Unpacking involves writing down all the prerequisite learning needed for mastery of a new standard. Pretesting on the prerequisites for each standard will assist teachers in making pertinent instructional decisions regarding students. Furthermore, questions for checking mastery of the new standard itself should be included in the pretest to prevent time wasted teaching what students already know. Because gifted students frequently achieve mastery of many processes and details of content quickly, teachers who make continuous efforts to assess prior knowledge and mastery have greater opportunities to address the students' needs for challenge and complexity in a more efficient manner. Moreover, careful assessment of prior knowledge and mastery of prerequisites allows the teacher to identify and remediate gaps in student learning that occasionally occur as a result of various acceleration and regrouping practices.

Attention Span

A student's attention span also affects his or her understanding and retention of knowledge. Many variables can affect one's attention span. Students may be developmentally ready for topics considered beyond their chronological age. For example, a gifted third grader may be emotionally and intellectually ready to comprehend the complexities in a story such as "The Giver" by Lois Lowry. If high-ability learners are required to read grade-level books that do not challenge their intellectual capabilities, they may become agitated or easily distracted. Students become bored and inattentive when faced with instruction that continually centers on material and skills they have already mastered. It is important for teachers to understand that attention span is also affected by age and learning disabilities, including Attention Deficit Disorder (ADD), and that a student can be both gifted and learning disabled at once, with the concomitant needs of learners in both of those groups (Johnson, Karnes, & Carr, 1987).

Motor and Cognitive Development

Commonly, preschool and early-elementary-aged gifted students' cognitive development is more advanced than that of their age peers. However, their motor development may be equal to or even lag behind that of their age peers (Silverman, 1997). When making instructional choices for gifted learners, activities should match the intellectual level of the gifted student. If they are not physically capable of mastering a task, then choices need to be made on how to keep the same advanced intellectual level of the task while utilizing age-appropriate physical requirements or rendering assistance with the manual task.

Gifted Characteristics

When determining instructional techniques to use with gifted learners, it is important to remember that this population has a quick mastery of factual information and principles. Typically, they possess a broad vocabulary, are intrinsically motivated, bore easily, and are independent thinkers; they do not depend on the judgments of others. In addition, gifted learners become very absorbed and involved in personal areas of interest. All of these characteristics, classified in Chapter 1 under the central traits of precocity, intensity, and complexity, have important implications for the pace, process, and challenge of instruction, as well as for curriculum development.

Preferred Learning Modality

The ways in which people learn vary from one individual to another, in terms of the learning areas of strength and weakness and in terms of preferred methods of encountering and expressing ideas (Gardner, 1983; Renzulli & Reis, 1997; Sternberg, 1988). Appropriate instructional choices should involve varying the modalities of lesson delivery to respond to the varied learning modalities among the students. Across subject areas and grade levels, students should be afforded opportunities to explore what modalities are best suited for them in terms of maximizing the learning experience. Moreover, teachers should help students to become cognizant of various modes and styles of learning so that they can capitalize on this information when trying to learn something new.

Beyond the varied learning modalities across the population of gifted students in general, teachers must also develop an awareness of the learning modalities of special populations of gifted students. As mentioned previously, students who are twice-exceptional demonstrate the needs and characteristics of more than one special population, requiring, for example, the time limits and structures characteristic of lessons targeted for students with ADD while still incorporating the complex, open-ended tasks designed to challenge identified gifted students. The Individualized Educational Plan, designed by a committee of educators and parents for each student qualifying for special education services, is a useful resource for teachers of twice-exceptional students in planning the instructional experience to serve different needs within the same child.

Cultural Diversity

In order to make appropriate decisions for students from diverse cultural backgrounds, instructors need to know the dominant learning characteristics of varied groups and be prepared to respond to them (Ogbu, 1994), while still recognizing that individual characteristics also vary considerably from child to child depending on personal traits and degree of identification with the cultural group (Banks, 1993). For example, Maker (1982) noted that gifted African Americans tend to have strengths in symbolic areas or logical reasoning where semantics are not a necessity; furthermore, they often place a high value on physical and creative expressiveness (Ford & Harris, 1999). In the affective area, African American students are often characterized by a strong cooperative and group orientation, with a heavy emphasis on family ties and group support. Similarly, Hispanic American students frequently come from backgrounds valuing social learning and cooperation, and they often demonstrate a preference for active, real-world learning experiences. Asian American students are often characterized by their emphasis on achievement through effort and a strong commitment to family and to education. Although learning characteristics of Native Americans vary considerably from one group to another, several common characteristics of the larger group include identification with a collective identity, leading to a focus on cooperation; emphasis on idealism and spiritualism; and nonaggressiveness (Ford & Harris, 1999; Sisk, 1989). Teachers of gifted students have a responsibility to be aware of these common characteristics of diverse cultural groups and how these traits may interact with characteristics of giftedness and other elements of their students' identities. Although no student's behavior is entirely predictable based on his or her cultural background or cognitive ability, multicultural awareness and respect improve the learning environment for all involved.

Grouping

Grouping is a complicated instructional issue that involves consideration of students, content, and context. When considering how to group students, teachers must think about their academic abilities within instructional areas and group them accordingly. In addition, however, students' personality and emotional characteristics must also be taken into account. Furthermore, as discussed elsewhere in this chapter, some content and models lend themselves better to working in groups, while others are more effective when taught to a whole class or explored individually.

The following questions address considerations of the influence of students in instructional decision making:

- What formal and informal approaches to pretesting will I use to gauge students' prior knowledge?
- What does student prior knowledge level imply for instructional planning? How will I group students based on these considerations?
- How will student attention span interact with the specific content to be taught and models to be employed?
- Do the individual strategies I use speak to students of different needs, abilities, and sociocultural backgrounds?
- Does my variety of strategies meet the needs of a diverse group of students?
- What group dynamics have I noticed among my students that will affect their performance in a certain activity?
- Are the planned strategies in alignment with the diversity of the group?
- Do my planned strategies provide opportunities for students with different learning modalities to be engaged?
- Are my planned strategies appropriate for the various levels of gifted learners in my class?

The Influence of the Teacher

In addition to all the considerations of content and student-specific needs, another key variable involved in making appropriate instructional choices relates to the teacher's knowledge, skills, and preferences. Even if two classrooms are very similar in terms of the range of students populating them and the content to be covered, they may still be very different merely because of the differences in teacher expertise, personality, and instructional style.

Much recent research has been conducted on identifying and generalizing the characteristics of good teachers (Darling-Hammond, 2000; Porter & Brophy, 1988). Furthermore, an ever-growing body of literature exists concerning what affects student learning, with increasing attention given to the role of the teacher (Darling-Hammond). Indeed, "at the heart of this line of inquiry is the core belief that teachers make a difference" (Wright, Horn, & Sanders, 1997, p. 57). In working to understand the complexity of teacher effectiveness, new research in the use of value-added accountability systems provides an important foundation for determining teacher effectiveness.

Value-added assessment measures the gain scores, or how much the individual student has learned within an academic year (Holloway, 2000). In the late 1960s, the Dallas Independent School District in Texas started to develop what has evolved into the Dallas Value-Added Accountability System, a complex system for collecting student achievement data that controls for variables such as ethnicity, gender, language proficiency, socioeconomic status, and prior achievement levels. Extensive data have been collected through this system and analyzed for results relating to teacher and school effectiveness: A recent study "strongly suggest[s] that negative effects of a teacher in the bottom third of effectiveness lasts through three years of teachers in the top third of effectiveness" (Mendro, Jordan, Gomez, Anderson, & Bembry, 1998, p. 262). Using classroom indices of math teachers, the study also found that "effective teachers knew subject matter, taught the entire range of the curriculum (including higher order thinking skills) with equal emphasis, and assessed students frequently through formal and informal methods" (p. 264). Furthermore, three consistent characteristics of effective schools emerged from this study: (1) achievement was a major focus, (2) staff expected students to achieve, and (3) principals did not tolerate ineffective teachers.

In response to demands from Tennessee business interests for greater accountability in public schools, the Tennessee Value-Added Accountability System, the first statewide accountability system of its kind, was developed (Ceperley & Reel, 1997). Profiles of academic growth for individual students were developed from value-added testing. A study of the cumulative gains throughout the entire state revealed that the racial composition, the percentage of students receiving free and reduced lunch, and the mean achievement level of the school were unrelated to gain scores (Sanders & Horn, 1998). The results of the research showed residual effects of teachers on the academic gains of students. Effective teachers facilitate academic growth in their students the year assigned to them; however, there are residual effects of prior assignments to ineffective teachers. It was discovered that ineffective teachers were ineffective with all students despite previous level of student achievement (Wright, Horn, & Sanders, 1997). Sanders and Horn (1998) analyzed math scores for students in two districts and discovered that achievement levels in grade 2 were very different from those in grade 5. Fifth graders who were assigned to three years of ineffective teachers had scores averaging 54 to 60 percentile points lower than students who were assigned to three years of highly effective teachers. Moreover, Sanders (2001) has noted both a "shed effect" in gain scores and a "peak effect," signifying that high-end learners are not gaining proportionately in their annual learning.

The implication of the Dallas Value-Added Accountability System and the Tennessee Value-Added Accountability System is that teachers make a difference. "Effective teachers appear to be effective with students of all achievement levels, regardless of the level of heterogeneity in their classrooms" (Wright, Horn, & Sanders, 1997, p. 63). It could be inferred from the above research that teachers need to be knowledgeable about how to differentiate instruction effectively for high-ability learners, implementing challenging curricula that incorporate higher order thinking processes and strategies.

Several scholars in gifted education have addressed the issue of what characteristics are important in an effective teacher of the gifted, and some of these characteristics relate to the instructional choices teachers make. Key characteristics of effective teachers of the gifted that are significant for instructional decision making include flexibility, willingness to accept diverse points of view, ability to serve as facilitator, and use of a simultaneous mode of processing (Silverman, 1993). Teachers of the gifted need to be comfortable with asking open-ended questions and receiving very diverse responses. They also must be prepared for students who are tremendously knowledgeable about the subject to be taught and need opportunities to explore that subject, *with guidance*, beyond what is required in the regular curriculum (VanTassel-Baska, 1992). Moreover, teachers of the gifted should be knowledgeable about when they need more instruction on how to meet the needs of special-needs learners, including highly gifted, twice-exceptional, and culturally diverse gifted students. Beyond the academic interactions with these students, teachers of the gifted must also be prepared to work with students whose humor and interpersonal styles are unusual for their age level and verge on adult behavior. Also, because gifted students are generally inquisitive and concerned about social and world issues, teachers need to be prepared for frequent questions that sometimes are difficult to answer. For example, a student may ask, "What is my purpose on earth?" or "What can I do as an individual to change the inequities that exist in a person's daily life?"

Teachers of gifted learners face the dilemma of whether they are giving too much or too little direct instruction and when this instruction should be modulated by facilitation. Direct instruction and classroom discussions are effective strategies for "teaching thinking skills, inducing understanding of complex, conceptual material, and teaching metacognitive skills" (Feldhusen, 1994, p. 370). For example, students need to understand concepts underlying a discipline, such as patterns in mathematics, before they are able to apply a concept to the content they are learning. In addition, direct instruction is imperative for proper implementation of learning models by the students. Learners need guidance when first being introduced to Paul's reasoning model (1992), creative problem solving (Parnes, 1967), or the Center for Gifted Education's research model (Boyce, 1997). With practice and direct instruction from the teacher, students will be able to know which model to employ in which circumstances.

Teachers of the gifted may find the following questions useful for a self-reflection of their effectiveness in the classroom as instructors:

- How much do I know about each content area for which I have responsibility?
- What is my preferred style of delivery? Do I prefer a more formal or informal style?
- How can I meet the special needs of my high-ability students?
- How can I instill more independent learning habits in my students?
- When do I employ direct and indirect instruction to facilitate learning?

The Influence of Context

The instructional context, in its broadest sense, encompasses all of the categories already addressed. However, some specific elements most clearly define this category. Decision making with the instructional context in mind must include attention to the following factors: time, grouping arrangements, physical arrangements of classroom space, and human and material resources and equipment.

Time

The variable of time is one of the most significant in all that a teacher does. Education today is defined by time as much as, if not more than, any other factor. The school day, the school year, and the entire K–12 spectrum of educational programming are all ruled by the clock and the calendar, despite the varying rates at which students learn, the ebb and flow of world events, and students' personal lives outside of the classroom. Indeed, mindful of the time problem, the National Education Commission on Time and Learning (1994) argued that students today are "prisoners of time," blocked by the clock and calendar from progressing and achieving at their individual rates because of the lockstep use of learning time.

Because of the structural restrictions placed by the schedule of the school day and year, teachers must consider the time variable side-by-side with their curricular goals, in both short-term and long-term planning. However, time may be viewed as an enabling factor as much as a restricting one, and it should be handled with some flexibility by the effective teacher. Teachers often complain that assessment takes up a considerable amount of valuable instructional time; and, indeed, assessment does take time as much as any other activity. However, rather than being seen as a subtraction from the allotted instructional time, assessment should instead be viewed as a necessary gauge for the best ways to reallot, reorganize, and reuse instructional time effectively. In instructional planning, teachers must begin, continue, and end with assessment in mind, and they should always be prepared to reassign planned time when assessment reveals that less time is needed to cover a particular aspect of the curriculum.

Gifted students need less time for mastery of basic material due to their ability to learn at an accelerated pace, their capacity to understand in greater depth and complexity, and their interests that vary from those of their age peers (Maker, 1982). When teachers are confronted with students who have already mastered basic skills, they should plan instruction that attends to academic and emotional needs and the degree to which they differ from the norm (Parke, 1995). Conversely, more time needs to be allotted for mastering higher level skills, in group or independent learning contexts, especially as they are applied to worthy student projects.

Pacing is another key factor in considering the all-important variable of time. One effective differentiation tool for serving the needs of students of varying abilities is to vary the pacing with which the curriculum is presented; however, as pacing is accelerated to support students who learn more quickly, teachers must take care to ensure that the time they save by so doing is reassigned to valuable learning, as well. Students should not come to school to "put in hours"; teachers must take advantage of their limited time and spend it as effectively and meaningful as possible.

Grouping Arrangements

Without employing grouping strategies, much of the power of any differentiated curriculum or instructional plan is lost, for it is in the grouping arrangement that the gifted have the potential to fully respond to any curriculum (Kulik & Kulik, 1992). A discussion of key grouping strategies follows that highlights popular approaches used in gifted programs.

Cooperative Learning Groups. Cooperative learning has become increasingly popular in recent years. All students in the group contribute actively to the problem under study, and group energy propels learners toward mastery of the material offered. To make cooperative learning effective for the gifted, however, ability and interest must be considered in establishing such groups. For example, cooperative learning can be a powerful way to organize gifted learners for a particular English project in which each student has a role to perform. Examples would include the following:

- writing skits;
- performing a play;
- developing an advertising campaign;
- organizing a literary exhibit;
- developing a literary magazine; or
- conducting research on a topic from a multiple-source/multiple-viewpoint perspective.

Cluster Grouping. In cluster grouping, a group of gifted students is assigned to one teacher as part of an overall class at a particular grade level. Thus, the gifted can be grouped and regrouped within the classroom to accommodate different instructional needs. For academic subjects, however, cluster groups generally work together on the same instructional plan, while other students in the room follow a different plan. Even in a secondary-level honors course, gifted students could be subgrouped in the class for targeted activities.

Tiered Instruction. One way of allowing students to benefit from different grouping formats within even one lesson is to utilize tiered instruction. In this model, students are involved in independent, small-group, and large-group work within the same time frame; by responding to a given stimulus independently, discussing it with peers, and then debriefing with the whole class, students are able to bring their full personal aptitude and interest to an activity, yet also benefit from sharing with others. Furthermore, varying the grouping throughout the activity allows the teacher to facilitate as whole-group leader, small-group consultant, and individual advisor. Moreover, after an activity has been discussed in the whole group, follow-up tasks should allow students to move back down through the grouping levels for further small-group discussion and independent reflection.

Grouping by Dyads and Triads. This strategy allows gifted learners to find one or two true peers in the classroom with whom they can work effectively. These pairings sometimes occur naturally, while other times an insightful teacher carefully nurtures them. This approach to learning is ideal for initiating independent projects and having students move ahead in parts of the curriculum somewhat independently, yet with the company of one or two similar students for elements of the task at hand. As long as the gifted learners are well motivated and interested in the learning task, some ability differences can be tolerated. This grouping approach should also encourage social development beyond the classroom in the form of study groups or less formal get-togethers.

Grouping by Learning Centers. Many gifted classrooms establish learning centers and have students actively participate in center activities according to a rotating schedule throughout the week. Gifted learners are typically accommodated by having either extended activities in each center geared to their level of need or by having a gifted center where all instructional activities are geared to their level. This approach provides instructional alternatives for all class members and enables students to develop responsibility for their own learning in selected areas of the curriculum. A center model might also be organized in a high school library, rather than a classroom. The important concepts are (1) freedom in choice of activities by the student, (2) voluntary movement toward desired learning opportunities, and (3) an organized system of center use and assessment.

Cross-Age Grouping. Cross-age grouping allows gifted learners who are within two or three grade levels of each other to work together in areas of strength and interest. Some high schools offer courses across grade levels. Others establish such groups of gifted students at predetermined times during the week. This technique is frequently used in small schools in which there are few gifted children at each grade level.

All of these approaches are important to consider in providing appropriate instructional options for gifted learners at the classroom level and beyond. Since even the most critical opponents of ability grouping voice support for instructional grouping (Oakes, 1985; Slavin, 1987), it is vital that schools enhance their programs with variations of the grouping strategies discussed above. Without such provisions, the gifted have limited access to appropriate challenges in the context of elementary and secondary classrooms and programs.

Physical Arrangements

The physical arrangements of a classroom are generally a less influential variable than the time factor; but, nevertheless, they must be considered in making appropriate instructional choices. As teachers plan their instruction, they must consider where students are located in relation to the teacher, to one another, and to the key materials to be used in a lesson. They must also consider the relationship of these physical arrangement variables to the time allotment. For example, if there is to be movement within the lesson, the teacher must consider how much time the physical rearrangement will take and whether it is worth the time it takes away from active engagement in the teaching-learning process.

Physical arrangements must also be carefully considered in terms of the specific students to be involved in a given lesson. The arrangement of desks; student proximity to certain other students, other facilitative or distracting influences, or both; and the overall climate for students that physical arrangements of a classroom can create can also affect learning outcomes.

Human and Material Resources

Available materials are not in and of themselves a curriculum, and they certainly are not instruction, but they have a powerful influence upon what the curriculum and instruction are in a classroom. A teacher may have access to an excellent curriculum, but if the materials to support that curriculum are not available, then the instructional implementation of the curriculum is limited or prevented. On the other hand, a teacher can buttress a weaker curriculum by enhancing it with the incorporation of powerful support materials in the instructional context.

Materials selection is addressed in more detail in Chapter 10, but it is worth mentioning here because of the powerful influence materials have over what happens in the classroom and because teachers must make decisions regarding the materials they use in guiding their instructional decision making. Generally, basal materials treat concepts and higher order thinking at a superficial level; therefore, diverse materials are essential if gifted students are to view topics from multiple perspectives (VanTassel-Baska, 1992).

Technology offers gifted students "expansive, almost limitless, intellectual and aesthetic horizons" (Howell, 1995, p. 155). Before integrating technology into their instruction, teachers must be cognizant of their own technological abilities and seek training on technology that would enhance the learning of gifted youth. Increasing one's technological knowledge and competence takes time, so teachers should be patient with their expertise in this area. The use of technology in the classroom ranges from word-processing and educational games, to telecommunications and intelligent computer-assisted instruction that collects diagnostic information pertaining to a student and modifies instructional strategies.

Technology fosters five types of learning: independent, individualized, interactive, interdisciplinary, and intuitive (Howell, 1995). An example of independent learning is a student using electronic databases, such as ERIC or DIALOG, to gather information for a research report, or students manipulating statistical data using SPSS. Students can be engaged in individualized learning using video, CD-ROM, or computer-assisted instruction. Gifted learners are involved in interactive learning when they present their products to others or exchange information with another through the computer. For example, high-ability students could create Web pages for the presentation of completed research or products. Understanding the habits of mind of more than one discipline and the similarities and differences among those disciplines is the focus of interdisciplinary learning. This goal can be accomplished through computer-generated simulations of real-world problems in which students are asked to gather, analyze, and report information. Intuitive learning involves experiences that have unintended learning outcomes that are both competitive and collaborative (Howell, 1995). Advanced simulations and virtual reality foster this type of learning.

In addition to the curricular resources a teacher may or may not have available to support instruction, the factor of human resources must also be carefully considered in the instructional decision-making process. Volunteers are a critical part of the gifted classroom. Community members are excellent resources for the habits of mind needed in specific professions, as well as for providing an extra hand in facilitating independent research. Content experts can be sought through local universities, businesses, and service clubs.

Mentors are usually thought of as individuals who shape the career aspirations of high-ability students; however a mentor can be anyone "who has an intense and personal relationship with a child that can influence the child on a sustained basis" (Seeley, 1998, p. 484). Teachers can carefully assign gifted learners to community individuals who are willing to assume the role of personal mentors. Personal mentors are individuals who assist a student with his or her intellectual development, influence the student's advancement through sponsorship, role-model appropriate behaviors, or some combination of these roles.

As a teacher considers any segment of the curriculum to be implemented—whether it be a unit, a set of lessons designed to respond to a given standard, or a single lesson—he or she must consider the following questions related to the instructional context:

- How much time is available to allot to the instructional module in question?
- How much time *should* be allotted to the module?
- What aspects of the physical arrangements of my classroom and school may enhance or impede planned instruction?
- Given the physical and time constraints, what are my possibilities for grouping arrangements for students?
- What technological resources are available to foster independent, individualized, interactive, interdisciplinary, or intuitive learning?
- What human resources are available to enhance the students' educational experiences?

Conclusion

Classrooms are dynamic environments influenced by instructional decisions in many dimensions. Content, students, teachers, and context all exert powerful influences on decision making. Teachers of the gifted should recognize logical linkages among the four influences and make appropriate instructional choices accordingly. In order to meet the needs of students, effective teachers must continually monitor and adjust their pedagogy. They understand that their practices matter in respect to what and how much students learn. Before making instructional decisions, teachers should consider students' prior knowledge, attention span, motor and cognitive development, preferred learning modalities, cultural diversity, and gifted characteristics.

When engaged in instructional decision making, teachers should also consider the time spent learning basic skills versus time spent on higher level activities, including independent mastery of content and projects. Another consideration is the grouping and space arrangements that best facilitate the learning that needs to be accomplished. Effective choices regarding human and technological resources are also crucial to the education of high-ability learners.

The instructional decisions that teachers make matter in very real terms for high-ability learners, many times constituting the difference between having a miserable year and a productive one.

Key Points Summary

❑ Content, students, teachers, and context all exert powerful influences on instructional decision making.
❑ The influence of content on instructional decision making includes the issue of aligning learning activities undertaken in the classroom to curricular goals and outcomes and managing activities so that appropriate attention is given to both variety and consistency.
❑ Students' prior knowledge, attention span, motor and cognitive development, gifted characteristics, preferred learning modality, and cultural diversity must be considered when making appropriate instructional decisions.
❑ When making instructional decisions, teachers need to be cognizant of their students' academic and emotional needs, be flex-

ible, be willing to accept diverse viewpoints, serve as a facilitator of learning, and model cognitive and metacognitive processes.

❑ The context of the teaching-learning environment, in respect to variables such as time, grouping, physical arrangement of classroom space, and human and material resources and equipment, is also central to making appropriate instructional choices.

References

Banks, J. A. (1993). Multicultural education: Characteristics and goals. In J. A. Banks & C. A. Banks (Eds.), *Multicultural education: Issues and perspectives* (pp. 3–28). Boston: Allyn and Bacon.

Bloom, B. S. (1956). *Taxonomy of educational objectives: Cognitive domain (Handbook 1)*. New York: McKay.

Ceperley, P. E., & Reel, K. (1997). The impetus for the Tennessee Value-Added Accountability System. In J. Millman (Ed.), *Grading teachers, grading schools: Is student achievement a valid evaluation measure?* (pp. 133–136). Thousand Oaks, CA: Corwin Press.

Cohen, S. (1987). Instructional alignment: Searching for a magic bullet. *Educational Researcher, 16,* 16–20.

Darling-Hammond, L. (2000). Teacher quality and student achievement: A review of state policy evidence. *Education Policy Analysis Archives, 8.* Retrieved January 24, 2000, ERIC database.

Dewey, J. (1916). *Democracy and education.* New York: Macmillan.

Eggen, P. D., & Kauchak, D. P. (1996). *Strategies for teachers: Teaching content and thinking skills* (3rd ed.). Boston: Allyn and Bacon.

Feldhusen, J. F. (1994). Strategies for teaching the gifted. In J. VanTassel-Baska (Ed.), *Comprehensive curriculum for gifted learners* (2nd ed., pp. 366–378). Boston: Allyn and Bacon.

Feldhusen, J. F. (1998). Strategies and methods for teaching the talented. In J. VanTassel-Baska (Ed.), *Excellence in educating gifted and talented learners* (3rd ed., pp. 363–379). Denver: Love.

Ford, D. Y., & Harris, J. J. (1999). *Multicultural gifted education.* New York: Teachers College Press.

Gallagher, J., & Gallagher, S. (1994). *Teaching the gifted child* (4th ed.). Boston: Allyn and Bacon.

Gardner, H. (1983). *Frames of mind: The theory of multiple intelligences.* New York: BasicBooks.

Holloway, J. H. (2000). A value-added view of pupil performance. *Educational Leadership, 57,* 84–85.

Howell, R. D. (1995). Technological innovations in the education of gifted and talented students. In J. L Genshaft, M. Bireley, & C. L. Hollinger (Eds.), *Serving gifted and talented students: A resource for school personnel* (pp. 155–172). Austin, TX: PRO-ED.

Johnson, L. J., Karnes, M. B., & Carr, V. W. (1997). Providing services to children with gifts and disabilities: A critical need. In N. Colangelo & G. A. Davis (Eds.), *Handbook of gifted education* (2nd ed., pp. 516–527). Boston: Allyn and Bacon.

Joyce, B., Weil, M., & Calhoun, E. (2000). *Models of teaching* (6th ed.). Boston: Allyn and Bacon.

Kulik, J. A., & Kulik, C. C. (1992). Meta-analytic findings on grouping programs. *Gifted Child Quarterly, 36,* 73–77.

Maker, C. J. (1982). *Curriculum development for the gifted.* Rockville, MD: Aspen.

Maker, C. J., & Nielson, A. B. (1996). *Curriculum development and teaching strategies for gifted learners* (2nd ed.). Austin, TX: PRO-ED.

Mendro, R. L., Jordan, H. R., Gomez, E., Anderson, M. C., & Bembry, K. L. (1998). *An application of multiple linear regression in determining longitudinal teacher effectiveness.* Retrieved August 6, 2001 from http://www.dallas.isd.tenet.edu/depts/inst_research/aer98rm2

National Education Commission on Time and Learning. (1994). *Prisoners of time.* Washington, DC: U.S. Government Printing Office.

Oakes, J. (1985). *Keeping track: How schools structure inequality.* New Haven, CT: Yale University Press.

Ogbu, J. U. (1994). Understanding cultural diversity and learning. *Journal for the Education of the Gifted, 17,* 355–383.

Parke, B. N. (1995). Developing curricular interventions for the gifted. In J. L Genshaft, M. Bireley, & C. L. Hollinger (Eds.), *Serving gifted and talented students: A resource for school personnel* (pp. 123–134). Austin, TX: PRO-ED.

Parnes, S. J. (1967). *Creative behavior guidebook.* New York: Scribners.

Passow, A. H. (1982). *LTI committee report.* Unpublished report, National/State Leadership Training Institute of the Gifted and Talented, Ventura, CA.

Paul, R. (1992). *Critical thinking: What every person needs to survive in a rapidly changing world.* Rohnert Park, CA: Foundation for Critical Thinking.

Porter, A. C., & Brophy, J. (1988). Synthesis of research on good teaching: Insights from the work of the Institute for Research on Teaching. *Educational Leadership, 45,* 74–85.

Renzulli, J. S., & Reis, S. M. (1997). The schoolwide enrichment model: New directions for developing high-end learning. In N. Colangelo & G. A. Davis (Eds.), *Handbook of gifted education* (2nd ed., pp. 136–154). Boston: Allyn and Bacon.

Sanders, W. L. (2001, June). *The impact of teaching on student achievement.* Presentation at the William and Mary School Leadership Institute, Williamsburg, VA.

Sanders, W. L., & Horn, S. (1998). Research findings from the Tennessee Value-Added Assessment System database: Implications for educational evaluation and research. *Journal of Personnel Evaluation in Education, 12,* 247–256.

Seeley, K. (1998). Facilitators for talented students. In J. VanTassel-Baska (Ed.), *Excellence in educating gifted & talented learners* (3rd ed., pp. 473–488). Denver: Love.

Silverman, L. K. (1993). *Counseling the gifted and talented.* Denver: Love.

Silverman, L. K. (1997). The construct of asynchronous development. *Peabody Journal of Education, 72*(3&4), 36–58.

Sisk, D. A. (1989). Identifying and nurturing talent among the American Indians. In C. J. Maker & J. W. Shiever (Eds.), *Critical issues in gifted education. Vol. 2: Defensible programs for cultural and ethnic minorities* (pp. 128–132). Austin, TX: PRO-ED.

Slavin, R. E. (1987). Ability, grouping, and student achievement in elementary schools. *Review of Educational Research, 57,* 293–336.

Stanley, J., Keating, D., & Fox, L. (1974). *Mathematical talent: Discovery, description, and development.* Baltimore: Johns Hopkins University Press.

Sternberg, R. J. (1988). A triarchic theory of intellectual giftedness. In R. J. Sternberg & J. E. Davidson (Eds.), *Conceptions of giftedness* (pp. 223–243). New York: Cambridge University Press.

Taba, H. (1962). *Curriculum development: Theory and practice.* New York: Harcourt, Brace, & World.

Tomlinson, C. (1999). *The differentiated classroom: Responding to the needs of all learners.* Alexandria, VA: Association for Supervision and Curriculum Development.

VanTassel-Baska, J. (1992). *Planning effective curriculum for gifted learners.* Denver: Love.

VanTassel-Baska, J. (1998). Appropriate curriculum for the talented learner. In J. VanTassel-Baska (Ed.), *Excellence in educating gifted and talented learners* (3rd ed., pp. 339–361). Denver: Love.

Wright, S. P., Horn, S. P., & Sanders, W. L. (1997). Teacher and classroom context effects on student achievement: Implications for teacher evaluation. *Journal of Personnel Evaluation in Education, 11,* 57–67.

Chapter 12

Assessing Student Learning

by
Li Zuo
and
Joyce VanTassel-Baska

You are a middle school teacher who would like to obtain a more complete profile of how your gifted students are progressing. You surmise that the annual state test does not begin to tap into their abilities, and tests you have created are also limited to factual information. If you knew more about their capabilities in your subject area, you would adapt the curriculum accordingly. How can you appropriately assess authentic learning in gifted students?

The purposes of student assessment[1] are to examine the effectiveness of classroom teaching and learning, as well as to plan for future instruction based on student learning needs.

---

1. *Student assessment* refers to all formal (and informal) practices associated with gauging student learning in a particular curricular module. It would include teacher-made and standardized measures, performance-based, portfolio, and paper-and-pencil.

Constructing an effective assessment tool is not an easy task in the sense that it must not only cover the objectives and content under assessment, but cover them in a way that is technically adequate. In the case of assessing gifted students' learning, it is also necessary to increase the task difficulty level so as to provide opportunities for those students to demonstrate the advanced thinking of which they are capable.

This chapter discusses some of the guidelines in curriculum-based assessment construction, with particular focus on high-ability learners. Examples of assessments from Advanced Placement, the International Baccalaureate, and the Center for Gifted Education's science units are provided to illustrate the concepts under discussion and their application.

Technical Considerations in Assessment

Depending on the use of a test, different levels of technical adequacy are required. A test that is used for the determination of eligibility for a special service (e.g., a gifted program) must be highly valid and reliable. For a teacher-made classroom assessment, however, the demand on its technical adequacy is less stringent.

Two major properties of technical adequacy are reliability and validity. Other important considerations are test fairness and, particularly in the case of high-ability learners, test ceiling. The following explanation of these constructs may be supplemented by test manual descriptions, if needed.

Reliability

Reliability refers to the consistency of examinees' test scores over repeated administrations of the same test or alternate test forms. Such consistency gives the assurance that the test is measuring an individual's true ability. There are several ways to estimate an instrument's reliability using test data. Administering the instrument twice to the same group of examinees with an interval in between, the so-called test-retest method, yields the reliability coefficient of stability. Administering two forms of the same instrument one after another to the same group of examinees, the so-called alternate form method, yields the coefficient of equivalency. Combining the two methods by testing and retesting with alternate forms yields the coefficient of both stability and equivalence. That reliability is usually lower because it combines both types of errors due to test construction and examinees' performance over time.

A reliability coefficient of .85 means that 85% of the observed score variance is attributable to true score variance (Crocker & Algina, 1986). A high reliability, typically above .85, is generally found in well-established intelligence tests and achievement tests. Teacher-made classroom tests generally are not subjected to reliability studies because of their relatively low-stakes nature, nor are they expected to meet a high reliability standard. Yet, it may be important to conduct a test-retest reliability check to ascertain stability of the measure.

Validity

While the reliability coefficient indicates the consistency of examinees' scores, it does not ensure defensible inferences drawn about examinees' knowledge or behavior. The basis for such inferences needs to be established through studies in which test developers or test users collect evidence to demonstrate an instrument's *validity*, which is the degree to which the test measures what it purports to measure and thus justifies the inferences made.

Content validity refers to the inference that can be made about an examinee's knowledge of a domain or construct of specific interest from his or her performance on the test (Crocker & Algina, 1986). It is the most relevant type of validity for classroom assessment. Content validity can be established by having content experts check the test items to determine whether or not they assess what they are supposed to assess. The test maker, of course, should make sure before seeking expert review that the test covers the instructional objectives and curricular contents for assessment. A helpful method of checking the coverage is to map out the test items against content or skills to be assessed in a table of specifications. The layout should present a balanced coverage if all the objectives or content areas are of equal importance. Table 12.1 gives an example of a table of specification. Matching the assessment with curricular goals or objectives also means selecting the right assessment approach for a particular goal or set of objectives. When the goal specifies that students should be able to conduct a scientific experiment, a paper-and-pencil approach will not adequately assess its attainment. For that particular goal, performance assessment is a superior tool.

Table 12.1
Table of Specifications

Content Goal Emphases

Test Item	Geography	Weather	Civilization	Political System	Economy	Religion
1	√					
2		√				
3			√			
4			√			
5				√		
6					√	
7						√
8				√		
9	√					
10					√	

Fairness

A good test should not be biased in favor of or against any individual because of his or her gender, culture, language, or experience. Bias occurs when a test contains vocabulary or tacit knowledge that is specific to a subculture, but is irrelevant to the test purpose; when a test is given to students who have different degrees of familiarity with the employed test format; and when the test calls for the use of a lab device to which students have had varied exposure. Students from another culture, students who speak another language, and students with learning disabilities are some of those for whom accommodations may need to be made in order to ensure a fair assessment of their ability.

Test Ceiling

Test ceiling refers to the maximum score allowed on a test. An easy test that allows too many students to achieve the highest score possible is said to have a low ceiling, which means it fails to discriminate for high-end students. Tests that are designed for use with gifted learners should pay special attention to this problem, providing sufficiently difficult tasks and scoring protocols with room for varied levels of performance near the top.

Authentic Assessment

In recognition of the limitations of standardized tests and the need to assess students' high-level skills, a movement toward more performance-based and authentic assessment is occurring, even in large-scale assessments. Products, portfolios, and other performance-based approaches that used to be advocated for gifted learners to demonstrate their ability to apply and synthesize knowledge (VanTassel-Baska, 1992) are now incorporated in large-scale assessment for all students. Powerful examples of this trend include the use of writing and mathematics portfolios in the Vermont statewide assessment at grades 4 and 8 and performance tasks and portfolios in writing, reading, and mathematics in the Kentucky assessment system at grades 4, 8, and 12 (Asp, 1998). Several considerations important in developing and implementing more authentic and performance-based assessment systems with high-ability learners are addressed below.

Target High-Level Skills

Given the depth and complexity of gifted learners' cognitive abilities, tests for this population should emphasize high-level thinking and processing skills. That is, the test should go beyond simple recollection of knowledge or facts and require students to operate at higher levels of application, analysis, synthesis, and evaluation. Task demands for gifted learners can make use of the following thinking processes often identified as central to differentiation (Marzano, Pickering, & McTighe, 1993):

- comparing;
- classifying;
- induction;
- deduction;
- error analysis;
- constructing support;
- abstracting;
- analyzing perspectives;
- decision making;

- investigation;
- experimental inquiry;
- problem solving; and
- invention.

By the same token, expectations for students' performance conveyed, for instance, through scoring rubrics should reflect the same high standards for complexity and sophistication to bring out the best products that gifted learners are capable of generating.

Use Multiple Approaches

To monitor student performance and inform instruction, a teacher needs to collect student performance data all the way through a learning module or unit, using formative and summative assessments. Formative assessments are used to monitor student progress during instruction, while summative assessments are given at the end of instruction for the purpose of certifying mastery or assigning grades (Gronlund, 1998). A sample set of formative and summative assessment tools in the area of writing is illustrated in Table 12.2. While some approaches are more suitable for one type of assessment (e.g., portfolios may be used for formative, rather than summative, assessment), some approaches can be used for both. In order to examine a student's performance from various perspectives and under different conditions, it is desirable for teachers to employ multiple assessment approaches in both oral and written form. A combination of approaches generally works to both the teacher's advantage and the student's advantage because different approaches can supplement one another to provide a more comprehensive picture of a student's performance.

Identifying Purpose

An emphasis on performance-based tasks does not need to replace entirely standardized tests when the latter may function effectively. For instance, although a performance task can allow students to demonstrate their actual writing ability, students may also construct their own sentences in such a way as to bypass their weak areas in grammar and sentence structure. If language mechanics are the focus of an assessment, then a standardized test can better cover a large number of grammar and language points in a relatively short time. It is, therefore, a more efficient tool for examining students' mastery in that area. The key is to select an appropriate approach based on the purpose of the

Table 12.2

Assessment Tools for Writing

	Writing Projects	Research Products	Metacognitive and Organizational Products
Formative tools • Portfolio of work in progress	Three graded essays in second draft form with peer and teacher commentary	Outline for research paper	Annotated bibliography of research paper references
Summative tools • Portfolio of completed work	Final draft essays (three or more)	Research paper	Self-assessment of completed portfolio

assessment. Generally, if content mastery is being assessed, a paper-and-pencil test with close-ended items may be preferable. If higher order thinking and problem solving are being assessed, a more performance-based approach would be appropriate.

Issues in Assessing Gifted Students' Learning

Differentiation for gifted learners typically calls for the use of advanced content, deep processing, and quality products. Where differentiation is occurring, gifted students tend to get harder books to read and more challenging projects to complete than their regular classmates. How do teachers assess their learning outcomes in such a way that these students feel properly rewarded for their extra labor? How can we encourage gifted students to strive for a higher level when they always compare favorably with their peers in the classroom? And, in attempting a challenging project, how should teachers appropriately weigh the emphasis on their efforts and final results? A finding that emerged from two districtwide evaluations of gifted programs is that gifted students are not evaluated regularly for their learning in the programs (VanTassel-Baska, Avery, et al., 2001; VanTassel-Baska, Zuo, Struck, & Avery, 2001). That, in part, speaks to the complexity of the problem.

Another technical issue with performance assessment is its typically low-scoring interrater reliability (Stiggins, 1991). Therefore, quality control in scoring and repeated use of such an assessment over time to collect multiple samples of student performance can help ensure a reliable assessment of a student's ability.

Models for Assessment

The examples that follow provide a concrete representation of performance-based assessment tools that have been and continue to be employed effectively with gifted learners. Both examples meet the technical adequacy requirements discussed in this chapter.

International Baccalaureate and Advanced Placement Assessments

At the high school level, the academic provisions for gifted and high-ability learners often primarily consist of International Baccalaureate (IB) and Advanced Placement (AP) courses. These courses are calibrated to be "advanced" to a typical college-level course at a selective school in various subject areas. For a more complete description of these programs, see Chapter 13. Because of their emphasis on advanced level work, the assessment approaches employed in IB and AP programs are illustrative of assessments commonly used with academically oriented gifted learners.

The IB assessment model measures the performance of students against the main objectives of the program by using a combination of external and internal assessment methods in both written and oral modes. External assessments are provided and scored by the International Baccalaureate Organization (IBO). Internal assessments, which are also provided by the IBO, are scored by classroom teachers who are required to send representative scores of high, low, and average levels to the IBO for verification of their having correctly used the scoring rubric. The purpose of this is to ensure that students are assessed fairly according to international standards. Take the IB Language A1 assessment model for an example. Its externally assessed components are commentary and essay papers on seen and unseen texts and two written assignments of comparative and imaginative/creative nature. The external assessments account for 70% of the overall Language A1 assessment. The internally assessed component consists of two compulsory oral activities, one commentary on a teacher-selected extract, and one oral presentation on a student-selected topic. The oral component accounts for 30% of the total assessment (International Baccalaureate Organization, 1999). Scoring rubrics for the written work typically contains six levels to differentiate the degrees of *none, little, some, adequate, good,* and *excellent* demonstration of required ability, skills, or presentation. These assessments demand such abilities as appreciation, interpretation, comparison, critique, analysis, evaluation, and creativity.

The AP exam in each course provides another example of carefully constructed and scored responses that require depth of knowledge and thought. The exams generally contain two question types: multiple choice and free response. The multiple-choice section emphasizes the breadth of the student's knowledge and understanding of the content. The free-response section emphasizes the application of these core principles in greater depth in solving more extended problems or analyzing complex issues and texts (e.g., College Board Advanced Placement Program, 1999a, 1999b, 1999c, 1999d). For example, a student taking an exam in English Language and Composition might be asked to analyze the rhetoric of a given passage; a student taking English Literature and Composition might be asked to use examples from literature selections he or she has read to support a generalization about character or about plot in literature. Students taking a science or statistics exam may be given a situation and asked to design an experiment to answer a question of interest. In general, the free-response questions are designed so that different students are able to draw upon the different experiences and texts they have encountered in their courses in order to respond to the question, thus allowing choice for both teacher and student while still maintaining a common course framework.

The free-response section is scored against carefully developed guidelines that are drafted by individual item developers, reviewed and revised collectively by task committee, and modified based on student responses. Scorers of the free-response section are trained to apply the guidelines using exemplary student responses. Sample free-response questions for all exams, demonstrating the emphasis on higher level thinking required of students, are available through the College Board at http://www.collegeboard.com.

Along with demonstrating emphasis on higher level skills, the AP and IB exams also illustrate the proper use of different test formats to serve different purposes of assessment. Moreover, these exams are exemplary for high-stakes testing in terms of their careful construction with consideration of the technical concepts discussed earlier in this chapter. For example, the free-response questions in the AP Physics exam (College Board Advanced Placement Program, 1999a) were first developed by members of the AP Physics Development Committee, then reviewed and revised by the committee collectively in a meeting, and finally combined with multiple-choice items written by physics content experts at the Educational Testing Service (ETS). Such a detailed and collaborative development procedure helps to ensure the quality of questions. Free-response questions are assembled with multiple-choice items in such a way that the two parts complement each other to cover the content and skills called for by the test specifications.

Although the resources available to the College Board and the IBO for developing their assessments far exceed the resources available to the average classroom teacher or district curriculum developer, the procedures used by these organizations are instructive in terms of developing even small-scale classroom assessments. The emphases on determining key principles, concepts, and content for assessment; using multiple formats for question development; encouraging review by a group of educators and content experts; and developing and revising careful scoring guidelines based on the test framework and student response are important considerations that teachers and curriculum developers may use as foundations for creating strong assessments.

Center for Gifted Education Science Units

Another example of the use of performance-based assessment tools may be found in the science units developed for high-ability learners by the Center for Gifted Education at the College of William and Mary (Center for Gifted Education, 1997), which assess learning in multiple ways. Student learning outcomes are an ultimate indicator of the effectiveness of curricular intervention. These outcomes include oral and written forms of assessment of product, process, and concept in accordance with the Integrated Curriculum Model (ICM). Ideally, curricular intervention that starts with a curriculum developer's theoretical conceptions should result in tangible student gain to complete the cycle of curriculum development. That successful translation from theory to reality depends on both the soundness of the theory and sensitive measurements well aligned with the theory.

This section will analyze an example of an assessment instrument used in the Center for Gifted Education's science curriculum, with exploration of key features that influenced the selection of the instrument and its incorporation into the curriculum. Specifically, the following pages will explore the two forms of the instrument, scoring, content validity and reliability, student examples, and instructional needs indicated by the assessments. This exploration will also serve to illustrate the importance of a reliable and valid instrument in the study of curriculum effectiveness.

Description of the Instruments and Scoring. The Diet Cola Test was developed by Marilyn Fowler Cain (1990) to assess students' understanding of experiments. It is an open-ended test that requires students to design an experiment to determine whether or not bumble bees are attracted to diet cola. A parallel form to the Diet Cola Test, the Earthworm Test, asks students to design an experiment to find out whether or not earthworms are attracted to light (Adams &

Callahan, 1995). Both instruments were adopted in the Center for Gifted Education's science units to be used on a pretest and posttest basis for their adequate reflection of the unit objectives to develop student experimental research skills, the similar age range targeted, and their sufficiently high ceilings (VanTassel-Baska, Bass, Ries, Poland, & Avery, 1998).

Students' responses are scored according to a checklist of science process skills, with points assigned for addressing each skill and additional points for skills addressed in greater detail:

- plans for *safety*;
- stating the *problem* or *question*;
- giving a *hypothesis*;
- describing three *steps* or more;
- arranging steps in a *sequential order*;
- listing *materials* needed;
- plans to *repeat testing*;
- defining *terms*;
- plans for *observation*;
- plans for *measurement*;
- plans for *data collection*;
- plans for *interpreting data*;
- plans to make *conclusions based on data*; and
- plans to *control variables*.

Reliability of the Instrument. The National Research Center on the Gifted and Talented at the University of Virginia conducted reliability and validity studies on the Diet Cola Test. The study included 180 students in grades 4–8 who were nominated by their teachers as being good in science and employed the method of test-retesting (10-week interval) with alternate forms. Researchers established the reliability of stability and equivalency of the instrument as .76 (Adams & Callahan, 1995).

Validity of the Instrument. The same study at the National Research Center on the Gifted and Talented at the University of Virginia investigated the instrument's content validity and construct validity. The purpose of content validation is to assess whether or not the items adequately represent a performance domain of specific interest (Crocker & Algina, 1986). In this respect, the instrument was said to "exhibit content validity with a clear match between the task and its indicators of success and the criteria of science aptitude suggested by the literature" (Adams & Callahan, 1995, p. 16). The purpose of construct validity is to examine whether or not the instrument correlates highly with other instruments that measure similar constructs of interest. Three instruments were selected to correlate with the Diet Cola Test: the science portion of the Iowa Test of Basic Skills, the Group Embedded Figures Test, and the Test of Basic Process Skills. The results showed low correlations with varied degrees of statistical significance between the Diet Cola Test and other instruments (Adams & Callahan). Therefore, the test was cautioned as not being a suitable identification instrument for making decisions about the specific aptitude of specific individuals.

Given the use of the Diet Cola Test in the Center for Gifted Education's science units, it is more relevant to establish its content validity by examining its match with the objectives of the units and its coverage of the targeted high-level skills in unit instruction.

Match Between the Instrument and Unit Objectives. In light of the findings from the analysis of the the National Education Longitudinal Study (NELS) data (Hamilton, Nussbaum, Kumpermintz, Kerhoven, & Snow, 1995) that the instructional variables of working on experiments in class, problem solving, and promoting scientific understanding were the best predictors of achievement in quantitative science by 10th grade, the William and Mary science units put emphasis on the scientific process, in which students conduct scientific inquiry through the use of experimental design. The units focus on the objectives of developing student abilities to explore a new scientific area, identify meaningful questions within that area, demonstrate good data as appropriate, evaluate results in light of the original problem, make predictions about similar problems, and communicate understanding to others (VanTassel-Baska et al., 1998). The Diet Cola Test, being a performance test that requires students to design an experiment in order to study a given problem, can evaluate fairly well student learning with respect to most of the objectives in the units.

Match Between the Instrument and the Instructional Approach. The specific approach used for instruction in the science units from the Center for Gifted Education is problem-based learning (PBL), discussed in more detail in Chapter 8. Each unit presents students with a problem scenario and proceeds to have them define the problem and ways to solve it. The related science and scientific experiments are introduced in the process of students' exploring and investigating the problem. This problem-based approach is reflected well in the Diet Cola Test, a desirable feature that adds to the authenticity of the instrument.

Match Between the Instrument and Targeted High-Level Thinking. As a science curriculum developed for high-ability learners, the units provide materials and instruction that are sufficiently challenging, in-depth, and varied to meet their learning needs. Through an integrated approach of teaching scientific topics and processes within an overarching concept of *systems*, the units aim to train students in their ability to perform systems thinking and apply what they have learned in an intradisciplinary or interdisciplinary way. Accordingly, the assessment for this kind of learning should give due emphasis to higher level thinking skills, as called for by the tasks in the instrument.

Students' Pretest and Posttest Performance. Most units (four out of six on which data were collected) showed a statistically significant effectiveness when treatment students were compared with their own prior performance or with their peers who received no curricular intervention. To illustrate students' increased understanding in experimental design and data collection after their exposure to the units, three sample responses from fifth graders were presented as follows (grammar and spelling are not corrected).

Earthworm/Diet Cola Test Responses

Student A
  Pretest Response:

  > First, I would put some earthworms in a container. There would be lights and some dirt. I would put several different earthworms in it. If more earthworms liked the light than that would be right. If more didn't like the light then that would be right. I would try this with about seven groups and decide if they liked light. (Score = 5)

Posttest Response:

> *Materials*: Diet Cola, 3 large containers, 3 small containers, 6 bees
>
> *Hypothesis*: If you give bees diet cola then they will be attracted to it.
>
> 1. Gather 6 bees, diet cola, 3 large containers, 3 small containers.
> 2. Put 2 bees in each large container.
> 3. Pour 5 ml of diet cola in each small container.
> 4. Set the small container of diet cola in each large container that has bees in it.
> 5. Watch and observe to see if the bees are attracted to the diet cola.
> 6. You should record if the bees like the diet cola on a chart like below.

Bees	*If they are attracted to Diet Cola*
1	
2	
3	

> (Score = 11)

Student B
Pretest Response:

> No, earthworms don't like light. How I know that is because I took an earthworm and put it on some dert and if it liked sun light it would stay on top of the dert but it didn't it went into the dert where it's dark. (Score = 4)

Posttest Response:

Title of experiment is — Are bees attracted to diet cola?

Materials: a room with nothing in it, 4 bees in a jar, a cup of diet cola, and a Pepsi

Step by step on how to do the experiment: First you take the diet cola & put it in the room when you take the Pepsi and put it in the room by the diet cola. Then you take the jar of 4 bees and release them in the room & then in about 5 mins. see which one they like better & if they don't like neither of them.

How will you know: Look in each cup & see how much they drink out of each cup. The data I will be collecting is: how much diet cola & Pepsi they drink.

Data Table

Diet Cola   Pepsi

(record information here)

(Score = 12)

Student C
Pretest Response:

I don't think earthworms like light, because most of them live underground unless it rains or something and they get washed out of the dirt. I could always do an experiment to make sure, thow. For an experiment, I might take an earthworm with some kind of light, and dirt, and see if it stays out in the light, or trys to get away from the light by going under the dirt.

(Score = 5)

Posttest Response:

Title: "Are bees attracted to diet cola?"

Hypothesis: I don't think bees are attracted to diets, just to regular. For example: Coke, Sprite, Dr. Pepper.

Materials: Bee, diet cola, container

Description of what I would do: Take one can of diet cola and pour about 1 cup of it into a dish, bowl, etc. Then release a bee about a foot away and see if it moves toward the diet cola. If it does—you know bees like diet cola, but if it moves away from the diet cola, or doesn't respond to it you know bees don't like diet cola. When you are done with your experiment carefully release your bee, pour out your soda, and put back the way you found them.

    What will you record: If the bees are attracted to the diet cola or if they are attracted to the non diet liquids.

Data Table:

Tries	1	2	3	4	5	6

Reactions:

(Score = 12)

Note. From "A National Study of Science Curriculum Effectiveness With High-Ability Students," by J. VanTassel-Baska, G. Bass, R. Reis, D. Poland & L. D. Avery, 1998, *Gifted Child Quarterly, 42*, p. 208. Copyright © 1998 by the National Association for Gifted Children, 1707 L St. NW, Ste. 550, Washington, DC 20036, (202) 785-4268, http//www.nagc.org. Reprinted with permission.

Treatment Effect and Revealed Instructional Needs. The implementation results of the science unit showed that, compared with students who did not use the unit, those who participated in unit instruction performed significantly better on the posttest after taking into consideration the pretest difference between the treatment and comparison groups. Content analysis of student performance showed that students were weak in (a) stating a plan for interpreting data, (b) stating a plan for making conclusions based on data, (c) planning to control variables, (d) planning to repeat testing, and (e) planning to practice safety (VanTassel-Baska et al., 1998). More instructional attention is needed in implementing the corresponding component of the curriculum.

Other Assessment Approaches

As mentioned before, teachers need to use formative and summative assessments in a variety of modes to monitor and evaluate student progress over time and to avoid putting undue weight on a single high-stakes test. The assessment opportunities for formative assessment in the William and Mary science units include the following:

- the student's problem log, which is a written compilation of the student's thoughts about the problem (each lesson contains suggested questions for students to answer in their problem logs, which can also be used by the student to record data and new information that he or she has obtained during the course of the unit);
- experimental design worksheets, which can be used to assess a student's understanding of experimental design and the scientific process, as well as to record information about what was done and what was found during student-directed experimentation; and
- teacher observation of student participation in large-group and small-group activities.

Opportunities for summative assessment include the following:

- the final resolution activity, which involves a small-group presentation of a solution to the unit's ill-structured problem, the quality of which will reflect the group's understanding of the science involved, as well as the societal and ethical considerations needed to form an acceptable solution; and
- final unit assessments, which allow the teacher to determine

whether or not individual students have met the science process, science content, and systems objectives listed in the goals and objectives at the beginning of the unit.

Conclusion

Effective and reliable assessment is not an easy task, and for gifted students it is even harder, given the nature of the learner and the nature of the learning in the program. Just as evaluation of gifted programs is a weak area in gifted education, so too is assessment for gifted students. While we can learn from the general assessment literature, we have a great need to build practice and experience in this area, creating performance and portfolio approaches that clearly demonstrate enhanced learning for this population of learners.

Key Points Summary

❑ Effective practice in assessment requires attention to technical details of reliability, validity, test fairness, and test ceiling. Test ceiling is a particularly important consideration in the development of assessments for high-ability learners.

❑ Expectations for student performance on assessments for high-ability learners should be at a high level, requiring the employment of analysis, synthesis, and evaluation skills; these expectations should be conveyed to students through both the questions asked and the rubrics employed for scoring.

❑ A combination of formative and summative, standardized and performance-based assessments should be employed to develop a clear understanding of student progress and learning needs in each area of the curriculum.

❑ The Advanced Placement and International Baccalaureate programs employ assessments that illustrate effective measurement practice for gifted learners by incorporating accelerated content, requirements for higher level thinking, and varied response tasks relevant to the subject areas.

❑ The Center for Gifted Education science curriculum provides another example of performance-based assessment for high-ability learners, incorporating emphasis on higher level task demands relevant to the subject area and a scoring rubric that has a sufficiently high ceiling.

References

Adams, C. M., & Callahan, C. M. (1995). The reliability and validity of a performance task for evaluating science process skills. *Gifted Child Quarterly*, *39*, 14–20.

Asp, E. (1998). The relationship between large-scale and classroom assessment: Compatibility or conflict? In R. Brandt (Ed.), *Assessing student learning: New rules, new realities* (pp. 17–46). Arlington, VA: Educational Research Service.

Cain, M. F. (1990). The diet cola test. *Science Scope*, *13*(4), 32–34.

Center for Gifted Education. (1997). *Guide to teaching a problem-based science curriculum*. Dubuque, IA: Kendall/Hunt.

College Board Advanced Placement Program. (1999a). *Released exams: 1998 AP Physics B and Physics C*. New York & Princeton, NJ: College Entrance Examination Board and Educational Testing Service.

College Board Advanced Placement Program. (1999b). *5-year set of free-response questions 1995–1999: English*. New York & Princeton, NJ: College Entrance Examination Board and Educational Testing Service.

College Board Advanced Placement Program. (1999c). *Released exam 1997: AP statistics*. New York & Princeton, NJ: College Entrance Examination Board and Educational Testing Service.

College Board Advanced Placement Program. (1999d). *Released exam 1998: AP environmental science*. New York & Princeton, NJ: College Entrance Examination Board and Educational Testing Service.

Crocker, L., & Algina, J. (1986). *Introduction to classical and modern test theory*. New York: Holt, Rinehart, & Winston.

Gronlund, N. E. (1998). *Assessment of student achievement* (6th ed.). Boston: Allyn and Bacon.

Hamilton, L. S., Nussbaum, E. M., Kumpermintz, H., Kerhoven, J. I. M., & Snow, R. E. (1995). Enhancing the validity and usefulness of large-scale educational assessments: II. NELS: 88 science achievement. *American Educational Research Journal*, *32*, 555–581.

International Baccalaureate Organization. (1999). *International Baccalaureate Language A1 Guide*. Geneva, Switzerland: Author.

Marzano, R. S., Pickering, D., & McTighe, S. (1993). *Assessing student outcomes: Performance assessment using the dimensions of learning model.* Alexandria, VA: Association for Supervision and Curriculum Development.

Stiggins, R. J. (1991). Facing the challenges of a new era of educational assessment. *Applied Measurement in Education, 4,* 263–273.

VanTassel-Baska, J. (1992). *Planning effective curriculum for gifted learners.* Denver: Love.

VanTassel-Baska, J., Avery, L., Reardon, M., Zuo, L., Rainen, L., & Struck, J. (2001). *Evaluation report of the Virginia Beach gifted program.* Williamsburg, VA: Center for Gifted Education, College of William and Mary.

VanTassel-Baska, J., Bass, G., Ries, R., Poland, D., & Avery, L. D. (1998). A national study of science curriculum effectiveness with high-ability students. *Gifted Child Quarterly, 42,* 200–211.

VanTassel-Baska, J., Zuo, L., Struck, J., & Avery, L. D. (2001). *Evaluation report of Chesterfield County gifted program.* Williamsburg, VA: Center for Gifted Education, College of William and Mary.

Aligning Curricula for the Gifted With Content Standards and Exemplary Secondary Programs

by
Catherine A. Little
and
Wendy T. Ellis

You are a district coordinator for a gifted and talented program in a state that is in the process of implementing high-stakes testing. You have spent the last few years collecting high-level curricular resources for use in your program, and the teachers working with gifted students have attended professional development workshops on the use of these materials and the development of similar ones for their own classrooms. Now, with the advent of the new testing program, district policy requires that teachers be able to demonstrate how all the materials they use relate to the state standards. Your teachers are in a panic because the curricular materials you have asked them to use were not designed under the standards, so they do not seem to have a one-to-one correspondence. In addition, the high school Advanced Placement coordinator wants to set up a meeting with you and the content-area curriculum coordinators to discuss how the K–10 programs prepare advanced students for AP courses in grades 11–12. How do you manage these varied issues?

The chapters in this book have focused on key elements of strong curricula for gifted and talented learners, providing guidelines for both selection of materials and development of curricular frameworks, instructional activities, and relevant assessments. A key emphasis of the book has been on the need to recognize the complexity of the curriculum, instruction, and assessment endeavor. Adding further complexity is the need to extend thinking about curricula beyond the particular classroom or content area and develop a clear sense of the scope and sequence of the overall educational program. The larger educational context in which gifted students experience their education requires that administrators and teachers working with this population have an understanding of how a curriculum for the gifted is aligned with the required standards for all students, as well as how the gifted curriculum is articulated. The development of documents demonstrating these alignments requires a macro-level understanding of the curriculum and the context, including both the intended student population and standards incorporated within state and local accountability frameworks.

The rationale for such macro-level awareness and suggested strategies for developing aligned curricular systems are the focus of this chapter, which will approach alignment of curricula for the gifted from three directions. First, this chapter will examine how existing local, state, and national content standards can be used as a foundation for developing curricula for the gifted in a way that supports alignment, but also raises the level of expectation for advanced learners. Second, it will address how packaged curricular materials for the gifted can be examined side-by-side with existing standards documents in order to demonstrate areas of alignment. Third, it will focus on Advanced Placement (AP) and International Baccalaureate (IB) program options as exemplary high school programs that are appropriate for gifted students (Avery, 1998), exploring how existing structures within these programs can serve as models for vertical alignment that prepare students for college-level coursework.

Using Content Standards
as a Basis for Curriculum Development

There has been a major initiative in the United States toward specifying standards at the national and state levels in the major content areas, and many states have begun implementing related high-stakes testing programs. Standards can be both a help and a hindrance to the educator seeking to develop curricula for classroom use with gifted and talented students (VanTassel-Baska, 2001a). Standards provide a starting point for curriculum development by illustrating the major content areas and processes to be addressed at each given grade level, subject area, or both. The national standards projects are based on expertise from practicing professionals in the various disciplines, who generally base their recommendations for student learning on the core content and key habits of mind required in professional practice. Connections between state-level standards and the national documents allow strong continuity from one place to another, and the accountability movement bears possibilities for improving teaching and learning practices. Moreover, there has been a call at the national level for curricular standards to be more challenging for all students, raising the ceiling for high-ability students even as they raise the minimum standards for all (U.S. Department of Education, 1993).

However, such ideals for raising both ceilings and minimum competencies are not always met in practice, and, in many cases, the standards developed do not represent sufficient challenges for the gifted (VanTassel-Baska, 2001a). Furthermore, the requirement to raise the performance level of all students in order to achieve required scores on high-stakes tests often results in curricula that use the standards themselves as the ceiling, thus limiting students for whom those standards represent only a starting point.

The National Association for Gifted Children's standards for curricula and instruction for gifted programs (Landrum, Callahan, & Shaklee, 2001) emphasize the importance of adaptation and modification of regular classroom curricula to meet the needs of gifted students, as well as articulation of differentiated curricula for the gifted across the K–12 span. This emphasis on the need for differentiation— encompassing placement and program decisions, scope and sequence of the curricula, and instructional objectives, assessments, and resources—underscores the notion that curricula designed primarily to bring all students up to the level of the content standards is unlikely to challenge gifted students sufficiently.

Consequently, curriculum developers in gifted education must use standards as guidelines, but primarily as *minimum* guidelines, then use specific principles related to the learning characteristics of gifted students to extend and expand the standards in the curriculum to be used for these students. Thus, the curriculum developer working to align curricula for the gifted with existing standards must understand two things deeply: the standards themselves and the learning needs of gifted students.

Understanding the Standards

National and state content standards provide useful frameworks for curriculum development practices. However, although some are quite prescriptive, their most effective use with gifted students can only emerge when the curriculum developer understands them deeply and holistically, with the following key principles in mind:

Flexibility. One danger in using the standards too closely as guidelines for curriculum development or for instruction is a tendency to treat them in a linear fashion. Following any set of standards in order with little deviation carries two negative implications. First, it is easy to run out of time and not address all standards in a semester or a year; second, a linear treatment precludes many opportunities to challenge students' higher level thinking by illustrating the connections among different aspects of the standards. For example, at a given grade level in social studies, state standards documents may have guidelines for history, political science, geography, and economics grouped separately, without clear explanations of possibilities for integrating the key ideas. Yet, some economics concepts may be made more understandable to students when explored within historical or political contexts, and study of history is well informed by integrating it with geographic ideas. This call for integration does not presume that all standards can be fully taught when integrated within other standards; however, flexibility in using parts and portions of several standards at once can encourage student learning at all levels.

Conceptual and Critical Thinking Connections. The issue of flexibility and the combination of standards described above presupposes the curriculum developer's ability to recognize the deep conceptual connections among the many aspects of the standards. Such recognition requires the developer to study the standards intensively around a given content area, including both the national standards and the relevant state- and local-level standards. In some cases, the rationale behind standards organization includes some of the disciplinary principles that guided development and may illustrate some of these conceptual connections; an effective strategy is to review the national standards documents first and then the state-level ones. Once conceptual connections have been established, the developer can use methods such as the concept development model discussed in Chapter 5 and conceptual applications suggested in Chapters 6–9 to ground the curriculum for the gifted in challenging, abstract ideas. The concepts, then, provide the foundation upon which standards are regrouped and addressed in different ways, also serving as the glue to hold together advanced content and higher level processes. Beyond the identification of key concepts, another feature of the standards to be addressed and deeply understood by the curriculum developer is the process demand of each of the standards. The developer must examine to what degree a given standard addresses higher level thinking processes and to what degree it represents factual recall or basic skills. A curricular reorganization is then necessary to provide opportunities for pretesting and compacting around basic skills to allow more focus on those processes that represent a higher level of cognitive engagement.

Cross-Subject and Cross-Grade Organization. Teachers generally recognize that they may have students in a class who have not fully mastered the standards assigned to an earlier grade level; thus, these teachers familiarize themselves with the prerequisite standards for what they must teach. Similarly, teachers and curriculum developers working with gifted students should familiarize themselves with the standards at grade levels 1–3 years higher that at which they teach. This allows the development of advanced task demands related to the skills required at the students' level of functioning, rather than their chronological grade level. Moreover, interdisciplinary connections that align the requirements for one subject area with another allow for more real-world and integrated product assignments and save time from addressing all the standards separately.

Intent versus Content. Beyond deeply exploring and understanding the standards across multiple grade levels, the next important principle for a curriculum developer to follow is the need to focus curriculum development on the *intent* of the standards, not just the *content* they include. Both curriculum developers and teachers need to keep in mind that, at their deepest level, the standards are about the ability to learn and think, not about knowledge of isolated factual details. Consequently, the focus of curricular goals and instructional practices, whenever possible, should be on the processes of inquiry that will guide students to discovery of the knowledge and concepts embedded within the standards.

The Learning Needs of Gifted Students

As addressed in Chapter 1 and throughout this text, gifted students demonstrate a number of distinguishing characteristics that are important to consider in developing effective educational programs for them; precocity, intensity, and complexity are the most salient among these characteristics with regard to curriculum development and alignment (VanTassel-Baska, 1995). Suggestions discussed thus far for adapting curricula to address these characteristics may be summed up as attention to a set of specific qualities that define a differentiated curriculum for the gifted: acceleration, complexity, depth, challenge, and creativity (VanTassel-Baska, 2001a). These five elements underscore the three dimensions of the Integrated Curriculum Model (ICM) and incorporate emphases on advanced levels in terms of activities and materials, targeted instructional strategies to engage students in challenging study of complex issues, and opportunities for in-depth and creative project work. The checklist provided in Figure 13.1, organized around the five specific qualities listed above, provides educators with some guidelines for reviewing standards and making appropriate modifications when establishing differentiated expectations for gifted students.

Use of these principles, in conjunction with a deep understanding of the standards, provides the curriculum developer with a solid foundation for writing or adapting curricula that fit within required standards frameworks and also for challenging and engaging high-ability learners. Such a foundation is essential for the curriculum developer seeking to meet the needs of the gifted within today's public school context.

However, although the ability to develop such differentiated and aligned curricula is certainly important, not all curricula that meet such requirements must be designed from scratch. In many situations, existing curricular materials, especially those developed with gifted students or key habits of mind within disciplines, also align effectively with standards and meet the differentiation needs of gifted students at the same time. In these situations, the alignment task is often as simple as taking two existing documents—the curriculum and the standards—and demonstrating how they match. The next section will discuss some guidelines for handling this task efficiently.

1. Acceleration
   - √ Fewer tasks assigned to master standard
   - √ Assessed earlier or prior to teaching
   - √ Clustered by higher order thinking skills

2. Complexity
   - √ Used multiple higher level skills
   - √ Added more variables to study
   - √ Required multiple resources

3. Depth
   - √ Studied a concept in multiple applications
   - √ Conducted original research
   - √ Developed a product

4. Challenge
   - √ Advanced resources employed
   - √ Sophisticated content stimuli used
   - √ Cross-disciplinary applications made
   - √ Reasoning made explicit

5. Creativity
   - √ Designed/constructed a model based on principles or criteria
   - √ Provided alternatives for tasks, products, and assessments
   - √ Emphasized oral and written communication to a real-world audience

Figure 13.1
Differentiation Features Checklist

Note. From *Curriculum Planning and Instructional Design for Gifted Learners*, by J. VanTassel-Baska, in press, Denver: Love. Copyright © 2002 by Love. Reprinted with permission.

Aligning Existing Curricula With Existing Standards

Ideally, curricula today should be designed with attention to the national and relevant state-level standards in the appropriate subject areas, for the appropriate grade level, and with a clear demonstration of how the curricula and the standards are connected. However, such a preorganized alignment is often not possible, either because standards are developed after the curriculum in question or because curricular materials designed under one set of localized standards are brought into use in another area. When this occurs, educators are faced with the task of demonstrating how the curricula they wish to use aligns with existing standards.

Once again, the steps for accomplishing this task relate to a deep understanding of existing standards and a willingness to explore the standards from a holistic, instead of a linear, perspective. Obviously, prewritten curricula are less likely to have a one-to-one correspondence with a given set of standards than are curricula specifically written to match them. Consequently, this type of alignment effort involves not only understanding the standards at a holistic, conceptual level, but also understanding the curricular document in question at such a level. This understanding begins with a review of the goals and outcomes given in the curricular document, compared to the fundamental goals and outcomes illustrated within the standards. Again, frequently the intent of the standard may be addressed more than the specific content, which is why understanding of the fundamental goals and outcomes of both the standards and the curricular document are key to demonstrating effective alignment. In addition to addressing process-level outcomes, the alignment process should also involve summarizing the major content addressed in the curriculum and how it fits with the content addressed in the standards.

Developing Alignment Documents

Depending on the specific requirements of a given situation (such as that addressed in the scenario at the beginning of the chapter), alignment of a curriculum with existing standards may be documented in several different ways. As a curriculum is developed, it is reasonable to indicate at the opening of a unit and within discrete lesson plans the specific standards addressed therein, although, in some cases, a caveat may be necessary to explain that the lesson may address only some portion of the standard(s) indicated. Another useful document is a summary document that demonstrates in chart form the connections between major emphases of the curriculum and the specific standards addressed. Such a document may be specifically organized around the goals of the curriculum, the goals of the standards, or the major emphases of either. Several examples of content area alignments between the Center for Gifted Education's curricula and relevant national standards appear in other chapters of this book (see Chapters 6–9); additional examples of alignment documentation are given in Tables 13.1 and 13.2.

Table 13.1
Social Studies Unit Aligned With State Standards

Unit Emphasis	Virginia Standards
Study of early Jamestown settlers, with emphasis on the following: purposes for colonization; daily life; government/leadership; social structure; interaction with environment; and interaction with local American Indians.	*History/Social Science* VS.3 The student will demonstrate knowledge of the first permanent English settlement in America by a) explaining the reasons for English colonization; b) describing how geography influenced the decision to settle at Jamestown; c) identifying the importance of the charters of the Virginia Company of London in establishing the Jamestown settlement; d) identifying the importance of the Virginia Assembly (1619) as the first representative legislative body in English America; e) identifying the importance of the arrival of Africans and women to the Jamestown settlement; f) describing the hardships faced by settlers at Jamestown and the changes that took place to ensure survival; g) describing the interactions between the English settlers and the Powhatan people, including the contributions of the Powhatans to the survival of the settlers.
Study of development of tobacco as major crop of the Virginia colony, with connection to the development of systems of indentured servitude and slavery.	VS.4 The student will demonstrate knowledge of life in the Virginia colony by a) explaining the importance of agriculture and its influence on the institution of slavery; b) describing how European (English, Scotch-Irish, German) immigrants, Africans, and American Indians (First Americans) influenced the cultural landscape and changed the relationship between the Virginia colony and England; c) explaining how geography influenced the relocation of Virginia's capital from Jamestown to Williamsburg to Richmond; d) describing how money, barter, and credit were used.

Note. "Unit Emphasis" from *Building a New System: Colonial America 1607–1790* (p. 5), by the Center for Gifted Education, 2001, Williamsburg, VA: Author. Copyright © 2001 by the Center for Gifted Education. Reprinted with permission. "Virginia Standards" from *Standards of Learning for Virginia Public Schools* (p. 14), by the Commonwealth of Virginia Department of Education, 2001, Richmond: Author. Copyright © 2001 by the Commonwealth of Virginia Department of Education. Reprinted with permission.

Table 13.2

Language Arts Curriculum Aligned With State Process Standards

South Carolina K–12 Language Arts Standards	Center for Gifted Education Language Arts Curriculum
Use language processes and strategies for continuous learning.	Major goal in linguistic competency emphasizes the development of advanced vocabulary and an advanced understanding of the grammatical system underlying the English language.
	Major goal in literary analysis and interpretation includes emphasis on noting and analyzing significant information in text.
	Emphasis on advanced vocabulary, grammar, and literature requires prerequisite skills in decoding, comprehension, and usage.
Use personal experience, the printed word, and information gained from observation as a basis for constructing meaning.	Major goal in literary analysis and interpretation center on constructing meaning and encourages the interaction between the reader and text, with students encouraged to bring personal reflections and experiences to bear on interpretations of the text along with careful examination of the text itself.
	Multiple opportunities to connect experiences with the world and with literature through discussions and journal writing.
Use language to clarify thought.	Major goal in understanding the concept of *change* emphasizes interdisciplinary connections at the level of the abstract concept as an important basis for constructing meaning.
	Major goals in literary analysis and interpretation and persuasive writing emphasize journal writing and draft development as tools for developing thoughts.
	Major goal in oral communication includes emphasis on discussion and debate as a method of elaborating thinking around literature selections and issues under study.
	Emphasis on peer and teacher review during the writing process encourages questioning for clarity and opportunities for revision.

Note. "Standards" from *Reading/English Language Arts Standards* (p. 6), by the South Carolina Department of Education, 1998, Retrieved May 31, 2001, from http://www.sde.state.sc.us/offices/cso/English_LA/standards.htm. Copyright © 1998 by the South Carolina Department of Education. Reprinted with permission.

In developing alignment documents that address curricula for gifted students, it is also useful to include relevant standards across several grade levels, with the recognition that these students are likely to be capable of managing content and processes above the level of their age peers. For example, a unit designed for elementary gifted students on colonial Virginia was examined for how it related to the Virginia standards at grades 3, 4, and 5 (Commonwealth of Virginia Department of Education, 2001). Several primary emphases of the unit and related standards are demonstrated in Table 13.1. Note that the unit emphases, outlined in the left-handed column, differ slightly in emphasis and orientation from the Virginia standards given in the right-hand column, yet address the same areas of content.

Similarly, existing curricula can be aligned with standards that are organized by process across grade-level groupings by focusing on the major emphases of a given unit. For example, Table 13.2 illustrates how a selection of general K–12 standards in the language arts from the South Carolina Department of Education (1998) are aligned with the Center for Gifted Education's language arts curriculum.

Another issue related to the alignment of existing curricula to existing state and national standards is the issue of aligning one set of curricular goals with another under the umbrella of standards. This issue may arise when educators in one department of a school district wish to incorporate one set of curricular ideas or guidelines, while another department has a different program in mind. Once again, a careful, holistic review of multiple sets of guidelines can often reveal conceptual connections that potentially deepen the learning experience for students by exploring ideas in different ways. For example, the *Understanding by Design* framework recommends that educators examine desired outcomes for students and determine the foundations of these outcomes in "enduring understandings" and "essential questions" (Wiggins & McTighe, 2001). The development of these understandings and questions is followed by a determination of their appropriate assessments of them and resources and activities to support them. Table 13.3 shows the alignment of an eighth-grade social studies unit from the Center for Gifted Education (2000) with one district's local standards and enduring understandings. In districts in which such a framework is in use, a key step of the process is to determine to what degree existing resources support the enduring understandings established as student outcomes. Thus, existing curricula for gifted students should be examined not only in light of appropriateness for advanced learners and connections to stan-

Table 13.3

Social Studies Unit Aligned With Local School District Standards

Lesson Title	Local Social Studies Standards Addressed	Understanding by Design Overarching Understandings Addressed
Introduction to the unit	Examine fundamental political principles. Structure, function, and powers of federal government. Describe the nomination and promotion of candidates for elective office. Demonstrate an understanding of the rights and responsibilities of citizens in America.	All governments have defined structures and functions that interrelate to provide a governing system for citizens. The structure of a government depends directly upon the functions that government is designed to serve. The degree and types of citizen participation in government is influenced by the political system serving those citizens.
Introduction to the topic of democracy	Examine fundamental political principles (constitutional government, democracy and republicanism, consent of the governed). Examine fundamental liberties, rights, and values. Compare the United States' political system to systems of other nations. Demonstrate an understanding of the rights and responsibilities of citizens in the United States.	Democracy is a way that people govern themselves or select representatives as a way to govern themselves. Political systems vary in their concepts of freedom, citizenship, and distribution of power.

Reasoning	Examine fundamental political principles (separation of powers, federalism). Examine fundamental liberties, rights, and values. Compare structure, function, and powers of federal and state governments.	The structure of a government depends directly upon the functions that government is designed to serve. The development of a government is a gradual process requiring compromise, experience, and tradition. Democracy is a way that people govern themselves or select representatives as a way to govern themselves.
Introduction to systems	NA (background for cross-disciplinary understandings).	Each nation has a government structure as established by historical documents, a constitution or set of governing principles, and traditions.
The Three branches of government	Examine fundamental political principles (separation of powers, checks and balances). Structure, function, and powers of federal government. Identify the division and sharing of powers within levels of government.	All governments have defined structures and functions that interrelate to provide a governing system for citizens. All governments have defined structures and functions that interrelate to provide a governing system for citizens. The structure of a government depends directly upon the functions that government is designed to serve.
Systems of government	Examine fundamental political principles (democracy, checks and balances). Structure, function, and powers of the federal government. Identify the division and sharing of powers within levels of government. Compare the United States' political system to systems of other nations.	All governments have defined structures and functions that interrelate to provide a governing system for citizens. The structure of a government depends directly upon the functions that government is designed to serve. Political systems vary in their concepts of freedom, citizenship, and distribution of power.

Note. "Lesson Titles" from *The Road to the White House* (pp. i), by the Center for Gifted Education, 2000, Williamsburg, VA: Author. Copyright © 2000 by the Center for Gifted Education. Reprinted with permission. "Local Social Studies Standards Addressed" from *History and Social Studies Standards of Learning for Norfolk Public Schools* (pp. 15–16), by the Department of Curriculum and Instruction, 1999, Norfolk, VA: Norfolk Public Schools. Copyright © 1998 by the Norfolk Public Schools. Reprinted with permission. "Understanding by Design" from *Draft: Social Studies Essential Questions and Overarching Standards* (pp. 1–3), by the Norfolk Public Schools, 2000, Norfolk, VA: Author. Copyright © 2000 by the Norfolk Public Schools. Reprinted with permission.

dards, but also in reference to how the materials may support other locally determined outcomes and understandings. Such an effort at determining alignment can prevent tension within the school or district organization regarding choice of materials and can also reduce the necessity for developing materials from scratch to match local objectives.

The sections above have illustrated opportunities for curricular alignment primarily within the context of national and state standards, with the central emphasis on *horizontal alignment*, or the connections across expectations for gifted and other learners at a single grade level or within a grade-level cluster. However, *vertical alignment*, or consideration of how a curriculum connects across grade levels, is also key to effective planning, especially when the acceleration needs of gifted students are recognized.

To illustrate guidelines for vertical alignment and also to spotlight two exemplary programs that are challenging and accelerated, the following sections will explore how International Baccalaureate and Advanced Placement are organized and how students in elementary and middle school may be prepared for these high school experiences.

The International Baccalaureate Diploma Programme

The International Baccalaureate (IB) Organization's Diploma Programme (see http://www.ibo.org) is geared toward highly motivated secondary students; in the United States, the program is implemented on the 11th- and 12th-grade levels. While IB utilizes rigorous international curricula, its parameters are broad enough to accommodate national, state, and local requirements. Because the same criterion-based assessments are used worldwide, students are measured by international standards. For this reason, students earning the IB Diploma are generally looked upon favorably by university admissions officers and are frequently granted college credit based on their final assessment scores.

The IB Diploma Programme curricular model encompasses a nucleus of three core components—the Theory of Knowledge course; the extended essay; and creativity, action, and service (CAS)—around which six subjects are centered. This nucleus facilitates interdisciplinarity among the six disparate content areas, encourages an understanding of diverse points of view, and spawns critical thinking (see Figure 13.2).

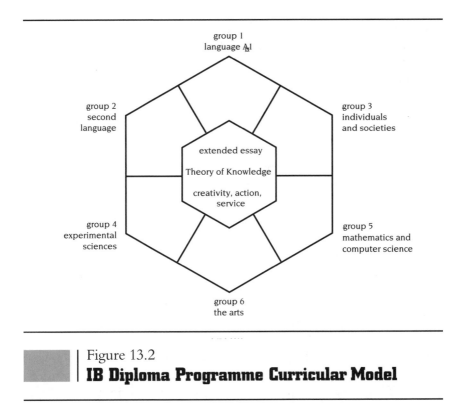

group 1
language A1

group 2
second
language

group 3
individuals
and societies

extended essay

Theory of Knowledge

creativity, action,
service

group 4
experimental
sciences

group 5
mathematics and
computer science

group 6
the arts

Figure 13.2

IB Diploma Programme Curricular Model

Note. From *The Diploma Program Curriculum* (n.d.), Retrieved August 2, 2001, from http://www.ibo.org/ibo2/en/ programmes/prg_dip_cv.cfm. Copyright © 2001 by the International Baccalaureate Organization. Reprinted with permission.

Core Components

The Theory of Knowledge course, which emphasizes the epistemological functions of various areas of knowledge and ways of knowing, allows for osmotic transfer among the subject areas. Knowledge systems—mathematics, natural sciences, human sciences, history, the arts, and ethics—are explored through the lenses of emotion, reason, language, and perception. The 4,000-word extended essay requires students to utilize extensive research and writing skills in the process of exploring a topic of their choice within IB guidelines. The CAS requirement entails 150 hours of active participation in areas of talent and interest and sharing these talents and interests in the form of community service. It is anticipated that CAS will help to produce responsible citizens who are sensitive to the needs of others, supporting the IB philosophy of educating the whole person.

Academic Subjects

The composition of the six academic subject areas is intended to provide balance to the International Baccalaureate student's educational program.

- *Language A1*: focuses on written expression and oral presentation skills in the student's native language coupled with the study of world literature.
- *Second Language*: focuses on written expression and oral communication in a second language.
- *Individuals and Societies*: includes areas that are, in the United States, traditionally associated with social studies and business.
- *Experimental Sciences*: includes biology, chemistry, physics, environmental systems, and design technology.
- *Mathematics*: various levels are available in the area of mathematics in order to speak to students' interests and abilities in this area.
- *Arts*: includes visual arts, music, theatre arts, dance, and film with an emphasis on student production and creativity.

Each student must study three of the subjects at the higher level (at least 240 teaching hours) and three subjects at the standard level (150 classroom hours). This allows students to study with more intensity those areas in which their strengths lie, while developing competence in other areas.

Global contexts and applications are addressed in all six subject areas. Final scores are awarded based on a combination of external assessments and externally moderated internal assessments. These assessments are intended to be summative in nature. Students achieving at least minimum scores in the six subject domains in addition to satisfactory marks in the Theory of Knowledge course, the extended essay, and the CAS components are awarded the International Baccalaureate Diploma.

**The International Baccalaureate Middle Years
and Primary Years Programmes**

In addition to the prestigious Diploma Programme offered at the secondary level, the International Baccalaureate Organization has also developed programs for students at the elementary and middle school levels with similar frameworks. Although these programs are not prerequisites for the secondary program, they nevertheless represent a strong example of vertical alignment. The earlier programs are clearly designed to prepare students at younger ages for the challenges they will confront in the Diploma Programme by emphasizing high-level learning and scholarly habits of mind.

The IB Organization's Middle Years Programme (IB-MYP) is a highly challenging program geared toward students in the middle grades; in the United States, IB-MYP is implemented in grades 6–10. As in the IB Diploma Programme, the IB-MYP curricular framework allows for national, state, and local requirements while maintaining its academic rigor and international focus. Again, criterion-based assessments are used worldwide, allowing for the measurement of student achievement based on international standards.

The IB Primary Years Programme (IB-PYP) is geared toward students in the elementary grades and focuses on the cultivation of internationalism, as well as a core body of knowledge relevant to students of all cultures. In keeping with the parameters set forth by the Diploma and Middle Years Programmes, the IB-PYP curricular framework is also flexible and allows integration with other standards. Unlike the programs for older students, however, all assessments in the IB-PYP take place internally by students and teachers; there are no external assessments or externally moderated internal assessments, although both summative and formative assessments are utilized.

The curricular frameworks for the IB-MYP and IB-PYP (see Figures 13.3 and 13.4) are analogous to the IB Diploma Programme in virtually all elements, demonstrating clear attention to developing core intellectual behaviors across the grade levels. At the center of each program is a set of core components, reflecting preparation for the Theory of Knowledge course in the IB Diploma Programme. Students in the IB-MYP engage in the study of *areas of interaction* that flow in and out of the content areas osmotically. Each area of interaction—including approaches to learning, community service, health and social education, environment, and *homo faber* ("Man the Maker")—becomes a different lens through which the academic domains are explored. Moreover, as central components in the program, they facilitate interdisciplinarity among the academic domains. The emphasis of the core components on aspects of community and the creativity of humankind also help to prepare students for the creativity, action, and service component of the Diploma Programme.

In the IB-PYP, the core of the program is a set of five components that function as the lenses through which the academic subject areas are viewed, lending an epistemic focus. These five compo-

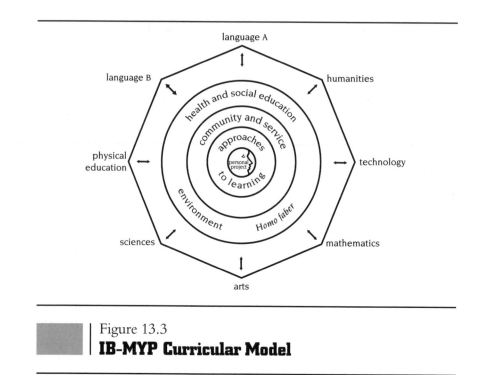

Figure 13.3
IB-MYP Curricular Model

Note. From *The MYP Curriculum* (n.d.). Retrieved August 2, 2001, from the International Baccalaureate Organization Web site: http://www.ibo.org/ibo2/en/programmes/prg_myp_cv.cfm. Copyright © 2001 by the International Baccalaureate Organization. Reprinted with permission.

nents—knowledge, concepts, skills, attitudes, and action—facilitate interdisciplinarity by encouraging connections about learning across subject domains, and they prepare students for the core areas of the programs at upper levels. Moreover, the IB-PYP has an additional level to the framework not found in the programs for older students, a set of six organizing themes. The themes of *Who we are, Where we are in place and time, How we express ourselves, How the world works, How we organize ourselves,* and *Sharing the planet* enable young students to seek a personal identity while simultaneously becoming aware of their role in our world culture. These themes are intended to be explored through the core components and subject areas, enhancing the interdisciplinarity of the program. They also help to prepare students for the "approaches to learning" concept of the IB-MYP and the community service requirements of both the Middle Years and Diploma Programmes.

In terms of academic subjects, the IB-MYP and IB-PYP emphasize the major subject areas and embed a heavy focus on global contexts

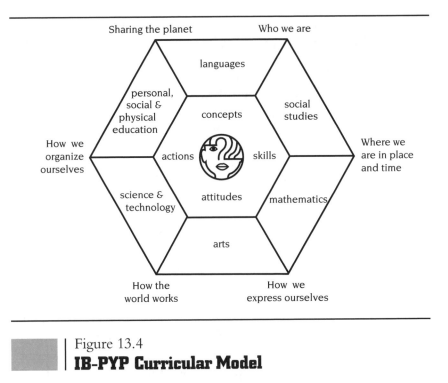

Sharing the planet   Who we are

languages

personal, social & physical education

concepts

social studies

How we organize ourselves

actions   skills

Where we are in place and time

science & technology

attitudes

mathematics

arts

How the world works   How we express ourselves

Figure 13.4
IB-PYP Curricular Model

Note. From *The PYP Curriculum* (n.d.), Retrieved August 2, 2001, from http://www.ibo.org/ibo2/en/programmes/prg_pyp_cv.cfm. Copyright © 2001 by the International Baccalaureate Organization. Reprinted with permission.

and applications. Instruction in both the student's first language and in a second language begins in the Primary Years Programme and remains throughout all the levels. Individual portfolios of products from all subject areas are kept to document student progress.

An additional area of alignment across programs is the culminating project. In the IB-MYP, students must complete a personal project on a topic of their choice that incorporates all of the areas of interaction. This project is analogous to the extended essay required of the IB Diploma candidates, although it utilizes a register that is personal, rather than scholarly. In the IB-PYP, students also develop a personal project for a PYP exhibition in the final year of the program, again with the emphasis on demonstrating competencies across the core components, academic subjects, and organizing themes of the program. Students are assessed on the culminating project and their portfolios at both of these levels before receiving program certificates.

Relationship of IB to Gifted Education and the ICM

The IB family of programs has important implications for curricula and instruction for practitioners in the field of gifted education. There are several specific components of IB that facilitate cohesiveness across K–12 and, therefore, lend themselves nicely to a discussion of curricular alignment.

If the three IB curricular frameworks were to be layered atop one another, a distinct pattern would emerges, one that could be translated into a framework for K–12 gifted programs that is consistent with the ICM. The framework illustrated in Figure 13.5 is fashioned after the IB and integrates the three dimensions of the ICM: the epistemological aspect, which reflects the issues/themes dimension; the emphasis on advanced academic content; and the process/product dimension. Their marriage mirrors the spirit of International Baccalaureate and lays the foundation for its application to K–12 gifted programs.

Epistemological Core. This framework's core serves, as in IB, an epistemological function. For gifted elementary students, this might mean, literally or metaphorically, wearing the different hats of experts in various fields in order to gain an early understanding of their differing approaches to knowledge. How, for instance, might an astronomer view the discovery of a new planet? Would a mathematician's approach be different? A historian's? How might a poet, an artist, or a songwriter respond to such a discovery? These are the types of questions that might be explored by young students in this epistemological realm.

As students enter the middle school years, approaches to epistemological thinking should become more sophisticated. At this point, students can go beyond "thinking like an expert" and be introduced to the concepts of paradigms and the different lenses that color our view of the world. How do differences in language, for instance, affect our understanding? How do individual perceptions alter information relayed, for example, by historians? How do we reconcile the emotions involved in compromising the environment with the practicality of economic considerations?

Utilizing the epistemological approach with gifted elementary and middle school students will prepare them well for advanced study in this realm when they enter high school. On this level, students are given opportunities to assess the relative value of various subject domains. For instance, they may explore the question of whether there

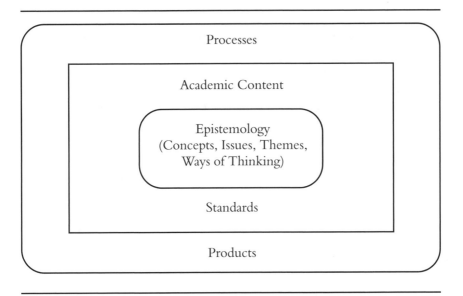

Figure 13.5
K–12 Program Framework
Reflecting IB and the ICM

is actually a hierarchy of languages; is one language "better" than another? Is science more "valuable," for example, than art? In addition, gifted high school students can be introduced to the study of logic; the study of logical fallacies is particularly useful in evaluation of practices used by experts in various fields.

In terms of instructional practices, epistemology is best approached through Socratic questioning, problem finding and problem solving, and vigorous discussion and debate, encouraging complex thinking that incorporates analysis, synthesis, and evaluation. It is important to remember that epistemology cannot occur in a vacuum; it is dependent on the next layer of the ICM, academic content, to exist. The core of epistemology must be integrated into the content areas to achieve optimum interdisciplinarity, a hallmark of appropriate gifted curricula.

Academic Content and Accommodation of Standards. As is illustrated above, the epistemological core is intended to be integrated into the study of academic content. Traditionally, the content model of gifted curricula involves a diagnostic/prescriptive approach that facilitates individualized acceleration of content (VanTassel-Baska, 1994). While moving students through mastered skills at a rapid rate is certainly a justifiable approach with the gifted, integrating epistemology with content provides the needed balance of breadth and depth.

As in the IB curricular models, the above framework implies a scope and sequence of course content that is cohesive from K–12. In order to ensure such cohesiveness, some subject areas should be introduced at an earlier level, most notably foreign languages in elementary school.

Processes and Products. The IB program contains a heavy emphasis on the creation of student products. Gifted curricula should also mirror this emphasis on products and the processes undertaken in their creation. As in IB, the ICM suggests that products created are not isolated in manner, but rather reflect an integration of approaches to knowledge (epistemology) and content.

The focus in the IB program at the middle and primary levels on maintaining a portfolio of students' work throughout their academic careers is an excellent model for gifted students' analysis of their own growth processes. With teacher as facilitator, young gifted students can begin to think metacognitively as they explore their progress over time. Older students begin to "find a voice" in their writing as they assess and reassess their work.

The concept of the public display of students' best work, as in the IB-PYP exhibition, is another excellent application for use with gifted students. This allows, among other things, for students to draw upon their epistemological studies to become "experts" for a day. Students can use the exhibition concept in conjunction with the portfolio, perhaps drawing from it their examples of products for public display.

On the middle school level, the IB-MYP personal project is illustrative of products suited for gifted students. Such a project allows students to integrate research skills, content, epistemology, and personal passions into a culminating educational artifact.

It is important to note that, with gifted students, the processes through which they arrive at their products are just as important as the products themselves. Student initiation of topics for exploration, problem finding and problem solving, and the teacher's role as a "consultant" to the project are key factors to keep in mind.

The College Board Advanced Placement Program

The College Board Advanced Placement (AP) program is similar to the IB Diploma Programme in that it, too, is geared toward able, highly motivated secondary students and is generally implemented on the 11th- and 12th-grade levels. AP courses are intended to provide students the equivalent of university-level coursework while still in high school, as well as the opportunity to receive college credit or advanced placement based on scores received on the corresponding AP Exams. AP Exams are at the heart of the program and can be taken by students regardless of their participation in AP courses; however, the courses provide substantial preparation for the exams, as well as academic challenges not traditionally offered to high school students (College Entrance Examination Board & Educational Testing Service, 1999c). Furthermore, AP courses' reputation for rigor means they are generally looked upon favorably by colleges and universities.

While both programs have developed reputations for academic challenge, AP and IB are quite different in terms of program structure. While IB offers a distinctive curricular model encompassing a student's entire 11th- and 12th-grade academic career, AP courses and exams are offered on an individual basis. A student may elect, for instance, to take only AP Calculus, or may choose to take as many of the 35 available AP courses as are offered by his or her school and are accommodated by his or her class schedule. In any case, students may elect to sit for any number of AP Exams for which the required fees have been paid. Students are measured by rigorous national standards via these assessments, consisting of a single test for each course, generally administered in the spring of the year the course is taken.

Specific curricular and instructional methods are left largely to the instructors responsible for their implementation; in this way, AP's parameters are broad enough to accommodate national, state, and local requirements. Although the program offers a great deal of flexibility in terms of specific curricular and instructional methods, the College Board has developed extensive teacher-training programs and supplemental materials that help to define exemplary content and suggest pedagogy that will facilitate students' success in the course, on the exam, and in university study. For example, the *Advanced Placement Program Course Description: English* (College Entrance Examination Board & Educational Testing Service, 1999a) provides goals and outcomes that suggest a framework within which teachers can develop a course that not only speaks to the rigors set forth by the program, but adapts to the specific needs of their own educational settings. In addition, the *AP English Literature and Composition Teacher's Guide* (College Entrance Examination Board & Educational Testing Service, 1999b) provides corresponding sample curricula, as well as accompanying demographic data about the schools in which theses examples of curricula are taught. This information enables teachers to develop their own courses using similar educational contexts as models. VanTassel-Baska (2001b) has analyzed the benefits of AP for gifted learners to include the following:

- accelerated learning;
- emphasis on higher order thinking skills;
- emphasis on advanced concepts;
- meaningful learning;
- high-level expectations; and
- incentives in the form of college credits, exemption from introductory courses, or both.

Such benefits are inherent in the course syllabi provided by the College Board, but also require strong teaching to ensure that the curriculum is delivered effectively. Ideally, AP teachers should receive advanced training in the nature and needs of gifted students and core research-based strategies that address those needs.

Vertical Teams

While the AP program is generally intended for implementation on the 11th- and 12th-grade levels, the last several years have seen the advent of a new phenomenon: Advanced Placement Vertical Teams (APVT). This concept is similar to the IB-MYP in that it provides for students on the 6th- through 10th-grade levels developmentally appropriate curricula that will prepare them for the rigors of AP on the 11th- and 12th-grade levels. APVT differs from IB-MYP in essentially the same way that AP and IB differ: The parameters for curriculum development and instructional methods are more broad in AP, with no specific model provided. It is up to the teachers to develop a specific program that suits the needs of the educational setting involved while maintaining the rigor inherent in AP. Furthermore, the concept of vertical teaming focuses, as its name implies, on the collaboration of the content-area faculty in grades 6–12. This focus, at first glance, appears to emphasize rigor of content over epistemological issues or process/product considerations; however, there is enough flexibility to allow teachers to utilize these theoretical models in an integrated manner.

APVT provide a scope and sequence that benefits gifted learners by eliminating redundancy and providing a skills base that enables them to move on to more complex concepts at an earlier age (Cannon & Kjos, 1999). For example, the concept of tone, the understanding of which is essential for success on the AP English Language and Composition Exam, can be introduced in the sixth grade. By anticipating the complex layers involved in using the concept of tone in literary analysis on the 12th-grade level, the English Vertical Team can then fashion a continuum of instruction that develops students' skills in this area to become progressively more sophisticated from the 6th through the 12th grades. Cohesion among the grade levels within each content area is most effective when a scope and sequence is set forth for as many domain–specific concepts as possible.

Relationship of AP to Gifted Education and the ICM

The Advanced Placement program and its corresponding Vertical Teams have important implications for curricula and instruction for practitioners in the field of gifted education. AP corresponds most closely with the advanced content emphasis of gifted curricula (VanTassel-Baska, 1994). This model allows for ease of alignment with national, regional, and local standards, while providing for acceleration of, and emphasis on, content. If using a team approach similar to Vertical Teams, teachers can decide at the outset the pace of the content coverage over the 7-year period, rendering classroom time more efficient by eliminating repetition. This increased efficiency allows not only for more breadth of content, but for increased depth, as well.

The utilization of a scope and sequence in developing gifted programming is essential in providing appropriate educational experiences for gifted learners (VanTassel-Baska, 2001a, 2001b). The APVT concept provides an excellent example of developing content-specific scope and sequence for grades 6–12. In order to extend its comprehensiveness, this type of team approach can and has been extended into the elementary level (Cannon & Kjos, 1999). Alignment suited for the gifted can be further enhanced by extending into the realm of interdisciplinarity. Representatives from the respective content-area teams can meet to form interdisciplinary subteams intended to ensure infusion of multiple content areas within each class. This extension allows for enrichment of the classroom experience though the incorporation of epistemological concepts.

Conclusion

The impact of the standards movement has clearly been felt in all aspects of curricular work at the K–12 levels, leading to the need for careful alignments and articulation of learning intentions, practices, and outcomes across the grade-level spectrum within and across subject area disciplines. Such alignment efforts must include attention to both horizontal and vertical connections among expectations and should involve collaborative teams of teachers who are capable of making the relevant connections at all levels of curricular analysis, from goals to activities. For gifted students to benefit from, rather than be cheated by, the standards movement, closer alignment with the secondary hallmark programs of IB and AP is called for. Through such processes, gifted students may someday experience a seamless web of learning that truly represents coherent challenge at each stage of their development.

Key Points Summary

❑ Alignment of gifted curricular practices to state standards is an essential part of program development.

❑ The use of vertical teams to work on a content curriculum across at least 3 years facilitates appropriate differentiation of the standards for gifted students.

❑ Scope and sequence planning provides school districts with a comprehensive, articulated set of offerings for gifted students at all levels of learning and in all core areas.

❑ Alignment of gifted curricula to other major district initiatives or local standards is essential to effective communication about curricula.

❑ Both Advanced Placement and International Baccalaureate offer articulated programs that extend from elementary through high school.

❑ Both Advanced Placement and International Baccalaureate programs, if taught well, embody the principles of the Integrated Curriculum Model.

References

Avery, L. D. (1998). Gifted curriculum at secondary level through Advanced Placement and International Baccalaureate. *Gifted and Talented International, 13*, 90–93.

Cannon, E., & Kjos, M. (1999, October). *English vertical teaming.* Presentation at the Advanced Placement Workshop, Richmond, VA.

Center for Gifted Education. (2000a). *Building a new system: Colonial America 1607–1790.* Williamsburg, VA: Center for Gifted Education, College of William and Mary.

Center for Gifted Education. (2000b). *The road to the White House: The American system of representative democracy.* Williamsburg, VA: Center for Gifted Education, College of William and Mary.

College Entrance Examination Board & Educational Testing Service. (1999a). *Advanced placement program course description: English.* Princeton, NJ: Author.

College Entrance Examination Board & Educational Testing Service. (1999b). *AP English literature and composition teacher's guide.* Princeton, NJ: Author.

College Entrance Examination Board & Educational Testing Service. (1999c). *A guide to the Advanced Placement program.* Princeton, NJ: Author.

Commonwealth of Virginia Department of Education. (2001). *Standards of learning for Virginia public schools.* Richmond, VA: Author.

Department of Curriculum and Instruction. (1999). *History and social studies standards of learning for Norfolk Public Schools.* Norfolk, VA: Norfolk Public Schools.

International Baccalaureate Organization. (2001a). *The diploma program curriculum.* Retrieved August 2, 2001 from http://www.ibo.org/ibo2/en/programmes/prg_dip_cv.cfm

International Baccalaureate Organization. (2001b). *The MYP curriculum.* Retrieved August 2, 2001 from http://www.ibo.org/ibo2/en/programmes/prg_myp_cv.cfm

International Baccalaureate Organization. (2001c). *The PYP curriculum.* Retrieved August 2, 2001 from http://www.ibo.org/ibo2/en/programmes/prg_pyp_cv.cfm

Landrum, M. S., Callahan, C. M., & Shaklee, B. D. (Eds.). (2001). *Aiming for excellence: Annotations to the NAGC pre-K–grade 12 gifted program standards*. Waco, TX: Prufrock Press.

Norfolk Public Schools. (2000). *Draft: Social studies essential questions and overarching standards*. Norfolk, VA: Author.

South Carolina Department of Education. (1998). *Reading/English language arts standards*. Retrieved May 31, 2001 from http://www.sde.state.sc.us/sde/educator/standard/langarts/gin_lafr.htm

U.S. Department of Education, Office of Educational Research. (1993). *National excellence: A case for developing America's talent*. Washington, DC: U.S. Government Printing Office.

VanTassel-Baska, J. (1992). *Planning effective curriculum for gifted learners*. Denver: Love.

VanTassel-Baska, J. (1994). *Comprehensive curriculum for gifted learners*. Needham Heights: Allyn and Bacon.

VanTassel-Baska, J. (1995). Developing talent through curriculum. *Roeper Review, 18*, 98–102.

VanTassel-Baska, J. (2001a). *Curriculum planning and instructional design for gifted learners*. Denver: Love.

VanTassel-Baska, J. (2001b). The role of Advanced Placement in talent development. *The Journal of Secondary Gifted Education, 12*, 126–132.

Wiggins, G., & McTighe, J. (2001). *Understanding by design*. Upper Saddle River, NJ: Merrill/Prentice Hall.

Implementing Innovative Curricular and Instructional Practices in Classrooms and Schools

by
Joyce VanTassel-Baska

This final chapter focuses on the implementation considerations necessary to make curricular innovation work on a larger scale than that of individual classrooms. It explores the importance of assessment as a part of the mosaic that charts student progress across years within and across learning areas and showcases the effectiveness data available to guide teacher practice.

This chapter will also explore research-based best practices in staff development that must be emphasized within and across schools in order to sustain innovative practice. Finally, it will address the leadership dimension so essential in institutionalizing meaningful school reforms.

Curriculum Effectiveness Research

Creating effective curricular and instructional models requires that a significant amount of attention go to the development of an effective accountability system. The use of assessment tools that facilitate student learning at the same time that they provide useful data for future instructional planning is the hallmark of performance- and portfolio-based assessment techniques, which have been discussed in the content and assessment chapters of this text (Chapters 6–9 and 12). Yet, it is systematic data collection on high-ability students over time that best demonstrates the effectiveness of any curricular model as a tool for enhancing significant and important learning. The Integrated Curriculum Model (ICM) has been tested substantially in the areas of science and language arts, using quasi-experimental research designs that compared pretest–posttest performance of students participating in the Center for Gifted Education units in these areas with the performance of similar students who were not taught using the units. The presentation of claims for student learning in each area follows, demonstrating specifically the results related to the specific curriculum, as well as supporting the notion of ongoing data-collection efforts to maintain high-quality curricular efforts.

Science Curriculum Effectiveness Data

The Center for Gifted Education's problem-based science curricular units for high-ability learners in grades 2–8 have been rigorously evaluated to ensure both effectiveness in promoting student learning gains and acceptance by teachers. Not only have the units and accompanying training materials undergone four major revisions in the course of their development, the next-to-last edition of the units was field-tested across multiple school districts.

The goals of the program across all of the units have consistently been threefold: (1) to develop student understanding of the concept of *systems*, (2) to develop specific content learning that is unit dependent, and (3) to develop scientific research processes. More specific learning outcomes have been delineated under each of these broad overarching goals, in keeping with the intent of the National Science Standards and the Benchmarks for Science Literacy that call for substantive content linked to high-level scientific processes and the understanding of meaningful scientific concepts (American Association for the Advancement of Science, 1990; National Research Council, 1996).

Although the units are designed to have assessments addressing all three of the major science learning goals given above, the research design investigating the curriculum's effectiveness focused explicitly on student application of the scientific method. Findings related to two of the units, *Acid, Acid Everywhere* and *What a Find!* (Center for Gifted Education, 1997a, 1997b), are presented here for illustrative purposes. Further discussion of the design of the units themselves may be found in Chapter 8.

Design. The sample for the evaluation of effectiveness of each unit was composed of volunteer teachers and their classrooms from our national network of schools, including districts from the states of Illinois, Florida, Connecticut, South Carolina, Ohio, Indiana, and Virginia. These same districts agreed to collect comparison data from classes of students of comparable ability in the same schools. The actual numbers of participating teachers varied by curricular unit being evaluated. Data were collected from 42 teachers covering 45 experimental classrooms for *Acid, Acid Everywhere,* with 10 comparison teachers covering 17 classrooms. For *What A Find!,* data were collected from 20 teachers covering 27 experimental classrooms, with 3 comparison teachers and classrooms. All teachers who participated in the field testing of units received implementation training lasting 2–5 days.

Students included in the sample were all average, above-average, or high-ability learners and were drawn from urban, suburban, and rural districts. All pull-out and self-contained classrooms contained only high-ability learners, but other organizational models were also represented in the sample.

Experimental and comparison classrooms were assessed on a pretest and posttest basis. Posttests were administered at the conclusion of the implementation process, after approximately 20–36 hours of instruction.

Instruments and Procedures. Claims regarding the evidence of effectiveness of the science curriculum in promoting student learning are based on the use of the Diet Cola Test (Cain, 1990). The Diet Cola Test measures a student's ability to apply the scientific method and to demonstrate scientific reasoning skills.

The instrument has alternate forms, which made it very useful for the pretest-posttest design employed in the evaluation. Its reliability was documented by the National Research Center on the Gifted and

Talented at the University of Virginia (Adams & Callahan, 1995), and its psychometric properties are reasonably high. It is an open-ended, performance-based assessment using a rubric with a ceiling of 21 points to rate student responses. It was the only instrument found in the literature to be appropriate for gifted students in science across the elementary and middle school age ranges due to its sufficiently high ceiling. It is also fairly quick to administer, taking only 30–40 minutes.

Data Analysis and Results. The analysis of the data for the two science units yielded statistically significant results, showing that students in the experimental or treatment classrooms outperformed students in the comparison classrooms on the posttest, with statistical controls in place for between-group differences in pretest scores. Effect sizes were also calculated to give a measure of how educationally important the significant differences are.

For *Acid, Acid Everywhere,* the experimental classrooms had an adjusted mean posttest score of 6.81 (statistical adjustment based on pretest scores in the two groups). The adjusted mean score for the comparison group was 5.41. For *What a Find!,* the adjusted mean on the Diet Cola Test for the experimental group was 5.95, and for the comparison group, it was 4.07. Both of these sets of results demonstrated statistical significance between treatment and comparison classes, indicating that the higher scores in the treatment group could be attributed to the use of the curriculum and not just to chance. The effect sizes also demonstrated that the differences were educationally important. More detailed descriptions of the study and the results may be found in other publications (see VanTassel-Baska, Bass, Ries, Poland, & Avery, 1998).

Teacher Questionnaire Results. In addition to student test data, the effectiveness of the science units was also assessed by asking teachers to respond to a curricular unit evaluation questionnaire. Forty-two teachers from 15 school districts completed the questionnaire for *Acid, Acid Everywhere.* Demographic data from this form demonstrated that the range of classes participating in the study included various grouping patterns, from self-contained gifted classes to heterogeneous classrooms, and that the teachers were generally experienced, with several years of working with gifted and talented students and of teaching science.

The questionnaire then asked teachers to indicate their perceptions of the unit, based on their experience teaching it. Most teachers reported positive perceptions of the unit. Teachers found the unit to be highly appropriate for high-ability students in terms of goals and outcomes, as well as exercises and activities. They also felt that it promoted active student involvement and that it was motivating for students. The overall judgment of the units by pilot teachers seemed to center on four main points:

- the units had applicability across a broad range of learners;
- the units were well designed and documented important curricular elements for teachers;
- the units were enjoyable and motivating for both students and teachers; and
- teachers would use the units again.

Language Arts Curriculum Effectiveness Data

The Center for Gifted Education's language arts curricular units have also been evaluated for effectiveness in terms of teaching literary analysis and interpretation and persuasive writing as language arts manifestations of higher level thinking (VanTassel-Baska, Zuo, Avery, & Little, 2002). As such, the study, discussed in the following sections, contributes to our understanding of the importance of embedding higher order skills into content and builds on prior understanding of effective research-based strategies for teaching writing (e.g., Burkhalter, 1995).

Design and Purpose of the Study. By using a quasi-experimental design, the researchers sought to demonstrate the effects of particular units of study on gifted learners at primary, intermediate, and middle school levels. Each unit was organized around the ICM (VanTassel-Baska, 1986, 1995) and, therefore, sought to enhance learning through an integrated approach of using advanced literature, embedding a reasoning model into the teaching of the language arts, requiring a high-quality student product, and teaching the major concept of *change* as it applies to literature, writing, language study, and oral communication.

Sample. Seventeen public school districts and one private school furnished student data for this study. The districts and schools were quite diverse, drawn from rural, urban, suburban, or exurban settings across 10 states: Colorado, Connecticut, Illinois, Indiana, Maryland, Ohio, South Carolina, Utah, Virginia, and West Virginia. The private school was located in an urban area. In all, 46 schools across these districts participated in the study.

Students participating in the study (N = 2,189) were all preidentified gifted learners in grades 2–8 in their local school district. Given the relative standard of giftedness applied to identification procedures at the local level coupled with the variety of state definitions of giftedness (Karnes & Stephens, 2000), the range of general ability and verbal aptitude varied in the sample to some extent. Identification criteria employed in the 10 participating states included ability and aptitude measures coupled with teacher recommendations. Threshold scores ranged from 94–99% for both identification on group ability measures and on group on-grade verbal aptitude measures.

Curricular Treatment. The curricular materials used in the study were four of a series of six units, organized around the ICM curricular framework developed under a federal Javits grant in the mid-1990s. The goals of the units are outlined in Chapter 6 on language arts. The units included pretests and posttests for literary analysis and interpretation and for persuasive writing. Other assessments, including both formative and summative measures, were also included. The four units included one written for grades 2–3, two for grades 4–6, and one for grades 7–9. This study focused on the pretest-posttest results of the literature and writing tests. Each of the teachers involved in the study received 1–4 days of training on the curricular materials. The training workshops were conducted by project staff, local teachers, or administrators who had themselves been trained for workshop leadership. Workshops introduced teachers to the curricular framework and to the specific teaching models used in the units, with discussion of how those models promoted accomplishment of the goals.

Instrumentation. The two assessments used in the study measured literary analysis and persuasive writing skills. The same task demands were consistent across the units, although different stimuli were used to evoke student responses in each unit. At the beginning and at the end of each unit, students were asked to read a selection and complete the two assessments based on that selection. Both assessments were piloted with relevant populations and formed the basis of an earlier curriculum effectiveness study (VanTassel-Baska, Johnson, Hughes, & Boyce, 1996). The first assessment was a performance-based test of literary analysis and interpretation. This test, modeled on the NAEP (National

Assessment Governing Board, 1992) assessment in reading, included four questions that addressed the following topics: (1) main idea, (2) analysis of a quote, (3) relationship of the concept of *change* to the selection, and (4) creating a title with a rationale to support it. The second assessment was a performance-based persuasive writing assessment that asked students to develop an argument to support whether or not they would require all the students in their grade to read the given selection (Center for Gifted Education, 1999). In each unit, students read and responded to a different selection in the pretest than in the posttest, although the two selections in each unit represented the same genre.

Scoring. The rubric for the literature test gave a range of 0–3 points for each of the four questions, for a total score range of 0–12. The rubric for the writing test was based on Toulmin's (1958) criteria for judging quality of claim, data, and warrant as adapted by Burkhalter (1995). This rubric gave a range of 0–20 total points, with a 0–6 range for each of the elements of claim, data, and warrant, and a 0–2 range for the conclusion (see Table 14.1 for a sample rubric).

Method. As in the science study discussed earlier in this chapter (VanTassel-Baska et al., 1998), the statistical test used to compare treatment and comparison classes in the language arts study was analysis of covariance (ANCOVA), which controls for between-group differences. The results of these analyses indicated statistically significant differences on the posttests for literary analysis and interpretation and for persuasive writing favoring the treatment group, which again means that higher mean scores on the posttests could be attributed to the use of the curricular units. For the literary analysis test, the adjusted mean score on the posttest for the treatment group was 6.86, while the comparison group had an adjusted mean score of 5.88. On the persuasive writing test, differences were even more dramatic, with the treatment group achieving an adjusted mean posttest score of 11.34, while the comparison group had an adjusted mean score of 7.59. The effect sizes were also medium to large, again indicating both educational importance of the results and statistical significance.

These analyses were conducted across four language arts units; the results of separate analyses, conducted at the unit level, are consistent with the results combined across units. In other words, virtually any language arts unit within the Center for Gifted Education's curriculum can be implemented and expected to generate significant treatment effect.

Table 14.1

Persuasive Writing Scoring Rubric

Score	Description of Response

Claim or Opinion:

0   No clear position exists on the writer's assertion, preference, or view, and context does not help clarify it.

2   Yes/no alone or writer's position is poorly formulated, but reader is reasonably sure what the paper is about because of context.

4   A basic topic sentence exists, and the reader is reasonably sure what the paper is about based on the strength of the topic sentence alone.

6   A very clear, concise position is given as a topic sentence, with some detail to explain context, and the reader is very certain what the paper is about.

Data or Supporting Points:

0   No data are offered that are relevant to the claim.

2   Scant data (one or two pieces) are offered, but what data exist are relevant to the claim.

4   At least three pieces of data are offered. They are relevant, but not necessarily convincing or complete.

6   At least three pieces of accurate and convincing data are offered.

Warrant or Elaboration on Data:

0   No warrant or elaboration is offered.

2   An attempt is made to elaborate at least one element of the data.

4   More than one piece of data is explained, but the explanation is weak and lacks thoroughness, or one piece of data is well elaborated.

6   The writer explains more than one piece of data in such a way that it is clear how they support the argument. At least one piece of data is convincingly and completely elaborated.

Conclusion:

0   No conclusion/closing sentence is provided.

2   A conclusion/closing sentence is provided.

Note. From *Autobiographies* (pp. 31–32), by the Center for Gifted Education, 1998, Dubuque, IA: Kendall/Hunt. Copyright © 1998 by the Center for Gifted Education. Reprinted with permission.

Additional tests were run to compare performance by gender and by socioeconomic status (SES) within the treatment group. In the gender comparison, results showed that there were no differences by gender for literature, but found a statistically significant difference for persuasive writing ($p < .01$). However, that difference was found to be of little practical importance when effect size was computed. This suggests that boys and girls benefitted relatively equally from their exposure to the literature curriculum. The SES comparison was conducted using schoolwide data on percentage of students on free or reduced lunch programs to categorize schools as high SES or low SES. This comparison yielded no statistically significant differences between the groups and demonstrated clearly, especially in writing, that students from high- and low-SES groups can benefit from using the curriculum. Additional details on the results of the language arts study may be found elsewhere (see VanTassel-Baska et al., 2002).

Discussion of Results. The data suggested that the use of the Center for Gifted Education's language arts units produces significant and important gains for gifted learners in key aspects of the language arts, as assessed by demonstration of high-level thinking on performance-based measures. Because of the integration of goals within the units, these findings contribute to our understanding of teaching literature and writing in an integrated way, teaching for deeper understanding, and teaching for thinking within a subject area. All of these are important aspects in enhancing learning when teaching to the new standards and to reflect research on teaching both literature and writing (e.g., Hillocks, 1986; McLaughlin & Talbert, 1993). The deliberate use of instructional models, such as the Literature Web, Hamburger Model, and the Paul model of reasoning, within the curriculum to promote student automaticity in thinking and writing about ideas appears to have impacted student learning positively (see Chapters 3 and 6 for explication of the relevant instructional models).

The treatment was effective with both economically disadvantaged and economically advantaged students. It was also equally effective with males and females when educational importance was used as the criterion to examine small differences. The grouping model used showed minimal evidence of impact on student performance, with all grouping models showing strong evidence of learning gains. Clearly, students benefitted from their exposure to the Center for Gifted Education's curricular units in language arts, and these benefits were

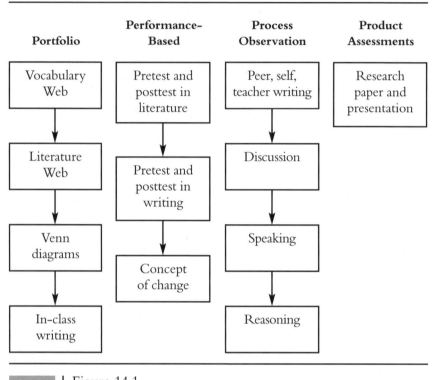

Portfolio	Performance-Based	Process Observation	Product Assessments
Vocabulary Web	Pretest and posttest in literature	Peer, self, teacher writing	Research paper and presentation
Literature Web	Pretest and posttest in writing	Discussion	
Venn diagrams	Concept of change	Speaking	
In-class writing		Reasoning	

Figure 14.1
Assessment Tools for Language Arts Units

documented in terms of learning outcomes of statistical and educational significance on performance-based assessment measures. Furthermore, this study showed how a curriculum derived from standards-based reform can be assessed using instruments that require demonstration of higher order reasoning in the language arts domain. Such assessments then provide data to support staff development and continuous improvement of curricular implementation.

Other Assessment Approaches

In addition to core assessments of accountability for student learning, a content-based system of assessment must also include formative approaches that understand how students are progressing and end-of-unit cumulative product assessments. The Center for Gifted Education's units contain several different assessment components so that teachers have maximum opportunities for student assessment information (see Figures 14.1 and 14.2).

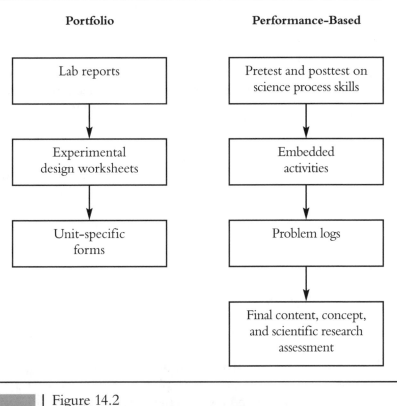

	Portfolio		**Performance-Based**

Lab reports	Pretest and posttest on science process skills

↓ ↓

Experimental design worksheets	Embedded activities

↓ ↓

Unit-specific forms	Problem logs

↓

	Final content, concept, and scientific research assessment

Figure 14.2
Assessment Tools for Science Units

Staff Development

A second area of need within a system of curricula and instruction is an effective plan and a follow-up evaluation mechanism for staff development. Guskey (2000) has argued that our accountability system for judging the efficacy of staff development is weak and has suggested that we need to consider several areas for assessing effectiveness. These include the following:

- participants' reactions;
- participants' learning;
- organizational support for change;
- use of knowledge and skills; and
- student learning outcomes (results).

When planning staff development programs for teachers of the gifted, there is a real need to focus on the elements that research suggests have been the most critical. These would include selecting content topics that respond to real, as opposed to perceived, need. Thus, in implementing reform-based principles, it is necessary to ascertain those principles teachers routinely employ and those they need to have skills for using. Based on a recent analysis of 165 classrooms (VanTassel-Baska, Avery, & Reardon, in press), it is clear that teachers of the gifted need more emphasis on the utilization of individualization techniques, critical thinking, problem solving, and metacognition, since the pattern of data suggests greatest discrepancy between observed and desired behavior in these dimensions. Thus, workshops on the implementation of appropriate curricular units should stress these skills.

A second research-based best practice in staff development involves emphasizing student learning in key areas as the goal and using student-learning data as the best evidence of effective staff development work. The Center for Gifted Education's staff development model (see Figure 14.3) encourages teachers to collect student data on the models taught through staff development and to use these data to make adjustments in their teaching. Only then can the claim of effective staff development be made.

A third area of research-based staff development practice involves the follow-up mechanisms that are in place in schools to encourage active experimentation with new teaching strategies and models (e.g., Joyce & Showers, 1983). It is clear that many schools are not positioned to engage in meaningful staff development practices based on the lack of organizational support for such activity. Principals and teacher teams must be actively engaged in ensuring that practices learned are tried out and supported in everyday practice. Evidence suggests that teachers practice a strategy or model before they make judgments about it based on how students react. If students respond favorably, then teachers are more apt to change their attitudes and beliefs about using a new model for learning (Guskey, 2000). Our experience with the Center for Gifted Education's staff development model suggests similar findings. Results from teacher implementation data in science, for example, consistently showed that teacher enthusiasm for problem-based learning increased as they saw their students' motivation increase with use of the pedagogy (VanTassel-Baska et al., 1998). An age of meaningful accountability calls out for school contexts in which teacher learning is as paramount a concern as student learning.

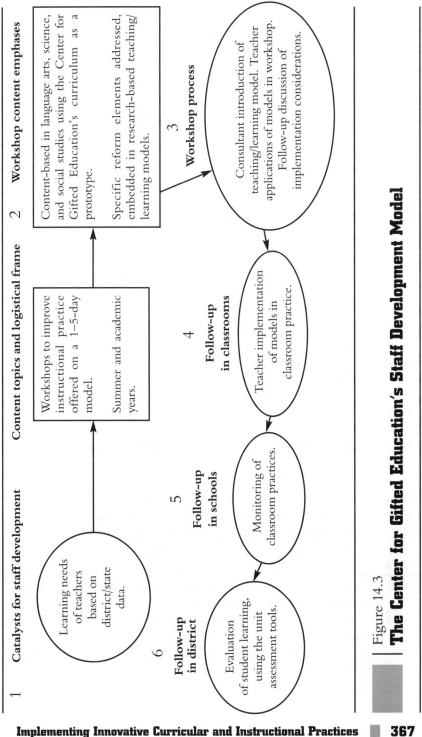

1 Catalysts for staff development	Content topics and logistical frame	2 Workshop content emphases

1   Catalysts for staff development

Learning needs of teachers based on district/state data.

6
Follow-up in district

Evaluation of student learning, using the unit assessment tools.

5
Follow-up in schools

Monitoring of classroom practices.

Content topics and logistical frame

Workshops to improve instructional practice offered on a 1–5-day model.

Summer and academic years.

4
Follow-up in classrooms

Teacher implementation of models in classroom practice.

2   Workshop content emphases

Content-based in language arts, science, and social studies using the Center for Gifted Education's curriculum as a prototype.

Specific reform elements addressed, embedded in research-based teaching/learning models.

3
Workshop process

Consultant introduction of teaching/learning model. Teacher applications of models in workshop. Follow-up discussion of implementation considerations.

Figure 14.3

The Center for Gifted Education's Staff Development Model

Another key finding from the staff development literature suggests that training on practices embedded in content and materials to be used in classrooms aids student learning, and, thus, it enhances the likelihood that teachers will continue employing the practice (Kennedy, 1999). This strategy for staff development work has been extensively employed in National Science Foundation (NSF) projects over the past decade, as well as in the curricular implementation workshops through the Center for Gifted Education at the College of William and Mary. A major emphasis in such training involves the teaching of a core model, practice, feedback, and then a demonstration of how and where it may be found in a unit of study or constructed into one. Closely linked to this demonstration is showing how the model is aligned to the teaching of the content area under discussion based on the demands of state standards. Thus, teachers leave a workshop with a contextual base for the use of the technique.

Finally, research-based best practice in staff development supports the need for a match between the sophistication of the learning and the duration of training opportunities. In-depth summer training options appear to work best if the learning to be accrued is complex, and more follow-up will be needed to ensure faithful implementation of such practices.

The staff development model, developed to help teachers implement the Center for Gifted Education's curricular model, addresses the assumptions of these research-based best practices.

The Role of Leadership in Reform-Based Practice

There has never been a time when instructional leadership has been in greater demand than it is now as we prepare to implement a substantial curricular learning reform agenda. The needs for such leaders must first evolve from a sound theoretical sense of what educational leadership is all about. Minimally, they must be schooled in the following principles, which are derived from theory:

- Leadership is about accepting the multiple realities of working in an organization (Bolman & Deal, 1991).
- Leadership is about integrity, using power to help people grow (Burns, 1978).
- Leadership is about building learning communities and managing them in contemporary educational environments (Gardner, 1990).

Table 14.2
Classroom Observation Form: Critical Thinking Strategies

The teacher used activities or questions that enabled students . . .	Yes	No	Comments
1. to make judgments or evaluate situations, problems, or issues	❏	❏	
2. to compare and contrast	❏	❏	
3. to generalize from specific data to the abstract	❏	❏	
4. to synthesize and summarize information within or across the disciplines	❏	❏	
5. to debate points of view or develop arguments to support ideas	❏	❏	

Note. From *Classroom Observation Form* (p. 2), by the Center for Gifted Education, 1999, Williamsburg, VA: Author. Copyright © 1999 by the Center for Gifted Education. Reprinted with permission.

- Leadership is about accepting and creating challenge through reflection, intention, and action (Kouzes & Posner, 1995).

In addition, school leaders must deliberately monitor classrooms on a regular basis to ensure that a given model is being implemented and done well. If the desired practice is critical thinking, for example, then the principal could use a simple checklist like the one in Table 14.2 to discern the use of these behaviors.

However, in order to implement such a checklist, the school leader must be able to discern these behaviors when they are in use. Since most of the reform strategies focus on higher level skill and concept development approaches, some training for administrators is warranted to ensure that reform practices are understood well enough to be effectively monitored. Thus, training for administrators in the models that teachers have learned, to the extent necessary for recognizing their use and judging the efficacy of their delivery, is crucial.

For example, a principal observed in an elementary school spent time in the classrooms every day, assessing the behaviors associated with the successful implementation of the Center for Gifted Education's language arts curriculum, and, based on his observations, he discerned the need for follow-up in-service in key areas for specified teachers only, thus successfully differentiating the staff development plan based on real data from the classroom.

Leadership must also be motivational and even inspirational in schools in order to lift the spirits of teachers and students who are engaged in the difficult work of enhancing learning. Thus, principals must be aware of the need for honoring the culture and symbolically rewarding the efforts that go on within it (Peterson, 2001). A high priority must be placed on accolades for enhanced learning. One school district, for example, rotates board meetings to each school in the district and asks the principal of each school to stage a performance demonstrating student learning. In addition, at each board meeting, students who received awards during the past month are individually recognized, along with their parents, for their accomplishments. The event is handled in such a way that the experience is one of celebration. This is an example of a learner-centered school district, in which learners are the focus of adult activities and evidence of learning is rewarded. Talent development must be recognized in order to demonstrate that it is valued sufficiently in a school context.

The Importance of Innovation in Schools

Ongoing innovative work serves many important functions in a school district. It serves to catalyze teachers and principals around authentic learning issues and to energize all school staff in proactive ways. Yet, the newness of innovative work also sparks self-doubt and forces teachers to use problem-solving skills in the best sense of Polya's (1957) notion that we are never problem solving until we hit situations that we can't handle.

Innovative work also underscores the importance of effort, persistence, and practice of new ideas until they are owned by the individual and institutionalized by the system. One of the realities of innovative work in schools is that it takes concentrated energy over time to make it work. Sufficient time must be allocated to working through implementation problems in order for teacher automaticity to set in and routine learning for students to be attained. Research on innovation (e.g., McLaughlin & Talbert, 1993) also suggests the need for collaborative work among the key human players in the process. Strong central-office leadership, the principal's involvement and support for key aspects of the given project, and teacher interest, enthusiasm, and deep understanding of the innovation are all essential to its success.

Some of the real values of establishing a climate for innovation in schools are the lessons on life-long learning that it provides. Teachers and principals become more attuned to their own learning states and the new insights that emanate from them. They become more aware of educational practices, more reflective about them, and more intellectually engaged with the world of schools beyond a single entity.

Finally, innovative work challenges us to examine the adequacy of current practices in ways that are healthy. We should question the fruits of reform, consistently asking what anyone is *learning* as a result of our efforts. Whether we are parents, teachers, or administrators, our focus has to be on the results of learning. This tenet should also guide educators engaged in the throes of innovation in order to stay focused on the goal, rather than just the means.

Creating a System of Learning

In order for curricula and instruction to result in authentic student learning, a systemic model for implementation has to be in place. This model must take into account ongoing assessment results in multiple areas and modalities, staff development that is both data-driven and needs-based, and leadership that is knowledgeable and proactive about the relationship between teacher behaviors and student learning. It must also be cognizant of the climate of innovation as a backdrop to the process. Such a systemic model would provide the annealing substance necessary to make quality content-based curricula for high-ability learners a reality in all classrooms (see Figure 14.4).

Connectivity among these elements is central to successful implementation of any instructional innovation. In the case of the ICM, such coherence is critical to success, as the sophistication level required by teachers to implement the curriculum is requisitely high.

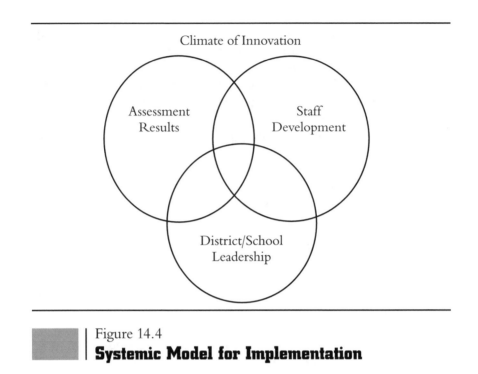

Climate of Innovation

Assessment
Results

Staff
Development

District/School
Leadership

Figure 14.4
Systemic Model for Implementation

Conclusion

In the final analysis, this book is about learning. It is focused on content-based learning, to be sure, but its real message lies in the recognition of the importance of serious and sustained efforts to enhance the learning of our best learners in schools. This group will not take care of itself. Research on talent development (Bloom, 1985; Csikszentmihalyi, Rathunde, & Whalen, 1993) suggests that these students need as much attention as, if not more than, other students in order to optimize their learning potential in life.

While successful practices in school are not life, they bear a strong resemblance, especially in relationship to habits of mind. If our best learners are not challenged by school, then these habits will not be instilled in such a way as to guarantee transfer and automaticity of response in meeting life's challenges. Do we not owe the gifted and high-ability students under our care the support necessary to have them thrive in the world as citizens, as well as professionals in their chosen areas?

This book has sought to provide the positive response to that question in the format of research–based approaches to achieving such a worthy goal. Future research will continue an emphasis on curriculum effectiveness studies in the subject areas of social studies and mathematics, as well as use of the curriculum with special populations of gifted learners, including at-risk and learning-disabled students. As we learn more about what gifted and high-ability learners can do at different stages of development, we are forced to tackle more advanced learning models that will challenge them even more in classroom settings, and we must have the courage to provide the level of differentiation for which they so desperately yearn.

Key Points Summary

❑ Successful implementation of new curricular and instructional approaches requires a supportive system of assessment, staff development, and leadership.
❑ The Center for Gifted Education's science curriculum has demonstrated significant and important learning gains in the area of experimental design. Moreover, teachers found it to be motivating and challenging for students.
❑ The Center for Gifted Education's language arts units enhanced student learning significantly and importantly in the areas of literary analysis and interpretation and persuasive writing.
❑ Research-based best practices in staff development include careful choice of topic, sensible time frame, the inclusion of follow-up strategies, and a plan for assessing student learning.
❑ Leadership in curricular innovation requires vision, integrity, a sense of community, and a proactive stance.
❑ A climate of innovation can facilitate implementation becoming institutionalized.

References

Adams, C. M., & Callahan, C. M. (1995). The reliability and validity of a performance task for evaluating science process skills. *Gifted Child Quarterly, 39,* 14–20.

American Association for the Advancement of Science. (1990). *Science for all Americans: Project 2061.* New York: Oxford University Press.

Bloom, B. S. (Ed.). (1985). *Developing talent in young people*. New York: Ballantine.

Bolman, L. G., & Deal, T. E. (1991). *Reframing organizations: Artistry, choice, and leadership*. San Francisco: Jossey-Bass.

Burkhalter, N. (1995). A Vygotsky-based curriculum for teaching persuasive writing in the elementary grades. *Language Arts, 72,* 192–196.

Burns, J. M. (1978). *Leadership*. New York: Harper & Row.

Cain, M. F. (1990). The diet cola test. *Science Scope, 13*(4), 32–34.

Center for Gifted Education. (1997a). *Acid, acid everywhere: A problem-based unit*. Dubuque, IA: Kendall/Hunt.

Center for Gifted Education. (1997b). *What a find!* Dubuque, IA: Kendall/Hunt.

Center for Gifted Education. (1998). *Autobiographies*. Dubuque, IA: Kendall/Hunt.

Center for Gifted Education. (1999a). *Classroom observation form*. Williamsburg, VA: Center for Gifted Education, College of William and Mary.

Center for Gifted Education. (1999b). *Guide to teaching a language arts curriculum for high-ability learners*. Dubuque, IA: Kendall/Hunt.

Csikszentmihalyi, M., Rathunde, K. R., & Whalen, S. (1993). *Talented teenagers: The roots of success and failure*. New York: Cambridge University Press.

Gardner, J. W. (1990). *On leadership*. New York: The Free Press.

Guskey, T. (2000). *Evaluating professional development*. Thousand Oaks, CA: Corwin Press.

Hillocks, G., Jr. (1986). *Research on written composition: New directions for teaching*. Urbana, IL: ERIC Clearinghouse on Reading and Communication Skills and National Conference on Research in English.

Joyce, B. R., & Showers, B. (1983). *Power in staff development through research on training*. Alexandria, VA: Association for Supervision and Curriculum Development.

Karnes, F. A., & Stephens, K. R. (2000). State definitions for the gifted and talented revisited. *Exceptional Children, 66,* 219–238.

Kennedy, M. (1999). Form and substance in mathematics and science professional development. *NISE Brief, 3*(2), 1–7.

Kouzes, J. M., & Posner, B. Z. (1995). *The leadership challenge*. San Francisco: Jossey-Bass.

McLaughlin, M. W., & Talbert, J. E. (1993). *Contexts that matter for teaching and learning: Strategies for meeting the nation's educational goals*. Washington, DC: Office of Educational Research and Improvement.

McLaughlin, M. W., & Talbert, J. E. (1993). How the world of students and teachers challenges policy coherence. In S. Fuhrman (Ed.), *Designing coherent education policy* (pp. 220–249). San Francisco: Jossey-Bass.

National Assessment Governing Board. (1992). *Reading framework for the 1992 national assessment of education progress.* Washington, DC: U.S. Department of Education.

National Research Council. (1996). *National science education standards.* Washington, DC: National Academy Press.

Peterson, K. (2001, June). *Shaping school culture for quality teaching and learning.* Presentation to the National Leadership Institute, College of William and Mary, Williamsburg, VA.

Polya, G. (1957). *How to solve it: A new aspect of mathematical method* (2nd ed.). Princeton, NJ: Princeton University Press.

Toulmin, S. E. (1958). *The uses of argument.* Cambridge, England: Cambridge University Press.

VanTassel-Baska, J. (1986). Effective curriculum and instructional models for talented students. *Gifted Child Quarterly, 30,* 164–169.

VanTassel-Baska, J. (1995). The development of talent through curriculum. *Roeper Review, 18,* 98–102.

VanTassel-Baska, J., Avery, L. D., & Reardon, R. M. (in press). Assessing teaching practices in gifted programs. *Gifted Child Quarterly.*

VanTassel-Baska, J., Bass, G., Ries, R., Poland, D., & Avery, L. D. (1998). A national study of science curriculum effectiveness with high-ability students. *Gifted Child Quarterly, 42,* 200–211.

VanTassel-Baska, J., Johnson, D. T., Hughes, C. E., & Boyce, L. N. (1996). A study of language arts curriculum effectiveness with gifted learners. *Journal for the Education of the Gifted, 19,* 461–480.

VanTassel-Baska, J., Zuo, L., Avery, L. D., & Little, C. A. (2002). A curriculum study of gifted student learning in the language arts. *Gifted Child Quarterly, 46,* 30–44.

Appendix: Standards for the English Language Arts Aligned With Curricular Emphases

The vision guiding these standards is that all students must have the opportunities and resources to develop the language skills they need to pursue life's goals and to participate fully as informed, productive members of society. These standards assume that literacy growth begins before children enter school as they experience and experiment with literacy activities—reading and writing and associating spoken words with their graphic representations. Recognizing this fact, these standards encourage the development of curricula and instruction that make productive use of the emerging literacy abilities that children bring to school. Furthermore, the standards provide ample room for the innovation and creativity essential to teaching and learning. They are not prescriptions for particular curricula or instruction. Although we present these standards as a list, we want to emphasize that they are not distinct and separable; they are, in fact, interrelated and should be considered as a whole.

Standards for the English Language Arts	Curricular Goals, Outcomes, and Emphases
1. Students read a wide range of print and nonprint texts to build an understanding of texts, of themselves, and of the cultures of the United States and the world; to acquire new information; to respond to the needs and demands of society and the workplace; and for personal fulfillment. Among these texts are fiction and nonfiction, classic and contemporary works.	Emphasis on multicultural and global literature and broad-based reading. *Goal 6: Students will develop understanding of the concept of change in the language arts.* *Sample outcomes:* • Interpret change as positive or negative in selected works. • Analyze social and individual change in a piece of literature.

2. Students read a wide range of literature from many periods in many genres to build an understanding of the many dimensions (e.g., philosophical, ethical, aesthetic) of human experience.

Broad-based reading in poetry, short story, biography, essay, and novel forms.

3. Students apply a wide range of strategies to comprehend, interpret, evaluate, and appreciate texts. They draw on their prior experience, their interactions with other readers and writers, their knowledge of word meaning and of other texts, their word identification strategies, and their understanding of textual features (e.g., sound–letter correspondence, sentence structure, context, graphics).

Goal 1: Students will develop analytical and interpretive skills in literature.

Sample outcomes:
- Cite similarities and differences in meaning among selected works of literature.
- Make inferences based on information in given passages.

4. Students adjust their use of spoken, written, and visual language (e.g., conventions, style, vocabulary) to communicate effectively with a variety of audiences and for different purposes.

Sensitivity to audience built into writing and research activities.

5. Students employ a wide range of strategies as they write and use different writing process elements appropriately to communicate with different audiences for a variety of purposes.

Goal 2: Students will develop persuasive writing skills.

Sample outcomes:
- Develop a written persuasive essay, given a topic.
- Complete various pieces of writing using a three-phase revision process.

6. Students apply knowledge of language structure, language conventions (e.g., spelling and punc-

Goal 3: Students will develop linguistic competency.

tuation), media techniques, figurative language, and genre to create, critique, and discuss print and non-print texts.

Sample outcomes:
- Analyze the form and function of words in a given context.
- Develop vocabulary power commensurate with reading.

7. Students conduct research on issues and interests by generating ideas and questions, and by posing problems. They gather, evaluate, and synthesize data from a variety of sources (e.g., print and non-print texts, artifacts, people) to communicate their discoveries in ways that suit their purpose and audience.

Goal 5: Students will develop reasoning skills in the language arts.

Sample outcomes:
- Define a problem, given ill-structured, complex, or technical information.
- Provide evidence and data to support a claim, issue, or thesis statement.

8. Students use a variety of technological and information resources (e.g., libraries, databases, computer networks, video) to gather and synthesize information and to create and communicate knowledge.

Incorporated in research model, writing task demands, and language and literature study extensions.

9. Students develop an understanding of and respect for diversity in language use, patterns, and dialects across cultures, ethnic groups, geographic regions, and social roles.

Applicable to the context of selected literature.

10. Students whose first language is not English make use of their first language to develop competency in the English language arts and to develop understanding of content across the curriculum.

N/A

11. Students participate as knowledgeable, reflective, creative, and critical members of a variety of literacy communities.

Contact with authors, use of peer review, major discussions of literary works.

12. Students use spoken, written, and visual language to accomplish their own purposes (e.g., for learning, enjoyment, persuasion, and the exchange of information).

Goal 2 (see above)
Goal 4: Students will develop listening/oral communication skills.

Sample outcomes:
- Develop skills of argument formulation.
- Evaluate an oral persuasive message.

Note. From *Standards for the English Language Arts*, by the National Council for Teachers of English, & International Reading Association, 1996, Urbana, IL: Author. Copyright © 1996 by NCTE & IRA. Reprinted with permission.

About the Authors

Joyce VanTassel-Baska is the Jody and Layton Smith Professor of Education at the College of William and Mary, where she initiated and serves as the director of the Center for Gifted Education. Formerly she initiated and directed the Center for Talent Development at Northwestern University. Joyce has also served as state director of gifted programs in Illinois, a regional director, a local coordinator of gifted programs, and a teacher of gifted high school students. Her major research interests are in the talent development process and effective curricular interventions with the gifted. She is the author of several books and has written over 200 other publications on gifted education. She is the editor of *Gifted and Talented International* and received the Distinguished Scholar Award in 1997 from the National Association for Gifted Children and the Outstanding Faculty Award from the State Council of Higher Education in Virginia in 1993. She is also the mother of an adolescent daughter. She holds a B.E., M.A., M.E., and Ed.D. from the University of Toledo.

Catherine A. Little is the curriculum and program development coordinator at the Center for Gifted Education at the College of William and Mary. Her background includes elementary teaching positions and 5 years of experience at the Center, including extensive work in curricular and professional development for teachers. She has coordinated several conferences and institutes for the Center, and she has given numerous conference presentations at state and national events, as well as many curriculum workshops for teachers. Catherine completed her Ph.D. in educational policy, planning, and leadership with emphasis in gifted education administration in the fall of 2001, with a dissertation study focused on metaphor development in young gifted children. She received the School of Education Award for Excellence for her master's work in gifted education and in 1999 received the NAGC Doctoral Student Award for Excellence.

Linda D. Avery served as the manager of center operations at the Center for Gifted Education from July 1999 until October 2001. In this role, she was responsible for providing oversight and guidance for all of the Center's programs and services, particularly for the coordination of two of the Center's largest initiatives, Project Phoenix and Project STAR. She previously worked in two state departments of education in Michigan and Illinois. Linda received her Ph.D. from the College of William and Mary in December 1999. She was the charter recipient of the Margaret, The Lady Thatcher Medallion for scholarship, character, and service conferred by the School of Education. She received her B.A. from Baldwin-Wallace College and her M.A. from Michigan State University.

Wendy T. Ellis is in her final year of coursework in the doctoral program in educational policy, planning, and leadership with an emphasis in gifted education administration at the College of William and Mary. She currently teaches English and Theory of Knowledge in the International Baccalaureate Programme at Henrico High School, where she has taught for 10 years. In addition to IB courses, Wendy has taught English in grades 9–12 on all levels, from standard to Advanced Placement. She has been a conference presenter on various topics regarding secondary gifted education. She holds an M.A. in gifted education from the College of William and Mary. She also holds a B.A. and a B.S. from Virginia Commonwealth University in English and English education, respectively. She is married with four sons.

Dana T. Johnson is an instructor in the mathematics department and the School of Education at the College of William and Mary. In her early teaching career, she taught middle and high school mathematics. Dana has worked on many projects with the Center for Gifted Education since its beginning in 1988, including curriculum development and teaching enrichment classes. She coedited the 1996 book *Developing Verbal Talent* with Joyce VanTassel-Baska and Linda Neal Boyce and authored "Mathematics Curriculum for Gifted Learners" in *Comprehensive Curriculum for Gifted Learners*.

Janine M. Lehane, a doctoral student and graduate assistant at the Center for Gifted Education, serves as assistant editor of *Gifted and Talented International* and has organized the Center's annual Talent

Search for Promising Student Authors. She has recently relocated from Brisbane, Australia. She has taught music, French, English, drama, and literacy and numeracy to pre-K–grade 12 students and adults. The abilities of these students ranged from severe intellectual disabilities to exceptional giftedness. For some years, Janine has also been engaged in research and writing for educational leaders and, more recently, for business leaders.

Molly M. Sandling is a social studies teacher at Jamestown High School in Williamsburg, VA, responsible for 9th- and 10th-grade courses in world history and world geography, as well as AP Human Geography. Molly received a bachelor's degree in history from the College of William and Mary and a master's in history from Yale University. She worked at the Center for Gifted Education while pursuing a master's degree in secondary social studies education and continues to work with the Center on curriculum development. Molly has authored or coauthored five of the Center's social studies units and has presented on social studies curricula for the gifted at several conferences and institutes.

Jeanne M. Struck serves as the director of precollegiate learner programs for the Center for Gifted Education. She is also the author of one of the elementary social studies units and has coordinated social studies implementation efforts as an intern with Norfolk Public Schools. She has taught 24 years in public schools, working with culturally and economically diverse gifted students. In 1999, she received the A. Harry Passow Teacher Scholarship from the National Association for Gifted Children. In 2001, Jeanne received both the Doctoral Student Award and the Research Division Dissertation Award from NAGC. Jeanne completed her Ph.D. from the College of William and Mary in May 2002.

Li Zuo worked as a postdoctoral fellow for research and evaluation at the Center for Gifted Education from August 1999 until April 2001. In this role, she coordinated the research agenda of the Center, conducting research studies, writing, and assisting staff and students in research design and other technical questions related to their research. Li received her Ph.D. from the University of Georgia. Both her B.A. and M.A. are from Hangzhou University in Hangzhou, China.

Index of Names

Abbs, P., 81, 85
Ablard, K. E., 170
Adams, C. M., 315–317, 358
Adler, M. J., 5, 54, 102, 105, 134, 146
Aldrich, P., 260
Algina, J., 307, 316
Alper, T., 166
Amabile, T., 7
American Association for the Advancement of Science, 9, 103, 172, 193, 195, 273, 356
Anderson, M. C., 291
Angus, D., 268
Apple, M. W., 3, 104–105, 148
Archambault, F. X., Jr., 18, 23
Arnheim, R., 80–83, 91
Asp, E., 151, 309
Austin, G. A., 110
Avery, L. D., 10, 26, 101–102, 104, 106, 108, 110, 112, 114, 116, 118, 120, 138, 255, 259–260, 262, 264, 266, 268, 270, 272, 274, 312, 316, 321, 328, 358–359, 366, 382

Bailey, J. M., 6
Banks, J. A., 5, 242, 289
Barrows, H. S., 198
Baskin, B. H., 141, 148
Bass, G., 10, 316, 321, 358
Beardsley, M. C., 83
Bembry, K. L., 291
Benbow, C. P., 9, 29
Beyer, B. K., 74, 234, 246–247
Binker, A. J. A., 247
Biological Sciences Curriculum Study (BSCS), 209, 273
Black, K. N., 35, 96
Bloom, B. S., 48, 51, 53–54, 76–, 283, 372
Bolman, L. G., 368
Boyce, L. N., 4, 10, 48, 69–71, 75, 92, 106, 141, 152, 209, 211–212, 260–261, 268, 293, 360, 382
Bragaw, D., 220, 242
Brophy, J. S., 290
Brown, E. F., 9

Brown, R. H., 246
Bruner, J. E., 110, 274
Buber, M., 81–82, 85, 87, 94
Burkhalter, N., 359, 361
Burns, J. M., 368

Cain, M. F., 315, 357
Calhoun, E., 279
Callahan, C. M., 316–317, 329, 358
Cannon, E., 351
Carr, V. W., 287
Cawley, C., 152
Cebulla, K., 162
Center for Civic Education, 268
Center for Gifted Education, 2, 9–11, 18, 31, 48, 67, 69–71, 73, 75, 86–87, 89, 92, 95–96, 106–107, 110–111, 114–119, 121, 126, 128–129, 131, 134–135, 137–140, 143–144, 147, 152–154, 167, 173, 176, 192–195, 198–199, 203–204, 222–224, 228, 232, 234, 237–238, 241–242, 256, 260–263, 268, 270, 293, 306, 315–317, 323, 334–337, 339, 356–357, 359, 361–364, 366–370, 381–383
Center for Talented Youth, 37–38, 206, 210–211
Chaney, A., 134,
Cohen, S., 281
Cohen, D. K., 49
College Board Advanced Placement Program, 44, 256, 312–314, 349–352
College Entrance Examination Board, 349–350
Commonwealth of Virginia Department of Education, 120, 335, 337
Corbett, J., 152
Cothron, J., 206, 274
Crocker, L., 307, 316
Csikszentmihalyi, M., 19, 372
Cunningham, C., 22

Daniels, H., 132
Darling–Hammond, L., 290

Daupert, D., 48, 57
Davis, G. A., 35
Deal, T.E., 49, 207, 268, 270, 349, 368
DeLong, P. D., 81–82, 87
Dessart, D. J., 163
Dewey, J., 48, 279, 282
Dobyns, S. M., 18, 23
Dods, R. F., 199
Downs, R. B., 134
Dugger, W. E., Jr., 149, 151

Edmonson, N., 97
Educational Testing Service, 314, 349–350
Edwards, B., 87
Eggen, P. D., 280–281, 283
Egner, R. E., 81
Ehrenberg, S. D., 104–106, 111
Eisner, E., 48
Eiss, N., 22
Elder, L., 50, 59, 73, 247
Eliot, T.S., 88
Emmons, C., 21
Ennis, 50
Erb, T., 11, 21
Evans, R. W., 268

Feldhusen, J. F., 18, 35, 50–52, 58, 73–74,
    102, 283, 293
Feynman, R. P., 208–209
Flanders, J. R., 164, 272
Ford, D. Y., 6, 289
Foundation for Critical Thinking, 58–59,
    157
Fox, L., 164, 283
Friedman, R. C., 174
Fullan, M., 103

Gallagher, J. J., 29, 43, 283,
Gallagher, S. A., 6, 29, 43, 199, 247, 283
Gardner, H., 5–6, 83–84, 91, 288
Gardner, J. W., 368
Gentile, C., 138
Gick, M. L., 103
Giese, R., 206, 274
Gomez, E., 291
Goodnow, J. J., 110
Goswami, U., 103
Great Books Foundation, 152, 157
Gregory, T., 260, 263, 268–270
Gronlund, N. E., 51, 310
Gross, M. U. M., 28
Grouws, D. A., 162
Guskey, T., 365–366

Hallmark, B. W., 152, 347, 352, 356
Halpern, D. F., 50
Halsted, J. W., 148, 157
Hamilton, L. S., 317
Hand, S., 56, 72–73, 80, 86, 214, 285, 296,
    298–299
Hansen, J., 18, 21
Harris, J. J., 289
Harris, K. H., 141, 148
Hauser, P., 148, 157
Hembree, R., 163
Hibbs, A., 208
Hillocks, G., Jr., 363
Hodges, H. A., 85
Holden, C., 209
Holloway, J. H., 291
Holyoak, K. J., 103
Horn, C., 55, 291
Horn, S. P., 290–292
House, E., 19
Howell, R. D., 298–299
Hughes, C. E., 360
Hunsaker, S., 22
Hutchings, E., 208
Hyde, A., 132

Imbeau, M., 22
International Baccalaureate Organization,
    313–314, 340–348
International Reading Association, 129, 131,
    157, 266, 380

Jacobs, H. R., 37, 184, 272
Jaffe, H., 91
Johnsen, S., 9, 21
Johnson, D. T., 4, 115, 141, 167, 173–174, 176,
    184, 211, 260–261, 263, 267–268, 270,
    360
Johnson, L. J., 287
Jones, E. D., 42
Jordan, H. R., 291
Joyce, B. R., 27, 279, 305, 355, 366, 381–382

Karnes, F. A., 18, 360
Karnes, M. B., 287
Kauchak, D. P., 280–281, 283
Kaufman, D. R., 199
Keating, D., 164, 283
Kennedy, M., 368
Kerhoven, J. I. M., 317
Kjos, M., 351
Kneip, W., 234
Kouzes, J. M., 369

Kreklau, H., 247
Kulik, C. C., 28, 295
Kulik, J., 18, 28, 295
Kumpermintz, H., 317

Ladson–Billings, G., 145, 157
Landrum, M. S., 329
Langer, J. A., 130, 157
Lapan, S., 19, 21
Lee, S. W., 174
Lehane, J. M., 26, 79–80, 82, 84, 86–88, 90, 92–96, 382
Leibowitz, W. R., 150, 157
Leighton, R., 208
Lerner, L. S., 193
Levinas, E., 80
Little, C. A., 10, 138, 359
Lockwood, A., 261
Louth, A., 84–85, 87
Lutz, L., 22
Lynch, S. J., 170, 211

Maddux, H. X. C., 172–173, 184
Maker, C. J., 9, 16, 28, 52–53, 283, 289, 294, 307, 343
Martin, D., 94, 247
Marzano, R., 7, 28, 51, 133, 157, 309
MathCounts Foundation, 38, 166
McKim, G., 260
McLaughlin, M. W., 363, 371
McTighe, J., 337
McTighe, S., 309
Mendro, R. L., 291
Miller, C. J., 170
Miller–Lachman, L., 145, 157
Mills, C. J., 170
Mirel, J., 268
Moore, B., 22

National Assessment Governing Board, 360
National Center for Education Statistics, 150, 157
National Center for History in the Schools, 221–222, 268
National Commission on Excellence in Education, 49
National Council of Teachers of English, 129, 131, 157, 266, 380
National Council of Teachers of Mathematics, 161, 165, 266, 272
National Education Commission on Time and Learning, 294
National Research Council, 193, 195, 356

Nelson, G. A., 148, 157
Néret, G., 91
Nielson, A. B., 283
Nussbaum, E. M., 317

O'Day, J. A., 11, 22
Oakes, J., 297
Ochse, R., 19, 21
Office of Educational Research and Improvement, 163, 204
Ogbu, J. U., 288
Olszewski–Kubilius, P., 43

Pang, V. O., 268
Parke, B. N., 294
Parker, J., 18, 22
Parnes, S. J., 56, 293
Passow, A. H., 283, 383
Patel, V. L., 199
Paul, R., 8–10, 12, 48, 50, 55–56, 58–59, 62, 68, 73, 76–, 131, 135, 139, 157, 223, 233, 247, 285, 293, 363
Peeples, S., 174, 178
Pence, M. M., 106
Perkins, D., 7, 9, 103
Peterson, K., 370
Phenix, P. H., 85
Pickering, D., 309
Pizzat–Timi, P., 22
Poland, D., 10, 316, 321, 358
Polya, G., 370
Porter, A. C., 272, 290
Posner, B. Z., 369
Proctor, T. B., 35,
Rathunde, K. R., 19, 372

Ravaglia, R., 166
Reardon, R. M., 366
Redfern, H. B., 83, 90
Reel, K., 291
Reid, L. A., 83
Reimer, B., 81–82, 87, 93
Reis, S. M., 10, 288, 321
Renzulli, J. S., 6, 288
Rezba, R., 206, 274
Ries, R. R., 316, 358
Rilke, R. M., 86, 94
Rimm, S. B., 35
Robertson, C., 22
Rosenblatt, H., 143, 157
Rosenthal, H., 199

Salomon, G., 7, 22

Salvin, T. J., 18, 23
Sanders, W. L., 290–292
Sandling, M. M., 219–220, 222–224, 226, 228, 230, 232, 234–236, 238, 240, 242, 244, 246, 248, 250, 252, 383
Saunders, R. M., 268
Saxe, D. W., 268
Schack, G., 103
Schecter, S. L., 234
Schiever, S. W., 28
Schunk, D., 138, 157
Seeley, K., 299
Seiger–Ehrenberg, S., 49
Seymour, D., 183, 272
Shaklee, B. D., 329
Shaver, J. P., 234
Sher, B. T., 6, 8, 25, 27–28, 30, 32, 34, 36, 38, 40, 42, 44, 106, 115, 167, 173–174, 176, 184, 191–192, 194, 196, 198, 200, 202, 204, 206, 208, 210, 212, 214, 216, 260, 263, 267, 270
Showers, B., 366
Silverman, L. K., 287, 292
Simpson, A., 80, 97
Sisk, D. A., 289
Skinner, B. F., 5, 22
Slavin, R. E., 297
Smith, M. S., 11
Smith, R. A., 80–84, 97
Snow, R. E., 113, 317
South Carolina Department of Education, 336–337
Southern, W. T., 42
Sowell, E. J., 166
Spillane, J. P., 49
Spivey, N. N., 144, 157
Stanley, J. C., 6, 9, 29, 35, 164, 283
Stephens, K. R., 360
Stepien, W. J., 199, 247
Sternberg, R. J., 288
Stiggins, R. J., 312
Stillinger, C., 166
Struck, J. M., 312
Suppes, P., 166
Swartz, C., 138, 157
Swiatek, M. A., 164, 166

Taba, H., 106, 110, 121, 134, 285
Talbert, J. E., 363, 371
Tangherlini, A., 170
Thomas, R., 81, 236
Thompson, M. B., 146,
Thompson, M. C., 132, 141, 146,

Tomchin, E., 22
Tomlinson, C., 18, 280, 284
Toulmin, S. E., 361
Tschudi, S., 142

United States Department of Education, 1n, 49, 204, 212, 329

VanTassel–Baska, J., 4, 6–7, 9–10, 16, 19, 29, 33, 43, 54, 90, 102–103, 128, 138, 141, 192, 260–261, 266, 268, 270, 283, 292, 298, 309, 312, 316–317, 322, 329, 332, 348, 350–351, 358–361, 363, 366
Vetrano, C., 247
Vygotsky, L. S., 3, 5, 23

Ward, V. S., 9, 102
Warren, R. P., 80, 273–274
Weil, J., 234
Weil, M., 279
Wesley, E. B., 234
Westberg, K. L., 18, 23
Whalen, S., 19, 372
Wheeler, R., 247
Whelan, M., 268
Wiggins, G., 337
Wolff, R. J., 91
Workman, D., 199, 247
Wright, S. P., 290–292
Wronski, S. P., 234

Zemelman, S., 132
Zhang, W., 21
Zuo, L., 10, 138, 312, 359

Index of Subjects

acceleration
  as curricular model, 5–6
  as differentiation feature, 9, 14
  content or subject acceleration, 33–35, 210
  grade advancement, 35
  in science, 192, 205, 210–212
  mathematics placement and, 164–166, 186
  myths about, 28–29
  science projects as, 198, 205–206
accountability (see also assessment), 2, 47, 133, 192, 265, 290–292, 328–329, 356, 364–366
administrators, 71, 192, 261, 275, 328, 360, 369, 371
advanced content
  as differentiation feature, 11, 88, 166, 193, 244, 312, 331, 351
  as dimension of ICM (see also substantive content, assessment), 7–10, 12
Advanced Placement (AP)
  AP Vertical Teams, 350–351
  assessments, 312–314
aesthetic education
  teacher role, 80–81
analyzing primary sources (see primary source documents)
AP (see Advanced Placement)
assessment of quality in art, 81–82
assessment of thinking, 68
assessment (see also authentic assessment, performance-based assessment)
  fairness of, 308
  technical adequacy of, 306–309
Attention Deficit Disorder (see also twice exceptional), 41, 287–288
attention span, 287, 290, 300
audience
  for writing, 133–134, 144–145, 148
authentic assessment
  as curricular reform element, 14–15, 309–312
  in language arts, 68, 128, 132–134, 151
  in mathematics, 164, 167–168
  in social studies, 244, 250–251

basal materials,
  appropriateness for gifted learners, 3–4, 261–262, 298
  in mathematics, 188
  in science, 207–213
Benchmarks for Science Literacy, 193–194, 356
Bloom's taxonomy, 48, 51, 53–54, 76, 283
breadth
  in mathematics content, 169–170, 172–173

calculators (see also graphing calculators), 34, 163
cause and effect (as curricular concept), 10, 12, 14, 115,
Center for Gifted Education research model, 48, 69–70, 73, 76, 152, 293
Center for Gifted Education staff development model, 366–367
Center for Gifted Education units
  assessments in, 12, 14
  conceptual emphasis of, 102–103, 118
  language arts, 12, 14, 31, 107, 115, 118, 134, 138, 144, 152–155, 359–364
  linkage to curricular reform elements, 6–7, 11–15
  mathematics, 115, 173–174
  science, 12–13, 115, 119, 198–199, 315–322, 356–359
  social studies, 12, 115, 118, 335, 337–339, translation of ICM, 9–11
Center for Talent Development, 211
Center for Talented Youth, 37–38, 206, 210–211
Challenge of the Unknown, 172–173, 184, 272–273
challenge, 3–4, 141, 148, 166, 221, 270, 286–287, 329–330, 332–333
change (as curricular concept), 10–14, 67, 102–103, 106–113, 115–116, 118, 120, 131, 134–137, 147–148, 154–155, 208, 235, 336, 359, 361, 364
classroom management (see learning environment)

classroom
 physical arrangements, 297
cluster grouping, 29–30, 32, 43, 45, 295
collaboration
 as mathematics habit of mind, 168–169
 in schools, 32, 252, 261–262, 314, 350–351, 371
community involvement in classroom, 44, 72, 203–204, 299
community service, 341, 343–344
compacting, 192, 331
competitions, 38–39, 206, 210, 216, 274
complexity (as learner characteristic), 6, 16–17, 286–287, 294, 309, 332
complexity (as differentiation feature)
 in mathematics, 163–164, 170, 173, 193
 in science, 196, 198, 204–205, 209–210, 214
 in social studies, 221–223, 234–236, 238, 244–245, 247–249
 of literature, 138, 146, 148–149
 of questions, 56, 347
 of tasks/outcomes, 51–54, 83, 129
computer programming, 188
concept applications, 114
concept attainment, 110
concept development/concept formation (see also concept emphasis)
 concept development model, 106–112, 114, 134, 285, 331,
concept emphasis
 as criterion for instructional and materials selection, 43, 260, 284–286, 298
 as curricular reform element, 11
 as dimension of ICM, 102, 106, 164, 283
 definitions of, 102–103, 104–106
 in IB, 314–315, 343–344, 346, 348
 in language arts, 102, 106, 115, 118, 134–135, 141, 146–148, 154–155, 336, 359
 in mathematics, 34, 115, 162–163, 167, 173–174, 185, 187–188, 267
 in science, 103, 106, 115, 119, 193, 199, 203–205, 207–210, 212, 267–268, 315, 356
 in social studies, 106, 115, 118–119, 233–238, 246–247, 250, 269
 in standards, 330–331
concept generalizations, 115
concept learning,
 assessment of, 118–119
 importance of, 102–104
concept mapping, 11

concept outcomes, 203
constructing meaning
 as curricular philosophy, 48
 as curricular reform element, 11, 15
 as instructional element, 50, 260, 270, 282
 in language arts, 142–144, 336
 in mathematics, 185–186
 in social studies, 247–248, 250, 252
content validity, 307, 315–317
contracts, 43
cooperative learning, 295
creative problem solving, 48, 51, 56, 76–77, 293
creative production
 as criterion for materials selection, 270
 role of teacher in, 87–88, 91
creative thinking
 definition, 50–51
 in problem solving, 56, 73
creativity (as differentiation feature)
 in mathematics, 168
 linked to content knowledge, 7
critical reading/literary criticism, 128–133, 152, 266,
critical thinking (see also higher order thinking skills), 22, 33, 48, 50, 58–59, 77–78, 135, 209, 245, 252, 330, 340, 366, 369
cross-grade grouping, 331
cultural diversity
 grouping and, 288–290
 as criterion in selecting materials, 266–267, 269
curiosity
 as habit of mind, 13, 19, 205, 267
curricular alignment (see also scope and sequence, national standards, state standards), 340, 346
curriculum articulation (see also scope and sequence), 329
curriculum effectiveness research, 356–364
curricular models (see also Integrated Curriculum Model), 1, 4–5, 9, 17
curricular philosophies, 4–6
curricular reform
 linkage to talent development, 6
 reform elements, 11–15

Dagwood Essay Model, 138, 140
debate, 35, 73, 268, 336, 347, 369
decision making
 as higher order process, 51, 58
 in instruction, 121, 264, 280–283, 289–290, 292–293, 298, 300

deductive thinking, 34
depth
    as criterion for materials selection, 184, 267–270
    as curricular reform element, 11
    as differentiation feature, 3, 43, 103
desktop publishing, 244
diagnostic-prescriptive approach, 3, 7, 32–33, 164
Diet Cola Test, 315–321, 357–358
differentiation
    features of a differentiated curriculum, 2–4, 332
    in heterogeneous classrooms, 18
    teacher knowledge and, 18–19, 290
direct instruction, 32, 292–293
discovery approach
    in mathematics, 183–184
divergent thinking, 48, 56, 76, 267
dual enrollment, 41

early entrance, 35, 44
early exit, 35, 45
Earthworm Test (see also Diet Cola Test), 315, 318–321
Education Program for Gifted Youth (EPGY), 36–37, 39, 166, 186
Elementary Science Study, 212, 273
Elements of Reasoning
    as model for reasoning, 58–62
    in language arts curricula, 10, 12, 138, 153
    in social studies curricula, 12, 223, 233
    linkage to research model, 69
    use of, 62, 68, 285
    use with ICM, 8–9
embedded assessment, 119
enrichment
    as curricular model, 6
    comparison to acceleration, 27–28, 34
    in mathematics, 172–173, 187
    science projects as, 205
ethics, 341
expectations for grade/age level
    reading level, 3, 9, 14, 17
expectations for performance
    in language arts, 129, 133
    in mathematics, 162, 173, 183–184, 188
experimental design, 181, 204, 206–207, 215, 282, 317–318, 322, 365, 373
extensions
    as criterion for materials selection, 265
    as instructional element, 283
    in language arts, 150

in mathematics, 184–185
in science, 208–209, 212, 214–215
in social studies, 249

foreign language, 33, 40, 146
formative assessment, 251, 322
Foundational Approaches in Science Teaching (FAST), 212
Full Option Science System (FOSS), 211
Future Problem Solving, 58

games and puzzles, 31, 173
gifted students
    characteristics of, 6, 16–17
grade advancement, 35, 45
grammar, 12, 37, 120, 132, 142, 151, 310, 318, 336
graphing calculators, 186–188
Great Explorations in Math and Science (GEMS), 215–216
Great Ideas: A Syntopicon of Great Books of the Western World, The, 102, 134
grouping,
    as instructional element, 289–290, 295–297
    with diagnostic-prescriptive approach, 30–32

habits of mind
    as context variable, 18
    as criterion for materials selection, 260, 265, 267–268
    as instructional element, 285–286, 298–299
    as curricular reform element, 13, 15
    as foundation for disciplines, 58, 62
    in IB, 343
    in language arts, 130–132, 146, 152
    in mathematics, 168–169, 183, 267
    in science, 193, 205–206, 213, 268
    in social studies, 220–223, 236–238, 242, 244, 248, 250
    linkage to reasoning, 58, 62
Hamburger Model for Persuasive Writing, 138–139, 363
hands-on approaches, 163, 198, 208, 282
heterogeneous classroom settings, 6–7, 10, 18, 252, 358
higher order thinking skills/higher order processes
    as criterion for materials selection, 266–267, 270, 298
    as curricular reform element, 11
    as dimension of ICM, 7–8
    as instructional element, 282, 286, 291–292
    assessment of, 312

in language arts, 135–141, 359, 266
in mathematics, 169, 174
in social studies, 223, 233
high-stakes testing, 192, 314, 327, 329
historical analysis, 10, 12, 126, 222
horizontal alignment, 340

IB (see International Baccalaureate)
ill-defined problem/ill-structured problem, 3, 131, 198, 202, 205, 247, 322
Illinois Math and Science Academy, 199
illustrations
    as literature selection criterion, 145
independent learning
    as criterion for materials selection, 270
    as instructional element, 15, 284, 293–294, 298
Individualized Educational Plan (IEP), 288
inductive thinking, 103
inquiry
    as criterion for materials selection, 260, 264, 269
    as curricular reform element, 13
    as element of higher order process, 48
    as element of ICM, 15, 84
    as instructional element, 264, 283
    as nature of science, 205
    assessment of, 310, 317
    in language arts, 33, 128, 141, 151–152
    in mathematics, 183–184
    in science modular curricula, 212
    in social studies, 221, 223, 245–247, 269
    through problem-based learning, 204–205
instructional alignment, 281
instructional leadership, 368
instructional strategies
    as criterion for materials selection, 264
    as differentiation feature, 3
    for supporting higher order processes, 48
Integrated Curriculum Model (ICM)
    assessment of, 118–119
    concept emphasis of, 102–103
    description of, 7–9
    linkage to AP, 351–352
    linkage to gifted student characteristics, 16–17, 332
    linkage to IB, 346–348
    rationale, 6–7
    to support interdisciplinary inquiry, 7, 84
    translation in language arts curricula, 9–10, 12, 129–130
    translation in science curricula, 10, 193–195, 199

translation in social studies curricula, 10–11
translation in mathematics curricula, 164–165
intensity (as learner characteristic)
interdisciplinary learning/interdisciplinary connections
    as criterion for materials selection, 265–266, 268
    as curricular reform element, 11, 13, 15
    based on concepts, 104, 119–121
    in language arts, 128, 145–148, 266, 336
    in mathematics, 184–185
    in science, 204, 208, 214, 268
    in social studies, 243–244
    linkage to ICM, 7, 84
    through standards, 266, 331
International Baccalaureate (IB)
    assessments, 312–313, 340, 342–343, 345
    alignment with ICM, 346–348
    IB Diploma Programme, 340–341, 343, 349
    IB Middle Years Programme, 343–345
    IB Primary Years Programme, 343–345
Internet resources,
    for language arts, 150
    for mathematics, 184, 186–187
    for science, 214
    for social studies, 244–245, 249–250
internships, 43
intradisciplinary connections
    as criterion for materials selection, 268
    as curricular reform element, 15
    in language arts, 145–148
    in mathematics, 184–185
    in science, 284
    in social studies, 243–244

journals
    math, 169, 183, 185, 188
    scientific, 205, 209
    student, 74, 135, 144, 154, 252, 336
Junior Great Books, 31, 33, 152

K–12 curricula (see curriculum articulation, scope and sequence)

lab reports, 214, 365
language arts
    acceleration in, 33
    applications of curricular reform elements, 12
    application of reasoning model, 67, 135, 138–141

conceptual emphasis, 106–107, 115, 118
curriculum effectiveness research, 359–364
language study, 10, 120, 129, 132, 142, 146–147, 155, 266, 359
Lawrence Hall of Science, 211, 215, 273
leadership (see instructional leadership)
learner outcomes of significance
    aligned with instruction, 282
    as criterion for materials selection
    as curricular reform element, 15
    concept outcomes, 114, 203
    for product development
    in language arts, 129–131
    in mathematics, 164–165
    in science, 192–195
    in social studies, 220–222
learning centers, 285, 296
learning disabilities (see special populations)
learning environment, 280, 289
learning modalities, 288, 290, 300
linguistic competency, 131, 336
literary analysis and interpretation
    as language arts goal, 118, 144, 336
literature selection
    criteria for, 145, 148–149
    for language arts curricula, 9, 128–129, 141–142
Literature Web, 89, 94, 142–144, 151, 285, 363–364
logic
    as science habit of mind, 205

manipulatives, 31, 52, 170, 264
Math Forum, 165, 184, 186–187
MathCounts, 38, 46, 166
mathematical mosaics, 172
mathematics
    acceleration in, 28, 34
    communication and, 162, 267
    conceptual emphasis, 115, 120, 173–174
media specialists, 72, 261
Mega Mathematics, 187
mentorships, 43
metacognition
    as curricular reform element, 13, 15
    as higher order process, 48, 51, 73–75
    in language arts, 152–155
    in mathematics, 185–186
    in science, 206–207
    in social studies, 251–252
    in staff development, 366
models (as curricular concept), 105, 115, 120, 167, 174, 208

modular curricula
    in science, 207–208, 211–213
motivation, 16, 29, 198, 210, 366
motor development, 287
multiage classroom (see also cross-grade grouping), 37,
multicultural emphases
    as criterion for materials selection, 264, 266, 269
    as curricular reform element, 14–15
    in language arts, 33, 144–146, 266
    in social studies, 238–243, 269
multiple-choice tests, 168, 250, 313–314
music, 13, 39, 41, 85, 93, 95, 120, 147, 208, 243, 342

Nation at Risk, A, 49
National Association for Gifted Children, 275, 321, 329
National Education Longitudinal Study, 317
National Excellence report, 1n, 49
National Research Center on the Gifted and Talented, 21, 316, 357
national standards
    curriculum alignment with, 329–331, 334–337, 349
    in language arts, 130–131
    in mathematics, 161–162
    in science, 192–195
    in social studies, 221–222, 268
Need to Know Board, 202–203, 207

observation
    as science habit of mind, 205–206, 214
open-endedness
    as criterion for materials selection, 268, 270
    in mathematics, 168, 170, 188
    in social studies, 246–247
    of activities, 3, 283, 288
    of inquiry, 55–56, 84, 118, 292
    of literature selections, 148
    of problem-based learning, 204
    of science projects, 205, 214, 268
oral communication/presentations
    as language arts goal, 12, 129–131, 133–134, 336
    of research, 10, 70

pacing
    as instructional element, 294
    in mathematics, 163–164, 169–170, 183
patterns (as curricular concept), 105, 120, 183–184, 186–188, 235

PBL (see problem-based learning)
peer assessment, 92
perfectionism, 90
performance-based assessment
    as authentic assessment, 14, 167, 309–310, 312
    content validity and, 307
    in language arts, 360–364
    in mathematics, 167
    in social studies, 251
    in science, 315, 358, 365
persuasive writing
    as higher order process, 11
    as language arts goal, 336
    assessment of, 359–364
    in social studies, 233
    linkage to standards of reasoning, 138–141
    models for teaching
placement (of students), 17–18, 42, 164–166, 329
portfolios, 14, 309–310, 345
power writing, 133
preassessment/pretesting
    as criterion for materials selection, 264
    as element of assessment, 86–87, 118–119, 166, 188, 251, 286
precocity
    as learner characteristic, 6, 16, 269, 332
    case studies, 36–42
prerequisites, 286–287, 342
primary source documents
    analyzing, 236–237, 248, 251
    in social studies, 12, 222–223, 236, 244–245, 249, 251
    use in Socratic teaching, 55
principals (see administrators)
problem log
    as assessment, 204, 322
    in science, 203, 207
problem solving
    assessment, 188, 310, 312
    as criterion for materials selection, 264, 269
    as curricular reform element, 13
    as higher order process, 49, 51
    in art, 83
    in mathematics, 162, 165, 172–173, 183, 188
    in social studies, 234, 269
    in staff development, 366
problem statements
    in creative problem solving, 57
    in problem-based learning, 199, 202

problem-based learning (PBL)
    and metacognition
    as instructional approach, 3, 366
    in Center for Gifted Education science units, 10, 12, 198–205, 317–318
    in integrated mathematics/science unit, 173
    in social studies, 247
product development/projects (see also science projects)
    as dimension of ICM, 9–10
    differentiated for gifted, 4, 14
    in IB, 342, 345, 347–348
    in language arts, 88–90, 133–134, 144, 364
    in mathematics, 183, 188
    in social studies, 250–251
    perfectionism and, 90
    quality/assessment of student products, 90–93
Project 2061, 193, 195, 373
PSAT, 40
pull-out programs, 6, 40

questioning
    as criterion for materials selection, 268
    as differentiation tool, 3, 19
    for literary analysis and interpretation, 116, 150–152
    Socratic, 48, 54–56, 76, 78, 151–152, 347
    to support metacognition, 207
    to support reasoning and inquiry, 60–62

reading
    acceleration in, 33
real-world problems/connections
    as criterion for materials selection, 267–269
    as basis for research, 69–70
    in mathematics, 162, 172, 184–185, 267
    in science, 198, 202, 204, 212, 268
    in social studies, 223, 234, 244, 247, 269
    through literature, 133
    through problem-based learning, 10
reasoning about a situation or event, 23–224, 226, 233
reasoning model (see reasoning, Elements of Reasoning)
reasoning (see also higher order thinking skills)
    as criterion for materials selection, 267, 269
    in language arts, 12, 132, 135, 138–141, 150
    in mathematics, 162–163, 165, 169, 174, 182, 267

in social studies, 221, 223–223, 233–234, 247–248, 250, 269
  linkage to concept development, 61, 103, 105
  reasoning questions, 137–138
reliability
  alternate form method, 306
  of assessment instruments, 306–307, 312
  of Diet Cola Test, 316
  test-retest method, 306
research model, 69–73
Rocky Mountain Talent Search, 211
rubrics
  for artwork, 91–92
  for assessing concept learning, 118–119
  for assessing writing, 133
  for literary interpretation and persuasive writing, 361–362
  for research project, 75
SAT, 40
school climate, 19, 297, 371
Science and Technology for Children, 212, 273
science concepts, 22, 235, 243, 268
Science Curriculum Improvement Study, 212, 273
science projects, 205–207, 216
science
  applications of curricular reform elements, 11, 13–14, 192
  application of reasoning model, 62, 66
  assessment in Center for Gifted Education units, 204
  conceptual emphasis, 106, 115, 119–120
  curriculum effectiveness research, 315–232
scientific process, 8, 12, 199, 204, 209, 212, 214–215, 317, 322
scope and sequence, 121, 256, 263, 328–329, 348, 351–352
secondary sources, 11–12, 70, 87, 236, 249–250
selection of materials
  as curricular reform element, 14–15
  as element of differentiation, 3–4
  in language arts, 3, 145, 148–149, 266
  in mathematics, 184, 266–267
  in science, 192, 207–216, 267–268
  in social studies, 220, 248–250, 268–269
  model for, 261–270
self-assessment, 51, 91–92, 264, 311
self-contained classroom settings, 358
simulations, 214, 238, 269, 298–299
skepticism
  in mathematics, 168–169, 267

small-group work, 143, 167, 183, 296, 322
social studies
  applications of curricular reform elements, 11–14
  application of reasoning model, 62, 65
  conceptual emphasis, 10, 106, 115, 118, 120
  Socratic questioning and, 55–56
Socratic questioning, 54, 56, 76, 152, 347
special populations, 288, 373
spiraling
  in science curriculum, 210
staff development, 256–257, 355, 364–368, 370–373
stakeholders
  in historical analysis, 236
  on issues, 60–61, 69, 71–72
standardized tests, 309–310
standards of reasoning, 68, 139
state standards
  conceptual emphasis, 120
  convergence with national standards, 265–266
  curriculum alignment with, 330, 335, 368
stereotypes
  in literature, 145
  in social studies, 211
substantive content
  as curricular reform element, 14–15
  as instructional element, 282–283
  in language arts, 141–142, 144, 151
  in mathematics, 169–170
  in science, 196–198, 356
  in social studies, 235–238, 247–248
  linked to higher order processes, 50
summative assessment, 12, 164, 167, 310, 322
systems (as curricular concept), 10–14, 21, 43, 61, 84, 103, 105–106, 115, 119–120, 174, 188, 193–194, 199, 204, 214, 235, 273, 290, 309, 318, 323, 328, 335, 338–339, 341–342, 356

table of specifications, 307–308
talent development, 6–7, 17, 211, 370, 372
Talent Identification Program, 211
teachers
  characteristics and skills, 18–19, 32–33
  education and training, 18–19
  effectiveness, 290
  facilitation roles, 56, 72, 87–88
  role in supporting acceleration, 42–43
  technological knowledge, 298
  translation of staff development learning, 366–370

teaching integrated math and science, 215, 272

teaching models, 26, 125, 281, 360

Techniques of Problem Solving (TOPS), 31, 183

technology
    as curricular reform element, 15
    as instructional tool, 298
    criteria for selecting, 265
    in language arts, 149–151
    in mathematics, 186–187
    in science, 203, 267–268
    in social studies, 244–245

tenacity
    as mathematics habit of mind, 168–169, 267

tessellations, 120, 172

test ceiling, 256, 306, 308, 323

Theory of Knowledge course, 340–343

Third International Mathematics and Science Study, 163, 266

tiered instruction, 295–296

time
    as variable in curricular implementation, 17, 293–295
    needed for curricular innovation, 370–371

traits of the reasoning mind, 247

twice-exceptional students, 288

underachievement, 29, 192

Understanding by Design, 337–339

Validity
    of assessment instruments, 307

value-added accountability, 290–292

vertical alignment (see also curriculum articulation, scope and sequence), 50, 340

Visual Thinking cards, 183

Vocabulary Web, 152–153, 364

vocabulary, 9, 12, 33–34, 54, 94, 126, 131–132, 141–142, 151–153, 236, 287, 308, 336, 364

wait time, 55

Wheel of Reasoning (see also Elements of Reasoning), 58, 62

William and Mary units (see Center for Gifted Education units)

word processing, 52, 149, 244, 298

writing (see also persuasive writing, writing process)
    as constructing meaning, 142–144
    as language arts content, 12, 128–129
    assessment tools, 86–87, 132–134

writing process (see also persuasive writing, writing)
    as curricular element, 9–10
    as habit of mind, 130
    linked to reasoning, 135, 138–141